Canadian Public Administration
discipline and profession

Kenneth Kernaghan, editor

Butterworths
Toronto

592240

Canadian Public Administration: Discipline and Profession

© 1983—Institute of Public Administration of Canada

Printed and bound in Canada

5 4 3 2 1 3 4 5 6 7 8 9/8

Canadian Cataloguing in Publication Data
Main entry under title:
Canadian public administration

Text in English and French.
Includes bibliographical references.
ISBN 0-409-83983-3

1. Public administration – Addresses, essays, lectures.
2. Canada – Politics and government – Addresses, essays, lectures. I. Kernaghan, Kenneth, 1940-

JL108.C36   354.71   C83-094150-9E

Données de catalogage avant publication (Canada)
Vedette principale au titre:
Canadian public administration

Textes en anglais et en français.
Comprend des références bibliographiques.
ISBN 0-409-83983-3

1. Administration publique – Discours, essais, conférences. 2. Canada – Politique et gouvernement – Discours, essais, conférences. I. Kernaghan, Kenneth, 1940-

JL108.C36   354.71   C83-094150-9F

The Butterworth Group of Companies
Canada:
Butterworth & Co. (Canada) Ltd., Toronto and Vancouver
United Kingdom:
Butterworth & Co. (Publishers) Ltd., London
Australia:
Butterworths Pty. Ltd., Sydney
New Zealand:
Butterworths of New Zealand Ltd., Wellington
South Africa:
Butterworth & Co. (South Africa) Ltd., Durban
United States:
Butterworth (Publishers) Inc., Boston
Butterworth (Legal Publishers) Inc., Seattle
Mason Publishing Company, St. Paul

JL
108
.C3564
1983

Contents

About the Institute

The Institute of Public Administration of Canada is a private non-profit organization of public servants from all orders of government: teachers, administrators and students in universities and colleges; and others interested in public administration.

The Institute's main goal is to contribute to better public administration in Canada. To achieve this, the Institute conducts, among other things, a broad range of research, seminar, and publication activities to help enlarge the body of knowledge about Canadian public administration.

These essays were written to mark the twenty-fifth anniversary of the Institute's quarterly journal *Canadian Public Administration/Administration publique du Canada.*

About the Editor

Kenneth Kernaghan is professor of political science and administrative studies at Brock University. He received his Honours B.A. in economics and political science from McMaster University and his M.A. and Ph.D. in political science from Duke University. He served as chairman of the Department of Political Science and founding director of the School of Administrative Studies at Brock. He is the author of several books, monographs and articles on Canadian public administration and public policy and is editor of *Canadian Public Administration*, the learned journal of the Institute of Public Administration of Canada.

This volume is dedicated
to the distinguished former editors
of *Canadian Public Administration*.

Ce volume est dédié
aux distinguées anciens rédacteurs
d'*Administration publique du Canada*.

Malcolm Taylor, 1958–1960
Albert S. Abel, 1961–1969
Douglas V. Verney, 1970–1974
Donald V. Smiley, 1974–1979

Kenneth Kernaghan **Canadian public administration: progress and prospects**

If you don't care where you get to, then it doesn't matter which way you go. This doesn't mean that when you do care about your destination there is "one best way" to go. So it is with the study and practice of public administration in Canada. We know where we want to go but we are, both by choice and necessity, travelling towards our goal by a variety of routes.

The routes to our goal of a high level of knowledge and performance in the public administration community include training and education programs, conferences, seminars, research, publication, and on-the-job public service experience. Academics and practitioners do not travel these routes together frequently enough; indeed, insufficient communication between these two sectors of the community remains a major impediment to our collective advance. Other significant obstacles in our path are scarce human and financial resources for scholarly research, especially on provincial and municipal administration, and inadequate opportunities for professional development.

The essays in this volume traverse the field of Canadian public administration to see how far we have travelled, the directions in which we are moving and the barriers still standing in the way of our progress. The publication of this volume marks the silver anniversary of *Canadian Public Administration*, the journal of the Institute of Public Administration of Canada.

This introductory essay provides a basis for subsequent essays on major themes (essays 3-6) and sub-fields (essays 7-16)[1] of public ad-

Professor Kernaghan is with the department of politics and the school of administrative studies, Brock University, and is editor of *Canadian Public Administration*.

1 Each of the ten sub-field essays, with varying degrees of emphasis, covers the following topics: the literature in the sub-field, current developments and problems, emerging trends and future prospects, the research agenda and, finally, the implications of all of these subjects for education and training in public administration. *Readers should note that each author was obliged to cover a large topic in a small number of pages.*

ministration in Canada. It begins with an analysis of the content and emphases of *Canadian Public Administration*. This is followed by a summary of the ideas and insights that emerged at a special seminar on the topic of "Canadian Public Administration: The Discipline and the Profession" at which the four theme papers were presented.[2] My summary of the seminar discussions doubtless suggests a larger measure of consensus and imposes a greater sense of order than actually existed. I have included some personal observations on the matters discussed but I have resisted the temptation to be a "creative rapporteur."

The good and the original

Dr. Samuel Johnson once wrote these words to an aspiring author: "Your manuscript is both good and original; but the part that is good is not original, and the part that is original is not good." Perhaps some of the articles published in *Canadian Public Administration* (CPA) since the journal's inception in 1958 deserved a similar response. But CPA has published many articles that are good and/or original in their entirety. Indeed, the body of literature represented by the one hundred issues of CPA published over the past twenty-five years is easily the single most important source of information and ideas on the theory and practice of public administration in Canada.

The evolution during this period of the administration of our public affairs is chronicled in the pages of the journal. Not surprisingly, the journal's content has reflected developments and problems of the time, especially in the practice of public administration. The journal has also examined, usually from a more theoretical perspective, enduring and recurring themes and issues.

A review of the journal's content does, however, reveal some noteworthy emphases and omissions. These are evident in the breakdown of articles by subject matter and authors for the years 1968 to 1981[3] (see Tables 1 and 2).

The political science emphasis has been reflected in the subject matter[4] and authorship of CPA articles; administrative science has been comparatively neglected. The subjects of structure/organization, public policy

2 The seminar was organized by the Institute of Public Administration of Canada and held in Lac Ste Marie, Quebec, May 12-14, 1982. The Institute acknowledges with deep appreciation the financial support of the Social Sciences and Humanities Research Council of Canada for the seminar and the silver anniversary issue of the journal.
3 For an analysis of the years 1958 to 1967, see Kernaghan, "An Overview of Public Administration in Canada Today," CANADIAN PUBLIC ADMINISTRATION, vol. 11 (Fall 1968), pp. 294-96.
4 The classification of subject matter is based primarily on the standard content of public administration texts.

TABLE 1 Distribution of Articles by Subject Matter:
Canadian Public Administration, 1968-1981

Subject Matter	no.	%
Scope of the discipline	3	.73
Methodology	18	4.40
Organization theory	8	1.96
Environment	14	3.42
Structure/organization	43	10.51
Public policy – process and substance	95	23.23
Intergovernmental relations	32	7.82
Management	28	6.85
Finance/budgeting	17	4.16
Personnel	39	9.54
Politics of public administration	38	9.29
Responsibility/values	14	3.42
Administrative law	5	1.22
Other	55	13.45
TOTAL	409	100.00

TABLE 2 Distribution of Articles by Author(s):
Canadian Public Administration, 1968-1981

Authors	no.	%
Academics		
Political science	131	26.89
Economics	45	9.24
Public administration	35	7.18
Business administration/		
management science	9	1.84
Others (sociology, history etc.)	76	15.60
SUBTOTAL	296	60.76
Practitioners and Others		
Federal public servants	83	17.04
Provincial public servants	57	11.70
Municipal public servants	13	2.66
Others (politicians, foreign		
public servants etc.)	38	7.80
SUBTOTAL	191	39.21
TOTAL	487	100.00

process and substance, politics of public administration, and intergovernmental relations constitute more than 50 per cent of the articles; the subjects of organization theory and management make up only 9 per cent
of the total.

Table 2 shows that a greater percentage of CPA articles have been
written by academics than by federal, provincial and municipal govern-

ment employees. Compared to the 1958-1967 period, there has been a slight increase in contributions from academics. There are of course many more teachers of public administration now than in 1967 and they have more time and incentive (e.g., salary, promotion, status) than public servants to write for publication.

More than half of the academic authors are political scientists. The small number of contributions from specialists in management science, sociology and social psychology explains the paucity of articles with an administrative science orientation.

The great majority of the authors (75.8 per cent) used an historical/descriptive methodological approach. The general tone of 20.8 per cent of the articles was normative/prescriptive and only 3.4 per cent of the authors used a behavioural/empirical approach.

The scarcity of CPA articles in the administrative science category is a reflection of the manuscripts submitted rather than of editorial policy. Indeed, books and monographs on Canadian public administration mirror the content and emphasis of the journal. Some Canadian contributions with an administrative science orientation are published in other social science journals in Canada and elsewhere. Doubtless this results in part from an understandable perception that CPA is much more a journal for academic political scientists and economists and for public servants than for academics with an administrative science bent. It is notable that the contributions of public servants are more management-oriented and practically-oriented than those of academics, but even most of these articles fall within the broad category of political rather than administrative science.

CPA's current terms of reference are "the examination of the structures, processes and outcomes of public policy and public management related to executive, legislative, judicial and quasi-judicial functions in the municipal, provincial and federal spheres of government."[5] These terms embrace an administrative science approach to public administration but they do not do so explicitly. If Canada's public administration community is to make an appropriate contribution to the practice of public administration, the imbalance in the literature between political science and administrative science must be remedied. This is not an original observation but it is a good one.

The remaining sections of this paper deal specifically with the major topics covered at the seminar mentioned earlier and by the four theme papers.

5   "Editorial Statement," vol. 23 (Spring 1980), p. 4.

KENNETH KERNAGHAN

The discipline and the profession

In an article published in 1968,[6] I examined the state of the discipline and the profession of public administration in Canada. Since that time the achievements of the discipline, as measured by research, publications, scholars and schools, has been greater than all the preceding years combined. The progress of the profession during this same period is more difficult to measure and more prone to political and popular debate. In general, the vastly increased volume and complexity of government activities have been met by a commensurate expansion in the number and quality of public servants. But in both the study and practice of public administration so much remains to be done – or done better – that self-commendation must yield to self-criticism. Moreover, there is no lack of external critics to suggest that our theoretical and practical achievements in public administration have been insubstantial.

Perhaps the seminar should have been entitled "Canadian Public Administration: Discipline? Profession?" There is certainly not universal, or even widespread, agreement that the study of public administration is a discipline or that its practice is a profession in the strict sense of these words.

The study of public administration is not – and is unlikely to become – a discipline in the restrictive sense of an intellectual endeavour with a body of coherent and accepted theory. Even if discipline is defined less rigorously as a field of study with a nucleus of uniting beliefs, public administration has not yet achieved agreement on those beliefs. The matter is complicated by the field's so-called "identity crisis" arising from the intellectual and institutional treatment of the subject as a sub-discipline or sub-field of both political science and administrative science (i.e., organization theory and management science). In Canada's universities, the two approaches co-exist, with the study of "public administration as political science" continuing its traditional role as the dominant approach. During the past decade, several schools of public administration have adopted a "policy-management" approach which combines elements of political science, administrative science and public policy in an effort to form a distinct field of public administration.

Similarly, the practice of public administration is not – and is unlikely to become – a profession in the sense of fulfilling the strict criteria normally associated with such traditional professions as law, medicine and engineering. These criteria include a high degree of knowledge and/or skill based on education and/or training, membership in a professional

6 "An Overview," *op. cit.* pp. 291-308.

organization with a high set of standards for admission, dedication to public service above personal interest, and a code of ethics.

The implications of seeking professional status for public service practitioners have not been carefully examined in Canada; moreover, no deliberate, concerted effort is being made by academics and practitioners to achieve a profession of public administration (or public management). It is clear that public administration is gradually moving closer to satisfying some of the criteria noted above but can only be considered a profession if a much looser definition of the term is accepted.

The advance of public administration need not await the resolution of philosophical and semantic debates over whether public administration is a discipline and/or a profession. In ordinary discourse, these terms are usefully applied to the study and practice of public administration respectively.

To see ourselves

At the seminar, teachers and practitioners of public administration were provided with external perspectives on the discipline and the profession by a sociologist, an economist, a businessman and a politician.[7] Seeing ourselves as others see us sometimes confirms our worst suspicions about them. In this case the experience confirmed some suspicions about ourselves.

Public administration can profit enormously from having its theory and practice critically evaluated by persons in other disciplines and professions. This is not simply because members of the public administration community may be unable to provide a sufficiently objective assessment of their field; it is also because public administration is a multidisciplinary enterprise which draws on ideas, insights, theories and techniques from several fields of study and practice.

The essence of Professor Sheriff's argument was that public administration is "an atheoretical discipline" because "most approaches are middle-range theory which are tied to a particular problem, but which are not used to tie together a wide variety of concerns within the public sector." She encouraged students of public administration to avoid middle-range models from related disciplines or sub-disciplines (e.g., the sociology of organizations) and to emphasize the "macro-level theories in which such partial models are embedded." Professor Sheriff, like many

---

7 Respectively, Professor Peta Sheriff (Department of Sociology, McMaster University), Professor Gilles Paquet (Faculty of Administration, University of Ottawa), Pierre Lortie (President, Montreal Stock Exchange), and Pauline Jewett (federal member of Parliament).

scholars studying public administration, sees the central question as one of power – "how it is exercised, by whom and in what direction."

Professor Paquet described the fields of economics and public administration as *modern* professions in that they have no clearly delimited boundaries, no strict controls on entry and no formal code of ethics. He contended that the instrumental rationality of economists can "help solve small problems and puzzles in public administration" but that economists are unlikely to contribute much to achieving substantive rationality. Second, he proposed that public administration should rediscover the distinction between *management*, where the economic approach can be useful, and *governance*. In his view, a theory of governance in public administration can be pursued by 1/ recognizing the normative nature of the discipline; 2/ adopting "the same process of internship which has proved the core element in the training of other professionals"; and 3/ acknowledging the counter-productive nature to date of instrumental rationality. Finally, Professor Paquet suggested that many of the failures of rational management techniques may be more the result of their "fundamental unsuitability" than "the craftiness of uncooperative bureaucrats."

Pierre Lortie discarded the public sector–private sector dichotomy in favour of a distinction between the market and non-market (i.e., government) sectors of the economy. He expressed concern about three broad tendencies in government. First, the focus on techniques of rational decision-making resulted in undue emphasis on "analytic and policy formulation jobs" to the detriment of effective management and program implementation. Second, bureaucrats, who play an important political role in government, are increasingly isolated from and consequently uninformed about the market sector. Third, the non-market sector is unable or unwilling to recognize its costs and failures. Mr. Lortie concluded that governments must "learn to distinguish what they can and cannot do efficiently and effectively" and must take "a more practical orientation to problem identification and programme delivery."

Pauline Jewett said that the remoteness which politicians and the public feel from the administration of public affairs is due in significant measure to the secretive and uncommunicative nature of bureaucrats. Among the other items on her list of concerns were discrimination against women in the public service, inadequate communication in many departments between Ottawa and the field offices, the "better do nothing than make a mistake" syndrome among public servants, and the weakness of parliamentary controls over the bureaucracy.

Several seminar participants took vigorous exception to certain of these views "from the outside." But there was support and, in some instances, strong endorsement for most of the observations and proposals of the external critics. The fact that academics and practitioners were divided amongst themselves on many of the issues precluded any effort to draw the wagons into a circle around either the academic or professional components of the public service community.

Top values

Values are critical determinants in both political and bureaucratic decision-making. The term "values" refers here to enduring beliefs that influence the choices made by individuals, groups or organizations from among available means or ends.

I have suggested elsewhere[8] as well as in a later essay in this volume[9] that certain *administrative* values have been dominant in the evolution of Canadian public administration as a field of practice. These values are political neutrality, accountability, integrity, responsiveness, representativeness, and economy, efficiency and effectiveness. A focus on these values serves as a useful framework for discussing the development and probable future of public administration in Canada.

The relative importance of these values has changed over time; their significance varies according to the bureaucrat's level and position in government; and some of the values compete with one another for priority in the bureaucrat's value system (e.g., efficiency versus responsiveness). Michael Pitfield observes that "government is inextricable from the interplay of contending values" and that no senior bureaucrat "can avoid confronting the reality of choice and balance among ethical and policy values . . . ." Administrative values must also be balanced with competing and complementary personal values (e.g., status, self-actualization). Finally, the core group of administrative values noted above provides a basis for normative judgments as to which values should be sought now and in the future and for speculative discussion of the impact of new developments on existing values.

J.E. Hodgetts, in his essay on implicit values in the administration of public affairs, asks whether the *bureaucratic* values of economy, efficiency and effectiveness can be melded with the *political* values of representation, responsibility and responsiveness. In the light of the definition of values provided earlier, one could argue that politicians and bureaucrats share many of the same values, but with differing degrees of intensity. Certainly politicians are more concerned with such values as representation and responsiveness and bureaucrats with such values as

---

8 "Changing Concepts of Power and Responsibility in the Canadian Public Service," CANADIAN PUBLIC ADMINISTRATION, 21 (Fall 1978), pp. 389-406.
9 "Merit and Motivation: Public Personnel Management in Canada" (with P.K. Kuruvilla).

efficiency and effectiveness. But both politicians and bureaucrats are concerned with all of the core values. Indeed, this fact helps to explain the nature of political-bureaucratic relationships in a democratic society. Bureaucrats are expected to reflect the values of their elected superiors; hence politicians are a major source of administrative values.

At present, accountability is widely viewed as the paramount value in the administration of public affairs. It is not easy to define. For example, Professor Hodgetts asserts that the traditional hierarchical notion of accountability has been supplemented – or supplanted – by a multi-dimensioned notion of accountability to a broader range of political and bureaucratic actors. Nor is accountability easy to achieve. For example, it is difficult in the area of transfer payments between governments to determine which government should be held accountable for the expenditure of the funds. There is no doubt that the attention of academics and public servants will continue to centre on the meaning of accountability and the means of achieving it.

Professor Hodgetts treats the merit principle as a major value in public administration; it could also be viewed as a broad objective of public personnel management and be examined in relation to the administrative values noted above.[10] Much of the vigorous debate over merit in the public service arises from confusion as to whether it is the merit principle or the merit system that is being discussed. The merit principle requires that all Canadians have a right to equal consideration for employment in the public service and that appointments and promotions be based on merit – that is, on fitness to do the job. But in the federal government, according to the Public Service Commission, merit is only one of "five principles that should govern staffing policies." The other four are equity, equality of access, sensitivity and responsiveness, and efficiency and effectiveness. These other principles (or values) are being incorporated into the merit system which is the administrative means for pursuing the merit principle. Discussion of definitions cannot, however, be allowed to obscure the fact that many seminar participants were unhappy about the extent to which the present system departs from the principle.

I shall return to the question of values in the final section of this paper.

The state of the union

The discipline and the profession of public administration can be significantly advanced through communication and cooperation between the field's preachers and practitioners. The preachers or "keepers" of the

10 See ibid.

discipline are a small band of dedicated but dispersed scholars. They are required to teach, administer, research and consult while satisfying academics that they are sufficiently scholarly and bureaucrats that they are properly practical. Moreover, compared to the other social sciences in Canada, the discipline of public administration is very young. It is not surprising, therefore, that the theme papers by Pitfield and Cameron leave the impression that the contribution of the discipline to the profession is potentially large but to date has been regrettably modest.

High expectations of the discipline are held by practitioners and, to a lesser extent, by social scientists in other disciplines. Among these expectations are an over-arching, unifying theory or a paradigm of public administration; middle-level or partial theories that explain and predict bureaucratic behaviour (e.g., in the area of political-bureaucratic relations); an extremely broad range of subject matter in MPA programs (ranging from Canadian history and politics to quantitative analysis and including relevant knowledge of economics, political science, law, sociology, psychology and management); analyses of systemic questions (e.g., the implications of parliamentary reform for the political and bureaucratic systems); critiques of innovations in government structures and processes; and consulting assistance which meets the needs of government without sacrificing academic integrity.

Taken individually, these expectations are neither unrealistic nor unrealizable; taken together, they pose an enormous challenge to the small number of university teachers of public administration. Fortunately, there are public administration scholars in the bureaucracy as well as in academe. Unfortunately, with some notable exceptions, scholarly professionals have contributed relatively little to the study of public administration, despite the fact that public employees in Canada outnumber the keepers of the discipline by a ratio of about 1:40,000. We need to consider not only what the discipline has contributed to the profession but also what the profession has contributed to the discipline. This defence of public administration scholars does not change the fact that their research and publications are widely viewed as irrelevant to the requirements of the profession. Both Pitfield and Laframboise identify areas that not only could be, but already should have been, the focus of scholarly research.

The discipline is not the handmaiden of the profession, but reality demands that academics be sensitive to the needs of practitioners. If academics want their research and ideas to affect practice, they must write on matters of current or perennial concern to the profession. Moreover, they must use a vocabulary that is easily comprehensible to the non-academic. The development of a common language for communication between the discipline and the profession is especially important for articulating shared values and assumptions. Those who share a common language are more likely to find common ground.

In the late 1960s, I suggested that the primary challenges to the discipline of public administration were "inadequate literature, insufficient research funds, difficulty of access to government documents, new approaches to the study and teaching of public administration and the need for contributions from fields other than political science. . . ."[11] Substantial progress has been made in several of these areas but the prospects for accelerating the pace of our progress depends significantly on assistance from the profession. A disproportunate amount of the greatly expanded body of public administration literature has been written by academics. The existence of much in-house research by practitioners, including those who have "drilled dry holes" in various policy fields, is not even acknowledged, much less publicized. Moreover, the profession has done little to encourage scholarly research in public administration by providing financial and other support to research and publication programs outside government.

While access to government documents will doubtless be improved by the Freedom of Information Act, scholars will require access to materials normally exempted from disclosure. Such access is especially important for the preparation of materials to support the increased use of case studies and simulations in the teaching of public administration. The case method, actively promoted since 1976 by IPAC's Case Program in Canadian Public Administration, is especially well suited to the classroom needs and writing talents of practitioners. Finally, contributions from fields other than political science, most notably economics, have gradually increased but a paucity of writings remains in the fields of organization theory, management science and law despite the many practitioners educated and/or working in these fields.

All four theme papers in this volume address the comparative virtues of MPA and MBA programs as preparation for government service. It has been suggested that MPA graduates tend to be interested and competent in policy analysis and contemplation whereas MBA's are more inclined toward problem-solving and management. This argument is not as valid as it was before the management component of public administration programs became as central as it is today. Practitioners, especially those involved in recruitment, should note this important change in program emphasis.

11 "An Overview," p. 308.

Turning solitudes into synergy

In general terms, the challenge to the discipline and profession of public administration is to transform several sets of solitudes into a network of cooperative action. There are varying degrees of separateness between theorists and practitioners of public administration, between government and private sector officials, between teachers of public administration and teachers in other fields, including business administration, between politicians and bureaucrats, and between middle-level and senior bureaucrats. In each case, at least one of the key actors is either a teacher or practitioner of public administration. Thus, the public administration community is in an excellent position to bridge the gaps in communication and perception among professors, politicians, bureaucrats and businessmen. The community's efforts must, however, be based on strong links between its academic and professional components. The activities of both professors and public servants should be based on knowledge of both the theory and practice of public administration.

Improved relations between bureaucrats and businessmen may be achieved in part by closer intellectual and organizational links between programs in public and business administration. Collaboration in research and instruction may also promote better understanding of government-business relations and of the feasibility of transferring business practices and technologies to the complex and political environment of government.

The pervasive influence of politics on public administration requires that scholars make a special effort to explain the nature and effects of interactions between bureaucrats and politicians at all levels of government. In particular, more attention should be paid to improving communication between bureaucrats and backbenchers.

It is critically important that politicians, bureaucrats and academics find ways to enhance the public's trust in government and, specifically, to improve the public image and thereby the morale of public employees. Morale can also be heightened by removing the solitudes between the senior and middle levels of the bureaucracy. Laframboise illustrates the problem by reference to the "middle manager-formal system" and the "deputy minister–short circuit system." Bureaucratic leaders who treat public service as a higher calling rather than a comfortable career provide an appropriate role model for their subordinates. But political leaders and their top advisers need to remember that only if human resources are well managed at the senior echelons will the influence of high performance and high morale trickle down the administrative pyramid.

Virtually all the essays in this volume touch on emerging trends and developments in the study and/or practice of public administration. But the crystal ball reveals only a hazy outline of the long-term prospects for Canadian public administration. We will undoubtedly encounter many challenges that we cannot now foresee. The structures and processes of government as well as the substance and pedagogy of public administration programs will be adapted to deal with new problems and technologies.

To cope with this prospect of constant change, we need a clear understanding of our values and value priorities. Such values as accountability, efficiency, integrity and responsiveness will continue to guide the choices we make among possible reforms. The relative priority of these and other values changes over time but the current consensus is that accountability will remain a dominant value in public administration for the foreseeable future.

The administrative values which the public administration community cherishes most highly must in practice be reconciled with one another and with personal values. Both academics and practitioners should insist that conflicting values be reconciled in the guiding light of the public interest. For a focus on the public interest is the central distinguishing feature of the profession and discipline of public administration.

Kenneth Kernaghan

L'administration publique canadienne: situation actuelle et perspectives d'avenir

Le chemin que l'on emprunte importe peu si l'on n'a pas de destination précise. Cela ne veut pas dire que lorsque l'on connaît sa destination, on trouve d'emblée le « meilleur chemin » pour y arriver. Telle est la situation de la théorie et de la pratique de l'administration publique au Canada : nous visons bien un objectif précis mais nous nous y acheminons, par choix et par nécessité, par divers chemins. La réalisation de notre objectif, soit un niveau élevé de connaissance et de performance dans la communauté de l'administration publique, passe par des programmes de formation et de perfectionnement, des conférences, des colloques, de la recherche, des publications et de l'expérience pratique. Les théoriciens et les praticiens ne parcourent pas assez souvent ensemble les chemins qui mènent à cet objectif; en fait, le manque de communication qui existe entre ces deux catégories de personnes demeure l'un des principaux obstacles à notre progrès collectif. Parmi les autres entraves importantes, on retient la rareté des ressources humaines et financières affectées à la recherche savante, particulièrement au niveau de l'administration provinciale et municipale, et l'insuffisance des possibilités de perfectionnement professionnel.

Les articles qu'il renferme parcourent le domaine de l'administration publique canadienne. Ils tentent d'établir la distance parcourue, de déterminer dans quelles directions nous nous dirigeons et de découvrir quels sont les obstacles qui gênent encore notre avance. Ce présent volume est publié à l'occasion du vingt-cinquième anniversaire d'*Administration publique du Canada*, la revue de l'Institut d'administration publique du Canada.

Ce premier article sert d'introduction; il fournit un fondement aux études ultérieures qui traiteront des thèmes principaux (études 3 à 6) et

Le professeur Kernaghan enseigne à la Section de politiques et à l'Ecole d'Etudes administratives de l'Université Brock, et il est rédacteur d'*Administration publique du Canada*.

des sous-secteurs (études 7 à 16)[1] de l'administration publique au Canada. Il débute par une analyse du contenu de la revue *Administration publique du Canada* depuis sa fondation. S'y trouve ensuite un compte rendu des idées et opinions formulées lors d'un colloque national spécial sur le thème « Administration publique du Canada : la discipline et la profession », au cours duquel quatre études thématiques ont été présentées.[2] Mon résumé des discussions donnera sans doute une impression de consensus et d'ordre ne correspondant pas véritablement à la réalité. J'ai inclus mes remarques personnelles sur les questions discutées mais j'ai résisté à la tentation de jouer au « rapporteur créatif ».

Qualité et originalité

Samuel Johnson fit un jour l'observation suivante à un jeune écrivain : « Votre manuscrit est à la fois bon et original; malheureusement, ce qui est bon n'est pas original et ce qui est original n'est pas bon ». Il se pourrait que certains articles publiés dans la revue *Administration publique du Canada* (APC) depuis sa création en 1958 méritent une critique de ce genre, mais il ne faudrait quand même pas oublier qu'APC a publié un grand nombre d'articles qui ont brillé autant par leur qualité que par leur originalité. On pourrait même ajouter que l'ensemble des textes publiés dans les cent numéros d'APC au cours des vingt-cinq dernières années constitue la principale source de renseignements et d'idées sur la théorie et la pratique de l'administration publique au Canada. Il est ainsi possible de se faire une idée, au fil des pages de la revue, de l'évolution de l'administration de nos affaires publiques au cours de la période couverte. Les articles reflètent bien sûr l'évolution et les problèmes de l'époque et, en particulier, ceux de la pratique de l'administration publique. Les thèmes et questions qui demeurent toujours d'actualité ou qui refont régulièrement surface y ont également été examinés, mais dans une optique plus théorique dans la plupart des cas.

Un examen du contenu de la revue révèle cependant que certaines questions ont reçu beaucoup d'attention tandis que d'autres ont été passées sous silence. Ceci ressort en particulier dans la répartition des arti-

---

1 Chacune des dix études sur les sous-secteurs traite, avec des degrés d'insistance variables, des sujets suivants : la documentation concernant le sous-secteur examiné, la situation actuelle et ses problèmes, les nouvelles tendances et les perspectives d'avenir, l'ordre du jour de la recherche et, enfin, la répercussion de toutes ces questions sur la formation dans le domaine de l'administration publique. Les lecteurs sont priés de noter que chaque auteur a dû traiter un vaste sujet en un nombre limité de pages.

2 Le colloque a été organisé par l'Institut d'administration publique du Canada et s'est tenu au lac Ste-Marie, Québec, du 12 au 14 mai 1982. L'Institut tient à exprimer sa profonde reconnaissance au Conseil de recherches en sciences humaines du Canada pour l'appui accordé pour le colloque comme pour le numéro de vingt-cinquième anniversaire de la revue.

cles par sujet et par auteur, de 1968 à 1981[3] (voir tableaux I et II). Ces tableaux de répartition[4] démontrent que l'accent a été mis sur les sciences politiques tandis que les sciences administratives ont été comparativement négligées. En effet, plus de la moitié des articles publiés traitent des sujets suivants : structure/organisation, processus et principes de base de politique publique, politique de l'administration publique et relations intergouvernementales; quant à la théorie de l'organisation et la gestion, elles ne représentent que 9% du total. On constate également, d'après le tableau II, que les universitaires ont écrit davantage d'articles que les fonctionnaires fédéraux, provinciaux et municipaux. Par rapport à la période de 1958 à 1967, on constate même une légère augmentation du nombre d'articles écrits par ces universitaires.

Il ne faut évidemment pas oublier qu'il y a plus de professeurs d'administration publique actuellement qu'en 1967, qu'ils ont plus de temps et qu'ils sont beaucoup plus motivés à écrire en vue d'être publiés, pour des raisons de salaire, de promotion ou de prestige, que ne le sont les fonctionnaires. Par ailleurs, plus de la moitié des universitaires auteurs d'articles sont des experts en sciences politiques. Le nombre réduit d'articles soumis par des spécialistes en sciences de la gestion, en sociologie et psychologie sociale explique la rareté des textes touchant les sciences administratives. Ainsi, si les articles de cette catégorie sont peu nombreux,

TABLEAU I: *Répartition des articles par sujet – Administration publique du Canada, du vol. 11, n° 1, 1968, au vol. 24, n° 4, 1981.*

Sujets	n	%
Portée de la discipline	3	0,73
Méthodologie	18	4,40
Théorie de l'organisation	8	1,96
Environnement	14	3,42
Structure/organisation	43	10,51
Politique publique – Processus et fond	95	23,23
Relations intergouvernementales	32	7,82
Gestion	28	6,85
Finances/budget	17	4,16
Personnel	39	9,54
Politique de l'administration publique	38	9,29
Responsabilité/valeurs	14	3,42
Droit administratif	5	1,22
Divers	55	13,45
Total	409	100

3 Pour l'analyse des années 1958 à 1967, voir l'article de K. Kernaghan intitulé « An Overview of Public Administration in Canada Today », *Administration publique du Canada*, vol. 11, automne 1968, pp. 249-96.
4 La classification des sujets se base essentiellement sur le contenu habituel des manuels d'administration publique.

TABLEAU II: *Répartition des articles par auteur(s) – Administration publique du Canada, du vol. 11, no 1, 1968, au vol. 24, no 4, 1981.*

Universitaires	n	%
Science politique	131	26,89
Economie	45	9,24
Administration publique	35	7,18
Administration des entreprises/Sciences de la gestion	9	1,84
Autres (sociologie, histoire, etc.)	76	15,60
Total partiel	296	60,76

Praticiens et autres	n	%
Fonctionnaires fédéraux	83	17,04
Fonctionnaires provinciaux	57	11,70
Fonctionnaires municipaux	13	2,66
Autres (hommes politiques, fonctionnaires, étrangers, etc.)	38	7,80
Total partiel	191	39,21
Total	487	100

cela n'est pas imputable à une décision prise par la rédaction, mais plutôt à la rareté des manuscrits soumis dans ce domaine. On retrouve d'ailleurs dans les ouvrages et monographies sur l'administration publique canadienne la même tendance, en matière de fond et d'orientation, que celle qui est reflétée dans la revue. Il est vrai que certains auteurs canadiens publient des articles ayant trait aux sciences administratives dans d'autres revues de sciences sociales, au Canada ou ailleurs. Il faut certainement attribuer cette situation au fait fort compréhensible qu'APC est considérée comme une revue destinée davantage aux professeurs de sciences politiques et d'économie et aux fonctionnaires qu'aux professeurs s'intéressant principalement aux sciences administratives. Signalons de plus que les articles émanant de fonctionnaires sont davantage axés sur la gestion et la pratique que ceux que produisent les universitaires mais même dans le cas de ces derniers, la plupart de leurs articles entrent dans la catégorie générale des sciences politiques plutôt que dans celle des sciences administratives.

D'une manière générale, la majorité des auteurs (75,8%) ont traité le thème de leur article selon une méthode historico-descriptive; 20,8% des articles ont reflété un ton normatif/prescriptif et 3,4% seulement des auteurs ont opté pour un traitement behavioriste/empirique.

Le mandat actuel d'APC comprend « l'examen des structures, des processus et des résultats de la politique et de la gestion publiques relatifs aux fonctions exécutives, législatives, judiciaires et quasi-judiciaires dans les ordres municipal, provincial et fédéral de gouvernement ».[5] Selon ce

5   « Communication du rédacteur », *Administration publique du Canada*, vol. 23, printemps 1980, p. 9.

mandat, l'administration publique est envisagée en partie sous l'angle d'une science administrative, bien que cela ne soit pas clairement énoncé. S'ils désirent apporter une contribution valable à leur secteur, les administrateurs publics du Canada devront donc redresser le déséquilibre qui existe entre les sciences politiques et les sciences administratives en ce qui concerne le montant de documentation. Cette remarque n'a certainement rien d'original, mais il est utile de l'exprimer.

Le reste de la présente communication porte sur les principales questions examinées lors du colloque du lac Ste-Marie et sur ses quatre exposés thématiques.

La discipline et la profession

Dans un article publié en 1968,[6] j'ai examiné la situation de l'administration publique au Canada en tant que discipline et profession. Dans les années subséquentes, la discipline a beaucoup plus progressé qu'au cours de toutes les années antérieures, si l'on en juge par le montant de recherche, de publications, de spécialistes et d'écoles. Quant à l'évolution de la profession au cours de la même période, elle est plus difficile à évaluer et fait davantage l'objet de discussions politiques et publiques. D'une manière générale, l'accroissement quantitatif et qualitatif du corps des fonctionnaires a été proportionnel à la masse et à la complexité des activités gouvernementales, qui ont connu une expansion considérable. Mais il reste tant de choses à faire, ou à améliorer, dans le domaine de la théorie et de la pratique de l'administration publique, qu'il vaut mieux éviter de se couvrir de gloire et pratiquer plutôt l'autocritique. Qui plus est, il ne manque pas de critiques extérieurs qui considèrent que nos résultats théoriques et pratiques dans le domaine ne représentent pas grand-chose. Il aurait peut-être mieux valu que le colloque mentionné s'intitule « Administration publique du Canada : discipline? profession? » Car il n'est certes pas reconnu universellement, ni même d'une façon générale, que l'étude de l'administration constitue une discipline et sa pratique une profession, au sens strict de ces termes.

L'étude de l'administration publique n'est pas et ne sera probablement jamais une discipline au sens étroit du terme, soit une démarche intellectuelle fondée sur un ensemble de principes cohérents et reconnus. Même si on prend une définition moins stricte du terme, soit un domaine d'étude regroupant des convictions unificatrices, on constate que l'accord ne s'est pas encore fait sur ces convictions. La question se trouve compliquée par la prétendue « crise d'identité » de l'administration publique, qui serait due au fait qu'elle est traitée sur le plan intellectuel et institutionnel comme une sous-discipline ou un sous-domaine des sciences politiques et des sciences administratives (soit la théorie de l'organisation et

6 « An Overview », *op. cit.*, note 3.

la science de la gestion). Dans les universités canadiennes, ces deux façons d'envisager la question coexistent; l'étude de l'administration publique continue, selon la tradition, à faire partie du domaine des sciences politiques. Cependant, au cours de la dernière décennie, plusieurs écoles d'administration publique se sont orientées vers une formule qui intègre à la fois des éléments de gestion et de politique, dans laquelle se retrouvent des éléments de sciences politiques, de sciences administratives et de politique publique, l'objectif recherché étant de faire de l'administration publique une discipline distincte.

De même, la pratique de l'administration publique n'est pas une profession et ne risque pas de le devenir, car elle ne répond pas à des critères précis comparables à ceux qui sont normalement adoptés par des professions traditionnelles comme le droit, la médecine et le génie. Parmi ces critères, citons des connaissances poussées et une compétence fondée sur des études ou une formation professionnelle, l'appartenance à un organisme professionnel ayant des normes d'adhésion strictes, un dévouement au service public passant avant les intérêts personnels et un code de déontologie. Nul n'a encore examiné minutieusement, au Canada, les conséquences de la recherche d'un statut professionnel pour les praticiens de la fonction publique; qui plus est, ni les théoriciens ni les praticiens ne déploient des efforts délibérés et concertés pour que l'administration publique (ou la gestion publique) devienne une profession. Il est évident que l'administration publique répond de plus en plus aux critères qui viennent d'être cités, mais pour qu'elle puisse être considérée comme une profession, il faudrait qu'une définition beaucoup plus large du terme soit acceptée.

Cependant, le développement de l'administration publique n'a pas à attendre l'aboutissement de discussions philosophiques et sémantiques ayant pour but de déterminer si elle est une discipline ou une profession, ou les deux. Dans la vie courante, ces termes s'appliquent à l'étude comme à la pratique de cette administration publique.

Ce que les autres pensent de nous

Lors du colloque, les enseignants et praticiens en administration publique ont pu connaître le point de vue d'un sociologue, d'un économiste, d'un homme d'affaires et d'un homme politique sur l'administration publique en tant que discipline et profession.[7] Une telle occasion de nous voir avec les yeux d'autrui peut parfois confirmer nos pires doutes à propos de ceux qui nous scrutent. Dans le cas de ce colloque, ce sont certains doutes sur nous-mêmes qui ont été confirmés. Il est certaine-

7 Respectivement, le professeur Peta Sheriff (département de Sociologie, Université McMaster), le professeur Gilles Paquet (Faculté d'administration, Université d'Ottawa), Pierre Lortie (président de la Bourse de Montréal) et Pauline Jewett (député fédéral).

ment très utile que la théorie et la pratique de l'administration publique fassent l'objet d'une évaluation critique par des personnes qui s'occupent d'autres disciplines et exercent d'autres professions. Des critiques extérieures ne sont pas simplement utiles parce que les professionnels de l'administration publique ne sont peut-être pas capables d'évaluer leur propre domaine avec suffisamment d'objectivité, mais aussi parce que l'administration publique est un secteur multidisciplinaire qui s'inspire des idées, opinions, principes et techniques propres à plusieurs autres domaines d'étude et de pratique.

D'après le professeur Sheriff, l'administration publique est « une discipline qui ne repose pas sur une théorie » car « la plupart des stratégies relèvent de théories intermédiaires qui portent sur un problème précis et elles n'ont pas pour but de réunir une vaste gamme de questions touchant le secteur public ». Les étudiants en administration publique sont encouragés à délaisser les modèles intermédiaires qui découlent de disciplines connexes ou de sous-disciplines (par exemple la sociologie des organisations) pour mettre l'accent sur les « macro-principes qui englobent ces modèles partiels ». Comme bien des théoriciens de l'administration publique, le professeur Sheriff considère que la question du « pouvoir » constitue le fond du problème, « comment il est exercé, par qui et dans quel but ».

Pour le professeur Paquet, l'économie et l'administration publique entrent dans le cadre des professions « modernes », car elles ne sont pas nettement délimitées, elles n'imposent pas une sélection initiale stricte et elles n'ont pas adopté de code de déontologie officiel. A son avis, la capacité de rationalisation des économistes peut « être utile lorsqu'il s'agit de résoudre de petits problèmes et difficultés propres à l'administration publique », mais il ne faut guère compter sur eux pour arriver à une rationalité indépendante. En second lieu, il suggère que l'administration publique établisse de nouveau une distinction entre « gestion », lorsqu'une optique économique peut être utile, et « gouvernance ». A son avis, le principe de gouvernance peut être appliqué à l'administration publique 1) en reconnaissant le caractère normatif de la discipline, 2) en adoptant « le système de stages qui s'est révélé fondamental pour la formation d'autres professionnels » et 3) en reconnaissant qu'un système fondé sur la rationalité instrumentale a, jusqu'à présent, nui à la productivité. Enfin, toujours selon le professeur Paquet, si les techniques de gestion rationnelle ne permettent pas souvent d'obtenir les résultats escomptés, c'est peut-être davantage dû au fait qu'elles sont « fondamentalement inadéquates » plutôt qu'à « des pratiques astucieuses adoptées par des bureaucrates récalcitrants ».

Pour sa part, Pierre Lortie rejette la dichotomie qui existe entre le secteur privé et le secteur public et lui préfère une distinction entre le secteur soumis au marché et le secteur non soumis au marché (soit gouvernemental) de l'économie. Pour lui, trois tendances générales au sein du gouvernement lui paraissent préoccupantes. Tout d'abord, par suite de l'importance accordée aux techniques de prise de décision selon des principes rationnels, on accorde une importance excessive aux « fonctions d'analyse et de formulation de politique », au détriment de l'efficacité sur les plans de la gestion et de la mise en application des programmes. En second lieu, les bureaucrates qui jouent un rôle politique important au sein du gouvernement sont de plus en plus coupés du secteur soumis au marché et par conséquent mal renseignés sur ce secteur. En troisième lieu, le secteur non soumis au marché est incapable de reconnaître ses coûts et ses échecs ou refuse de le faire. En conclusion, M. Lortie considère que les gouvernements doivent « apprendre à faire une distinction entre ce qu'ils peuvent et ne peuvent pas accomplir efficacement et rentablement » et «aborder l'identification des problèmes et l'exécution des programmes dans une optique plus réaliste ».

Pour Pauline Jewett, il faut attribuer dans une large mesure à la nature secrète et fermée des bureaucrates le fait que les hommes politiques et le public ne se sentent pas directement concernés par l'administration des affaires publiques. Elle cite ensuite un certain nombre de préoccupations, dont la discrimination envers les femmes dans la fonction publique, l'incapacité de nombreux ministères à assurer la communication entre Ottawa et les bureaux régionaux, l'attitude des fonctionnaires qui préfèrent « ne rien faire plutôt que de courir le risque de commettre une erreur » et la faiblesse des moyens de contrôle parlementaires sur la bureaucratie.

Plusieurs participants au colloque se sont élevés avec véhémence contre certains points de vue émanant de ces observateurs « de l'extérieur ». Mais la majorité des observations et propositions formulées par ces critiques ont été reçues avec intérêt et bienveillance et, dans certains cas, fortement appuyées. Comme la dissension régnait parmi les théoriciens et les praticiens eux-mêmes à propos de nombreuses questions soulevées, tous les efforts tentés pour créer un consensus soit au sein du groupe des théoriciens soit au sein de celui des professionnels de la fonction publique se sont soldés par des échecs.

Les valeurs suprêmes

Les valeurs sont des facteurs déterminants en matière de décisions politiques et bureaucratiques. Par valeurs, on entend ici des convictions durables qui influencent les choix faits par des individus, des groupes ou des organismes parmi différents moyens pour aboutir à diverses fins. J'ai avancé ailleurs,[8] ainsi que dans un autre article de ce volume,[9] que cer-

8   « Changing Concepts of Power and Responsibility in the Canadian Public Service », *Administration publique du Canada*, vol. 21, automne 1978, pp. 389-406.
9   « Merit and Motivation: Public Personnel Management in Canada » (avec P.K. Kuruvilla), dans ce volume.

taines valeurs « administratives » ont fortement influencé l'évolution de l'administration publique canadienne en tant que domaine de pratique. Il s'agit de la neutralité politique, de l'imputabilité, de l'intégrité, de la sensibilité, de la représentativité, puis de l'économie, de l'efficience et de l'efficacité. Ces valeurs servent de cadre utile à la discussion du développement et de l'évolution probable de l'administration publique au Canada.

L'importance relative de ces valeurs a évolué avec le temps; leur portée varie en fonction du niveau et du poste qu'occupe le bureaucrate au sein du gouvernement; de plus, certaines de ces valeurs rivalisent entre elles pour avoir la priorité chez le bureaucrate (par exemple efficacité contre sensibilité).

Michael Pitfield fait remarquer que « le gouvernement n'échappera jamais à l'interaction de valeurs opposées » et qu'aucun haut fonctionnaire ne peut « éviter d'avoir à faire face aux impératifs de choix et d'équilibre entre des valeurs déontologiques et politiques... » Il faut également déterminer la place des valeurs administratives par rapport aux valeurs personnelles, qui sont en concurrence avec ces dernières ou les complètent (le prestige ou la réalisation du potentiel personnel). Enfin, les valeurs administratives fondamentales citées plus haut permettent d'arriver à des décisions normatives à propos du choix des valeurs à retenir dans l'immédiat et à l'avenir, ainsi que de spéculer sur l'impact des nouvelles tendances sur les valeurs existantes.

Dans son exposé sur les valeurs implicites dans l'administration des affaires publiques, J.E. Hodgetts se demande si les valeurs « bureaucratiques », comme l'économie, l'efficience et l'efficacité, peuvent être combinées aux valeurs « politiques » de la représentation, de l'imputabilité et de la sensibilité. A la lumière de la définition des valeurs proposée précédemment, on pourrait avancer que les hommes politiques et les bureaucrates adoptent des valeurs « identiques » mais avec un degré d'intensité différent. Pour les hommes politiques, il ne fait aucun doute que la représentativité et la sensibilité sont des valeurs privilégiées, alors que les bureaucrates mettent davantage l'accent sur l'efficience et l'efficacité. Il reste que les hommes politiques et les bureaucrates ne négligent aucune des valeurs fondamentales. Cela explique d'ailleurs la nature des relations politico-bureaucratiques dans une société démocratique. On s'attend également à retrouver chez les bureaucrates les valeurs de leurs supérieurs élus, ce qui fait que les hommes politiques sont une autre importante « source » de valeurs administratives.

A l'heure actuelle, l'imputabilité est considérée par la majorité comme une valeur primordiale dans l'administration des affaires publiques. Ce n'est pas une notion facile à définir. Ainsi, le professeur Hodgetts affirme que la notion traditionnelle et hiérarchique de l'imputabilité a été élargie – ou remplacée – par une notion d'imputabilité multidimensionnelle, qui s'étend à un éventail plus large d'hommes politiques et de bureaucrates. La mise en application de ce principe d'imputabilité n'est pas non plus chose facile. Ainsi, dans le domaine des paiements de transferts entre gouvernements, il est difficile de déterminer quel gouvernement devrait être tenu responsable de l'affectation des crédits. Il est certain que les universitaires et le fonctionnaires continueront à examiner la signification du terme imputabilité et les moyens de mettre en oeuvre ce qu'elle implique.

Pour le professeur Hodgetts, le principe du mérite constitue une valeur importante en administration publique. Cette notion pourrait également constituer un objectif général de la gestion du personnel du secteur public et être examinée à la lumière des valeurs administratives citées plus haut.[10] La question du mérite suscite une forte controverse au sein de la fonction publique du fait de la confusion régnant à propos de l'objet même de la discussion. Il faudrait ainsi savoir si elle porte sur le principe du mérite ou sur le système du mérite. Selon le principe du mérite, tous les Canadiens doivent avoir des chances égales d'emploi dans la fonction publique et les nominations et avancements doivent être fondés sur l'aptitude à l'exécution de fonctions déterminées. Mais d'après la Commission de la fonction publique du gouvernement fédéral, le mérite n'est qu'un des « cinq principes qui doivent régir les politiques de dotation en personnel ». Les quatre autres sont l'équité, l'égalité d'accès, la sensibilité et l'efficience et l'efficacité. Ces autres principes (ou valeurs) sont incorporés dans le système fondé sur le mérite, qui constitue le moyen administratif de mise en pratique du principe du mérite. Il ne faut cependant pas que la discussion des définitions puisse faire oublier que les fonctionnaires et les universitaires sont loin d'être d'accord sur la distance qui existe ou qui devrait exister entre le système du mérite et le principe du mérite. Je reviendrai sur la question des valeurs à la fin de cette communication.

L'état de l'Union

L'administration publique en tant que discipline et profession pourra faire des progrès certains grâce à la communication et la collaboration entre les prédicateurs et les praticiens. Les prédicateurs ou « défenseurs » de la discipline sont des gens convaincus de la valeur de ce qu'ils prêchent, mais ils sont aussi dispersés et peu nombreux. Il leur faut enseigner, administrer, faire de la recherche et des consultations tout en prouvant aux universitaires qu'ils connaissent suffisamment bien la théorie et aux bureaucrates qu'ils ont un sens pratique bien développé. En outre, comparée aux autres sciences sociales au Canada, la discipline de

10   Voir notes 8 et 9.

l'administration publique est très jeune. Il ne faut donc pas s'étonner que les propos de Pitfield et de Cameron donnent l'impression que le potentiel d'apport de la discipline à la profession est vaste malgré la regrettable modestie dont elle a fait preuve jusqu'à présent.

Les praticiens attendent beaucoup de la discipline; il en va de même pour les spécialistes des sciences sociales appartenant à d'autres disciplines, quoiqu'à un degré moindre. Ils en attendent, entre autres : un principe unificateur et dominant ou un modèle d'administration publique; des théories partielles ou intermédiaires qui expliquent et annoncent le comportement bureaucratique (par exemple dans le domaine des relations politico-bureaucratiques); une gamme extrêmement étendue de sujets couverts par les programmes de maîtrise en administration publique (qui vont de l'histoire et de la vie politique canadiennes aux analyses quantitatives, en passant par les connaissances pertinentes en économie, sciences politiques, droit, sociologie, psychologie et gestion); des analyses des questions relatives au système (par exemple les implications de la réforme parlementaire pour les systèmes politiques et bureaucratiques); les critiques des innovations touchant les structures et processus gouvernementaux; et le recours à des consultants pour répondre aux besoins du gouvernement sans sacrifier l'intégrité académique. Individuellement, ces espérances sont à la fois réalistes et réalisables, mais prises ensemble, elles posent un défi considérable aux universitaires professeurs en administration publique, dont le nombre est plutôt restreint. Réjouissons-nous cependant qu'il y ait des chercheurs en administration publique parmi les bureaucrates comme dans les établissements d'enseignement. Malheureusement, à quelques notables exceptions près, les professionnels versés en théorie de l'administration publique n'ont guère contribué à l'étude de ce domaine bien que, au Canada, le rapport numérique entre les fonctionnaires et les défenseurs de la discipline soit de l'ordre de 1/40 000. Nous devons envisager non seulement ce que la discipline a apporté à la profession, mais aussi ce que la profession a apporté à la discipline.

Cette défense des chercheurs en administration publique ne change rien au fait que leurs recherches et publications sont dans l'ensemble considérées comme sans rapport avec les exigences de la profession. Pitfield et Laframboise précisent les domaines sur lesquels la recherche pourrait porter et même aurait déjà dû porter. La discipline n'est pas la servante de la profession, mais la réalité exige que les universitaires soient attentifs aux besoins des praticiens. Si les universitaires veulent que leurs recherches et leurs idées aient un effet sur la pratique, il leur incombe de traiter de questions courantes ou permanentes, qui intéressent la profession. En outre, ils doivent utiliser un vocabulaire aisément accessible à tous. L'expression de valeurs et d'hypothèses communes doit se faire dans une langue de communication commune à la discipline et à la profession. La compréhension est nettement facilitée lorsque les interlocuteurs parlent la même langue.

Vers la fin des années 1960, j'ai déclaré que la discipline de l'administration publique souffrait principalement « d'un manque de documents appropriés, d'une insuffisance de crédits de recherche, d'une difficulté d'accès aux documents gouvernementaux, d'une carence en nouvelles méthodes d'étude et d'enseignement de l'administration publique, et de l'insuffisance des apports de domaines autres que les sciences politiques... »[11] Des progrès très nets ont été enregistrés dans plusieurs de ces domaines, mais l'accélération du rythme de ces progrès ne se fera qu'au prix d'une aide accrue de la profession. Dans la masse des documents sur l'administration publique qui a connu une expansion considérable, un nombre disproportionné d'écrits est attribuable aux théoriciens. Les efforts de recherche déployés par les praticiens, y compris ceux qui se sont lancés, sans aboutir nulle part, dans divers domaines de politique, ne sont pas reconnus et aucune publicité n'est faite à leur égard. Qui plus est, la profession n'a pas fait grand-chose pour encourager la recherche en administration publique en finançant ou en appuyant d'une manière quelconque les programmes de recherche et de publication en dehors du secteur gouvernemental.

L'accès aux documents gouvernementaux sera certainement facilité par la loi sur l'accès à l'information, mais les chercheurs devraient tout de même pouvoir prendre connaissance de documents dont la divulgation est normalement interdite. Un tel accès est indispensable pour la préparation des documents que requiert l'emploi de plus en plus fréquent de cas et de simulations dans l'enseignement de l'administration publique. La méthode d'étude de cas a fait l'objet d'une promotion vigoureuse depuis 1976 grâce au Programme de cas en administration publique canadienne de l'IAPC. Elle convient particulièrement à l'enseignement en classe et elle est utile aux praticiens désireux de faciliter la compréhension de leurs écrits. Enfin, l'apport provenant de disciplines autres que les sciences politiques, en particulier l'économie, a progressivement augmenté, mais on ne peut que déplorer que les textes consacrés à la théorie de l'organisation, à la science de la gestion et au droit demeurent toujours aussi rares, bien que de nombreux praticiens aient fait des études ou travaillent dans ces domaines.

Les quatre exposés thématiques publiés dans ce volume examinent les avantages comparatifs des programmes de MAP et de MAE comme moyens de se préparer à entrer au service de l'Etat. Certains considèrent que les titulaires d'une MAP ont tendance à s'intéresser à l'analyse et à l'étude

11   « An Overview », *op. cit.*, note 3.

des politiques et à être compétents dans ces domaines, alors que les titulaires d'une MAE seraient beaucoup plus portés à s'intéresser à la résolution des problèmes et à la gestion. Cet argument était beaucoup plus valable autrefois, c'est-à-dire avant que l'élément « gestion » des programmes d'administration publique ne prenne la place prépondérante qu'il occupe aujourd'hui. Les praticiens, et surtout ceux qui s'occupent du recrutement, devraient prendre note de cet important changement d'orientation des programmes.

De l'isolationnisme à la synergie

D'une manière générale, il faut que l'administration publique en tant que discipline et profession réussisse à transformer diverses factions isolationnistes en un réseau de collaboration. Les divers groupes en jeu sont séparés par des fossés plus ou moins profonds; c'est ce que l'on constate entre les théoriciens et les praticiens de l'administration publique, entre les dirigeants du secteur gouvernemental et ceux du secteur privé, entre les professeurs d'administration publique et les professeurs d'autres disciplines (y compris l'administration des entreprises), entre les hommes politiques et les bureaucrates, et entre les bureaucrates de niveau intermédiaire et ceux de niveau supérieur. Dans chaque cas, au moins un des protagonistes est soit un enseignant, soit un praticien. Par conséquent, les membres de la communauté de l'administration publique sont bien placés pour combler les écarts existant au niveau de la communication et de la perception entre les professeurs, les hommes politiques, les bureaucrates et les hommes d'affaires. L'effort des administrateurs publics doit cependant reposer sur des liens solides unissant les théoriciens et les professionnels. Les activités des professeurs comme celles des fonctionnaires devraient reposer sur la connaissance à la fois de la théorie et de la pratique de l'administration publique.

On réussira peut-être à améliorer les relations entre les bureaucrates et les hommes d'affaires en resserrant les liens intellectuels et organisationnels existant entre les programmes d'administration publique et ceux d'administration des entreprises. La collaboration dans le domaine de la recherche et de l'enseignement favorisera peut-être aussi une meilleure compréhension des relations gouvernements-entreprises et des possibilités d'adapter les pratiques et techniques du secteur privé au milieu complexe et politique du gouvernement.

Par suite de l'influence envahissante de la politique sur l'administration publique, les chercheurs devraient faire un effort particulier pour expliquer la nature et les effets des interactions entre les bureaucrates et les hommes politiques de tous les ordres de gouvernement. Il est particulièrement important que l'on s'efforce d'améliorer la communication entre les bureaucrates et les députés sans portefeuille.

Par ailleurs, les hommes politiques, les bureaucrates et les universitaires doivent absolument trouver le moyen de promouvoir la confiance du public dans le gouvernement et, en particulier, d'améliorer l'image de marque des fonctionnaires, ce qui contribuera à relever leur moral. Ce moral peut également être relevé en inversant la tendance au compartimentage, qui existe entre les bureaucrates de niveau intermédiaire et ceux de niveau supérieur. Laframboise illustre bien le problème en parlant du « système formel imposé au chef de service de niveau intermédiaire » et du « système de court-circuit réservé au sous-ministre ». Les hauts fonctionnaires qui considèrent que la fonction publique est une noble vocation plutôt qu'une carrière de tout repos donnent le bon exemple à leurs subordonnés. Mais les dirigeants politiques et leurs conseillers supérieurs ne doivent pas oublier que les ressources humaines doivent d'abord être bien gérées au niveau supérieur pour que la base de la pyramide administrative puisse avoir un rendement élevé et garder un bon moral.

La quasi-totalité des articles figurant dans ce volume traite des tendances naissantes et de l'évolution de l'étude et de la pratique de l'administration publique. Malheureusement, la boule de cristal ne nous révèle que de très vagues perspectives à long terme. Nous rencontrerons certainement de nombreuses difficultés que nous ne pouvons pas encore prévoir. Les structures et processus de gouvernement ainsi que la matière et les méthodes d'enseignement des programmes d'administration publique seront adaptés en fonction des nouveaux problèmes et des innovations technologiques. Pour pouvoir faire face à ces constants changements que l'on prévoit déjà, nous devons nous faire une idée précise de nos valeurs et de leur ordre de priorité. Des valeurs telles que l'imputabilité, l'efficience, l'intégrité et la sensibilité continueront à guider nos choix en matière de réformes éventuelles. L'ordre de priorité attribué à ces valeurs est relatif et change avec le temps mais, à l'heure actuelle, on s'accorde généralement à reconnaître que l'imputabilité restera la valeur dominante dans le domaine de l'administration publique pour les années à venir.

Finalement, les valeurs administratives qui sont particulièrement chères aux administrateurs publics doivent, dans la pratique, être conciliées les unes avec les autres ainsi qu'avec les valeurs personnelles. Les universitaires comme les praticiens doivent insister pour que l'on rétablisse la compatibilité entre des valeurs contradictoires dans le but de servir l'intérêt public. En effet, le souci de l'intérêt public demeure la caractéristique véritablement propre à l'administration publique en tant que profession et discipline.

J.E. Hodgetts | Implicit values in the administration of public affairs

In this restrospective *tour de horizon* of Canadian public administration we should, I suggest, seek to focus on what could be called our "administrative culture." What are the implicit values or working assumptions that infuse, inspire, colour and constrain the attitudes and behaviour not only of those who make their careers in Canadian governmental affairs but also of those who have occupied themselves with research and teaching in the field of public administration? Just as I hypothesize that practitioners and preachers practice and profess within the context of what I call our administrative culture, so too is that culture itself formed and re-formed by the changing societal, economic and political forces which establish the environment within which both practitioners and students of public affairs carry on their daily labours. In short, our administrative culture should be as dynamic as the forces that impinge upon it and with which it constantly interacts in a pluralist, open society.

Our investigation may most usefully be undertaken by pursuing answers to these questions: From whence cometh the values that have dominated our administrative culture? What are they and how have they changed over time? Once we have answers to these questions we open up the more immediate issues before us, namely, by what means have these values been made flesh amongst students and practitioners of public administration; and in what ways have these values left their imprint on the modes and means of studying and practising the administration of public affairs?

Administrative culture and its values

Students of government, since the advent of what is known as the "behavioural revolution" in the study of politics, have familiarized us with the concept of "political culture." It is probable that the delay in applying the same term to administration has been occasioned by the lag in

The author is visiting professor, School of Public Administration, Dalhousie University.

our perception of public administration as a legitimate field of study in its own right. Applying the concept retrospectively, it seems to me that Canada's administrative culture consists of the British heritage of institutions and conventions mingled with American ideas and practices, with adaptations of both to meet indigenous features of a federal state, overlaid by regional and cultural factors. Over time, our administrative culture has swung between these two poles, gyrating uncertainly in the attraction and repulsion of the powerful magnetic field to our south.

During our first forty years, it would appear that Canada's administrative culture was overwhelmingly attracted to the British heritage in which the value espoused was the merit principle to be applied against the contrary value of patronage, or what Max Weber referred to as a "personalized" bureaucracy. Not only did early Canadian reformers use Britain as their reference point but in the United States as well – if we take the influential study of Dorman B. Eaton that glowingly sang the praises of British reforms and their applicability to the United States as a case in point[1] – the same value was dominant. Parenthetically, I would here raise the question as to why in Canada particularly, the value of the merit principle came to be enshrined as a sacred icon to which we, more than its British progenitors, have been prone to render unquestioning obeisance. Perhaps the answer lies in the fact that the merit principle acquired the cachet of a moral value: it is not without significance that prominent supporters of the principle were also in the front ranks of those espousing the temperance movement. In the United States also, the overtones of this moralistic identification, even if in a negative sense, are to be found in the sarcastic reference to administrative reformers as "snivel service reformers," and we can also remind ourselves that the murder of a president by a disappointed patronage seeker has a very direct moral message. Finally, as will become more apparent below, the serendipidist support for the merit principle from the scientific management movement may have contributed to its enshrinement as basic dogma of reform – a support which was not so available in Britain where the scientific management movement seems never to have taken hold in the same fashion as in the United States and Canada.

Indeed, it is through the scientific management movement, with its values of economy and efficiency, that American administrative culture made its major imprint on Canada's. The link connecting this movement to the merit principle and making the two sets of values mutually supportive is to be found in the way in which public administration evolved

---

1   Dorman B. Eaton, *Civil Service in Great Britain. A History of Abuses and Reforms and their Bearing upon American Politics* (New York, 1880).

as a discipline worthy of concentrated study. The take-off point is usually associated with the seminal article by Woodrow Wilson in 1887. Thereafter, the progress of the study was marked by efforts to define and establish territorial rights that would establish a clear-cut separation between politics and administration. Frank Goodnow's 1900 work bearing this title set the stage and established the parameters within which his apostles and their critics worked in two solitudes, adumbrated as either politics *or* administration.

Lending support to the separated study of the two fields was the virtually simultaneous promotion of the scientific management movement which may have taken its roots in the realm of the administration of private affairs but whose precepts of efficiency and economy were seen to be equally applicable to the administration of public affairs. Throughout the first three decades of this century, in the name of these values, there was a concerted drive to reform local and state governments, and then the national government.

Clearly, the successful application of scientific principles depended, in the view of their promotors, on the maintenance of a rigorous dichotomy between politics and administration – where, as between ends and means, only a science of means was possible of attainment. In this perception the scientific management movement found itself in league with the supporters of the merit principle as a value because the latter, in their battle to eradicate patronage, had an equal stake in maintaining the segregation of administration from the nefarious intrusions of politics.

The Canadian–United States border proved as permeable to these elements of the American administrative culture as it has to the enveloping influences of the Big Mac–Coca Cola culture. Canada had the same indigenous conditions that promoted patronage as the instrument ready to hand for parties engaged in the task of aggregating support across a continent. There was, accordingly, common ground in seeing the merit principle as the answer to this perceived evil. The old Civil Service Assembly of the United States and Canada, with this principle as its primary plank, indicates the commonality of this value. There was also the same reinforcement of this value by the scientific management movement, which in the most literal sense was imported into Canada from the United States. Early enthusiasm for the strong mayor and city manager forms of local government was one manifestation of the movement's influence. The most prominent evidence of the importation of scientific management values was provided in the immediate post-World War One period with the introduction of position classification plans at the federal level and, less successfully, in the province of Ontario. The other provinces' heavy reliance on such sources of external aid was largely a post-World War Two phenomenon.

A sweeping generalization that could be used to characterize the course of events since the heyday of the modes of thought enshrined in the scientific management and merit movements is that our struggle today is to rebuild the bridges that were deliberately torn down in the effort to preserve the two solitudes of politics and administration. For the single-minded pursuit of a pure science of means can become at the least a sterile enterprise dissociated from the ends it is established to serve; at worst it can lead to a technocracy, all the more subversive (because it has now become a meritocracy) of the maintenance of those values incorporated in the notion of accountability which it is the function of "politics" to guarantee.

It is the recognition of the impasse created by the autonomous pursuit of the values of efficiency and economy (to which must now be added effectiveness and productivity) that has brought on the contemporary attempt to re-unite administration with politics. Thereby, we have now raised the question of whether the bureaucratic values of economy, efficiency and effectiveness can be melded with the political values of representation and responsibility, and yet still retain their salutary influence on the work-a-day world of bureaucracy. Nor is this problem of blending potentially conflicting values rendered more amenable to solution by trends in the sixties that called not so much for a responsible bureaucracy but insisted that it be more directly *responsive* to its clientele publics – many of which, finding representative institutions wanting, were clamouring for "participatory democracy." Since knowledge is power, it is but a short step to argue in the name of participation for freedom of information. And, from the perspective of the student of public affairs, it is a natural step to broaden one's inquiries to include an examination of the values that make a bureaucrat behave as he does when vested with growing discretionary powers. Hence the interest in the notion of "representative bureaucracy."

In short, even as we seek to come to grips with melding of bureaucratic values with political values, we find new pressures of a populist order that inject yet other values that cut athwart the hierarchical institutions of "overhead democracy" which have been traditionally relied on to provide accountability. What I conceptualize as the multi-dimensioned nature of accountability (that is, not only the traditional upward-downward dimension, but outward, inward and even sideways) is a reflection of the increasing interaction between administration and politics, where the values at play, as in days of yore, are no longer so clear-cut nor so mutually supportive.

How and by whom are values of administrative culture transmitted?

Having educed the values of our administrative culture, it is now appropriate to inquire as to the mode and manner of their transmission to students and practitioners of the administration of public affairs.

I would suggest that the best place to seek for evidence of the assertion of these values would be at those points in time when significant proposals for change – always cast in terms of administrative reform – have been made. In the Canadian case, looking back we observe that royal commissions were the major carriers and transmitters; indeed, the very first royal commission created by the new dominion government was one to inquire into the civil service. In each succeeding decade between 1867 and the outbreak of World War One, there was at least one major royal commission established to undertake similar inquiries. They all had in common a pre-eminent concern for the merit principle value. Their definition of the problems and the answers they provided depended heavily on the inspiration provided by similar reforming emissaries in Britain, beginning with the Trevelyan-Northcote Report of 1857. There the focus was on the primacy of merit ("a career open to the talents") to be secured by a politically neutralized Civil Service Commission, selection examinations (to be made by open competition after 1870), and a simple person-ranking classification into "intellectual" and "mechanical" workers.

These constituted the hallmarks of our own administrative reform proposals which remained with us from 1867 to 1914. An interesting feature of these royal commissions was their virtually total preoccupation with what for us today is only one concern, namely personnel administration. The narrowness of focus that delineated the area thought of as public administration is nicely captured in the first academic study of the civil service of Canada by MacGregor Dawson, published in 1929. It might well have been subtitled "From Patronage to Proficiency," for all the attention it gave to the range of matters now assumed to be legitimate subject matter for the discipline and practice of public administration. Professor Dawson was particularly hostile to the first intrusion of the scientific management movement into the federal public service manifested by the installation of the detailed position classification plan of 1919 (some four years prior to the adoption of a comparable plan for the civil service of the United States).

Apart from this singular attempt to incorporate the values of the scientific management movement into the federal bureaucracy – and even these had as their primary focus the improvement of personnel administration and were supportive of the merit principle – there is little evidence throughout the thirties that the focus had changed or that other values might be at stake. A royal commission on scientific and professional personnel in the public service, reporting at the outset of the decade, simply continued the tradition of its predecessors; while the reversion to the use of parliamentary committees to scrutinize the operations of the Civil Service Act did little more than point up the problem of preserving the merit principle and the Civil Service Commission standing as guarantor for the separation of politics from administration.

The explanation for this relatively static situation may be found in the state of the discipline. The fact is that, in an academic sense, there was no discipline. Dawson's seminal work, for all its narrowness of focus, stood alone, supplemented in the mid-thirties by a few articles in the journal of the recently resuscitated Canadian Political Science Association. It is important to remind ourselves that what I would still claim to be the parent discipline of public administration, political science, had at this period less than two dozen card-carrying members operating out of only seventeen universities, and many of these doubled as historians or economists. My first exposure to public administration occurred when, as a graduate student, I studied under Leonard White, one of the small handful of American scholars who had managed to assemble the scattered data into textbooks; but I recall that our major work of reference was the Report of the President's (Brownlow) Committee on Administrative Management which appeared in 1937. Viewing my own progression for a moment as revelatory of the transmission process, I can report that this heavily Americanized approach to the discipline constituted my first course in public administration at Queen's University in 1945. And it was another fifteen years before some of us attempted to inject Canadian content by producing compilations of readings which still had to lean heavily on external sources, especially for the theoretical perspectives in which the values I have been seeking to identify were still very much in the ascendency.

It is a sign of the times that Professor Kernaghan, who took up the torch alongside the late A.M. Willms, now has difficulty in deciding amongst the rich variety of fare now available for such a compilation. It would be an oversight were I to fail to acknowledge the debt early compilers of such readings owed to *Canadian Public Administration*, the journal of the Institute of Public Administration of Canada. And it is a mark of the continuing high quality of its offerings that this journal still continues to provide useful fodder for any would-be compiler of readings in public administration. In so far as the journal provides the forum where preacher and practitioner can meet, we have at hand one of the essential instruments for transmitting information, ideas and, indeed, even the values underlying these ideas, to the public sector.

What may appear to have been a prolonged digression away from the main thrust of this paper has been introduced to make the point that, if we are looking to the modes and means by which a field of discipline is conceptualized and the inherent values it promotes are transmitted, we must look to its "carriers." I have concluded that because the progenitor discipline of political science in Canada was just getting off the ground in the thirties, the discipline of public administration has been a late bloomer of the sixties and seventies; the number of academics professing the discipline is still not large but student interest is growing, even as the body of material for study and analysis has made an exponential leap. I have already noted the important contribution that a vehicle like *Canadian Public Administration* has made to this growth. It should also be added that the most significant transmitters of values and ideas will be those students who have been exposed to the formal teaching of the discipline of public administration. It must be of more than passing concern, particularly to those who have mounted specialized graduate programs, that their "product" still by no means enjoys a strong "market" preference. Indeed, the student of business affairs would still appear to have the competitive edge for government employment.

If this perception is accurate then I believe we must retrace our steps to examine the implicit value lurking within this preference. The usual answer – that we are a capitalistic, mixed-enterprise economy dominated by the businessman's ethos and values – is not altogether conclusive or adequate. However, if we revert to the values of the earlier scientific management movement we may be able to detect how pervasive and persistent its influence has been and continues to be.

In their writings and recommendations the exponents of scientific management were disposed to promote the notion that administration is administration is administration, whether private or public. Obviously, as I have argued, it is easier to maintain this position if one can preserve the old administration/politics dichotomy. It is even easier if one substitutes, as we are increasingly prone to do, the word "management" for "administration". For the former term, to my mind, speaks to narrower, more technically related tasks that lend themselves more readily to segregation from the "political" component that I believe is implicit in the term administration. I am probably expressing a minority opinion here, as I note the recent adoption of the term "senior management" for the upper level of the federal bureaucracy. Nevertheless, I suspect deputy ministers would be the first to agree that there is validity to the distinction made here as they wrestle with the dual burden of being managers as well as policy advisors to their ministers. If values can be inferred from the titles we attach to official functions (as I believe they can), then the growing preference for the term management as opposed to administration demonstrates the durability of the values espoused by the scientific management movement. To me, this tendency flies in the face of the current acknowledgment of the need to break away from the old politics-administration dichotomy in order to give full play to the pre-eminent values enshrined in notions of accountability – notions that focus on the linkages between administration and politics, not on their separation.

What explains the durability of the values identified with the scientific management movement? I have already referred to the first manifestations of the movement in the immediate post-World War One period through the hiring of what we would today call a firm of management consultants (a subsidiary of an American firm at that) to bring into being a new position classification plan for the federal public service. But, from Griffenhagen and Associates in the early twenties to the Glassco Commission of the early sixties, what is the evidence of the scientific management precepts being applied? As already indicated, the thirties continued on the path of the old administration-politics dichotomy with the emphasis on merit and its protector, largely viewed through the window of highly partisan, often hostile parliamentary committees. The forties and fifties showed a reversion to royal commissions: the Gordon Commission on Administrative Classifications (note again the emphasis on personnel administration and the influence of a British Treasury official, paralleling Sir George Murray back in 1912). Then in the fifties came the Heeney Committee on the Civil Service Act, followed in the sixties by Heeney II on collective bargaining. The fact that these inquiries were conducted by "insiders" is important because it signifies a growing capacity within the system to generate its own programs for self-improvement. This growing sophistication within the bureauracy may help to account for the comparative paucity of evidence on the public record of the on-going influence of the scentific management movement: it had been "internalized." Apart from the open and clear-cut manifestations of this influence attendant upon the post-War Two "modernization" of provincial bureaucracies that nearly all relied on a second-generation school of classification and personnel experts (primarily Public Administration Services, Chicago), the scientific management precepts were left to bore from within. In the thirties and forties, for example, organization and methods and machinery of government units began to appear in the Civil Service Commission. My recollection is that, at least in the early stages, those in charge of such operations viewed themselves as the equivalents of management consultants and the most successful operators were deemed to be those with a degree in engineering – once again a preferred training for those in the scientific management movement (like President Hoover, from stationary engineer to social engineer).

Budgeting and financial management were also arcane matters that were developed, as far as I can see, entirely by insiders, including the office of Comptroller of the Treasury (with much prompting by a businessman prime minister, R.B. Bennett) and the Financial Administration Act – the first in the early thirties and the second in the early fifties. (Autobiographically, I can say that my unwitting contribution to the Financial Administration Act was to round up for the first time all the crown corporations that were subsequently listed in schedules which I had nothing to do with designing.) It would be interesting to explore with the actors of the day who may still be with us what sources they looked to for inspiration; but I suspect that they would say that the reform of procedures and practices was a pragmatic response, in the name of economy and efficiency, to resolving day-to-day problems.

Whatever may have been the reference points for this process I have characterized as "internalized" reform, there can be no question that in the range of issues addressed the perception of what constituted the subject matter for the discipline of public administration was extended far beyond its historical preoccupation with personnel administration. Thus, when the fledgling discipline began to take its place in the offerings of universities about the mid-forties the way had been prepared for the inclusion of such matters as machinery of government, organizational theory, financial management and budgetary processes.

The period of internalized reform was brought to a halt – or, more accurately, brought out into the public domain – with the appointment of the familiar device of a royal commission. In 1960, the appointment of the Royal Commission on Government Organization (Glassco Commission) marked the full flowering of the scientific management movement. The chairman, a businessman and accountant by training, was flanked by another businessman, leaving the third member, a retired auditor general with experience dating back to the late twenties, to ride herd on the operation with his insider's experience. Senior staff consisted of a rising young executive from the private business world, two seconded civil servants, and a lone academic. What was unique about this enterprise was the appointment of some two dozen task forces to undertake the most far-ranging investigation to which the public service has ever been exposed. With few exceptions, the personnel for all these task forces was drawn from the staffs of management consultancy firms. At the time, this was a very young and relatively untried profession which had sprung mainly from firms of chartered accountants. For most, it was their first exposure to public sector administration. For a few the experience proved so much more challenging than the private sector that they stayed on. Others left with the same conviction they initially had held that administration is administration, regardless of the context. In hindsight, my own impression was that the enthusiasm with which they promoted their wares was dictated not so much by their perception that public administration should be brought up to the standards of private administration as by the prospect of getting government to adopt their ideas so that it could better secure favour from the private sector clientele. In short, it was a reversal of the adage that what is good for General Motors is good for government.

The terms of reference of the Glassco Commission were such as to constitute an open invitation to the task forces to adhere rigorously to the politics-administration dichotomy and to concentrate on the old, tried and true values of economy and efficiency. The reference was explicit on both counts. First, the institution of Parliament was declared out of bounds, an adjuration that was taken so much to heart that I can recall anxious discussions as to whether it would be proper to offer comments on the Auditor General's functions, since he was an officer of Parliament. Second, in the general charge to the Commission, it was directed to recommend changes "which they consider would best promote efficiency, economy and improved service in the despatch of public business."

The public service was not unreceptive to many of the recommendations of the Commission, largely because insiders had been seeking to measure up to the same set of values as those to which the Commission and its task forces were wedded. Indeed, in many instances, the recommendations were based on the informed judgments of those within the service. There was opposition to contracting out services for government and scepticism about the accountants' conviction that one could determine real costs or that accrual accounting was possible. The earlier conviction of the Manpower Task Force of the Glassco Commission – that the merit principle and its guardian commission were redundant – gave way to a more sophisticated critique that made a valid distinction between the merit principle (a good thing) and the merit system (a bad thing). In the important area of financial management, where there were significant procedural reforms, particularly as applied to the Estimates and the expenditure budget, the Commission was much influenced by the Plowden Inquiry in Britain and the MacNamara reforms in the United States that gave rise to what ultimately became known as Program, Planning and Budgeting. Undoubtedly, the actions taken to implement reforms in this area left the most indelible mark on the bureaucracy and, together with the many variations on the theme, were still echoing through the bureaucratic corridors when the Lambert Commission arrived on the scene in 1976.

However, the theme by which the Glassco Commission is best known derived from its perception that public administration had become so huge and complex that efficient management depended upon a systematic attempt to delegate: let departmental managers manage. The Commission, contrary to some views, did appreciate the fact that if one is to delegate, the recipient of the delegation must receive clear delimitation of the charge and be held accountable for the way in which the assigned duties have been performed. At this point, we must recall the constraints imposed by the Commission's terms of reference for, as I have suggested, they preserved the old values associated with the administration-politics dichotomy and at the same time prohibited the Commission from commenting on the ultimate instrumental link in the accountability chain, namely Parliament. The lesson to be learned from Glassco is that, if we want to add accountability to the armoury of values surrounding the practice of public administration, it cannot be pursued in isolation from politics and its final resting point, the representative legislature.

The Glassco Commission triggered several provincial inquiries of a comparable nature, notably in Saskatchewan, Ontario and Newfoundland. In the case of Ontario, the Committee on Government Productivity (a single word to embrace economy, efficiency and effectiveness) differed from its federal counterpart in mingling practitioners with the outside consultants, presumably with the objective of melding the implementation process with the on-going investigative-recommending process. Royal commissions, as major articulators and transmitters of values, suffer from the fact that once they have reported they cease to exist, and therefore they have no hands-on relationship with the implementation process. It is true that the Glassco Commission was unique in that it successfully engineered the creation of an on-going ginger group that, as an adjunct to the Privy Council Office, assumed responsibility for supervising the extended dialogue over implementation of key elements of the report. In addition, particularly for the implementation of its recommendations concerning program budgeting, management consultants were kept busy for several years revising the format of the Estimates. Indeed, one of the most important consequences of the extensive use by Glassco of the management consultancy fraternity was that it opened the door for them, at all levels of government, to a great many special assignments. Even with the strengthening of in-house consultants (an extension of the old organization and methods work of the forties and fifties and now provided by Supply and Services), this trend has continued unabated.

Another thrust for administrative improvement in the late sixties and early seventies, which was undoubtedly stimulated by Glassco but surfaced most explicitly in Ontario's COGP report, was precipitated by the new emphasis on planning and programming as an integral element of the expenditure budgetary process. If this process was to go beyond the "bottom-up" incrementalism of the past, it required a rationalization of top structures at the cabinet level. Borrowing from the experience acquired by consultants who were grappling with the conversion of a sprawling Department of Transport into a co-ordinating ministry, the COGP boldly designed a comprehensive plan which embodied the notion of policy sectors and co-ordinating ministerial "Secretaries" for each policy grouping. Under the chairmanship of the premier, these co-ordinating ministers operated a Policy and Planning Committee of Cabinet. The endeavour to create a top-down planning process had similar institutional outcomes at the federal level with the creation of the Priorities and Planning Committee of the cabinet in 1969. Not until the emergence in the late seventies of the budgetary envelope system did the federal government institute the ministries of state for the sectoral policy envelopes.

As I have suggested, working within the context of the maintenance of a clear separation between administration and politics in pursuit of the bureaucratic values of economy, efficiency and effectiveness, the accountability loop had to be left dangling at both ends. Seventeen years later, the Lambert Commission on Financial Management and Accountability was appointed with terms of reference that permitted it to close the accountability loop by plugging the two dangling ends into Parliament.

While we are all familiar with the immediate reasons for appointing the Commission – the lengthening litany of complaints from the Auditor General that financial management was well below acceptable standards – these would help to explain only the first part of the task assigned to the Commission. In this respect, the Commission would have had to consider its inquiry wedded to the traditional norms. Yet accountability was deliberately added to the reference and was not regarded by those who established the terms of reference nor by the commissioners themselves as a perfunctory after-thought but as the very heart of the matter. Was it the ominous statement of the Auditor General that the government and Parliament were in danger of losing control of the administration of public affairs that gave such priority to the value of accountability?

Whatever the answer to this question, the fact remains that the Commission came to the view that accountability, viewed not as a system but rather as discipline for the major actors in the system, had to be got right this time around, if the broad delegation (which it saw as even more essential for a government that had grown much more complex and unwieldy since the days of Glassco) was to take place. Their reason for optimism on this score was founded on the perception that while part of their inquiry had to be grounded on the traditional bureaucratic values of economy, efficiency and effectiveness, they had also to consider the linkages to the popularly elected forum where mandates originated, delegations were authorized, and where ultimately there had to be a rendering of account. Thus, the Commission sought to provide the means by which we could secure answers to the questions: Who is accountable? For What? To Whom? How? and So What? (i.e., where are the sanctions when the account is rendered and found to be wanting?). If we are unable to provide answers to these questions then accountability is in question, the links in the fragile chain are weakened or broken, and the discipline we hope to instil thereby will be produced instead by invoking once again the detailed top-down controls from central agencies – which is another way of saying that delegation has had to be withdrawn.

Lurking just beneath the surface of all the questions which we must answer with respect to accountability is the need for evaluation. Even had the new legislation for the Audit Office not included the power to audit departmental systems to ensure that wherever practicable evaluation programs were in place, I am sure that the need for them would have been perceived as a vital element in making viable the new value of accountability. The jury is still out with respect to our capacity to evaluate, but in view of its importance to the proper working of accountability a strenuous but sensibly balanced endeavour to do what is possible should be pursued and would be expected to include evaluation of both programs and personnel.

At an early stage in this paper the point was made that accountability is multi-dimensional. In our tradition of overhead democracy, accountability is perceived as flowing upward-downward, hierarchically. The terms of reference for the Lambert Commission, though significantly extended beyond the Glassco Commission's to implicate Parliament, were also constraining in their turn; for the Commission was prevented from reaching outside the conventions of individual and collective ministerial responsibility which are the means of channelling accountability in the upward-downward dimension. If one considers the Coombs royal commission in Australia that reported just before the Lambert Commission was appointed one can see that it did go beyond the traditional dimension of accountability to explore the "outward" dimension or the issue of bureaucratic responsiveness.

Clearly, we have not heard the last word on accountability as the value that has opened the way to bridging the two solitudes that have for so long been unnaturally separated in the study and practice of public administration. With populist pressures urging more open government and fuller direct participation, the growth of a direct "interface" between bureaucracy and its clientele publics, the proliferation of regulatory and deciding tribunals making such direct interchanges possible, and the extensive resort to crown corporations which renders even hazier the always grey area between what is public and what is private, I conclude that the Lambert Commission has simply touched off a debate on the full implications of this many-dimensioned value of accountability which should provide grist for the profession and the discipline of public administration for years to come.

Michael Pitfield

The discipline and the profession of public administration: a practitioner's perspective

Introduction

The silver anniversary of the journal *Canadian Public Administration* is an occasion welcome both for itself, and for its prompting of reflections upon personal experience. For both reasons I very much appreciate the Institute's invitation to provide a practitioner's perspective of the relationship between the discipline and the profession of public administration.

At the outset one is tempted to investigate the terms "discipline" and "profession" as they are applied to public administration: To what extent is it a discipline for those who teach and those who study it? To what extent is it treated as a profession by those who practise it?

Let me pose two qualifications of my own: First, I use the term "public administration" in its broadest, most general sense, encompassing what in Canada used to be called "political economy" and what in the United States is still called "government." The narrow meaning of public administration may buttress its claim to be a unique science, but it does so at the cost of turning the subject into either an academic amusement or a study of mechanics. Similarly, I will presume that the discipline of public administration encompasses not only those two or three dozen persons who are formally keepers of that discipline, but also the larger number of academics who involve themselves in questions and issues of public administration, affiliated as they may be to various other disciplines.

Secondly, I must confess to being unconvinced of the utility of regarding public administration as a discipline at all. Public administration should be treated as a broad subject; but the best student or practitioner of public administration usually has also a complete grounding in a particular discipline – be it law, economics, political science, psychology, mathematics, or what have you. Public administration can and should be superimposed on a disciplinary base, but it may be self-defeating to regard public administration as a discipline itself. If this leads to the suggestion that administration is essentially a post-graduate field of study,

The author is Clerk of the Privy Council and Secretary to the Cabinet.

so be it. Similarly, I am not convinced of the utility of regarding the practice of public administration as a profession. Professions, after all, tend to regard themselves as self-regulating bodies of independent practitioners. Public administrators surely must have professional standards, but I prefer to regard public administration as something blending an occupation and a vocation. Public administration should be a calling, not merely an undertaking.

My point of view is obviously conditioned by the fact that I come from the Canadian federal government; that the largest part of my career has been spent in dealing with policy rather than with the administration of programs; that in those activities I have been principally involved at the interface between the politicians and the permanent officials.

This said, it will not surprise you that I regard the relevance of the discipline to the profession as vital. Relevance is the key, the test. Let me outline what I mean by recalling elements of past relations between the discipline and the profession, by touching on the present balance between them, and – most important – by seeking to illuminate some of the implications for both of future challenges in public administration.

Looking back

Looking back over the twenty-five years of my involvement as a student, practitioner and teacher of public administration, I recall a situation in the 1950s when the literature regarding the Canadian system of government was quite thin. Canadian studies were few, sketchy, often superficial, frequently outdated. Surprisingly large areas could only be explored by trying to apply to the Canadian scene the writings of British authorities who seldom had Canada in mind and naturally reflected their own British circumstances and conditions – conditions that had often developed from Victorian times.

Today all this has changed. The literature, though still not vast, is sizeable, its quality significant, its orientation largely Canadian (though, it must be said, now often reflecting American methods, priorities and even American values and biases). We are still touched by a colonial tone – now American – but the situation has nonetheless greatly improved. This is largely to the credit of the Institute of Public Administration of Canada and the learned societies, along with certain of our universities and a number of our publishers.

As I recall the situation in the mid fifties, the teaching of public administration was largely given over to the description of process and organizational facts. The focus was on operations and programs, comparatively little attention was given to public policy. The students produced from these courses were rarely found at the higher levels of government. Those rarefied commands belonged to the graduates of places such as Oxford, Queen's and Harvard; more especially, to students of political economy and law.

Looking back we can see those as simpler days of small government. I am sure they did not seem so then, but they were less confusing and less debilitating. At the time there was an aura in the country at large of challenge and growth, of brave new fields to conquer. Into that expansion the practitioners were led by a number of great public administrators whose names are now legendary in the Canadian government and whose great strengths were not only first-class minds but firm knowledge of the principles of the system, credibility, and authority in what they did. Public administration as it was being taught in academia at the time, whether by that name or as part of other disciplines, was not regarded as very relevant amongst these practitioners.

Today much of the teaching of public administration has been reformed into sizeable schools or departments. To some degree these developments reflect the increased complexity and scope of modern government. The extraordinary success of the business schools has also stimulated a considerable soul-searching amongst teachers and students of public administration with a wide variety of resulting institutional and disciplinary arrangements.

From the point of view of government, today's graduates who have studied public administration are of no more mixed quality than one would e .pect of any educational system. But their utility in government naturally reflects the peculiarities of the courses that each has followed. When a good student with a relevant background finds his way to the right job, the results are outstanding. Unfortunately, such instances are not as common as one would like. Consequently, though the situation is gradually improving, the discipline of public administration has continued to carry amongst practitioners of government much of the image of irrelevance it carried twenty years ago.

By way of contrast, the attractiveness to government employers of business school graduates has been remarkable. Even though comparatively unfamiliar with even the rudiments of government organization, political science and law, MBA's are being sought because of their problem-solving orientation, initiative and sensitivity to conflict situations. They are quick learners, used to dealing with systems, and favourably disposed to the idea and precepts of management. Those are characteristics that only recently have characterized graduates in public administration, and even then, only the graduates of some schools.

The practitioners in government, on the other hand, have been increasingly well disposed to many of the sorts of things that business schools are concerned with. In a sense this inclination stems from, or at least coincides with, the Glassco Report. In 1963, whether by its report or by its example, that commission set off a wave of reform that has swept through not only the methods and process of, but ultimately basic thinking about, public administration at the federal level in this country.

So the last twenty years have been a time of great innovation in the federal government. What the federal administration has done has been frequently treated as a model by the provinces, especially the larger ones, and even by other countries and by international institutions. In turn, the development of thinking in Ottawa has been clearly influenced by proposals in other countries – Britain, the United States, Australia and Sweden, for example – and by Canadian provinces – Ontario, Saskatchewan and Quebec, for example. But by far the largest proportion of thinking with regard to government, not only with respect to methods and process but more especially with regard to the adaptation of the fundamental principles of our system of government to the modern condition, has come from within the government of Canada itself.

The process of change was initiated by Prime Minister Pearson and has been stimulated by Prime Minister Trudeau, but it has been driven by such leading figures of the Parliament and public service as Pickersgill, Heeney, Robertson, Bryce, Davidson, Balls, and the Saskatchewan mafia of Johnson, Shoyama and Tansley. What they did was not motivated by any grandiose view of change for the sake of change, any obsession with the accretion of power, or any idealistic pursuit of comprehensive symmetry as a positive good in itself. To the contrary, it seems to me the approach has been remarkable for its sense of responsibility, its pragmatism, its incrementalism and, in these senses, its conservatism – however significant the ultimate consequences. It has been an effort to cope wisely, respectfully, always mindful of long-term consequences, with the realities of big government, and a big economy and a complex society constantly but unpredictably exposed to difficult problems; to cope always mindful of the importance of consistency with the principles of parliamentary democracy, responsible government, and collective and individual ministerial responsibility.

What the practitioners have tried to do is to take what is known and has been experienced in public administration and apply it to the problems of today and to the anticipated problems of tomorrow. Inevitably this has been to launch into unknown territory with only common sense, an empirical appreciation of policy, program and political interrelationships, and a firm grasp of the basic principles of our system of government as a guide. It is a journey that has led from exploring the dichotomy between policy and program to the development of the concept of the fiscal framework, to new methods of resource allocation and planning, techniques of coordination and restraint, processes in decision-making, manpower planning, personnel administration, government organization and so on and on.

There are a number of observations that can be made with respect to this voyage, observations which reflect upon the relationship between the profession and the discipline of public administration. I begin from the point of view of an official immersed in the daily challenges and frustrations of government.

A first observation is that the planning, exposition and development of reforms has been done almost entirely inside government. The literature of the discipline of public administration and its affiliates has been of little help, especially in terms of prescribing what should be done by way of change and the alternatives that are available. This is not to say that there have not been experts in the discipline of public administration who have participated within government in the elaboration of reforms, but even those have been remarkably few and far between, notwithstanding efforts to recruit them.

Apart from the question of inputs into the process of reform, another observation to be made is how little critique there has been of reforms once they have been made. I think, for instance, of the policy and expenditure management system initiated in 1979, of developments in the cabinet committee system, of the interrelationships among ministers, their political advisors, and top permanent officials. One does not even have to talk in terms of "balanced," "informed" or "objective" criticism and thereby run the risk of being accused of paranoia. In fact, with few exceptions, scholarly criticism – whether informed or not – has not been all that frequent. Nor have more than a few scholars sought to inform themselves of goings-on in government in order to seek to develop generalizations which would relate practice to theory and theory to practice.

A third observation to be made is to note how often the practitioners when they seek out keepers of the academic disciplines for advice and guidance run into a plea of academic independence either as an excuse for not giving help or as a justification for treating government in a confrontational mode. Of course this is by no means universally the case, but it is frequent enough that it seems worthy of remark here. Naturally I do not deny the importance of academic independence, but I think its application by students of public administration to their involvement in the practice of government has to be very carefully handled. The approach which I hope will be reinforced over time is one which recognizes that the independence of the scholar is to be found in his own intellect and sense of integrity. It is not dependent upon building walls that separate the discipline from the profession; far less is academic integrity enhanced by holding disciplinary purity above the muck and mire of involvement in the practice of the profession. Indeed, separation and purity seem to me inherently self-defeating of the discipline's raison d'être. Even more would credentials of scholarship be undermined should more keepers of the discipline adopt a priori attitudes of confrontation, of criticism for the sake of criticism, of seeking to establish the reputation of independent thinkers simply by being against everything – if not, indeed, of seeing in every act the basest possible motivation or crassest possible ignorance.

I put this view strongly but I have not forgotten that there is another side to the question. I have shared with the keepers of the discipline a number of their frustrations too, both during my own experiences in academia and as I reflect now upon that experience.

A first frustration is the feeling of being cut off from what is going on inside government, of lack of relevant information, of being swept aside by the press of events before being allowed to gain an adequate understanding of the situation, much less to make a meaningful contribution. Secondly, there is the reality that teaching and administrative responsibilities in any university must come first, and that one's involvement with the profession can only be at best part-time. Thirdly, it is true that officials eagerly pursuing their own prejudices and ambitions do try to coopt support and are impatient – sometimes even vengeful – with regard to those whose duty it is to maintain the intellectual integrity of the discipline. Finally, the financial resources and support staff available to government cannot but make the scholar positively envious, though here it must be added that the variety of sources from whom money can be found, though it be only in trickles, is surprisingly large.

There are doubtless many other aspects, pro and con, that can be pleaded to describe how the mutual support of the discipline and the profession is not as full or productive as one would expect it to be, as it certainly is in the United States from my own experience, as it must be if the interests of the public – much less of the discipline and the profession – are to be well served.

Looking forward

This relevance of the discipline and the profession to the public is after all the fundamental reason for seeking to encourage the relevance of the discipline to the profession. It is to improve government – and thereby add to the peace, happiness and prosperity of individuals – that we are all devoted. In the words of the charter of the Institute of Public Administration of Canada: "To promote ... the study of public administration with a view better to serve the public interest." Let us not lose this simple idealism in the daily welter of facts and opinions. And in this regard we have great and compelling opportunities.

Public administration today stands at the threshold of advances in efficiency and effectiveness such as the study of business administration encountered at the beginning of this century. If we apply ourselves to the opportunities before us our contribution to the improvement of government – to the greater peace, happiness and prosperity of our compatriots – could be truly remarkable.

In this light the professional cannot but be struck by the extraordinary benefits available from a more relevant relationship with the discipline: economic benefits in the sense of greater efficiency; benefits of effectiveness in the sense of a better chance to do the right thing; and benefits to democracy in terms of more informed debate and the bringing to bear of well-informed views from outside government.

There is a greater variety of methods available to us for the improvement of relevance:

– The government could encourage permanent officials to publish articles of scholarly excellence.

– Greater use could be made of seminars and guest lectureships.

– Term appointments into the more important government departments could be instituted for scholars to act as historians (using the term loosely) in ferreting out and telling the story of what the department has been doing and why.

– The keepers of the discipline and practitioners could work together in the development of more numerous, more detailed, and more relevant case studies.

– Greater contractual arrangements of part-time or term appointments are needed to make particular skills available to departments while at the same time deepening and broadening those skills amongst teachers and students.

– We could develop further exchange appointments of public administrators into universities (what we now, perhaps misleadingly, tend to call sabbaticals), and appointments of academics into government not only on short-term, project bases but also where medium or longer-term undertakings are possible. Here I include the possibility of senior, retiring public servants arranging, or having arranged, as a last assignment a post at a university or school of public administration.

– We might develop greater acceptance in the public service and universities of "inners and outers" – that is, of a system whereby people might normally expect over a lifetime that their careers would take them out of one camp and into the other several times. Let us not underestimate the potential utility and importance of such a process to the provision of a graceful, honourable and temporary "cooling off" period for top officials who may have become closely identified, rightly or wrongly, with policies which are to be abruptly changed.

– Finally, perhaps there should be a joint council set up between the federal government and the keepers of the discipline – either as the representatives of an association or, if by no other means, simply by bringing together a group of interested schools of public administration – to work on securing a closer involvement and greater relevance.

These are as yet sketchy possibilities, each with advantages and disadvantages in different circumstances. Together they do not, and are not intended to, amount to a systematic program. Such possibilities can only be realized if they are fleshed out in further discussion among the keepers of the discipline and practitioners.

Amongst various problems to be worked out, let me mention two: first the necessary willingness among academics to become more engagé; and secondly, the work that will have to be done on guidelines with regard to the treatment of information. On its side, government will have to be more forthcoming and less security-conscious; and amongst scholars there must be the maturity – more prevalent in my experience in the United States than it is in Canada – that gives government some control over the publication by scholars of classified information made available to them. We must face up to the fact that without a mutually understood and accepted system of ensuring the responsible handling of classified information, it simply will not be made readily and comprehensively available; and both the discipline and the profession will be immeasurably the poorer, the more irrelevant and the more out of date in consequence.

If we could harness the discipline and the profession more closely together in ways such as these, then there is an enormous field of public administration to be more usefully cultivated than heretofore, not only by each of us for our own purposes but also by both of us for a higher, common purpose. At the moment the federal government is in the course of major initiatives concerning the forms and methodology of decision-making, the methods of decentralization for programs as well as policy, and the total reform of the systems of personnel management both in public service and Governor-in-Council appointments. Federal officials feel rather proud, and greatly challenged, by what is being done in these and other areas. But we also feel that the scholarly community has a tremendous contribution to make in ensuring that what is done is right.

Besides these immediate initiatives, there are even greater opportunities in the immediate future. We are going through a great sea change in terms of the management of big government and big economies and big social forces. These are dangerous as well as challenging times and tackling them is going to require very thorough thinking. What is required is more of a return to basic principles and less of a reliance upon contemplation of recent experience as a guide to future action; more comprehension and surer handling of the complex interrelationships of policies, and less defining of problems in neat boxes, one by one. One need only consider the present outlook for the economic situation and for national unity in this country to realize how profound are the changes facing us and therefore the thinking that will have to be brought to bear on our reaction to them.

All of this is likely to lead us to the consideration of questions as fundamental as the role of the permanent public service and the role of Parliament. We must squarely confront the pressures for the politicization of the one and the bureaucratization of the other. To do so, of course, we had better be clear – and not merely rhetorical – about what we mean and, even more important, about what root causes must be addressed. I do not believe, for instance, that the merit principle in the public service has ever been stronger than it is today. In that sense, the public service has not been politicized. Nor do I believe that the public service would not strive with equal diligence to assist different governments. The danger of politicization which I do see involves the gradual drawing of officials into political situations where they will almost inevitably be politically attacked from all sides while trying, from their own point of view, to do their best under adverse circumstances: bluntly, to make the best of a bad situation. If the nature of the permanent public service is to be changed, it should be not casually but in full realization of the implications and the consequences.

Indeed, the root issue behind the major symptoms of politicization and bureaucratization, seems to me a singular one – namely, the present uncertainty about the role of Parliament and parliamentarians. I am utterly convinced that in our system of government, the role of Parliament remains the prime determinant from which all else flows – including the position of the ministry, the role and responsibilities of ministers, and the roles of the officials supporting them. There is today a crying need for fundamental, sensitive, constructive reflection on the role of Parliament and its elected members.

Permanent officials cannot undertake that reflection; it is ideally the elected representatives who should do so; yet because of the demands and pressures upon them, they probably need the help of the discipline of public administration and its affiliates. Until that process of reflection is carried through, Parliament – faced with the overwhelming mass of government business and daily political tensions – will likely respond to uncertainty about its own role in largely ad hoc ways. That in turn would generate even more uncertainty, and could increasingly lead Parliament to disparate attempts to scrutinize all that government does in detail rather than overseeing and holding responsible those who are in fact responsible and who have the means to fulfill that responsibility. That road leads toward the bureaucratization of Parliament, in the sense that Parliament would submerge itself in process rather than principles, in details rather than directions, and in dealings at the level and from the perspective of bureaucrats rather than on the political bases and from the political perspectives which have been Parliament's strength.

In these circumstances, with Parliament and its role so fundamental to our entire system of government, neither civil servants nor politicians nor the press and public can be certain in their expectations. A climate of overall uncertainty can build which would involve sufficient obscurity in the chains of responsibility and accountability that circumstances of public service politicization would develop.

The other side of that coin is that Parliament may not focus on its primary levers of constitutional power and political control, on the key functions it is uniquely able and essential to fulfill. Only when the larger uncertainties are clarified – whether or not by fundamental changes in the roles of Parliament and parliamentarians, perhaps even simply by a clearer definition of the role of Parliament today – can the role of the public service be clarified or changed accordingly.

Clearly, then, more than ever, we in the profession will want to be able to look to the keepers, and the products, of the discipline of public administration for concrete contributions both of intellect and of labour. More than ever, the discipline faces great opportunities for involvement and for contributing work of practical value as well as theoretical import – indeed, for linking the two *through* involvement. Public administration is above all a human discipline and a human profession, with a subject matter that can be experienced as well as observed. We do not need to *reduce* our common subject matter to an observer's science; instead we have the great advantage of being able to participate *and* to examine our own participation.

Conclusion

Whatever our métiers, the common ground for both the discipline and the profession is our mutual concern with the most important qualities public administrators will need to possess in order to respond to the challenges facing public administration as a whole. If the discipline of public administration is to increase its relevance to the profession, judgments will be made on the basis of the kinds of graduates we are going to need from that area of academic and scholarly investigation and training particularly related to the profession. Let me then contribute in conclusion certain points of direction which seem to me particularly important:

– We must return to a greater emphasis upon broad basics – a knowledge of history, of our country and of the principles of the main disciplines closely related to public administration (economics, law, business administration). This is knowledge essential to officials in the upper echelons of government. The fostering of these disciplinary interrelationships can contribute to better public administration not only through the training of graduates and the cross-fertilization of their teachers, but also through contributions to immediate policy problems. For instance, fostering better mutual understanding and dialogue between business and government can be assisted by working links between business and public administration schools, ensuring that graduates in each are exposed to the preoccupations and perspectives of the other.

– We must ensure there is still room for the degree of generalization which provides an awareness of science, culture, and all that goes into what used to be called the rounded personality, or what Cardinal Newman called the "educated man." I do not refer simply to culture for its own sake (though I do not denigrate that); but if government is to have the scope which it does and will have, we cannot permit the discipline of public administration to come to be regarded as sufficient in itself. It is a means, not an end.

– We must foster skills in problem-solving and the sensitivity, confidence and initiative required for that purpose. The fundamental discipline required is a discipline of the mind's working. Lawyers, economists, even philosophers, are valuable public servants because they are trained rigorously to think and reason within the constraints of a model. Government is a system; the discipline of public administration should be able to provide similarly rigorous training in thinking about, and training in, that system, not simply the latter.

– It follows that the minds of both students and practitioners must be well stocked with knowledge of our system of government – its law, the constitution, and the structures and consequences of the administration.

– We must seek to regain in graduates of public administration the capacity for brief and articulate expression.

My last point is one which ought to emerge clearly from the challenges which face us. It is the tremendous significance for public administration of the recognition and handling of the ethical dilemmas and conundrums inherent in government. I refer not only to matters such as conflict of interest or the legitimacy of perquisites, but to truly fundamental questions of duty, honour and responsibility. To, for instance, the agonizing and complex balancing of ethical imperatives which is involved in determining security and intelligence policies, and to the built-in structural issues which require every senior public servant to continuously reason through the proper balance between his official duty of service to his minister and his professional duty of impartial responsibility. Government is inextricable from the interplay of contending values. No governor, no government, no senior public administrator can avoid confonting the reality of choice and balance among ethical and policy values which in other lines of work can often be separated into different spheres. It is above all the full appreciation of this dimension of public administration which is so easily missed when the discipline is not engaged with the profession.

I began this paper by speaking of relevance as the key and the test. If the reader finds it surprising that the pursuit of relevance leads me to call for the recognition of the ethical problems inherent in public administration, I can only re-emphasize that public administration is an engaged profession – *and* an engaged discipline. From that point of departure, both can go far. Without it, the profession and the discipline are only nodding acquaintances.

The discipline and the profession of public administration: an academic's perspective

David M. Cameron

If one were to accept that the proper test of the value of a discipline of public administration is its usefulness to practitioners or professionals, one would be accepting a common but regrettably short-sighted notion of scholarship and higher education. To borrow and emasculate a phrase, this would be "demand-side" academics. It stems from a view of universities ultimately as instruments of manpower policy, their utility judged by the extent to which what they study and teach fits vocational requirements perceived by contemporary employers. Clients define the product required; universities produce that which is demanded. Not only does this notion neglect the important responsibility of universities to question as well as train, but it quite falsely presumes that the public administrator alone is the best judge of what is relevant and useful to public administration.

I am no advocate of the "ivory tower"; I certainly do not wish to suggest either that universities need not serve vocational purposes or that the study of public administration should proceed without close and continuous contact with the practice of public administration. Universities do train as well as educate. The study of public administration must be related to the profession of public administration.

The "public" in public administration denotes more than administration which happens to be carried on in the public sector, however. The public must be seen as both participating in, and the object of, public administration and not merely as providing the context for the professional practice of administration. It follows, then, that the test of the value of public administration – discipline and profession – is political. Both must ultimately be judged in relation to their contribution to the good of the society they serve. From this perspective, the value of a discipline of public administration in terms of its usefulness to a profession is too narrow an approach. Both discipline and profession must be assessed in terms of their usefulness in promoting the good of society.

The author is executive director, policy and planning, Dalhousie University.

This demands a broader and more appropriate framework. In developing such a framework, it is important to explore in slightly greater depth the essential nature of public administration itself.

The nature of public administration

Public administration can be defined in a variety of ways, and I do not wish to embark upon any review or analysis of alternative definitions.[1] We can disregard the more subtle and esoteric characteristics and distinctions and take public administration quite simply to be the administration or management of public affairs. The management of public affairs is ultimately and essentially a political process, centred in the institutions of government and having two principal dimensions: the management of government and management in government.[2]

This distinction between the management of government and management in government may seem to be not wholly different from the more traditional distinction between policy and administration. The latter distinction is inadequate, however, not only because it limits "administration" to that which is not policy but also because it tends to diminish the significance of "public" in public administration.

This is not to suggest that the policy-administration distinction has no utility. I think it does and, despite what some of my more zealous academic colleagues may say from time to time, there *is* much in public administration which is essentially similar to, if not the same as, business administration. The problem is not so much with the distinction between policy and administration as with the suggestion that the former is not part of the latter. To suggest that the formulation of public policy is not part of public administration is, quite simply, to remove from public administration its most important and distinguishing characteristic.

The management of government may be seen to contain two principal components: the formulation of public policy and the design and maintenance of the machinery of government through which policy is formed and implemented.[3] Management in government comprises those activities more traditionally associated with "administration": personnel and finan-

---

1 While this has not been the subject of great concern to Canadian scholars, the best overview of the field is probably found in A. Paul Pross and V. Seymour Wilson, "Graduate Education in Canadian Public Administration: Antecedents, Present Trends and Portents," CANADIAN PUBLIC ADMINISTRATION, 19, no. 4 (Winter 1976), pp. 515-41.
2 I am indebted to Peter Aucoin for this distinction and for many of the ideas which surround it.
3 The notion of organization as policy is suggested in Peter Aucoin's fascinating concept of "positional policy" developed in his "Theory and Research in the Study of Policy-Making," in G. Bruce Doern and Peter Aucoin, eds., *The Structures of Policy-Making in Canada* (Toronto: Macmillan, 1971).

cial administration, and the associated processes of planning, directing, reporting, evaluating and accounting.

With this very brief excursion into the nature of public administration, how do we come to an assessment of the contribution of the discipline? In seeking an answer to that question, I propose to discuss in relation to both the management of government and management in government, the three major areas of academic endeavour – teaching, research and professional activities with particular reference to consulting.

Teaching

One jaundiced citizen reacted recently to a description of the teaching program of a school of public administration by asking incredulously, "You mean to say you actually *train* people to be bureaucrats?" I suspect some academics might be somewhat unsettled by this question. Nonetheless, it captures rather well the essential test of the contribution of teaching programs to the profession of public administration. That test must be administered in two parts, however. First, we must ask how it is, if at all, that public administrators ought to be trained. Second, we can then examine the contribution of academic programs to such training.

An argument is frequently made against the teaching efforts of university programs based on the assertion that public administrators cannot and should not be trained at all. Such a view may be motivated by concerns over restricted access to government employment or by the belief that administration is ultimately an art and cannot be taught. A general education and practical experience are frequently cited as more important than professional training. This proposition is often associated with the recruitment of Britain's administrative generalists from the playing fields, if not the classrooms, of certain well-known schools.

It is difficult to disagree with this perspective, up to a point. Certainly it would be folly to take the position that a general education and pracical experience are not valuable, perhaps even essential, for effective public administration. Accepting that these are necessary does not lead logically to any basis for concluding that they are sufficient.

Contemporary teaching programs in public administration, and especially MPA programs, are certainly not premised on the assumption that technical training offers a better preparation for a career in public administration than a liberal education. Quite the contrary, these programs have specifically rejected such a dichotomy and invariably require an undergraduate degree as a prerequisite for admission. The range of academic backgrounds found amongst MPA students is almost as wide as the university curriculum itself. MPA programs combine a liberal *and* professional education. Ironically, a criticism frequently levelled at MPA programs is that they are too liberal, too academic and too much oriented toward the social sciences, especially political science and economics. If one accepts that professional training is appropriate, one still must assess the appropriateness and quality of existing programs.

There is, of course, general agreement that training in a profession is necessary for many practitioners of public administration, especially those engaged in specialized functions associated with management in government. Legal officers must be trained in the law, accountants must be trained in accountancy, and similarly with a variety of specialties. Governments would not likely hire engineers, architects or foresters without demanding appropriate professional training.

Does not the logic that supports professional training in these areas encompass professional training in more general management practices as well? Certainly the private or corporate sector has long since recognized this role for the MBA. The argument that training in an MBA program contributes to more effective management in the private sector must logically extend to comparable training in the public sector as well. Surely training oriented to the private sector cannot in itself be the most appropriate training for managers in the public sector. If managers can be trained in one sector, they can surely be trained in both. And insofar as public administration differs from business administration – and it does differ in the fundamental sense that it is public – then the effective training of managers in the public sector would seem to be training which embodies the public nature of public administration.

There is nothing inherent in the idea of teaching public administration which renders it inferior to a more traditional general education (the great value of which is presumably its contribution to critical thinking). Furthermore, there is nothing which suggests a priori that training in a professional discipline other than public administration, and particularly business administration, is more appropriate as preparation for a career in public administration. Therefore, the test of the contribution of the discipline to the profession, through teaching, must lie in the nature and quality of the academic programs themselves. The principal object of any such test would be the MPA degree and its several manifestations in Canadian universities.

Space does not permit a thorough description or comparison of all MPA and closely related programs.[4] It should be noted, however, that careful and deliberate concern for curriculum development through more than a decade of growth and experimentation has now yielded substantial agreement on the nature of a core program and, at the same time, a remarkable variation in the particular orientation and concentration of

4   See G. Bruce Doern, "The Teaching of Public Administration in Canadian Universities," in *Executive Manpower in the Public Service: Make or Buy*, edited by Kenneth Kernaghan (Toronto: Institute of Public Administration, 1975), pp. 80-102.

each school. As a result, Canada's schools of public administration, taken together, offer a rich blend of common requirements and unique opportunities. And, while a systematic review of all programs is beyond the scope of this paper, the nature and quality of the programs may fairly be represented by a more intensive examination of a program at one of the schools.

Admission is competitive, requiring an undergraduate degree with first or high second-class standing. Fewer than one-third of those applying are likely to be admitted, and this fraction has steadily declined over the past decade. All manner of undergraduate degrees are represented, but those in political science, economics and commerce continue to be predominant.

The first year of the two-year program (or the equivalent for those studying part time) normally consists of six courses. The core courses include government structure and organization, policy formulation, quantitative methods for public management, applied economics, the management process in government, and public sector financial management and accounting. A general picture of the range of content and requirements may be gleaned from course descriptions from two of these courses.[5]

The course in government structure and organization "includes the structures for the management of government in Canada, including attention to all three orders of government: federal, provincial and municipal; the organization of central executive functions in both parliamentary and council systems of government; the organization and role of central staff agencies; the organization of regulatory and corporate agencies; and, in conjunction with the above, the structures and processes of policy planning, resource allocation, regulation and evaluation. These phenomena are examined in respect to both the organizational principles which inform their design and the organizational politics which shape their behaviour."

The course in financial management and accounting recognizes that "the effective public administrator must have a well-developed understanding of the techniques and processes of financial management . . . (and) must recognize how financial decisions affect and are affected by policy and organizational decisions. . . . The course examines the basic concepts and practices of accounting, the procedures for the translation of operating and capital-acquisition transactions into accounting terms, the preparation of financial statements and reports and, most important, the techniques of analysis of financial information."

---

5   These excerpts are taken from the 1981-82 student handbook of the School of Public Administration, Dalhousie University.

Having completed this core program, students advance to the second year where they encounter a more concentrated and applied curriculum. Again, using the MPA program of one of the schools as illustrative of the discipline generally, the second year offers five specializations or concentrations: financial management, personnel administration, policy analysis and program evaluation, municipal management, and health services administration. In order to give some flavour of this second-year program, it might be useful to describe the course in policy analysis which is one of the two advanced core classes in the policy analysis and program evaluation concentration. Students taking it as part of the concentration would also be taking a second core course in program evaluation, intensive management courses (advanced financial management, collective bargaining, etc.), and courses in substantive policy areas (regional development, natural resources, etc).

Policy analysis "... is a senior course intended to synthesize the conceptual and technical material introduced in the first year of the MPA program and to provide students with an opportunity to apply this material to the analysis of government policy problems of a nature similar to those confronting administrative agencies. In addition, the format of these analyses is intended to resemble those employed by practising administrators.

"To achieve these objectives, the course proceeds on three fronts: (1) it discusses the process of policy analysis including an examination of the elements of such analysis and techniques and procedures to be used in practice; (2) it requires that each student review and assess a case study of some policy problem ...; and (3) it requires that students, as part of a team consisting of about five people, undertake three demanding policy analysis exercises on problems that have been suggested by practising public servants and politicians ...."[6]

There are, no doubt, some weaknesses in the MPA programs offered at Canadian universities. One might suggest a greater presence for economics relative to political science. One might wish to see more emphasis on quantitative skills. Perhaps there should be closer ties with the study of law. And, of course, there is the long-standing criticism that MBA and MPA programs should be more closely integrated. The last point will be taken up below. Criticisms or suggestions regarding the appropriate disciplinary balance, as with those concerning practical versus theoretical approaches, are now matters of emphasis. As the above review of one program illustrates, the several disciplinary contributions and the two approaches are present, leaving critics to quarrel only about whether each is present in the appropriate degree. This search for balance is bound to continue, and it will continue to inform the process of curriculum devel-

6   Ibid.

opment. It must be emphasized as well that each school offers its own unique balance. For every criticism of one school, there is likely to be another school whose program answers the criticism. But, of course, emphasizing one dimension diminishes others, and any search for the perfect balance is bound to be elusive.

The one arena where criticism may validly extend beyond questions of emphasis and balance concerns relations between the disciplines of, or programs in, public and business administration. The degree of isolation of the two is unfortunate and weakens both. Explanations of the isolation are not difficult to find. Business administration achieved institutional maturity before its public cousin, and efforts to organize programs in public administration were frequently opposed by faculties of business who either saw the field as theirs or in competition with theirs. This opposition, and the resentment it engendered, still lingers. In addition, many of those who argued for integration did so in support of the concept of a single discipline of administrative studies in which public and business administration would be but applications or specializations. Irrespective of the dubious quality of the concept, the relative sizes of the established and emergent areas were virtually bound to yield programs in administrative studies which were, in fact, business administration with some options in public administration. For those in doubt, the experiment at York University seemed to offer adequate proof of the likelihood of such an outcome. Unfortunately, opposition to programs in administrative studies has often left a legacy of opposition to business administration itself. In the present context, this can be quite irrational.

Both the discipline and at least some of the schools of public administration are now sufficiently mature that there is no longer justification to fear closer cooperation with business administration. Cooperation could occur most profitably in areas directly concerned with management in government or business: accounting, finance, personnel, quantitative methods, etc. The principal advantages would be twofold. First, students in each discipline would be exposed to developments in the other. Secondly, areas still underdeveloped in public administration (accounting, organizational behaviour, operations research, for example), would stand a much better chance of support and development if undertaken jointly. For many universities resource constraints will preclude growth except that which results from rationalization and cooperation. Also, these are often the very areas where recruitment in business schools is most difficult, and therefore where cooperation might be facilitated by staff turnover and the consequent possibility of joint recruitment. Obviously, cooperation is a joint endeavour, and would require a significant change in attitude in most of our schools of business administration. Such cooperation would both strengthen and mark the maturity of teaching programs in public administration. It might also add breadth to current research efforts in public administration.

Research

While research and teaching are inextricably interrelated, the former is much broader and less easily classified than the latter. For example, it is reasonable to see MPA programs as central to the teaching of public administration. It is not so reasonable, however, to presume that the research of those who teach in MPA programs is equally central to the total research effort in public administration. The questions of who does what research in public administration logically precede questions of the contribution of the research that is actually done. But what is public administration research? When is research public administration, and when is it political science, economics, sociology, or some other discipline?

A study undertaken in 1978 sheds considerable light on the nature and location of public administration research.[7] Undertaken for the Research Committee of the Institute of Public Administration of Canada, the study defined research in public administration as falling within three areas: public policy, management, and organization. These three areas represent a different subdivision but the same totality as the division suggested earlier in this paper between management of government and management in government.

The authors constructed a list of 367 people potentially engaged in research in public administration in Canada, to whom questionnaires were sent. Replies were received from 151, or 41 per cent. Of these, 119 were engaged in research at the time or had been engaged in research over the previous five years.

The largest group of respondents identified their discipline as both political science and public administration (31 per cent). An almost equal number considered their discipline to be political science, even though they saw their research as public administration. Twenty-seven per cent identified solely with public administration as a discipline, while economics and business administration were each claimed by 16 per cent.[8] Eighty-four per cent of the respondents were located in universities.

The 119 respondents engaged in research identified 275 specific research projects undertaken over the previous five years and another 188 projects currently under way. Sixty per cent of these projects were reported as being fully funded from university or external sources. In terms of areas, 41 per cent of the projects were defined as studies of

7 David M. Cameron and Murray G.K. Davidson, "Alive and Well and Living in Universities: A Survey of Research in Public Administration," Unpublished paper, School of Public Administration, Dalhousie University, October 1978.
8 Ibid., p. 15.

public policy, 16 per cent as studies in public sector management and 25 per cent as studies in public sector organization (the remaining 18 per cent were not classified). Fully 95 per cent of all the projects either had been or were expected to be published.[9]

To a self-confessed "supply-side" academic, these are impressive data. They suggest quite forcefully that the discipline of public administration is active and productive in research. That many people who considered themselves to be engaged in public administration research did not identify this as their principal discipline does not seem particularly significant. It could be used to open up the question of whether or not public administration is a true discipline as opposed to a field of study to which several disciplines contribute. But does it make any difference? Surely the fact that research is being carried out in public administration is more important than whether the research contributes to a field or a discipline. Has` this research made a useful contribution to public administration? There cannot be any serious doubt that research has added to our knowledge of public policy and public administration. The productivity of academics in public administration (whether in schools or related academic departments) has been very impressive in the past few years. The schools of public administration in particular have without exception maintained a commitment to serious scholarship and research. Indeed, it is no exaggeration to suggest that the priority attached to scholarly research is one of the characteristics distinguishing public administration from some schools or faculties of business administration.

At the same time, the question of the utility of research is very difficult to answer. On the one hand, the usefulness of research in public administration, like public administration itself, must be judged in terms of its contribution to the public good. The public good, however, is a political object and not susceptible to objective definition. On the other hand, the usefulness of any research defies simple analysis precisely because the very essence of research is the exploration of the unknown or the unstudied. This is why research must always be speculative and why the most useful research is probably that about the usefulness of which no questions are asked. If research must, in the philosophical if not the monetary sense, be free, the same cannot be said for consulting.

Consulting

The impressive and extensive contributions of the discipline through teaching and research embody all the strengths and advantages of "supply-side" academics. They have developed within an academic profession, conform to high professional standards of objectivity and quality, and

9   Ibid., pp. 17-20.

yield "products" that are offered freely to the interested employer, colleague or reader. There are no external standards of relevance or usefulness, standards that were they ever established would almost surely yield mediocrity if they yielded anything at all. Research is not normally commissioned,[10] and graduates are not licensed to practise a profession. Instead, the schools of public administration are free to do what they judge to be right, proper and important. If the results are useless, this will soon become evident in unread publications and unemployed graduates. This is clearly not the case at present. There is a lively literature, especially associated with the publications of the Institute of Public Administration and the Institute for Research on Public Policy. MPA graduates are doing well even in a very tight job market. Surely this is sufficient to presume that the basic approach of the discipline to teaching and research is appropriate and useful.

The same test cannot always be applied to academic consulting, and I think this constitutes a very serious impediment to the realization of the full potential contributions of the academic discipline to public administration. I am concerned with two dangers that seem to be virtually inherent in the present practice in which professional advice or analysis is offered through a paid client-consultant relationship between public servants and academics.

The first danger arises from the earlier assertion that the value of the discipline must be judged not merely by its utility to practitioners but, ultimately, by its contribution to the public good. In teaching and research, this is possible but, insofar as consulting involves a confidential relationship between client and consultant, then the contribution of the discipline can *only* be judged by its usefulness to the public servant, or client. If the only effect of this were on the incomes of professors, we might well pay it little heed. It may have another, and more serious, consequence, however.

That second consequence, or danger, arises from the possibility that consulting may displace research. The enticements to consult go beyond personal income. There is a powerful professional lure in being, or being seen to be, "on the inside." The danger is that academics may direct their research to questions of departmental interest and neglect the critical and theoretical inquiry that may not be either lucrative or immediately appreciated by practitioners.

Paradoxically, while consulting may represent the most dangerous aspect of the relationship of discipline to profession, it is also the most promising. The promise lies in the possibility of a real blending of values

---

10   This observation reflects the author's opinion that commissioned research, unless part of a shared enterprise, seldom yields results of high quality.

and a real ability to communicate as between the discipline and the profession. The division might then be one of labour, rather than of purpose.

The purpose of both discipline and profession ought to be public service. The discipline ought to be as much the intellectual home of the practitioner as the profession is the outlet for direct public service by the academic. Consulting at present operates too frequently on the "demand side" of the relationship. The challenge is to transform consulting into a professional activity of both practitioner and academic. Consulting, in a sense, must become institutionalized in a two-relationship. As such, of course, it would no longer be consulting.

The academy must be far more open to the practitioner. It must become increasingly a place where public servants study, reflect and improve their management skills. This they should do with each other and with their academic colleagues. This should occur in the true academy – the university – and not in professional staff colleges. The latter would far too likely lack the institutional autonomy that is so important to developing scholarly rigour in the pursuit of truth.

The government department must be far more open to the academic. It must become increasingly a place where students and faculty gain practical experience and confront policy and managerial problems.

This objective will require changes by both practitioners and academics. It will require that the profession come to understand and support scholarly research and not just consulting. It could include encouraging students to undertake university assignments within departments, on departmental problems but meeting academic standards. It could entail a more creative use of consulting such that academic expertise, and not merely an immediate product, is deliberately fostered. Many of the instruments are already available, they need simply to be used more strategically. Change will also have to occur in universities. Certainly time spent in government and working for government ought to be recognized and rewarded. Schedules and terms may need to be more flexible to permit students and faculty to work in government departments when they are actually needed, and not only between May and September.

The words are easy; the task is difficult. We have come a long way, however, and the potential rewards for further efforts are considerable. We have some of the most competent professional public services in the world. We have strong, active academic schools and departments. The challenge is to bring the two closer together in a way that is mutually reinforcing. Only then would we be able to realize the possible contributions, not merely of the discipline to the profession, but of both to the public good.

H.L. Laframboise

The future of public administration in Canada

> "It should teach you to dismiss all your philosophies of progress or of a governing reason as the babble of dreamers who walk through one world mentally beholding another."
> – George Santayana addressing young British soldiers after the 1914-18 War

The purpose of this paper could not be more aptly stated. There is a world that we are walking through that may be quite different from the one we mentally behold, and some features of that real world, as they affect both the present and the future of public administration, are what I am going to attempt to describe.

"The babble of dreamers" accurately describes, also, much of what has been said, written and taught about public administration, and about how it can be improved. We have all witnessed the dreary succession of panacea solutions taken from the private sector, from the discipline of economics, from the field of politics and from the United States. The massive reappraisals – by Glassco, D'Avignon and Lambert, to name a few of the more prominent – have failed to improve the overall quality of public administration in the perception of practising managers. As a consequence, public administration as a discipline, and as a unified sub-set of management theory and political science, is decreasingly perceived as an authoritative source for the solution of problems. It is my view that a failure by the discipline and the profession to keep up to date on the evolving real world, both externally as reflected in the changing values and behaviour of Canadians and internally as reflected in the way we manage our public service, is the underlying reason why the discipline of public administration, as a body of knowledge, suffers from diminishing relevance.

This paper is structured into a series of sections, leading from what is happening among our political leaders and among the people they are

The author is with DREE-ITC Amalgamation, Government of Canada.

elected to serve, into the universe encompassed by the public service in the arrangement of its internal functions.

The struggle for jurisdictional recognition

The three jurisdictions – federal, provincial and municipal – are engaged in a three-way war for the affection, respect and loyalty of the Canadian voter, and for the control of those activities through which the citizens' gratitude can be evoked.

The federal government wants to be thanked by the voting public for the programs financed by federal funds. The provincial governments compete equally for the attention and gratitude of voters through their programs, and in particular seek to get voters to identify themselves primarily with the province in which they live. Regional and municipal governments, the runts of the jurisdictional litter, are to a lesser extent seeking greater self-containedness in matters of purely local concern.

The intensity of the struggle for jurisdictional recognition and ascendancy is at an all-time peak in Canadian history. There are no signs of abatement and this rivalry will colour the practice of public administration for the foreseeable future.

The previous practice of sectoral departments in one jurisdiction working out solutions to shared problems with their counterparts in another jurisdiction is being displaced by one which is dominated by federal and provincial commissars who oversee the totality of intergovernmental relations on behalf of their respective governments. The proliferation of departments of intergovernmental affairs in provinces and the strengthening of central coordinating agencies in the federal government are consequences of the struggle for jurisdictional recognition. On the federal side, the recent announcement establishing branches of the Office of Federal-Provincial Relations and the Ministry of State for Economic and Regional Development in provincial capitals, and the ascendancy of central information agencies such as the Canadian Unity Information Office, are firm evidence of the federal government's resolve to strengthen its visibility and increase the pace of federal image-making.

The wave of federal measures to recapture a voice in fundamental programs administered with federal financing or tax concessions, such as health programs and post-secondary education, or to administer directly and locally programs of economic assistance now jointly financed but administered through provincial agencies, has just started.

Where it will take us is a matter of conjecture but there is no doubt that officials will face increasing discomfort as their dedication to overall progress in their fields of interest becomes subordinated to a loyalty to their jurisdiction. This chauvinistic closing of ranks within jurisdictions means that the slogan "My sector right or wrong" stands in danger of being replaced by "My jurisdiction right or wrong."

The discipline and profession of public administration have always had an implicit responsibility for maintaining the fabric in which the three jurisdictions are interwoven. The adrenalin that flows from interjurisdictional battles, and the responses to the siege mentalities of political leaders, must not be permitted to cloud our judgment, nor to transform public administration as a profession into a series of armed camps.

The prospects for maintaining a balanced and cooperative framework for the management of interjurisdictional affairs are, to say the least, gloomy.

Rights-seekers and rights-protectors

The exquisite refinement of the overall field of human rights into a multitude of rights-seekers and rights-protectors has been a major development over the past ten years, and as the principal growth industry in government, rights have become a major preoccupation of public administrators.

Canada is in danger of becoming a rights-ridden country and if an observer from another planet were to base his judgment solely on the perceived horrors brought before his or her eyes by rights-seekers, he or she would get the impression that Canadian governments and Canadian society have been, and continue to be, the epitome of repression, injustice and discrimination.

As rights become entrenched, instruments and mechanisms are put in place to ensure their enforcement. These include not only human rights commissions and ombudsmen, but also hundreds of regulations and conditions being built into the social and economic structures of our nation. The Charter of Rights embedded in our new constitution will be controlled by judicial interpretation, and as precedents are set by the courts through their decisions, so will those precedents govern the application of the Charter to Canadian life and Canadian law.

A recent satirical book, *The 80's, A Look Back on the Tumultuous Decade, 1980-89*,[1] takes the children's rights movement to an ultimate conclusion:

With the 1987 Supreme Court decision in *Chip Jr.* v. *Chip Sr.*, children were granted the right to divorce their parents.

We have not reached that level of apparent absurdity but, in the overall, we are getting there.

There is very little that can be done to contain the growth of the

1 Tony Hendra *et al.* (New York: Workman Publishing Co., 1979).

rights movement, given the difficulty of justifying opposition to any kind of right. In Stephen Potter's terms, rights-seekers are experts in one-up-manship and through a sincere form of moral bullying and blackmailing have little difficulty in keeping their opponents in a "one-down" position.[2]

Looking to the future, administrators of public affairs will continue to be required by governments to lead the way in incorporating rights into the management of their programs. The game of "quota-filling" in appointments is in full swing in the federal government, constituting an affirmative action program for under-represented categories of Canadians of impressive proportions.

Secondly, the armies of rights-protectors – investigators, inspectors, arbitrators, boards, commissions and ombudsmen – will continue to grow in number as governments become more and more interventionist in the assurance of rights.

Thirdly, the negotiations between governments and rights-seekers will become more and more heated as governments try to draw the line before demands so extreme as to be unacceptable.

The expansion of the selectivity mode in government programming

In the design and administration of programs, there is a strong trend away from the universal application of relatively simple and objective criteria toward the judgmental consideration of individual cases. This "selectivity mode" is spreading in the field of economic assistance, in federal-provincial agreements, in the push for reducing regional economic disparity, in the management of labour and industrial adjustment programs, in the granting of exploration rights for oil and gas, and so on.

This trend away from universality and toward selectivity is important for the profession and discipline of public administration because it constitutes a significant shift away from the Weberian model of an impersonal bureaucracy, operating under standard rules and job descriptions, toward one where the judgmental and negotiating skills of the individual official are of paramount importance.

The expansion of the selectivity mode in government programming is driving the bureaucracy away from the dominance of expertise in public administration toward the dominance of expertise in the subjects within which cases must be judged. The development and application of the National Energy Program, and within that program, the negotiations of the Alberta-Canada oil agreement and the drafting of the Canada Oil and Gas Act, are examples of where negotiating and policy-development skills, coupled with a thorough knowledge of the oil business, far outweighed managerial skills in importance.

2 *One-Upmanship* (London: Hart-Davis, 1960).

All of this leads me to the conclusion that the talents of the individual official increasingly outweigh in importance the formal job descriptions according to which positions are graded and salaries determined. There are other conclusions, but these will have to wait until I've described the following further contributing factors.

The policy route

The managerial model is increasingly being displaced by the high-flying policy analysis, negotiating and development model as the route to the top in the federal bureaucracy. The rewards do not go to the efficient manager nearly as much or as quickly as they go to the official who can offer imaginative solutions to difficult problems, perceptive analyses of particular cases, and successfully negotiated agreements.

The difficulties this creates for traditional bureaucratic practice were particularly evident in the recent conversion of executive positions in the federal government to a new system of classification, the so-called Management Category Conversion. This position-based system of grading, using a modified Hay Plan,[3] is a private-sector model that favours positions with direct operating responsibilities and large operating budgets.

We made the system work in the conversion exercise but only after a great deal of agonizing adjustment and interpretation needed to do justice to positions whose impact was of a non-managerial nature.

The tension between jobs and people

There has always been a certain amount of tension between standard job classification systems and traditional organization principles on the one hand, and the particular talents of individuals on the other. In this tug-of-war, until, say, the 1970s, the job classification system dominated the skills of individual incumbents in the determination of grade levels, and the stability of the Weberian model was thus maintained. With the emergence of the selectivity mode in programming, the emphasis on negotiating skills, the dominance of policy analysis as the route to the top and the importance of subject matter expertise, the system is giving way to the individual case, to the tailoring of jobs to suit particular persons and to authority relationships based on the talents of incumbents.

As we move up through the 1980s, the trend toward destabilization will accelerate and means must be found for establishing a new norm for the relationship of people to jobs. Among the means could be flexible organization structures which permit duties to be shifted around among jobs and reporting relationships to be changed without going through the dreary business of rewriting job descriptions and generating massive

3 See Canada, Treasury Board, *The New Management Category - What It Means to You*, Introduction (September 1980).

reorganizations, and the grading of people according to the importance of their contribution rather than according to the box they fill on the organization chart.

The federal government has put its toe in the water through a moderate appointment-to-level policy for senior executives but a great deal more thinking is needed by the discipline and the profession to assess the significance of the changes I've outlined.

I hope I have overstated the problem because if I haven't, there is a rough road ahead in transforming some principles of administration to meet these new conditions.

The phenomenon of the creeping mandates

Since one of the prevalent driving forces among public administrators is the urge to tell others how to run their business, or to run their business for them, we are witnessing the phenomenon of the creeping mandates, a phenomenon in which organisms set up to perform a specific and limited function gradually extend their authority over functions that properly belong to others, and in which they have no particular expertise.

This phenomenon is of two types. One type consists of the inclination of central agencies with narrow mandates and professional skills to drape themselves with the mantle of experts in public administration; witness the Office of the Auditor General which got its nose into the tent with its "Value for Money" theme, and its consequent SPICE studies, and the Office of the Comptroller General, which has done so through its Management Practices Branch and its IMPAC studies.

Set up, respectively, to ensure propriety in the spending of public funds, and to ensure quality in the design of financial control systems, these offices have succeeded in extending their mandates into that of critics-at-large. When I read of the breath-taking scope of Comprehensive Auditing as defined by the Office of the Auditor General, and of IMPAC Action Plans, as defined by the Office of the Comptroller General, I perceive public administration, as a rounded body of knowledge, as having fallen into the hands of bookkeepers.

Instead of having only one camel in his tent – the Treasury Board Secretariat – a deputy head now has three camels. There is very little room left in the managerial tent for its principal occupant.

Henry Ford, in his rough and ready wisdom, dealt with the problem by periodically clearing out his whole accounting staff, as a matter of principle, thereby ensuring that his managers could proceed freely with the business of making and selling cars, unhampered by the creeping acquisition of power by an embedded bookkeeping elite.

In the matter of responding to non-financial requirements imposed by the offices of the Auditor General and the Comptroller General, the following quote from Henry Fielding's *Tom Jones* is appropriate:

And here I must desire all those critics to mind their own business and not to intermeddle with affairs and works which no ways concern them; for till they produce the authority by which they are constituted judges, I shall not plead to their jurisdiction (Tom Jones, Book 1, chap. 3).

To paraphrase Cicero: authority cannot prevail unless it is supported by reason.

One of the challenges faced, then, by the discipline and the profession is to recapture its field of expertise.

The second type of mandate-creeping takes place among line departments who take advantage of the prevailing view that everything in government is interconnected in order to grab a share of someone else's turf. I wrote about one aspect of this years ago in an article entitled "Here Come the Program Benders,"[4] but the situation has developed to a more alarming state since then. It is worth a section of its own.

Interdepartmental diplomacy: a new profession

The blurring of departmental boundaries, coupled with the spread of collegial decision-making, the proliferation of watchdog agencies and the creeping extension of mandates, has made necessary an emphasis on interdepartmental negotiations, and this emphasis has been translated into a corps of interdepartmental diplomats of considerable dimensions.

Not only has negotiation become a dominant function in dealing with outside pressure groups and other jurisdictions, but it has emerged as a distinct activity within the federal bureaucracy itself. This activity is becoming increasingly formalized through written contracts between parties such as memoranda of understanding between ministers, and letters of agreement between deputy heads. The form and content of these various pacts and treaties have reached a level of fastidious refinement that would do credit to Talleyrand.

Much as it is to be deplored, there is no diminution in sight of this unfortunate trend toward formality, a trend that reflects a prevailing, and often warranted, distrust of one another's motives within the same jurisdiction.

Creative negotiation

The art and practice of negotiation has become a central element of public administration both in its internal relationships and in its relationships with the outside world. The struggle for jurisdictional recognition,

4 *Optimum*, vol. 7 (1976), pp. 40-48.

the lobbying of rights-seekers, the expansion of the selectivity mode, the phenomenon of the creeping mandates, and the growth in interdepartmental diplomacy all require skills in negotiation that are more finely honed than would have been required ten years ago.

There is a ritual associated with creative negotiation which can be learned and can be taught; the initial taking of extreme positions by the opposing parties, the catharsis of rhetorical references to principles and mandates, the gradual identification of points of agreement, the sensing by both sides of what is negotiable and what is not, the exchange of concessions, the attempt at bullying, the recognition of the need to save face, the appeal to a third party, and eventually the closing of the gap or the agreement to disagree.

Without a knowledge of the dynamics of the foregoing process, a public servant is at a disadvantage in an activity that is becoming an important part of his or her work. If there is a single skill that should be learned, it is that of negotiating.

Two solitudes

Middle managers are required to follow the rules laid down by central agencies in matters of administration, rules that are applied and policed by departmental agents representing the various administrative specialties – personnel, finance, accommodation, purchasing and supply, and so on.

As an example, the burden created by these rules, often rooted in law, is such that in the federal service, if all the prescribed processes are respected, it takes a minimum of sixty working days to fill a position of indeterminate duration from outside the service. There is no better example of the way a bureaucratic process intended for one purpose, in this case getting good people quickly into needed positions, becomes instead a process with every conceivable barrier to achieving that purpose.

The world of the middle manager, beset by rules such as these, constitutes one solitude. But there is a second system in operation, the one in effect for the power-brokers among top officials who can, by a series of phone calls to their counterparts in central service and control agencies, achieve quick results in ways that are denied their subordinates. This is the second solitude. The difference between the two systems is aggravated by Janus-headed managers of administrative specialties in departments, who insist on conformance with procedures by middle managers, yet participate, with deputy heads, in finding ways to get around the rules in matters of direct interest to those deputy heads.

The consequence of having two systems of administration, the "middle manager–formal system" and the "deputy head–short circuit system," coupled with the growing distance between deputy heads and their internal departmental operations, is that there is little interest or pressure by deputy heads to force control agencies to simplify the rules that are constipating the bureaucracy. Accustomed to short-circuiting the prescribed rules, it is hard for deputy heads to appreciate the burden that the conformance with those rules places upon their subordinates.

As long as these two solitudes continue to exist, there is little hope for the reform and simplification of administrative systems. The deputy head who, by two quick phone calls, has just cleared the appointment of an outsider at a specific grade, is unlikely to be interested in cries for relief by his or her harried, rules-ridden middle manager.

The triumph of mediocrity

On this subject, my thoughts have been in part directed by Andrew Hacker who in his book, *The End of the American Era*,[5] gives a much broader and better view of it than I, using the academic world as his model.

Bright people with good judgment are always in short supply, and this should constitute a genuine limitation on the number entrusted with policy and program development, both on the issues arising from the people we serve, and in the ways by which we arrange our internal affairs. This iron law of the limitation of talent is now widely disregarded, and we have created "think" positions in numbers far out of proportion to the availability of individuals with the talents needed to fill them. The result is that analytical and developmental work is cluttered by thousands of individuals who, in a more rational world, would be filling routine positions more consistent with their limitations.

Since no policy is better than bad policy, the overall quality of developmental work would be raised immensely if we could discipline ourselves in future to limiting "think" positions to a number more in line with the availability of individuals with the necessary intellectual, judgmental and communications skills. Although this point is patently elitist, it is not unfair in its effect on people who are not up to the demands of their analytical jobs. Long years of "drilling dry wells," in the sense of doing analytical work that never makes it off the drawing board, is cruel and unusual punishment from which many could be spared.

Cutting back and political judgment

One of the problems facing almost all jurisdictions is the relative stagnation in the growth of revenues by comparison with the growth in expenditures, and a desire by legislators not only to achieve a better bal-

5　New York: Atheneum, 1973.

ance in absolute terms, but to shift spending from less desirable to more desirable programs. As we all know, this is more easily said than done. The withdrawal of funds and services from a clientele that has come to perceive them as permanent is one of the most painful decisions that elected officials have to face. For civil servants, the pain comes from choosing among their activities those which could be offered up for sacrifice.

It would be nice if the relative merits of competing programs could be quantified and ranked, and if that ranking could govern the choices to be made. There are other factors to be considered, and to illustrate how critical these can be, I have composed a hypothetical letter to a minister from his or her deputy minister which sharpens and dramatizes the conflict between narrow rational evaluation and broad political judgment, and which illustrates the tendency for programs to constantly extend the eligibility of benefit recipients.

LETTER TO: THE MINISTER OF NATIONAL HEALTH AND WELFARE
      FROM: THE DEPUTY MINISTER
   SUBJECT: SUPPORT SYSTEM FOR RED-HEADED PEOPLE

Dear Minister:

It is now twelve years since the Government decided to act on the findings of the Holmes Commission that people with red hair, because of the sensitivity of their skin to atmospheric radiation, were likely to have a reduced life expectancy by comparison with people whose hair was another colour.

When these findings were made public, red-headed people, as you will remember, established a strong lobby group, and since their representations took place shortly before an election, it was decided to incorporate a promise of a system of recompense into your party's platform.

When your Administration was re-elected, this Department, at the direction of the then Minister, prepared a proposal which, with slight modifications, was accepted by Cabinet. The essence of the proposal, given effect by statute on January 1, 1969, was that red-headed citizens and landed immigrants in Canada would receive monthly cheques of fifty dollars, indexed annually to to the consumer price index. These cheques are now in the sum of $122.00 monthly and constitute a significant proportion of the income of red-headed individuals. In one extreme case, where both parents are red-headed and have seven red-headed children living at home, the monthly family income is $1,098.00.

You will no doubt recall our early difficulties in establishing qualifications for the income supplement. First, we had to establish the colour range into which an applicant's hair had to come in order to qualify. This was settled between strawberry blond and auburn.

Our next problem came from the discovery that many applicants were not really red-heads but were dyeing their hair in order to qualify. Accordingly, we required clippings from each applicant to be analyzed for hair dye at a laboratory before approval.

Many applicants with grey hair applied on the grounds that they had red hair in their youth, were as vulnerable to atmospheric radiation as ever, and were being discriminated against because of their age. Taken to a tribunal of the Canadian Human Rights Commission, their case obtained a favourable ruling and we set up a system for obtaining affidavits from reputable witnesses who could confirm that the applicant's hair did indeed, during his or her youth, fall between a strawberry blond and auburn.

With this ruling by the Human Rights Commission, we had to extend the affidavit system to bald people. As a consequence of all this, there are now 1.2 million Canadians in receipt of the red-headed supplement at an annual cost of some $1.8 billion dollars.

When the Holmes Commission report was prepared, there was no statistical evidence that red-headed people had a shorter life expectancy than others, since people were not identified in mortality statistics by the colour of their hair. The Holmes findings were based purely on theoretical conclusions derived from the assumption that the skins of red-headed people were as excessively vulnerable to atmospheric radiation as they were to ordinary sunlight.

Now, after twelve years, we have sufficient statistics on the mortality rate of red-headed people, gathered through the income support program, to determine conclusively that the life expectancy of red-headed people is no different than that of people whose hair is of another colour.

You will appreciate the dilemma this creates for your Government. On the one hand, the continued payment of the income supplement cannot be justified on any rational grounds whatsoever and should therefore be discontinued. On the other hand, the cancellation of the program, particularly in view of the election that will likely be called in the next year, could have disastrous effects on your party's electoral results.

The conclusions of our mortality statistics, destroying any rational basis for the continuance of the program, are now known by only a handful of my officials. If it were decided to suppress the report, it would have to be done immediately, while the report was still a closely held draft.

Could I have your guidance please.

Your obedient deputy,
XXX*

People practising the profession of public administration, in its fullest sense, must be skilled in bringing the political dimension to bear on problems, as well as the managerial and quantitative ones. Accountability for how well this skill of political sensitivity is applied does not fit neatly into the various "cause and effect" chains that are so dear to measurement-oriented counter-managers in central agencies. As a consequence, administrators have often found themselves unable to explain to the satis-

---

*[Editor's note] Events do overtake hypothesis. From the *Toronto Star* dated October 23, 1982:
RED PRIDE REARS ITS FIERY HEAD IN U.S.
MISSION VEIJO, Calif. (UPI) – Hundreds of delegates to today's first annual convention of Redheads International bring a crimson tide of fiery-tressed members convinced that blondes have nothing on them when it comes to a good time.

"I've had letters from a family in Saudi Arabia, from people in Denmark, Japan, Germany and a lot from Canada," [Steve] Douglas [the club founder] said.

Redheads from around the world have been flocking to join the Southern California-based club dedicated to promoting "red pride." An estimated 3,000 people have paid the $10 membership fee in just the last three weeks.

faction of inquisitors why their actions do not conform with the quantitative-managerial model.

When I speak then about the need for the discipline of public administration to regain control of its field, I include the need for political judgment to be restored to a position of respect as a factor in decisions, difficult as it may be to quantify in accountability terms.

Agenda for research and reform

An ignorant man, who is not fool enough to meddle with his clock, is, however, sufficiently confident to think he can safely take to pieces and put together, at his pleasure, a moral machine of another guise, importance and complexity, composed of far other wheels and springs and balances and counteracting and cooperating powers. Men little think how immorally they act in rashly meddling with what they do not understand.
– Edmund Burke, 1791

The urge to reorganize functions, authorities and relationships is evidently one of the most fundamental drives of senior public servants. If one thinks of organization structures as skeletal arrangements, then we suffer from a surfeit of radical chiropractors, who believe that manipulating the bones will somehow cause the organic diseases to disappear.

Second to this urge to reorganize is an urge to add on new layers of management, either under central agencies or within departments. If management is perceived as poor, we simply add more of it until the swamp is so full of swamp-drainers that managers have neither the time nor the clean line of sight for shooting the alligators.

There is a need then for a return to simplicity, clarity and speed of decision-making in the arrangement of functions and authorities, and a willingness to forego the highly ornamental refinements that have given a rococo cast to our organizational designs. Much as research is needed on how to weed the organizational garden, I am not optimistic that it will be undertaken. There is little or no interest in projects designed to use the lessons of the past to construct models for the future.

Next, I would like to see research done on the effectiveness of the "coordinating" authority centres that have proliferated in the past few years. The merits of the coordination function are in my view highly over-rated. First of all, the term "coordination" is often a euphemism for "direction" and when the coordinating centres are situated outside the departmental pyramid, they constitute an order-giving authority that subjects managers to unintegrated dual supervision, one from within the pyramid and another from without.

Conflicts of views between the two authority sources can only be resolved by escalation to a common superior. Since the line manager usually has a much longer ladder to climb to a common superior than the coordinator, and since the escalation of differences is often perceived as stubbornness, the line manager is reluctant to join battle and the coordinator usually wins by default. If someone wants to examine this question, I would suggest that he start by looking at the public information function in the federal service, and especially at a booklet recently published on this subject by the Privy Council Office.[6]

Thirdly, I would like someone to identify the effects of pursuing, at one and the same time, accountability and dispersed decision-making. A more perverse pursuit of contrary goals would be hard to imagine. On the one hand, "accountability" has become a faddish word in public service jargon, and accountability is spoken of as if it had never before existed. On the other hand, the principle of participative decision-making is being extended far beyond the limits intended by its early proponents.[7] The principles of participative decision-making, enumerated by their proponents as important between closely associated managers within a discrete organizational pyramid, have been extended in the federal service far beyond these practical limits to inter-agency relations. Since the top of the inter-agency pyramid is the Prime Minister, and since he is obviously beyond reach as the arbiter of departmental disagreements on powers and processes, the result is perpetual squabbling without an accessible referee.

Pinning down accountability while dispersing decision-making powers is like trying to square the circle, and handing out bits and pieces of authority all over the place is a sure way to obscure the trail between cause and effect. As a veteran of dozens of interdepartmental committee meetings, I can attest to how good ideas can be ground down to pedestrian programs, and to how everyone is given a little piece of the action as tribute for letting proposals move forward. I liken these concessions to permitting lamprey eels to attach themselves to noble lake trout.

Fourthly, as an omnibus proposal, I would like to see someone start toward the resolution of the many problems I have raised in this paper. In the overall, the pursuit of simplicity and speed, and the reduction of clutter and obfuscation should dominate. Freedom to act, with control measures only to the extent needed to prevent impropriety and gross errors and to ensure general responsiveness to government policies, is the manager's dream. Why is it becoming farther and farther from realization?

6 Canada, Privy Council Office, *Government Communications: Principles and Mandate*, 1981.
7 Rensis Likert, *New Patterns of Management* (New York: McGraw Hill, 1961).

From system to serendipity: the practice and study of public policy in the Trudeau years

"The many techniques of cybernetics," Pierre Elliott Trudeau told us in 1969, "by transforming the control function and the manipulation of information, will transform our whole society. With this knowledge we are wide awake, alert, capable of action; no longer are we blind, inert pawns of fate."[1] Thus Prime Minister Trudeau ushered us into the 1970s, creating at the centre a policy-making system intended to fulfill the rationalistic aspirations of his philosophy.[2] His vision, as we all know, was short-lived. In a few days in October 1970, Ottawa plunged from rational planning to "crisis management." Two years later a cabinet demoralized by near defeat at the polls abandoned policy planning and opted for political survival, though it resumed a form of planning in the priorities setting exercise of the mid-1970s.[3]

Subsequent years have not restored the heady atmosphere of the late 1960s, with its confidence, its optimism and its technological fix. Rather,

The author is professor, School of Public Administration, Dalhousie University. The author acknowledges, with appreciation, the comments of two reviewers of this paper and discussions with M. Paul Brown, of Dalhousie University, and V. Seymour Wilson, of Carleton University, which have contributed to the development of this paper. He also wishes to thank Dean T.W. Kent, of Dalhousie University, for discussing his own experience in public policy-making. The author, of course, is entirely to blame for any errors, misinterpretations or pernicious opinions in the paper. He is aware that some readers will disagree strongly with those opinions but feels that it is the function of a survey piece like this to bring a perspective to bear on a body of literature, rather than to undertake a neutral, thoroughly documented assessment of each and every contribution that has been made to the recent literature.

1 Office of the Prime Minister, "Notes for Remarks by the Prime Minister at the Harrison Liberal Conference," Harrison Hot Springs, British Columbia, Nov. 21, 1969, p. 7, quoted in G. Bruce Doern, "Recent Changes in the Philosophy of Policy-making in Canada," *Canadian Journal of Political Science*, 4, 2 (1971), p. 248.
2 See ibid. for an excellent discussion of those rationalistic aspirations, and of their inherent difficulties.
3 See M.J.L. Kirby and H.V. Kroeker, "The Politics of Crisis Management in Canada: does planning make any difference?" in C.F. Smart and W.T. Stanbury, eds., *Studies on Crisis Management* (Montreal: Institute for Research on Public Policy, 1978), pp. 179-95.

Ottawa has moved somnambulistically, if not from crisis to crisis, then from problem to problem. By 1980 most observers agreed with Richard French's conclusion that "the technocratic planning theories of the Sixties and Seventies have been irreparably devastated by the critiques of both right and left. . . . There are no obvious technical solutions."[4] Chance, incrementalism, at best serendipity, not system, dominate Canada's policy processes.

Yet Trudeau's much-quoted, ill-fated pronouncement is still significant. It expresses the aspirations and the self-confidence not of a man, but of a time. It is symbolic. In it we see the penumbra of the late 1960s: the confidence in technology, the rejection of the past. Out with the old has gone the incrementalism that led, in the United States to Vietnam, and in Canada to a tiresome, rancorous federalism. In with the new is the cybernetic revolution, the promise of rational policy-making and the hope that with a new leader with a new style Canada will emerge from the cocoon of cooperative, and not-so-cooperative, federalism.

Thus, when Trudeau spoke of the cybernetic revolution he conveyed to many a sense that he was prepared to challenge the existing ideology and to bring about a new politics. His rhetoric built on a growing public conviction that far more is changing than merely the methods that are used to develop public policy. For many of his supporters he was speaking of something fundamental – something that could be addressed best through the process of rational policy-making of which he spoke so often. His failure to bring the cybernetic vision to life has therefore been more than a personal defeat; it is a defeat in which a generation shares. Consequently, the cybernetic vision lingers into the present time as a reproach and a reminder that we, like the rest of the industrialized world, have not come to terms with the essence of modern political life. To understand why this is so, we in this paper will cast our discussion in the framework laid out, also in the late 1960s, by Theodore Lowi,[5] and we shall suggest that the turbulence in public policy formation that we have observed in the last two decades reflects a fundamental shift in the nature of western politics – a shift from distributive to redistributive politics.

Three streams of development have led us to a politics of redistribution. The most venerable has been concerned with the institutionalization of social security, the acceptance of the view that in modern society "the risks to an individual's social security are part of the social costs of operating such a society," so that the community "should not

4 R. French, *How Ottawa Decides* (Ottawa: Canadian Institute for Economic Policy, 1980), p. 157.
5 Theodore J. Lowi, *The End of Liberalism: Ideology, Policy, and the Crisis of Public Authority* (N.Y.: Norton, 1969).

allow the costs of its progress to fall upon individuals and families, but should protect and compensate people who experience more than their fair share of the costs."[6] An increasingly prominent feature of Canadian politics since World War Two, the institutionalization of social security had developed considerably during the 1960s as the country implemented medicare, the Canada Pension Plan and regional development policy and began to debate the reform of income security programs and policies affecting native peoples. Redistribution, in its traditional sense, then, was very much on the public agenda when Trudeau assumed office and probably enjoyed a wider acceptance then than it has since.

The general public was less aware of the second force pushing Canada toward redistributive politics, though it, too, had been many decades in the making and its implications were becoming evident to economists, the business community and the self-styled "managers" of the economy. For J.K. Galbraith, whose writings have since drawn public attention to these developments, what has evolved is a new type of political economy, one in which mature corporations have sought and obtained a symbiotic relationship with the state. This has occurred because modern, complex business organizations have found the market economy too uncertain and too constraining a mechanism for the regulation of business life. Affiliation with the state offers these corporations, or the planning system, as Galbraith calls them, levels of demand and supply management which ensure security and growth.[7]

The third stream of development, fast rising to public prominence in 1969, was environmentalism. It was fashionable to talk of "the environmental crisis" in a way which made the Canadian public conscious of the wastefulness of modern industrial societies and of the limited resource base upon which they depended. The environmental movement thus gave point and urgency to the trends inherent in the institutionalization of social security and the demands of the planning system.

What were those trends? They can be summed up in the word "redistribution." The word suggests an authoritative reallocation of community resources, but to achieve that reallocation far more is involved, notably planning, which in turn implies centralized decision-making, and ultimately increased state intervention in all aspects of social and economic life.

Fundamentally, these central requirements of redistributive politics threaten the established political order. Redistributive politics are the reverse of distributive politics, a political process in which, because it is

6 Dennis Guest, *The Emergence of Social Security in Canada* (Vancouver: University of British Columbia Press, 1980), p. 2.
7 J.K. Galbraith, *The New Industrial State* (N.Y.: Mentor, 1971) and *Economics and the Public Purpose* (Boston: Houghton, Mifflin, 1973).

assumed that there is enough for all, the function of government is primarily to act as a dispenser, a broker. The state is relatively passive, taking its cue from the dominant ideology, liberalism, which with its emphasis on individualism and pluralism, is supremely adapted to distributive politics. By contrast, in a redistributive system, the state tends to become *dirigiste* and the ideology of liberalism, now inappropriate, has to be replaced. Thus it is hardly surprising that once Prime Minister Trudeau began to operationalize the cybernetic vision, the inherent contradictions between redistributive and distributive politics became sufficiently apparent to alarm many who had unwittingly accepted the new rationalism. In effect, then, a paradigm shift in public philosophy and political ideology, something which is achieved neither smoothly nor gracefully – witness the recent rise of neo-conservatism in western democracies – serves as the backdrop for developments in Canadian public policy throughout the 1970s, the course of structural change during the period and the limited success with which change has met. In other words, the threat and the promise of redistributive politics has run through the practice and theory of policy-making throughout the last fifteen years.

At first blush this suggestion may seem far-fetched. Usually the recent attempts to reorganize the federal policy system are explained in terms of the struggle to make the federal public service more responsive to the public, and more manageable.[8] Thus changes in the central policy structures themselves tend to be associated in the literature with the quest for manageability: the reassertion of political control and the institutionalization of federal-provincial relations.[9] Without doubt the literature is correct in suggesting that these are the concerns of the policy-makers themselves and that they should also concern those who write about policy-making. But something even more significant may be going on below the surface which should also capture the attention of practitioners and theorists. After all, the argument that the politicians were seeking to re-establish political control does not really hold water unless we assume that something more than simply increased complexity was affecting the relationship between ministers and their departments. More important, how else can we explain the trend toward coordination? To priorities setting? To planning? The existence of these trends does not

8   As for example, in P.M. Pitfield, "The Shape of Government in the 1980's: Techniques and Instruments for Policy Formulation at the Federal Level," CANADIAN PUBLIC ADMINISTRATION, 19 (Spring 1976), pp. 8-21.
9   See for example, Richard J. Van Loon's two useful recent articles, "Kaleidoscope in Grey: The Policy Process in Ottawa" in Michael S. Whittington and Glen Williams, eds., *Canadian Politics in the 1980s* (Toronto: Methuen, 1981), pp. 292-313, and "Stop the Music: the current policy and expenditures management system in Ottawa," CANADIAN PUBLIC ADMINISTRATION, 24 (Summer 1981), pp. 175-200.

prove that the thrust of development in policy studies, policy institutions and policy practice reflects a shift from distributive to redistributive politics, but it does suggest that it might be a useful conceptual framework for looking at Canadian developments in this field in the last few years. The literature has admirably recorded these developments.[10]

The policy literature: reflections of reality

As Bruce Doern pointed out in 1971, the study of policy-making had not to that point, "occupied a central place in Canadian political science."[11] The field had not entirely escaped notice, of course. Dawson had studied the conscription crisis of 1944;[12] Hodgetts in 1957 published a piece on "The Civil Service and Policy Formation";[13] various studies of policy fields appeared,[14] and *Canadian Public Administration* presented a number of articles on the relationships between ministers and their senior advisers.

An interesting feature of these studies (with the exception of Dawson's work, which focused on the deliberations of cabinet itself) was their concern about bureaucratic influence in policy making. Many of the CPA articles were attempts at role definition. Issues were becoming more complex, agencies less tractable, interests more outspoken. Civil servants and ministers asked themselves what could properly be left to officials, what attitude civil servants should take to interest groups, and how far their own perceptions of policy needs should influence the advice they gave to politicians. Long gone were the days when a subordinate of one British Prime Minister and Foreign Secretary could say "Lord Palmerston . . . never consults our Under-Secretary. He merely sends out questions to be answered or papers to be copied . . . and our only business is to obtain from the clerks the information that is wanted."[15] Nevertheless, the myth of the master-servant tradition was hard to dislodge and as late as the mid-1960s Mitchell Sharp still maintained that "civil servants do not

10 It is impossible to pick up a publisher's catalogue or a copy of CANADIAN PUBLIC ADMINISTRATION, *Canadian Public Policy*, *Policy Options* or the *Canadian Journal of Political Science* without being impressed by the number and quality of recent writings on Canadian public policy. The author regrets that he has not been able to keep up with it and that therefore the following summary will overlook some contributions and inadequately appreciate others.
11 Doern, *op. cit.*
12 R. MacGregor Dawson, *The Conscription Crisis of 1944* (Toronto: University of Toronto Press, 1961).
13 J.E. Hodgetts, "The Civil Service and Policy Formation," *The Canadian Journal of Economics and Political Science*, 23, no. 4 (1957), pp. 467-80.
14 Notably in the fields of international relations and fiscal policy under the aegis of the Canadian Institute of International Affairs and the Canadian Tax Foundation.
15 Quoted in Zara Steiner, *The Foreign Office and Foreign Policy, 1898-1914* (Cambridge: Cambridge University Press, 1969), p. 3.

make policy, all rumours to the contrary notwithstanding."[16] More recent veterans of the executive arena take public service policy-making as a matter of course.[17]

Just as significant as the debate over the role of the senior civil service in policy-making was the fact that the majority of these studies dealt not with central policy-making, as later studies would, but with policy-making in the departments. The legacy of Howe and Gardiner was still strong and the modifications of cabinet procedure and of the central policy structures received little attention, though they had been under way, albeit tentatively, since 1927 when King offered Burgon Bickersteth the post of personal assistant to the Prime Minister and the prospect of becoming secretary to cabinet.[18] Nevertheless changes at the centre were going forward and would become dramatically apparent in the first months of the Trudeau regime.

It is an exaggeration to claim, as Campbell and Szablowski do, that Trudeau's leadership victory coincided with the realization that "at the institutional level, the existing structure of government became visibly inadequate to meet the rapidly multiplying demands made on government by various segments of Canadian society."[19] However, Mr. Trudeau's own approach to the modification of the central policy structures drew attention to the emergent policy-making system in a way that could not be ignored. Scholars, and practitioners with a bent for writing, responded with a spate of studies that have flooded bookstores, journals and government files ever since. In the following passages we will consider all this industry from four perspectives: as the development of theory; the study of policy systems; the investigation of specific fields of policy-making and the elaboration of approaches to policy analysis.

Theory

Canada's recent policy literature does not owe its existence purely to Ottawa's "kaleidoscope in grey" nor even to the totality of changes in policy systems that have occurred recently across the country at, and between, various levels of government.[20] The literature has been in-

16 Mitchell Sharp, "The Bureaucratic Elite and Policy Formation," in W.D.K. Kernaghan, *Bureaucracy in Canadian Government* (Toronto: Methuen, 1969), p. 86.
17 See for example, J. Hugh Faulkner's account of the minister's role in "Pressuring the Executive," CANADIAN PUBLIC ADMINISTRATION, 25 (Summer 1982), pp. 240-53.
18 J.M. Mallory, "Mackenzie King and the origins of the cabinet secretariat," CANADIAN PUBLIC ADMINISTRATION, 19 (Summer 1976), pp. 254-66.
19 Colin Campbell and George J. Szablowski, *The Superbureaucrats: Structure and Behaviour in Central Agencies* (Toronto: Macmillan, 1979), p. 8.
20 See Kenneth Bryden, "Cabinets" in David J. Bellamy, Jon H. Pammett and Donald C. Rowat, eds., *The Provincial Political Systems* (Toronto: Methuen, 1976), pp. 310-23; Marsha A. Chandler and William M. Chandler, *Public Policy and Provincial Politics* (Toronto: McGraw-Hill Ryerson, 1979); and D.V. Smiley, *Canada in Question: Federalism in the Eighties* (Toronto: McGraw-Hill Ryerson, 1980).

fluenced as well by theoretical debates initiated outside the country. From public choice theory to political learning, from pluralism to operations research, international debates have impinged on the field in this country, stirring controversy and informing research.[21]

A few of these have had a significant impact. The debate between the incrementalists and the rationalists, though often set aside today, contributed to a climate of opinion which found practical expression in the reorganization of the central policy structures. Its most prominent articulation appeared in the eighth annual report of the Economic Council of Canada, entitled *Design for Decision*. Influenced by Yehezkel Dror's plea for better policy-making,[22] the Council urged the adoption of systematic approaches to policy-making, particularly the use of social indicators to monitor policy achievements and the emergence of new needs. Douglas Hartle and his supporters spent the mid-1970s championing this cause from one of the towers of Treasury Board.[23] Their campaign now appears quixotic, but it served to advance the practice and teaching of systematic policy analysis and thus has contributed to the development of competence in the policy process.

Some support for the rationalists appeared in the Canadian literature,[24] but the majority of commentators, though endorsing the goal of achieving "better" policy-making, were skeptical of the techniques that were to

21 For example, we see public choice theory expressed in the work of Jean-Luc Migué, *L'Economiste et la chose publique* (Québec: Presses de l'Université du Québec, 1979) and in Mark H. Sproule-Jones, *The Real World of Pollution Control* (Vancouver: Westwater Research Centre, 1980); Hugh Heclo's concept of "political learning" which is developed in his *Modern Social politics in Britain and Sweden* (New Haven: Yale, 1974) influences Christopher Leman's "Patterns of Policy Development: Social Security in the United States and Canada," *Public Policy*, 25 (1977), pp. 261-91; Mildred Schwartz has reviewed the impact of pluralism on some aspects of Canadian policy studies in "The Group Basis of Politics" in John H. Redekop, ed., *Approaches to Canadian Politics* (Scarborough: Prentice-Hall, 1978). Finally the utility of operations research and related approaches is discussed in the Economic Council of Canada, *Eighth Annual Review: Design for Decision-Making* (Ottawa: Information Canada, 1971). These citations, of course, simply illustrate the range of theory that has been used to illuminate Canadian public policy-making. Two recent and more orderly reviews will be found in Robert F. Adie and Paul G. Thomas *Canadian Public Administration: Problematic Perspectives* (Scarborough: Prentice-Hall, 1982) and V. Seymour Wilson, *Canadian Public Policy and Administration* (Toronto: McGraw-Hill Ryerson, 1981).
22 Yehezkel Dror, *Public Policy-making Re-examined* (San Francisco: Chandler, 1968).
23 Malcolm Rowan, "A conceptual framework for government policy-making," CANADIAN PUBLIC ADMINISTRATION, 13 (Fall 1970), pp. 277-97; Douglas G. Hartle "A proposed system of program and policy evaluation," ibid., 16 (Summer 1973), p. 243 and "Techniques and processes of administration," ibid., 19 (Spring 1976), pp. 21-33; "The Public Servant as Advisor: The Choice of Policy Evaluation Criteria," *Canadian Public Policy*, 2 (1976), pp. 424-38.
24 As in George J. Szablowski, "The Optimal Policy-Making System: Implications for the Canadian Political Process," in Thomas A. Hockin, ed., *Apex of Power* (Scarborough: Prentice-Hall, 1971), pp. 135-46.

be used to effect improvement.[25] For all their talk of public participation and of the use of social indicators, the rationalists seemed remote from the realities of the policy-making world. Academic observers and officials alike found the theory a poor guide to reality. Case studies reinforced their suspicions, whilst the down-to-earth assessments of practising policy-makers confirmed them.[26] Furthermore, the rationalists were discredited by events. Difficulties in implementing the new policy-making technology, the intelligence failures evident in the FLQ crisis and the economic turbulence that followed the 1973 oil embargo were a few of the events that cast the rationalists into disrepute.[27] The literature rediscovered process.

The revival was most clearly signalled by Richard Simeon who, in his 1976 article "Studying Public Policy," argued that "we have not really advanced very far in increasing understanding of how government policies and actions are to be explained or understood. There is a proliferation of isolated studies, and of different methods and approaches, but precious little in the way of explanation."[28] For Simeon, too much emphasis on isolated case studies and on technique had led to a situation in which we had "too many independent variables chasing too few and too vague dependent ones."[29] Furthermore, we had tended to skip a basic prerequisite to understanding: the development of a competent description of the actors involved in policy-making, their roles and their interrelationships. To effect a more orderly and productive approach to the field, Simeon recommended a process approach, one in which the policy process is seen as "the impact point" of the other variables in the equation: the environment, ideas, power and institutions.[30] It was a perspective to which many in the field were already attuned and which has since become predominant in Canadian policy studies.[31]

25　Khalid B. Sayeed, "From system's analysis to policy analysis," CANADIAN PUBLIC ADMINISTRATION, 15 (Winter 1972), pp. 641-47. See also Robert J. Jackson and Michael M. Atkinson, *The Canadian Legislative System* (Toronto: Macmillan, 1974), pp. 18-21.
26　Hubert L. Laframboise, with his customary deftness, provides both case study and down-to-earth assessment in his "Moving a proposal to a positive decision: A case history of the invisible process," *Optimum*, 4, no. 3 (1973), pp. 31-41.
27　See Hartle, "Techniques and processes"; Richard French and André Beliveau, *The RCMP and the Management of National Security* (Montreal: Institute for Research in Public Policy, 1979); Larry Pratt, *The Tar Sands: Syncrude and the Politics of Oil* (Edmonton: Hurtig, 1976).
28　*Canadian Journal of Political Science*, 9 (1976), p. 549.
29　Ibid., p. 580.
30　Ibid., p. 578.
31　Many would argue that Simeon's characterization of Canadian policy studies was unjust, that, if anything, a sense of process has consistently informed them. On the other hand, his call for a more orderly and systematic approach to analysing the factors which lead to public policy is well taken. Unfortunately, the perspectives from which environment, ideas, power and institutions can be approached are so numerous that no two scholars have yet offered us comparable case studies or theoretical discussions. Consider, for example, the contributions made by three scholarly,

The debate over rationalism had tended to focus policy studies. The turn to process fragmented them. Whether one was a supporter or not, the rationalist argument, with its normative overtones, forced the observer to consider the systemic quality of policy-making, its strengths and weaknesses and the possibilities for improvement. But the new technology had proven unequal to the complexities of the policy process and the spate of discussion dried up in an arid debate over technique. The new concern with process promised a broader approach, taking greater account of the human element in policy-making and exploring the dynamics of institutional relationships. Unfortunately it opened so many avenues for research that individual investigators were soon lost in a jungle of inquiry. Some contributed to the proliferation of case studies.[32] Others pursued the enigma of elite interaction.[33] For a few the concern for technique continued and contributed to a growing refinement of policy analysis (or perhaps more accurately, to the program evaluation aspects of policy analysis). The fear of bureaucratic dominance surfaced again and led to several related but loosely connected discussions dealing with the administrative state,[34] freedom of information,[35] questions of access and participation by individuals and groups,[36] and, above all, the role of Parliament in the policy process.[37] It is hard to discern either theme or direction in all of this discourse.

The development of theories of the policy process has not received

excellent discussions: Neil A. Swainson's *Conflict over the Columbia* (Montreal: McGill-Queen's, 1979); Malcolm G. Taylor, *Health Insurance and Canadian Public Policy* (Montreal: McGill-Queen's/Institute of Public Administration of Canada, 1979) and Mildred A. Schwartz, *The Environment for Policy-Making in Canada* (Montreal: C.D. Howe Institute, 1981).

32 For example, those in the Canadian Public Administration series, published by the Institute of Public Administration of Canada under the editorship of J.E. Hodgetts and in the publications of the Institute for Research in Public Policy.

33 Robert Presthus, *Elites in the Policy Process* (Cambridge: Cambridge University Press, 1974) and *Elite Accommodation in Canadian Politics* (Toronto: Cambridge University Press, 1973); Rianne Mahon, "Canadian public policy: the unequal structure of representation" in Leo Panitch, ed., *The Canadian State* (Toronto: University of Toronto Press, 1977).

34 O.P. Dwivedi *et al.*, eds., *The Administrative State: Canadian Perspectives* (Toronto: University of Toronto Press, 1982).

35 For example, Donald C. Rowat, *Administrative Secrecy in Developed Countries* (N.Y.: Columbia University Press, 1979).

36 A. Paul Pross, ed., *Pressure Group Behaviour in Canadian Politics* (Toronto: McGraw-Hill Ryerson, 1975); Fred Thompson and W.T. Stanbury, *The Political Economy of Interest Groups in the Legislative Process* (Montreal: Institute for Research in Public Policy, Occasional Paper No. 9, 1979) and Pross, ed., "Governing under Pressure: The Special Interest Groups," CANADIAN PUBLIC ADMINISTRATION, 25 (Summer 1982), 14th Annual Seminar issue.

37 W.A.W. Neilson and J.C. MacPherson, *The Legislative Process in Canada: The Need for Reform* (Montreal: Institute for Research in Public Policy, 1978) and Jackson and Atkinson, *The Canadian Legislative System*.

very much attention, Simeon's exhortations notwithstanding. There have been several excellent reviews of the theoretical literature which have been written self-consciously from the Canadian perspective.[38] A number of case studies have been used to evaluate, if not test, some of the major theories developed elsewhere.[39]

A number of studies have served as vehicles for applying aspects of theory. For example, Robert Presthus' comparative study of elites in the policy process makes a valuable contribution to theories of elite inter-action in Canada. As well, in chapters that deserve more recognition than they have received, he makes some progress in developing the cultural context within which Canadian public policy is set. More recently, Mildred Schwartz, also writing in the comparative United States–Canada vein, has widened this environmental perspective.[40]

These discussions, and the many like them that we have not been able to refer to, are valuable and they contribute to the development of theory, but they are not primarily concerned with theory-building. Perhaps that is unfair. It is often difficult to distinguish between the study of a particular phenomenon which seeks to explain that phenomenon through the application or development of theory, and a study which is primarily concerned with developing theory, and uses a case study to that end. Presthus' work, for example, clearly contributes to theory development, as does McRae's on-going work on consociationalism in multi-lingual societies.[41] A good deal of the work of the political economy school is also simultaneously and self-consciously an exploration of political phenomena and a development of Marxist theory.[42] Even so, there is a need for more work which is concerned with nothing other than the development of theories of the Canadian policy process. For example, Ronald Manzer's stimulating application of the concept of paradigm shift to policy development deserves much fuller exposure than it receives in its present mimeographed form.[43] The present writer, too,

38 Adie and Thomas, *op. cit.*; Wilson, *op. cit.*; Schwartz, "Group Theories of Politics" and P.C. Aucoin, "Public-Policy: Theory and Analysis," in G. Bruce Doern and Peter Aucoin, eds., *Public Policy in Canada* (Toronto: Macmillan, 1979), pp. 1-27.
39 Swainson, *op. cit.*, Taylor, *op. cit.*
40 *The Environment for Policy-Making.*
41 K. McRae, ed., *Consociational Democracy: Political Accommodation in Segmented Societies* (Toronto: McClelland and Stewart, 1974).
42 Panitch, *op. cit.* or Robert J. Brym and R. James Sacouman, *Underdevelopment and Social Movements in Atlantic Canada* (Toronto: New Hogtown Press, 1979).
43 Ronald Manzer, "Public Policies in Canada: A developmental perspective," (Paper given to Canadian Political Science Association, 1975) and "Public School Policies in Canada: A comparative, developmental perspective," (Paper given to International Studies Association, 1976). A short application of the approach has appeared recently in his review article "Social Policy and Political Paradigms," CANADIAN PUBLIC ADMINISTRATION, 24 (Winter 1981), pp. 641-48. See also Aucoin, *op. cit.*, pp. 14-16.

would appreciate having the opportunity to discuss with a theoretically oriented circle his own attempts to build and synthesize a theory of the Canadian policy process.[44]

Perhaps it is premature to ask for theory-building in the Canadian context. Any serious scholar has a sense of how little we know about our own condition and just how limited our attempts to test even the theories of others have been. In the strictest sense, theory-building is impossible in the field today. In a looser sense, however, it is not and there is probably much to be gained from attempting it. It might, for example, help us think more clearly about Canadian conditions. Reading the theoretically oriented literature in Canadian public policy is rather like subsisting perpetually on TV dinners; the basic cooking has been done elsewhere. Policy making, involving as it does the authoritative allocation of value in the community, is the quintessential political act. Therefore, to understand the policy process in a country is to understand a fundamental aspect of that country. We cannot achieve that understanding if we confine ourselves to applying to our own condition alien explanations of reality, however much theories developed in or about other places may sharpen our own self-examination. Hence we must be informed by those explanations, but we must break away from being dominated by them and we must develop our own understanding of our own reality. Only when we have done this can we contribute usefully to public debate in this country.

Systems

If our contributions to theory-building have to be considered insubstantial, the reverse is true of our efforts to describe and explain the environment, the institutions and the dynamics of our policy processes.

In the early 1970s we focused on the federal government and the processes used in the central policy structures. The work of Doern and Aucoin was most prominent here, and doubtless encouraged others to enter this particular area. That they did so is evident in the pages of *Canadian Public Administration* which during this period published a dozen articles discussing policy-making at the centre. Academics and senior officials

---

44 This is a process approach. Parts of it have had some exposure in the author's "Pressure Groups: Adaptive Instruments of Political Communication" in Pross, *Pressure Group Behaviour,* and "Pressure groups: Talking Chameleons" in Whittington and Williams, *op. cit.* These build on the assumption that political communication between the modern state and its publics is largely determined by the organization structure of the public sector and the major players in the private sector. In *Duality and Public Policy,* a discussion paper published (1980) by the Dalhousie Institute of Public Affairs I have tried to set this in a broader framework, one which recognizes and explores the environmental context (cultural and economic) of the process approach.

alike described and commented upon the radical changes that were occurring. In a sense, we may have seen too many articles written from this perspective. For a time, because the bulk of our literature on policy-making tended to focus on the machinery and processes of central structures, we tended to speak as though the rationalistic aspirations of Mr. Trudeau and his acolytes had been realized and that policies were both cohesive and the product of relatively rationalistic processes. Because the functions of the central policy structures are to review and coordinate, to impose some order on a chaotic process, it is not surprising that these activities should figure quite prominently in descriptions of the Privy Council Office, Treasury Board, cabinet secretariats and so on. We also tend to attribute too much cohesion to government policies because so many contributions to this particular literature have come from prominent political and administrative decision-makers. Without wanting to detract from the illuminating and useful contributions of Gordon Robertson, Marc Lalonde, A.W. Johnson, R.B. Bryce, Mitchell Sharp, Michael Pitfield and others,[45] in the view of this observer it is important to remember that they occupy the "overview" positions and, by the time policy issues reach their desks, the constituent elements have been refined to a few significant policy alternatives. Except in the case of major issues, the most senior officials may be aware of the maelstrom of policy competition, but not generally affected by it. By the time these officials exercise their influence on the policy process, the business of packaging is well under way. Hence, their view of the policy process may be that it is more orderly, more rational, and more capable of producing a cohesive package than is in fact the case. Finally, they may not fully appreciate how much the implementation of policy diverges from its conceptualization at the centre.

Interest in the central policy structures is still vigorous, and in the last few years has found expression in several book-length treatments.[46] Recent changes will doubtless precipitate more.[47] However, current writing

45 R. Gordon Robertson, "The changing role of the Privy Council Office," CANADIAN PUBLIC ADMINISTRATION, 14 (Winter 1971), p. 487; Mitchell Sharp, "Decision-making in the federal cabinet," ibid., 19 (Spring 1971), p. 1; Marc Lalonde, "The changing role of the Prime Minister's Office," ibid., 14 (Winter 1971), p. 509; A.W. Johnson, "Management theory and cabinet government," ibid., 14 (Spring 1971), p. 73; R.B. Bryce, et al., "The Cabinet and the Public Service Establishment," in Hockin, op. cit., pp. 116-27, and M. Pitfield, op. cit.
46 Viz. French, How Ottawa Decides; Gillies, Where Business Fails; Campbell and Szablowski, The Superbureaucrats.
47 Already several articles have appeared, notably the two by Van Loon, previously referred to; R. Dobell, "Pressing the Envelope," Policy Options, 2, no. 5 (1981), pp. 13-18; and Sandford F. Borins, "Ottawa's Expenditure Envelopes: Workable Rationality at Last?" in G. Bruce Doern, ed., How Ottawa Spends Your Tax Dollars (Ottawa: School of Public Administration, Carleton University, 1982), pp. 63-87.

is more questioning and probing than that of ten years ago. It is often highly critical.[48] Some of the reasons for this have been touched upon. The policy traumas of the early 1970s and the switch to crisis management doubtless influenced thinking and writing about the evolving system. Furthermore, by the end of the decade enough was known about the operations of the central agencies to occasion serious debate. We are now engaged in a major discussion of the capacity of these institutions to deliver sound policy advice to the political leadership. This concern is most clearly expressed in Richard French's account of the inter-institutional warfare which convulsed the senior federal bureaucracy through most of the 1970s, and in James Gillies' argument that the central policy structures have cut themselves adrift from the lines of communication which tie line departments to their primary constituencies.[49] There is mounting evidence that, despite the elaboration of structures and procedures at the cabinet level, policy is taking much longer to make than it did in the disorganized days of the mandarins and the *prima donna* cabinet ministers; that it is less informed by the views of the public at large, the government caucus, or the interested publics than it is by the rival claims of competing policy bureaucracies, and that it is simply bad policy.[50] In introducing his case study *The Draft Memorandum to Cabinet*, Douglas Hartle carefully explains that the events he describes are fictional but a reasonable reflection of reality.[51] The processes he describes are very different from the cybernetic vision of 1968. They are disturbing in the extent to which they are dominated by institutional rivalries, the calculus of personal ambition and, above all, by chance. In the case study serendipity lends a hand. In reality, observation of Ottawa policy-makers of recent years suggests that serendipity, "an apparent aptitude for mak-

---

48   It appears to this reader at least that there is a stronger evaluative note in most of the recent literature cited than was usually the case in the early seventies and the sixties. Certain writers (French, Gillies, for example) are clearly much more critical and there appears to be more support for schools of thought that are critical of the system as a whole (for example, the political economy school; see the journal *Studies in Political Economy*). In the past, too, it was unusual for leading figures in the discipline to attack government policies and policy-making with the vigour that Alan Cairns has expressed in "The other crisis of Canadian federalism," CANADIAN PUBLIC ADMINISTRATION, 22 (Summer 1979), pp. 175-79.
49   French, *op. cit.*; Gillies, *op. cit.* It is also expressed in the recent major federal management studies of the Lambert Commission (see Canada, Royal Commission on Financial Management and Accountability, *Report*, [Ottawa: Supply and Services, 1980]) and the d'Avignon Committee (see *Report of the Special Committee on the Review of Personnel Management and the Merit Principle* [Ottawa: Supply and Services, 1979]).
50   This was a prominent theme of IPAC's October 1981 national seminar on special interest groups. See Pross, "Governing under pressure."
51   Douglas Hartle, *The Draft Memorandum to Cabinet* (Toronto: Institute of Public Administration, 1976).

ing fortunate discoveries accidentally," has superseded system as a guide to successful policy-making. Perhaps this is a reaction to the failure of the systems approach. However, those of us who are not Ottawa policy-makers have considerably less faith in serendipity as a tool for decision.

Though we were initially preoccupied with changes in Ottawa, parallel developments in the provinces soon found commentators. The most widely publicized of these activities was initiated by the Ontario government and though not entirely successful, it did address a central issue: the question of whether or not policy-making would be enhanced through the application of the concept of an inner and outer cabinet.[52] This was an issue that Ottawa approached crab-wise through the creation of the Priorities and Planning Committee and did not address frontally until the brief and innovative premiership of Joe Clark. Of the other provinces, only Quebec needed, or took the trouble, to develop central policy structures comparable to Ottawa's.[53] All, however, undertook some revisions, most of which were reported in the literature.[54]

The literature was also contributing to the deepening understanding we were obtaining of the role of intergovernmental relations in Canadian public policy-making. Its growing significance had been evident since the Depression, but our awareness expanded considerably in the 1960s as cooperative federalism gave way to confrontational federalism and institutionally oriented models of federal-provincial relations were superseded by models drawn from the study of politics among nations.[55] The analogy to international relations was sharpened as the politics of oil tilted the balance of power in the country a little away from the centre towards the West. In this context Pratt pointed to the extent "province-building" by provincial governments contributed to the expansion of intergovernmental tension.[56] Cairns, impressed not only with the growth of Canadian governments but with their ineptitude, broke with the international relations analogy and opted for one more primeval. Canadian politics and policy-making, he argued, is suffering from the fact that eleven oversized governments, each with limited vision but well-developed territorial in-

---

52 See the various *Reports* of the Committee on Government Productivity published between 1970 and 1973 by the Ontario government, and James D. Fleck, "Reorganization of the Government of Ontario," CANADIAN PUBLIC ADMINISTRATION, 15 (Summer 1972), p. 383.

53 See Pierre O'Neill and Jacques Benjamin, *Les mandarins du pouvoir: L'exercice du pouvoir au Québec de Jean Lésage à René Lévesque* (Montreal: Québec/Amerique, 1978).

54 Bryden, *op. cit.*, Chandler and Chandler, *op. cit.*

55 As in Richard Simeon, *Federal-Provincial Diplomacy: The Making of Recent Policy in Canada* (Toronto: University of Toronto Press, 1972).

56 L.R. Pratt, *The State and Province-Building: Alberta's Development Strategy, 1971-76* (Edmonton: University of Alberta, Department of Political Science, Occasional Paper, 1976).

stincts, are forever getting in each other's way. It is as though, he argued, eleven elephants were blundering their way through a maze.[57]

Though we may treat intergovernmental policy-making lightly, we cannot afford to do so. As Smiley and others have shown, executive federalism has become a very real factor in the development of Canadian public policy.[58] Not everyone would agree with this writer's view that it is our policy crucible, but when one takes into account not only the apparatus of the first ministers' conference, but also the various sector conferences and the networks of officials and interest spokesmen, it is hard to escape the conclusion that much public policy is promoted, reviewed and brought to fruition at this level.

The central policy structures and intergovernmental relations occupy centre stage in the Canadian policy process, but the literature has not ignored other aspects of our little drama. As we have noted, the process orientation of the literature has led to some discussion of environmental influences. The policy role of pressure groups is receiving increasing attention, and the declining policy role of political parties has been the object of concern.[59] This, of course, also extends to the part that Parliament plays in initiating and shaping public policy. Here the literature alerts us to a critical problem: executive federalism, the growth of the central policy structures, and the dominance in their fields of specialized agencies and their attendant policy communities have all undermined Parliament's legitimating role in policy-making. If nothing is done to revive and enhance Parliament's significance in the policy process, the legitimacy of public policy itself will become suspect.

Field studies and policy analysis

The study of public policy can be all-encompassing. Not only does it embrace the furthest reaches of government activity, the study of process, as we have indicated, can scan the range of political life. While stimulating, this breadth does raise obvious problems of inclusion and of synthesis. We shall deal with those problems here by not attempting to be inclusive and by looking only very briefly at synthesis.

As far as field studies are concerned, an impressive range of analyses have appeared in recent years. The student of public policy no longer

57 Cairns, *op. cit.*
58 Smiley, *op. cit.*
59 Notably in Gillies, *op. cit.*, but also in Robert L. Stanfield, "The Present State of the Legislative Process in Canada: Myths and Realities," in Neilson and MacPherson, *op. cit.*, pp. 39-51; and Harold D. Clarke, Colin Campbell, F.Q. Quo and Arthur Goddard, *Parliament, Policy and Representation* (Toronto: Methuen, 1980). This author has discussed the relationship between parties and groups in "Space, Function and Interest: The problem of Legitimacy in the Canadian State," in Dwivedi, *op. cit.*

has any excuse for not being reasonably well informed. Many of these studies have shed a good deal of light on the processes of policy-making. Taylor's work on health policy is a good example. Amongst the many others, Langford's should be singled out because it sheds light on decision-making within a ministry system.[60] Aucoin and French's work on the Ministry of State for Science and Technology, taken together with Doern's critique of horizontal agencies helps to explain the failure of that form of policy co-ordination in Canada.[61] The Economic Council of Canada's "regulation reference" fostered extensive new writing in that area,[62] whilst the many intergovernmental aspects of policy-making have been amply discussed in case studies of specific policy development. Nor has the impact of the central policy structures been ignored. It is difficult, for example, to read Sally Weaver's *The Making of Canadian Indian Policy* without becoming vividly aware of what Atkinson and Jackson mean when they say that "while the central organs of policy-making ... have attempted to drive governmental goals into the departments, they have faced ministerial and departmental intransigence."[63]

Of the many points made in these studies, two should be singled out. The first is a reflection on the role of line agencies in policy formation. It is clear that while the policy process differs from field to field, sectoralism tends to play an extremely important part in defining the relationship between actors operating in each field. In other words, because government programs are implemented by functionally, or sectorally, defined agencies, policies related to those programs tend to be initiated, discussed, promoted and eventually implemented by the "policy communities" which cluster around those agencies. Thus Transport Canada is at the centre of a network which includes related federal agencies, provincial departments, interested groups, "think tanks" and so on. This policy community dominates the formation of federal transportation pol-

60 John W. Langford, *Transport in Transition* (Montreal: McGill-Queen's/Institute of Public Administration of Canada, 1976). See also Michael J. Prince and John A. Chenier, "The rise and fall of policy planning and research units: an organizational perspective," CANADIAN PUBLIC ADMINISTRATION, 23 (Winter 1980), pp. 519-42.
61 Peter Aucoin and Richard French, *Knowledge, Power and Public Policy* (Ottawa: Science Council of Canada, 1974); G. Bruce Doern, "Horizontal and Vertical Portfolios in Government," in G. Bruce Doern and V. Seymour Wilson, eds., *Issues in Canadian Public Policy* (Toronto: Macmillan, 1974), p. 316.
62 See Economic Council of Canada, Regulation Reference, *Final Report* (Ottawa: Supply and Services, 1981); the survey article "Regulatory Agencies," by Richard J. Schultz, in Whittington and Williams, *op. cit.*, pp. 313-34 and his *Federalism and the Regulatory Process* (Montreal: Institute for Research on Public Policy, 1979); W.T. Stanbury, ed., *Government Regulation in Canada: Scope, Growth, Process* (Montreal: Institute for Research in Public Policy, 1980).
63 Jackson and Atkinson, *op. cit.*, p. 61; Sally M. Weaver, *Making Canadian Indian Policy: The Hidden Agenda, 1968-1970* (Toronto: University of Toronto Press, 1981).

icy, and is checked, or even challenged, only when the "level of conflict," to use Schattschneider's phrase, concerning a particular policy cannot be contained within the community.[64] Transport Canada is not alone in possessing a policy community. In fact, case studies testify overwhelmingly to the presence of policy communities within virtually all policy fields.

A host of fascinating and important issues flow from this observation. It raises, for example, the question of policy dominance by specific communities and the problem of achieving effective intervention on the part of cabinets themselves. It suggests that the growing influence of sectoralism – as opposed to the traditionally geographic orientation of single-member constituency systems – in policy-making may be fundamentally responsible for the diminishing policy role of political parties and of Parliament. It has implications for intergovernmental relations. Brown, for example, has argued that problems in the implementation of regional development programs in the Maritimes may be related to the fact that the coordinative orientation of provincial cabinets and regional federal ministers was insufficient to off-set the sectoral approach of departmental specialists.[65]

The relationship between the sectorally oriented institutions and the policy-making centre has generated considerable discussion. Gillies argues that as the central policy structures have become powerful, so they have also grown remote from the line agencies and the policy communities that guide them. "The departments and their deputies became more the vehicles through which the overall policies of the government, as developed in the Committee on Priorities and Planning, were carried out, rather than the source of new ideas. The department – which for most Canadians has always been the liaison point between the governed and the governing and the place for the input of policy – no longer serves that function in anything like the manner it did a decade ago."[66] Richard Schultz, in an impressive analysis of the sources of departmental power,[67] rejects this position, maintaining that despite the efforts of the pro-active policy centre, the departments and their networks still possess sufficient

---

64   E.E. Schattschneider, *The Semi-Sovereign People* (N.Y.: Holt-Rinehart, 1960). The concept of the policy community is developed more fully in my *Duality and Public Policy* and succinctly in my "Pressure Groups: Talking Chameleons."
65   M. Paul Brown, "The Political Economy and Public Administration of Rural Lands in Canada – New Brunswick and Nova Scotia perspectives" (Ph.D. dissertation, University of Toronto, 1982).
66   James Gillies and Jean Pigott, "Participation in the legislative process," CANADIAN PUBLIC ADMINISTRATION, 25 (Summer 1982), p. 262.
67   Richard J. Schultz, *Federalism, Bureaucracy and Public Policy: The Politics of Highway Transport Regulation* (Montreal: McGill-Queen's/Institute of Public Administration of Canada, 1980), pp. 180-89.

control over the flow of information and over the day-to-day implementation of policy to effectively dominate it. It could be that both are correct, but that while policy communities dominate on-going policy and its incremental modification, the central policy structures and the governmental leadership, because they have hived themselves off from agency communication networks, do indeed operate in a vacuum when they intervene in a policy field. If this is the case, there are clearly enormous problems of public participation and of educating the centre which must be addressed.

Schultz's argument takes us further than this, however. He raises the possibility that power and influence, rather than flowing upward, may have "flowed downward, past ministers, past deputy ministers, into the middle ranks of the bureaucracy."[68] In other words, the central dominance that worries Gillies is, in fact, a myth that masks a near complete absence of power at the centre and at the top of departmental hierarchies. Thus the private sector has little policy influence not, as Gillies argues, because departmental leaders are disregarded by the centre, but because neither they nor officials at the centre have any real control over those parts of the administrative machine which are "interfacing" with the public. Schultz may be right.[69] Bureaucratic pluralism, at least at the federal level, may be endemic to the emerging Canadian system, just as political pluralism pervades the American. The possibilities and the problems of bureaucratic pluralism are truly Kafkaesque: a centre that is merely symbol; functionaries with a limited immediate power, but no role in the broader development of policy; a public baffled by a government that is arbitrary in small things, ineffectual in larger ones. Hopefully, both the literature and the policy-makers themselves will address these issues further.

A final point which becomes clear in reading case studies in policy-making is that the art of policy analysis[70] is not always well developed in this country. There is a tremendous variation in the quality of advice policy-makers receive; a variation from sector to sector and from govern-

68 Ibid., p. 188.
69 Faulkner, *op. cit.*, after several years as a cabinet minister, argues that the diffusion, not the concentration, of power is the major problem. The present writer has also noted the tendency of relatively junior officials to play a very active role in developing policy. See *Duality and Public Policy*, ch. 5.
70 The term "policy analysis" is used here in the narrow sense. as the process through which alternative courses of action are reviewed and evaluated in order to assist policy-makers to reach decisions. The term is, however, often used to refer to more general discussion of policy issues or the ex-post facto review of policy decisions such as those frequently published by research institutes such as the C.D. Howe Institute, the Institute for Research in Public Policy or the Economic Council of Canada. In this discussion these have been dealt with as field studies.

ment to government. As far as this writer is aware, this is an issue which has not been addressed by Canadians since the early 1970s.[71] It died as an issue then because the reform movement was too sweeping in its thrust, threatening to entirely sublimate politics in technique. It would be a pity, however, if an interest in developing the art, as well as the mechanical skills, of giving policy advice were to be suppressed forever.

In summarizing this lengthy, though incomplete, review of the recent Canadian literature in policy studies, perhaps we should suggest that the condition of the country and the state of development of the descriptive literature is now such that a far-reaching discussion of theoretical issues should, and can, be undertaken. It is not surprising that our recent literature has been primarily concerned with description. A proper understanding of the policy system must be built on sound description, and with the rate of change that has occurred in Canadian policy-making in recent years both observers and practitioners have had difficulty keeping up to date. Consequently, the literature has tended to reflect reality but not to reflect upon it.

Nevertheless, the time has come for us to look beyond description to underlying trends, to try to discern what is really happening in the "real world" of policy-making. This involves theorizing. It involves identifying the purely indigenous forces which are at work in the Canadian political system and demonstrating how they interact with generic tendencies (specialization of function, or bureaucratization, for example) and international forces (the influence of the multinational, the interdependence of world economies) to produce conditions which apply in Canada alone. In short, we must follow Wilson's recent example and we must build upon it.[72]

Many Canadian practitioners will scoff at what they will doubtless see as a typical academic retreat into theorizing. Once again, they will argue that the country needs "relevant" mission-oriented research and writing, not more "ivory-tower stuff." Nevertheless, while there is a definite and important place for highly practical research, we need much more urgently to strengthen the theoretical underpinnings of both research and writing and ultimately of policy-making itself. In the following paragraphs perhaps the reasons for saying this will become clear.

Recent developments: implications for practice, theory and education

This discussion began with the cybernetic vision of the late 1960s. It suggested that that vision addressed fundamental realities. Those realities

71 The Prince-Chenier article previously cited makes some useful points on the subject, however.
72 V. Seymour Wilson, *op. cit.*, especially ch. 11 and the Epilogue.

are still with us. We must still adjust policy systems that are built on a distributive ideology to a world in which redistributive politics are becoming determinant. The fact that the cybernetic vision has become a bad dream should not dismay us. The tumble from system to serendipity suggests that the adjustments we sought to make were much more difficult to achieve, and much less fully understood, than we had anticipated. It does not suggest that the attempt should not have been made. Clearly it should, and it will have to be made again.

The developments we have referred to throughout this discussion exemplify what Hugh Heclo calls "political learning." The political system moves sometimes sequentially, sometimes crab-wise; sometimes incrementally, occasionally systematically, to understand and respond to changes within the larger environment. It is an heuristic process and the Canadian development of policy systems has been heuristic. It began shortly after the Second World War and has continued, with varying intensity, to this day. The post-Glassco reforms of Ottawa's central policy structures had a major impact. They unleashed massive organizational development at the federal level, triggered a prolonged positional battle between the central agencies, and dislocated both resource allocation and policy communication processes. Periodic adjustments responded to these difficulties, sometimes successfully, sometimes not. Thus, the Pearson-Trudeau development of cabinet structures and procedures offset the growing influence of Treasury Board. The creation of horizontal portfolios was less successful; coordination was not enhanced thereby. It took much longer to tackle the problems in resource allocation created by the separation of Treasury Board from Finance. The development of Priorities and Planning and subsequently the annual celebration of the marriage of the fiscal framework and the expenditure budget were important but not entirely satisfactory moves in the right direction. The more recent acceptance of the inner cabinet concept coupled with the adoption of the program expenditure management, or "envelope," system, is more promising. This approach is held by some to be less effective as a planning and political control instrument than PPBS,[73] but it does have the advantage of meshing policy and resource allocation decisions and it appears, at least to this writer, to conform more realistically to Ottawa's power and institutional arrangements than did the latter.

Perhaps the most important thing that can be said about the new system is that it designates a planning centre. The Privy Council Office seems to have won supremacy over the policy bureaucracies of Treasury Board and Finance, though the role of the latter is still vague and it is quite possible that it, the Ministry of State for Economic and Regional

73   See Dobell, *op. cit.*

Development, and the Ministry of State for Social Development will in time come to rival the core group which serves the inner cabinet. If that should happen, the federal public service and policy-making in particular will once again suffer the indecisiveness and the upheavals which follow clashes at the top. For the moment, however, the Privy Council Office appears to have won its way. If it can balance its challengers off against one another; if it can command the support of the inner cabinet; and, above all, if the prime minister not only endorses its role but works the cabinet effectively, there is a reasonable chance that we can at last achieve effective direction to policy-making in this country. While we cannot avoid a degree of bureaucratic pluralism emanating from the inevitable tension between line agencies and the policy-making centre, that pluralism can be kept in hand as a healthy contributor to the development of public policy. In other words, after a decade of turbulence, if we have created a strong centre we may have built a central policy system that is appropriate to our needs.

What are our needs? To repeat: we must adapt to a world in which the redistributive mode is dominant. A world in which the institutionalization of universal social security is taken for granted; in which the physical constraints of resource utilization are accepted and taken into account; and a world which has come to terms with a new economic structure. This last is currently our most pressing concern. It is not simply that mature corporations, the planning system, depend on government for demand and supply management, and consequently must find in the public sector a much greater capacity to plan – and to realize those plans – than government has yet attained. In a sense, this may be a relatively tractable problem. What will be far more difficult will be the achievement of a proper balance in the economy between the predominating influence of the planning system and the necessary preservation of the competitive market economy.[74] For it seems likely that the competitive market economy, the traditional sector, will survive and will continue to be a political force, albeit as a peripheral influence. It will be the task of policy-makers to ensure that public policies are not so skewed to the needs of the planning system that life in the traditional sector becomes barely tolerable. This is particularly important in Canada where the uneven distribution

74 Galbraith, *op. cit.*, whose terminology has been used here, tends to dismiss the competitive market economy as of little account. Other theorists writing in the tradition of dual labour market theory are not as sure. See particularly, Suzanne Berger and Michael J. Piore, *Dualism and Discontinuity in Industrial Societies* (Cambridge: Cambridge University Press, 1980) which makes a strong case for the continued existence of the traditional sector and looks not only at the economic but at the political aspects of economic duality.

of the planning system and the competitive market economy often lie behind inter-regional discord and exacerbate centre-periphery tensions.[75]

We began to address these needs in the mid and late 1960s, but the machinery of government, the policy machinery in particular, was inadequate to the task. We spent the 1970s sorting out the machinery. We are by no means finished, but if we have indeed established the decision-making centre, other institutional reforms can now be addressed. The reform of Parliament is crucial and should have been tackled before had not the need to reform cabinet taken precedence. It is now on the public agenda and hopefully will remain there. The literature has identified possible reforms, and experience, notably the establishment of parliamentary task forces, has suggested others. Surely, too, hand in hand with enhancing the policy role of Parliament should come a renewal of the policy role of political parties, a step that must be achieved if sectoralism is to be contained and a place found for the expression of the general interest. Finally, we must restore the institutional linkages which ensure an adequate flow of policy information between line agencies and the centre. The complexity of modern government is such that we can never hope to restore – even if we wanted to – the days of departmental dominance, but the diffusion of power, the vacuum at the centre which developed during the 1970s, cannot be permitted to reappear without doing serious damage to the country.

These are broad-brush conclusions. They are far more optimistic than the current tone of the literature would warrant. They involve sweeping generalizations concerning the basic meaning and long-term impact of recent changes in federal policy-making processes, and they introduce concepts concerning fundamental trends that are not generally accepted. They flow from the relatively rare opportunity to survey and consider the events and the literature of the last decade and a half and they are offered here partly to stimulate discussion and partly because it is important to take the longer view and to look for underlying trends.

Even if these optimistic projections are realized, we still have plenty to worry about. One of the most vexing is the problem of policy-making

75 The application of theories of dualism to the situation of Canada's maritime provinces has been the subject of a major research undertaking at Dalhousie University's Institute of Public Affairs. See Donald H. Clairmont and Fred Wien, "Segmentation, Disadvantage and Development: An Analysis of the Marginal Work World, Its Linkages with the Central Work World and its Role in the Maritime Provinces" (Halifax: The Institute, 1974). The greater part of the research has focused on economic and social aspects of dualism, but some preliminary findings on political aspects have been presented in Richard Apostle and Paul Pross, "Marginality and Political Culture: A New Approach to Political Culture in Atlantic Canada," paper presented to the Canadian Political Science Association, 1981.

at the intergovernmental level. Would some of these problems diminish if Ottawa achieved a better understanding, through its line agencies and their policy communities, of regional aspirations and concerns? Perhaps. Perhaps, too, reform of Parliament and a restoration to the party system of a recognized role in the policy process would enhance the regional perspective of the federal government. On the other hand, we must also deal with the problem of the eleven lumbering elephants, and the changes which we have discussed have not addressed the problem of intergovernmental conflict. It is hard to see any grounds for believing that the difficulties we have experienced in the last fifteen years will not continue or even become worse as regional communities struggle to express and protect themselves through their provincial governments. Unless, of course, the dissenting premiers were right, and the patriated constitution will, so to speak, put down ten of the eleven elephants. We must wait for a generation or two to find out whether it will.

In the meantime, there are more immediate tasks. The most urgent relates to the need for planning. Whether the argument that we are engaged in the politics of redistribution is accepted or not, it is hard to deny that modern governments are engaged in the business of planning. Nor is it hard to deny that modern governments have generally failed in their efforts to achieve effective planning regimes. Aaron Wildavsky has persuasively explained why.[76] Seductive though Wildavsky's argument is, however, it must be rejected for the simple reason that while it may, as Wildavsky argues, take a religious faith to believe in planning, it takes an even greater faith to believe that market forces will ensure social equity, an orderly economy and the sensible use of natural resources. Practitioners and theorists alike must turn their attention again to the problems of achieving planning which is sensitive both to the needs of people and communities and to the vagaries of the laws of cause and effect. In other words, we must take another look at the problems of systematic politics.

Thus far these concluding comments have dealt with the practice rather than the study of policy-making. As our retrospective discussion has shown, many opportunities for scholarship flow from the day-to-day operations of the machinery of policy-making. Without doubt the practical agenda we have just sketched out will provide fertile ground for every type of scholarly inquiry, from the purely descriptive to mission-oriented research and to dispassionate analysis. Our discussion has touched on some of these possibilities: to continue our descriptive endeavours so that we have a sound, and useable, understanding of Canadian processes; to revive our interest in the problems of forecasting and planning; to refine

76 Aaron Wildavsky, "If Planning is Everything, Maybe It's Nothing," *Policy Sciences*, 4 (1973), pp. 127-53.

the techniques of policy analysis. Implicit in the discussion have been other items which belong on the research agenda. For example, we have suggested that liberal ideology is inappropriate to the politics of redistribution and that we are in the midst of a paradigm shift as far as ideology is concerned. This single generalization conjures up a host of research possibilities, beginning with the obvious one: Is it tenable? If it is, then we must investigate the nature of the ideology that is appropriate. We must ask whether it is yet emergent and if it is, how its development will occur given the present myth and idea systems which currently pervade our political culture. These are important questions, for paradigm shifts in ideology do not occur uneventfully. They involve the breakdown and reconstruction of consensus and frequently social dislocation and disorder. Timely inquiry might ameliorate these difficulties.

On a less rarefied plane, it is clear that even more scholarly effort must be devoted to understanding the roles of the institutions engaged in public policy-making and clarifying the extent to which they contribute to or detract from the attainment of democracy. The forces of sectoralism are indeed powerful. A century ago Weber described the power of a fully developed bureaucracy as "over-towering." Today we are still discovering what he meant and we are even further today from containing that power than we were in Weber's day. By studying and properly understanding the policy role of Parliament and of our political parties we can contribute something to harnessing the power of bureaucracy within our own polity. By studying the central policy structures and the communications links between the centre, line agencies and policy communities we can better ensure that policy is a reflection of the needs of the public and not merely the self-serving divinations of government agencies.

In all of this there must be a much stronger effort to develop theory. It is not enough to describe and bemoan the declining policy role of Parliament. We must ask why that decline is taking place and we must come up with more powerful explanations than those which currently suffice. In this writer's view, the influence of differentiation of function – sectoralism, bureaucratization – is significant, but we need much more profound development of theory relevant to the Canadian case before we can be sure and before we can usefully apply such an understanding.

Scholarship is expressed in the classroom as well as on paper and here it is in many respects more immediately applicable. Though it may appear not to be the case, today's student – tomorrow's practitioner – is going to be influenced by what is said in the classroom. The mood in the classroom today is disturbing. The literature describes a policy process in disarray and the conclusions reached by students are harsh and contemptuous. Canada has not yet experienced serious, widespread political disenchantment, but it could easily do so if the student generations of the

1980s can find no firm evidence that their policy system is workable, responsive and sound. In this context the performance of Canada's policy-makers will greatly affect the conclusions our students reach. But so also will the scholarly work of their teachers. This work, as we have argued, is concerned with describing, analysing and explaining immense change. It should be vigorously developed in the classroom so that students have a firm understanding of process fundamentals. This will not make life any easier for the policy-makers of the 1990s, but on the principle that an informed public is superior to an uninformed one, it does hold out the promise of a constructive rather than a destructive response to our problems on the part of tomorrow's citizens and public servants. This is not to suggest that we should down-grade the courses in substantive policy or in policy analysis that are taught in most schools of public administration. These are an important aspect of political science and public administration education and they should be enhanced, not down-graded. However, it does mean that they should be built on a thorough understanding of process. Without such an understanding substantive policy will be considered out of context and policy analysis and policy advice will be unrealistic.

In sum, we have recently lived through a vexing period in the evolution of Canadian policy processes. Doubtless there are more difficulties ahead. However, it is possible that the most recent developments have achieved an equilibrium in the core policy institutions and that, as a result, the time has now come to effect important and long overdue reforms in other key institutions. We can at least hope that this is so and we can also hope that in effecting these reforms study and practice will achieve a rare moment of cooperation.

The influence of organizational theory in Canadian public administration

V. Seymour Wilson

The ideas of economists and political philosophers, both when they are right and when they are wrong, are more powerful than is commonly understood. Indeed the world is ruled by little else. Practical men, who believe themselves to be quite exempt from any intellectual influences, are usually the slaves of some defunct [theorist] . . . the ideas which civil servants and politicians . . . apply to current events are not likely to be the newest . . . I am sure that the power of vested interests is vastly exaggerated compared with the gradual encroachment of ideas. Soon or late, it is ideas, not vested interests, which are dangerous for good or evil.

John Maynard Keynes

Introduction

To embark on a study of organizational theory and its relevance to public administration is analogous to undertaking Homer's Odyssey: like Ulysses one is never quite sure if the journey has begun, where one is located at any point of time, or when the whole nightmarish experience will eventually end. Part of this bewildering experience is undoubtedly due to the proliferation of possible routes open to the unsuspecting traveller; for although a vast number of studies, concepts and approaches have been developed for the study of organizations there is little apparent unity among them. This state of affairs is partly due to the number of "basic" and "applied" disciplines involved – psychology, economics, industrial management, political science, sociology to name a few.[1] Partly it may also be due to the absence of an integrative framework to guide and give sharper focus to the disparate strands of research.[2] Indeed, we are now being conditioned to the idea that our long journey of discovery may lead us to scores of integrative frameworks – an impossible task to comprehend if ever there was one. As V. Subramaniam

The author is associate professor of public administration, Carleton University.

1 See for example the treatment given this theme in James G. March, ed., *Handbook of Organization* (Chicago: Rand McNally, 1965).
2 For the exposition of this position see the work of Mayer N. Zald, particularly in Mayer Zald, ed., *Power in Organizations* (Nashville, Tenn.: Vanderbilt University Press, 1970).

recently warned us, our study of organization theory may be more complex than an "elephantine problem": "What academics are researching in organization theory is not the same animal with several parts but a whole species with several sub-species . . . [thus] the same type of organization [has possibly developed] different sub-types in different cultural surroundings."[3]

This interesting insight opens up a series of queries to the academic mind which unfortunately cannot be pursued here.[4] Rather I would like to turn to another aspect of our bewildering experience which does attract the attention of both academics and practical men who believe themselves to be exempt from any theoretical influences, to paraphrase Lord Keynes. This is the general relationship between organization theory *writ large* and the practical world of public administration. Despite its apparent confused state has theory said anything to practice? Indeed, are not practical politicians and public servants "closet theorists", as Keynes implies?

For purposes of simplicity, most students of organization theory would not take strong exception to the statement that in the study of organizational goals, social environment and structures, the theoretical formulations which have informed practice in some measure have come from four broad schools of organizational theory: scientific management (subsequently refined and known as classical theory); human relations; systems theory; and, of recent vintage, the action theory of the New Public Administration movement. For purposes of this essay the corpus of organization theory is therefore examined under these four classifications. Our first task will be to demonstrate to what degree these four broad classifications have affected administrative practices in Canada.

Before doing so, one point should be emphasized. Much traditional writing in the field of organization theory was the work of reformers who had some practical knowledge of administration but whose approach to the subject matter was overwhelmingly influenced by the causes they wish to promote.[5] Indeed, traditional as well as present-day theories share this characteristic of a heavily normative content. Thus there is a constant dialectic between normative values and the need for practical solutions to problems in administration. This is evidenced in all four

3 V. Subramaniam, "Reflections on Trends in Organization Theory," in Ross Curnow and Roger Wettenhall, eds., *Understanding Public Administration* (London and Sydney: Allen and Unwin, 1981), p. 120. This argument is also explicit in Golembiewski's proposal for "mini-paradigms" for public administration. See Robert T. Golembiewski, *Public Administration as a Developing Discipline*, Part I (New York: Marcel Dekker, 1977).
4 This theme is admirably treated in Subramaniam, "Trends in Organization Theory." I highly recommend this article.
5 Peter Self, *Administrative Theories and Politics* (Toronto: University of Toronto Press, 1973), pp. 11-16.

broad categories of organization theory examined here; scientific management as well as systems theory sought creative leadership and humane manipulation of workers while embracing the relentless logic, precision and certainty of technology.[6] Human relations sought the Holy Grail of displacing the effects of the internal contradictions in managerial practice by removing labour/management conflict and substituting in its place "cooperation."[7] Finally the New Public Administration, presented in recent years as a radical action theory of decidedly normative implications, openly proclaims social justice and equity for all while seeking to achieve this through more administrative discretion.[8]

Theoretical developments and practical applications

It is a common observation that Canada has, throughout both her colonial and national past, been poised somewhat uncomfortably between two differing models of national development, the American and the British. It is hardly daring, indeed, to state that much of our history can be read as the process of conscious choice within a highly dualistic international context.[9] When, in the early twentieth century, a certain consensus began to form around the proposition that some new form of conscious control had to be instituted over the federal bureaucracy, the question also arose of the proper model to be followed: the British service, with its tradition of the administrative generalist, or the American system, with its new-found emphasis on the technical specialist. As suggested elsewhere, the concrete reality of the existing structure – itself a product of the Canadian historical experience up until that time – was a predetermining factor in deciding which bureaucratic model was to be emulated, and this factor militated for the acceptance of the American system.[10] But to at least a limited extent there *was* scope for conscious choice, a fact demonstrated by an interesting example.

6 H.S. Persons, ed., *Scientific Management in American Industry* (New York: Harper and Brothers, 1929), see especially pp. 427-39.
7 Elton Mayo, *The Human Problems of an Industrial Civilization*, 2nd ed. (Boston: Graduate School of Business Administration, Harvard University, 1946).
8 Bayard L. Catron and Michael M. Harmon, "Action Theory in Practice: Toward Theory without conspiracy," *Public Administration Review* (Sept./Oct. 1981), pp. 535-41.
9 The other form of dualism in Canadian history, the English-French division within the country, also raises a multitude of questions about administrative ideology, but that in itself is a subject for another paper.
10 For the development of this theme see J.E. Hodgetts *et al.*, *The Biography of an Institution: The Civil Service Commission of Canada 1908-1967* (Montreal: McGill-Queen's University Press, 1972). See also A. Paul Pross and V. Seymour Wilson, "Canadian Public Administration: The Discipline's Ugly Duckling," in Michael Stein *et al.*, eds., *Aspects of the Discipline: Political Science in the Twentieth Century* (Toronto: University of Toronto Press, forthcoming).

The Haldane Report of 1918 is usually acknowledged to be the classic discussion of the problems of government growth and the issue of ministerial responsibility. Few realize that it had important antecedents in Canada. The proliferation of non-departmental agencies – the very proliferation that so exercised Haldane – created enough concern in this country, that in 1912 Dr. Adam Shortt persuaded Sir Robert Borden to set up an investigatory committee on the Canadian machinery of government to review the problem. Not surprisingly, Sir George Murray, a recently retired British civil servant, was brought here to investigate the matter. Murray, who later served on the Haldane Committee, wrote a report which not only anticipated Haldane, it anticipated Lambert.[11] It argued for an "inner" and "outer" cabinet to rationalize the growth of the Canadian ministerial portfolios; the abolition of the Treasury Board and the setting up of a department of the Treasury with sweeping financial and personnel powers (shades of Lambert's Board of Management); and the need to abolish all these proliferating boards and commissions in a return to a pristine form of ministerial departmentalization.[12]

In any event, it was the American influence, in the form of scientific management, which eventually became the predominating reform for the Canadian public service. The general outlines of this theory as well as its well-defined relationship to bureaucratic reform in Canada have been comprehensively outlined elsewhere,[13] but a few parenthetic observations here serve to round out this discussion. The links between scientific management and the classification system used in the Canadian reforms have already been established.[14] However, it is interesting, by a process of historical inquiry, to reconstruct in part the social and intellectual environment of the time of reform as a means of isolating some of the philosophical assumptions which led to the concrete reforms being put in place.

The literature on the subject suggests that if the growth of private enterprise in the late nineteenth century led to the demand for structural rationalization in industry to which scientific management was an answer, then the progressive era of the early twentieth century led to an unprecedented growth in governmental functions which in turn gave rise to a demand for classification studies to rationalize the growing bureaucratic

11 Sir George Murray, *Report on the Public Service of Canada* (Ottawa: King's Printer, 1912).
12 V. Seymour Wilson, *Canadian Public Policy and Administration* (Toronto: McGraw-Hill Ryerson, 1981), chapter 11.
13 Hodgetts, *Biography of an Institution*, chapters 9, 10.
14 V. Seymour Wilson, "The Relationship between Scientific Management and Personnel Policy in North American Administrative Systems," *Public Administration* (Autumn 1973), pp. 193-205.

structures.[15] And it is interesting to note that, like scientific management which began to assume in the eyes of its followers a quasi-messianic role as a panacea for all society's ills,[16] so too classification study took on certain emotional overtones in the United States. Significantly, it was known as the classification "movement," and became inextricably linked to various other such movements in the progressive era, such as the drive for economy and efficiency in government.[17]

But the new administrative ideology had very concrete consequences, a fact which was not lost on both the American and Canadian reformers. One study of the progressive era has suggested that the breakdown of the old laissez-faire ideology of the nineteenth century was succeeded by what might be called bureaucratic thought, which looked to science to solve all the societal problems which unregulated enterprise had created: in effect the application of scientific management to society as a whole.[18] It is therefore scarcely surprising that classification analysis came to be applied to the governmental structures themselves.

The classification movement tied in with the rising support for the merit system and the attack on patronage. Obviously if the merit system were to be practical, a scientific classification of the duties of all positions as well as a precise description of the qualifications necessary to fulfill these duties was a prime requirement. Economy and efficiency in the administration of government would obviously be enhanced if all functions were clearly specified and lines of authority clearly drawn. It cannot be overemphasized how chaotic and poorly organized governments tended to be in the early twentieth century. This chaos was no less a concern of government employees than it was of the taxpayers. As Leonard White suggests, it was one of the general objectives of the classification movement to "lay the foundation for equitable treatment for public employees by the accurate definition, orderly arrangement, and fair evaluations of positions in the public service."[19]

To round out this discussion of the general factors encouraging scientific management the influence of World War One must be noted. For

15   This point was made specifically by Griffenhagen and Associates, the American firm which devised the 1918 classification system for Canada. See "A Farewell Contribution from Griffenhagen and Associates Ltd.," in *The Civilian*, Canadian civil service staff publication (February 1921), p. 69.
16   Nicos Mouzelis, *Organization and Bureaucracy: An Analysis of Modern Theories* (London: Routledge and Kegan Paul, 1964), p. 84.
17   William E. Mosher and J. Donald Kingsley, *Public Personnel Administration* (New York: Harper and Brothers, 1936), p. 355.
18   R.H. Wieke, *The Search for Order, 1877-1920* (New York: Hill and Wang, 1967), pp. 133-77.
19   Leonard White, *Introduction to the Study of Public Administration* (New York: The Macmillan Co., 1926), p. 279.

the first time the United States and Canada found themselves engaged in a total war which required the massive mobilization of economic re- sources and activity under the centralized authority of the federal gov- ernments in both countries. Such an effort required not only a vastly expanded bureaucracy but also demanded an effective means of rational- ly organizing this expanded administration. In the United States the armed services were faced with some enormous personnel problems. A new appreciation of personnel as a specific area of interest for manage- ment was one apparent result, and new standardized personnel specifica- tions and means of testing for the required skills were developed.[20]

At a more specific level, new principles of centralized financial control were being developed: a uniform system of accounting required a uni- form job terminology.[21] Moving away from private enterprise into the field of governmental administration, this consideration took on impor- tant new dimensions. For example, one dimension is that the earliest scholarly study concerned exclusively with a problem in Canadian public administration was carried out by two members of the U.S. civil service reform movement, H.S. Villard and W.W. Willoughby, who applied to the Canadian budgetary process the searching concern for sound finan- cial management which has been such a prominent part of American studies in the field.[22]

Another dimension is the necessity for intelligible information upon which the peoples' elected representatives might base their attempts to control the operations of the civil service. A set of common symbols (or a common working language) was needed for communication be- tween politicians and administration and for communication within the bureaucracy itself. It has been pointed out, both by American and Canadian scholars of urban government, that scientific management re- forms were spurred on primarily due to municipal leaders' sheer inability to make rational decisions on appropriations for administration in the absence of any standardized information on its organization.[23]

Scientific management theorists also argued and demonstrated how a classification plan would allow for a more specific examination system, one that would test candidates for the exact skills required.[24] One theo-

20 Cyril C. Ling, *The Management of Personnel Relations: History and Origins* (Homewood, Illinois: Irwin, 1965), pp. 322-37.
21 Mosher and Kingsley, *Public Personnel Administration*, p. 355.
22 H.S. Villard and W.W. Willoughby, *The Canadian Budgetary System* (N.Y.: Appleton, 1918).
23 Fred Telford, "The Classification and Salary Standardization Movement in the Public Service," *The Annals of the American Academy of Social and Political Science* (1924), p. 206.
24 Lewis Merriam, "The Uses of a Personnel Classification in the Public Service," ibid., p. 216.

rist in particular mentioned two points which illustrate how deeply the roots of the classification movement lay in the soil of Taylorism. The classification, he argued, made possible the precise planning of salaries as rewards for efficiency. This idea was in fact a central concern of Taylor himself who developed complex incentive schemes. And the theorist assimilated what may well have been the central core of Taylor's thought when he maintained that classification would be a move away from the imperfect discretionary authority of senior administrative officers and toward a scientific method of efficiency rating.[25] It is therefore no accident that presentations made to the 1946 Royal Commission on Administrative Classifications (Gordon Commission) supporting the classification scheme then in place since the reforms of 1918 steadfastly maintained these two characteristics as the central cornerstones of the merit system.

So much for a detailed look at the early contribution of scientific management to Canadian administrative practice. One more point should be made in parting, however. Reinhard Bendix has made the significant observation that scientific management theory served as an ideological tool for American management in convincing workers that hard work was a reward in itself rather than a means of rising from the bottom to the top.[26] Yet Bendix also noted management's reluctance to make this point too explicit because it ran so contrary to the American myth of success – from office boy to the president. The same ambiguity was the dogged problem of the Canadian classification scheme for well over fifty years of our history. The scheme and its theoretical justification was infused with echoes of the spirit of Horatio Alger and yet the actual system was a labyrinth of passageways with dead ends. The paradox is that in turning for advice to the United States, famed for its progressive business methods and traditions of liberal enterprise, Canada received a plan for a civil service structure of great hierarchical complexity, with a good deal of built-in rigidity within which upward mobility proved to be extremely difficult. The 1946 Royal Commission of Administrative Classifications echoed this central complaint on almost every page of its report.

Within this limitation, then, the first American ideological impact on the Canadian civil service rested. It was an impact which was in one sense profound, but in another sense, curiously restricted. Far from importing old American ideas of employee mobility upwards, the reforms made such movement perhaps less likely than before. It did, however,

25   Ibid., pp. 216-17.
26   Reinhard Bendix, *Work and Authority in Industry: Ideologies of Management in the Course of Industrialization* (New York: John Wiley and Sons, 1956), p. 285.

impart a tone, that of the philosophy of scientific management to the administration of the civil service. Efficiency and economy after this period became more like operational concepts than political slogans, and it is this contribution of scientific management that has remained enduring up to the present day.

This enduring concern for the "rationalization" of bureaucratic structures can be demonstrated in various ways, but a good example where both theory and practice in this area meshed is in the legitimizing and subsequent growth of central agencies. Scientific management theory in the form of classical theory provided the theoretical justification for the growth of the institutionalized presidency under President Roosevelt in the late 1930s. The theoretical papers of the Brownlow Committee created by Roosevelt at that time are now generally acknowledged as the *locus classicus* of classical management theory.[27] These papers written by Gulick, Urwick, Fayol, Mooney and others popularized such concepts as PODSCORB, staff and line, and span of control. The establishment of the Executive Office of the President was a direct result of the recommendations of this committee, instituting the concept of staff agencies and centralized leadership by the executive office at one of the highest levels of governmental authority in the United States. "The president needs help" was the cryptic conclusion of the Brownlow Committee after surveying the awesome administrative responsibilities heaped on the shoulders of the chief executive of the United States. Thus the growth of the institutionalized presidency has come to be viewed as one manifestation of the continuing and interminable struggle to achieve political dominance between Congress and the president, and the theoretical concept of staff played an important role in this evolution.[28]

In Canada Mackenzie King sat and watched these developments. Persuaded as he was by Roosevelt's New Deal legislation, it is hardly surprising that he saw this rationalizing of the institutionalized presi-

27 Few commentators make the subtle distinction between *scientific management* and *classical management* theory. By the late 1920s and early 1930s scientific management had been severely criticized for its inflexibility and inhumane implications for the individual worker. Human relations theory of course was instrumental in this criticism, but by then much of scientific management was concerned with efficiency and economy from a different perspective: instead of concentrating its concern at the individual level (time and motion studies classification, etc.) it now looked at the organization from the top downwards, that is, the managerial level (leadership, span of control, planning, organizing, budgeting "staff and line" etc.). The contribution of Taylor's counterpart in France, Henri Fayol, whose emphasis has always been from the managerial level downwards, became widely known through the translation of his works.
28 See Luther Gulick and Lyndall F. Urwick, eds., *Papers on the Science of Administration* (New York: Columbia University Press, 1937).

dency as a good thing and wished something akin to it in Canada, although by no means on the same scale.[29] Thus the theoretical roots of strong central agencies lay in the significant reforms of the American presidency in the 1930s. By osmosis it was transformed to Canada where some two and a half decades later it grew into a rather sturdy sapling. It is no accident that the strengthening and further developments of staff agencies around the Canadian federal executive has been viewed by some as the "presidentializing of the Prime Minister's Office" and that there has been considerable debate both in the popular and academic literature as to the nature of this growth.[30]

The sociologist Reinhard Bendix, amongst others, has pointed out that between the two world wars organization theory in the form of "human relations" ideas had a distinct influence on both the public and private sectors in the United States of America.[31] Basically this body of theoretical literature made two substantive points: 1/ the work group, not the individual, is the unit of production and therefore the proper focus of managerial concerns;[32] and 2/ improvements in reaching organizational objectives can be best obtained by "a freer and more pleasant working environment, a supervisor who is not regarded as a 'boss' [and who therefore fosters] a 'higher morale' [amongst his subordinates]."[33] Put simply, the push was on both in theoretical and practical circles to displace the ill effects of labour/management conflict and substituting in its place "cooperation."[34]

In Canada no developments of this sort surfaced in the public sector. The federal government, for example, continued in its well-established role as omnipotent employer. Institutions of employer-employee relationships created during this time (the revitalization of the Treasury Board

29 For the development of this theme see V. Seymour Wilson, *Canadian Public Policy and Administration*, chapter 9.
30 In one of the most lengthy and satisfying interviews I have ever had with a senior public servant, the late A.D.P. Heeny, who was given the job to refurbish the PCO/PMO complex, recalled that King reminded him to look at the American reforms of the institutionalized presidency. Heeney added that he was impressed by the evolving changes and on one of his wartime visits to Washington, King insisted he speak to the officials involved. Heeney recalled that King, however, had a hazy view of these changes, and Heeney preferred to look at the more modest administrative reforms made by the longtime secretary to the British cabinet, Sir Maurice Hankey. By 1968 Heeney was lamenting Trudeau's "Americanization" of the PMO/PCO complex. It had, he felt, "gone too far."
31 Bendix, *Work and Authority in Industry*, pp. 283-85. See also C.S. George, *The History of Management Thought* (Englewood Cliffs, N.J.: Prentice-Hall, 1968); Ling, *Management of Personnel Relations*.
32 Mayo, *Human Problems of an Industrial Civilization*, p. 116.
33 Ibid., p. 78.
34 Ibid., p. 177; Bob Hoke, "The Game of Work: Key to On-the-Job Behaviour," *Management Review*, 58 (December 1969).

in the 1930s and the creation of the National Joint Council in the 1940s) had as their central focus "the problems of the government as employer and not those of the employees."[35] The creation of the 1946 Royal Commission on Administrative Classification was an attempt to infuse the public service with new ideas for change in the personnel field. But this effort only met failure. Commenting on the state of affairs in the public service in the late 1940s and early 1950s the chairman of the Public Service Commission said it all when he exclaimed that "the use of the title personnel officer or training officer [at that time] would have been sufficient to have one tried for witchcraft."[36] During this time it was also generally held by many "that in a democratic society, government is benevolent and will treat its employees according to the best standards, whereas private employers are out to make a profit and so will tend to exploit their employees unless they are protected by a strong union."[37] This implies that the concerns for conflict management and various theoretical techniques and practical devices developed and encouraged by the private sector really had no place in government (or at least in Canadian government).

Change came very slowly between the mid forties and the early sixties. Personnel administration started in the public service after the severe indictment of the Gordon Commission, but the standards of selection for personnel officers were low and training almost non-existent. Perhaps the most important area where theory would begin to inform practice was the beginning of O & M (Organization and Methods) in the public service in 1946.

When it hired O & M specialists in 1946 the Civil Service Commission reminded its public that "management consciousness" had spread in the governments of the United Kingdom, the United States, France and others, and that advisory services on organization and methods had been established in these places as an aid to operating departmental agencies. The commission was further aware that "great benefits, in terms of increased efficiency and economy, can be realized by the intensive study and adjustment of organizational structure and the simplification and modernization of systems and methods."[38]

The word "systems" in postwar managerial thinking holds a status

35 Hodgetts, *The Biography of an Institution*, p. 194.
36 Sylvain Cloutier, "The Personnel Revolution: An Interim Report," Speech given at the Royal Military College, Kingston, June 19, 1965 (mimeograph), p. 2.
37 W.R. Dymond, "The Role of the Union in the Public Service as opposed to its Role in Private Business," Paper presented to the fifth annual conference, IPAC, Saskatoon, September 9-12, 1953. *Proceedings*, p. 59. It should be noted that Dr. Dymond did not prescribe to this view.
38 Civil Service Commission of Canada, *Annual Report*, 1947, p. 12.

equivalent, from a symbolic viewpoint, to that occupied by "scientific" in the prewar period.[39] Indeed, the practical implications of the systems approach – bringing "society under control in the same way as nature by reconstructing it according to the pattern of self-regulated systems of purposive-rational action and adaptive behaviour" – seem quite analogous to those of scientific management. So, too, does the methodological basis of systems analysis. Its proponents refer to it, in a manner reminiscent of Taylor's "mental revolution" as "primarily a way of thinking about the job of management"[40] as a "frame of mind."[41] Operations research was inaugurated during World War Two first in the United Kingdom and later in the United States. This rationalizing process was a long, steep climb by working out methods of integrating diverse subunits around the talk of solving complex technical problems.[42] Finally, cybernetics and computer technology lent respectively a sort of soul and body to the systems idea. It is very difficult to gauge to what extent these new theoretical ideas applied to organizations influenced the Canadian administration, but within the bowels of the bureaucracy there was certainly a growing awareness of the manner in which such theory was informing practice, especially in the United States.[43] Much of the literature on cybernetics and computer technology was being readily absorbed by the private sector in the United States immediately after the war. Canadian practitioners were very much aware of this and our literature reflects a constant preoccupation of our practitioners with the "new concerns for economy and efficiency" and growing interest in the pros and cons of applying the same management techniques found in the private sector to the public sector.[44] This major concern finally culminated in the Glassco Commission's statement that:

39 I am indebted to the excellent exposition of "systems" found in Michael E. Urban, *The Ideology of Administration: American and Soviet Cases* (Albany: State University of New York Press, 1982), pp. 53-59.
40 Richard A. Johnson *et al.*, *The Theory and Management of Systems*, 2nd ed. (New York: McGraw-Hill, 1967).
41 Herbert A. Simon, *The New Science of Management Decision* (New York: Harper & Row, 1960), p. 15.
42 Stafford Beer, *Decision and Control* (London: John Wiley and Sons, 1966).
43 Jack Byrd, *Operation Research Models for Public Administration* (Lexington, Mass.: Lexington Books, 1975).
44 C. James Gardner, "Staff Organization and Work Procedures," *Proceedings* of the eighth annual conference, IPAC, Victoria, B.C., September 5-8, 1956, pp. 47-56, especially p. 52-55. The early volumes of CANADIAN PUBLIC ADMINISTRATION provide substantial evidence for this assertion. I provide some random examples from one year, 1961: the article by Hugh Whalen, "The Peaceful Coexistence of Government and Business" (4, no. 1); Stanley Mansbridge, "Organization Theory and Practice" (4, no. 3); and the articles by Ross Davidson, J.J. Macdonell and Elmer B. Staats under the heading "Administrative Management in Government and Business" (4, no. 4).

The immediate aim of the techniques of management developed for industry is to attain the organization's goals with the greatest possible economy of effort. Consequently, most of the techniques of management developed for business can be adapted to governments, due allowance being made for the different tests by which economy and productivity must ultimately be judged.[45]

The Glassco Commission saw its task of introducing not only the new system technologies (which now heavily influenced the literature on organizational theory, especially decisional theory) but also helping to create a theoretical and practical revolution in "human resourcing" (of personnel management). The royal commission is strident in its criticisms:

> The charges laid at the doorstep of the personnel management system and largely confirmed by our investigation can be bluntly stated: there is a waste of human resources, because of the failure to give orderly consideration to the best methods of providing and utilizing people and the consequent frustration of many individual careers.[46]

The winds of change which affected the public service of Canada in the mid 1960s seemed to reach hurricane proportions for both personnel and systems management. Indeed, taking a clue from Robert Bogustaw's scathing critique of "the new utopians"[47] senior managers in the public service warned of signs of a "saturation psychosis"[48] as the conversion of all these theoretical ideas into practical methods of operation proceeded along. A large number of management science theoreticians and senior practitioners from the private sector as well as university economists and mathematicians enamoured by systems analysis entered government to direct the new revolution. The rise and fall of this revolution has been amply recorded elsewhere, particularly at the central agencies level, and we need not deal with describing the vicissitudes of that experience here.[49] Suffice to state that the results of the revolution has been mixed and have been judged rather harshly by some of its early foes and even former advocates, but I leave this critical judgment of an historical experience for other papers in this collection.[50]

45 *Report of the Royal Commission on Government Organization*, I. *Management of the Public Service* (Ottawa: Queen's Printer, 1962), pp. 46-47.
46 Ibid., p. 255.
47 Robert Boguslaw, *The New Utopians* (Englewood Cliffs, N.Y.: Prentice-Hall, 1965). What Boguslaw warns against is the negative impact on society of the work of reformist social engineers, *those theorists of action*, who apply the ultra-rational concepts of such disciplines as management science too far from rational social structures.
48 H.L. Laframboise, "Administrative Reform in the Federal Public Service: Signs of Saturation Psychosis," CANADIAN PUBLIC ADMINISTRATION, 14, no. 3 (Fall 1971), pp. 303-25.
49 R.D. French, *How Ottawa Decides: Planning and Industrial Policy-Making 1968-1980* (Ottawa: Canadian Institute for Economic Policy, 1980), chapters 1 and 2.
50 See especially the article by H.L. Laframboise, this volume.

Many readers of this essay would readily recall the social and political ferment of the 1960s in the United States due to the Vietnam War. This war's impact on the United States still remains a matter of debate and conjecture but in the area of organization theory it is readily acknowledged that its impact has been profound.[51] The New Public Administration reflected, more specifically, a critical reaction to conventional public administration. Advocates argued that previous organizational theory missed or completely de-emphasized "the essential notion of the political nature of public bureaucracy."[52] Those who identified with this movement were generally critical of previous theories of organization and optimistic about a new theory, one with proper values, high motivation and correct administrative means. The primary normative premises of public policy and administration were expressed as "the purpose of public organization is the reduction of economic, social and psychic suffering and the enhancement of life opportunities for those inside and outside the organization. . . . New Public Administration seeks to change those policies and structures that systematically inhibit *social equity*."[53]

Three themes have emerged over the years as important in this area of theory. First was the notion of "client-centred bureaucracy," encompassing the notion that administration was almost exclusively the delivery of programs aimed at achieving equality, both racial and other, and projected towards revitalizing the urban core of American cities. Efficiency in delivery and sensitivity to basic human needs were the important characteristics of this aspect of the theory.

The second theme was active participation – not only in program delivery but to some extent in the definition of what the program should be before implementation is sought. This meant active participation of employees or staff in the decision-making roles which were part and parcel of both program formulation and implementation.

Finally, there was the notion of representative bureaucracy. Representation of the people in a democracy cannot rely only on the electoral process; it must also be achieved by reflecting the citizenry in the bureaucracy in terms of race, ethnicity, geography, class and other social criteria.[54] This representation was seen as encouraging true participation

---

51 Dwight Waldo, *The Enterprise of Public Administration: A Summary View* (California: Chandler & Sharp Publishers, Inc., 1980).
52 Fred A. Kramer, *Dynamics of Public Bureaucracy* (Cambridge, Mass.: Winthrop, 1977), p. 5.
53 H. George Frederickson, "Towards a New Public Administration," in F. Marimi, ed., *Toward a New Public Administration* (Scranton, Pa.: Chandler, 1971), p. 312.
54 Waldo, *Enterprise of Public Administration*, pp. 95-96; V. Seymour Wilson and W.A. Mullins, "Representative Bureaucracy: Linguistic/Ethnic Aspects in Canadian Public Policy," CANADIAN PUBLIC ADMINISTRATION, 21, no. 4 (Winter 1978), pp. 513-38.

in policy-making by identifying those administering with those for whom the administration was intended. To sum up, this "theory of action," as it is called by its proponents, argues that responsibility in policy and administration is the key to unlocking the door for the *summum bonum*, the supreme good of democratic politics – namely, responsiveness to societal demands. And this responsiveness can only be realized in two ways: the recovery of relevance in the study of public policy and administration, and a critical examination and call for new directions in the style in which it is practised. To action theorists it is not inconsistent with the doctrine of popular sovereignty to accord the bureaucrat – the "real" decision-maker in the administrative state – his rightful inheritance to make decisions and to accept full responsibility for so doing. The administrator now has a moral imperative to rid society of alienation and other ills through style and process in administration.

Action theory in its various manifestations has caused considerable debate in the United States, particularly in regards to new policies for urban renewal and in school assignments and employment policies. The last in particular has generated the most heated controversy under the concept of "affirmative action": if discrimination or at least some condition of inequality has been demonstrated through comparisons of statistical patterns, then the remedial policy to be followed calls for racial, sexual and ethnic quotas to be imposed for employment purposes and for the admittance to public educational institutions.

Numerous books and magazine articles have been written on the topic, and court decisions continue to flow from the consequences of this new direction in American public policy. In Canada governmental responses to affirmative action have been less controversial. With the sole exception of the armed forces, Canadian policy-makers have not opted for legislated quota systems to be applied in the area of public employment. This does not mean that vigorous representations have not been and continue to be made to rectify institutional conditions which foster inequality of opportunity for women and certain select groups in society. The historical record of this discrimination in public service employment in Canada is so well documented that evidence of this assertion need not concern us here.[55]

The case of francophones is similar. Lack of ethnic representation of one of Canada's "founding races" in the bureaucracy was a central theme of the Royal Commission on Bilingualism and Biculturalism.[56] The vigorous efforts of the Trudeau administration, fully supported by the opposi-

---

55 See Hodgetts, *Biography of an Institution*, pp. 482-93.
56 Canada, *Report of the Royal Commission on Bilingualism and Biculturalism*, III, *The Work World* (Ottawa: Queen's Printer, 1969).

tion parties in the House of Commons are also well known and documented.[57]

The continuing evolution of these areas of policy concern is shown by the government's attempt in the late 1970s to create a new philosophy of management which would develop the traditional concerns for effective personnel management while introducing changes which incorporate affirmative action programs for women, the handicapped and native Canadians.[58] Various recruitement programs fostered by the Public Service Commission, and the departments of Unemployment and Immigration, Indian Affairs, and the Secretary of State are in reality the practical beginnings of a policy of affirmative action in governmental employment. The policy has been much more gradual than in the United States, and it has avoided much of the controversial aspects of American policy by thus far de-emphasizing the notion of legislated quota systems in hiring practices.

Emerging trends in the 1980s and beyond

What lies in the near future and beyond? The management theories resurrected or reaffirmed by both the Lambert and D'Avignon reports, and the pre-eminent question about the very nature of the federal government's powers following on the constitutional settlement, have yet to show clearly the shape of things to come. But some central themes seem to be emerging even if crystallization remains problematical for the present.

We have hinted throughout this essay that in a modern industrial society such as Canada bureaucratic forms of organization predominate and that this situation stands in opposition to the formal set of public norms which is rooted in the democratic tradition. The situation seems to be more acute in the United States; nevertheless, it remains somewhat of a lesser problem in the Canada of the 1980s.

Influential Canadian commentators have identified this problem as the central concern for the management of public affairs in the 1980s and beyond. During the spring of 1980 Dr. Michael Kirby, the former president of the Institute for Research on Public Policy and until recently a senior mandarin in the federal public service spoke at length on the shape

---

57 V. Seymour Wilson, "Language Policy," in G. Bruce Doern and V. Seymour Wilson, eds., *Issues in Canadian Public Policy* (Toronto: The Macmillan Company, 1974), pp. 253-85.
58 *Report of the Special Committee on the Review of Personnel Management and the Merit Principle*, September, 1979 (Ottawa: Supply and Services Canada). Also known as the D'Avignon Committee after its chairman G.R. D'Avignon.

of governmental managerial ideology in the 1980s in a series of lectures entitled "Reflections on the Management of Government in a Democratic Society in the 1980s."[59]

Kirby's speech is not used here as a straw man. His pronouncements are useful for two good reasons. First, they are the latest and perhaps the clearest musings relevant to our subject matter which has come out of the Canadian cabinet secretariat in the last decade. Secondly, while these pronouncements emphasize some of the traditional themes related to organizational theory and practice, there is an attempt to place these themes within the broader question of the maintenance of democratic governance in Canada. This is particularly relevant in a time when the retrenchment in government resources is a reality and the role of government is being seriously questioned by various groups in our society.

But let us return to the title of Kirby's lectures for a moment. First the term "management of government" suggests an emphasis on rationality in the direction of the public business. Secondly, the phrase "democratic society" is evocative of the representative bureaucracy and the so-called consultative planning. Why is this so? It is so because, in precise usage, it is not "societies" *per se* which are "democratic." Rather, it is the method by which the society manages state power – the authoritative allocation mechanisms of the society – which is or is not "democratic." In a word, it is the mode of government, itself one aspect of the society, which usually takes the adjective. A "democratic society" is something much looser than a "democratic government," probably referring more to a mood or spirit of life than a mechanism for doing public business.

And, indeed, this interpretation is supported by the text of the lectures. Kirby's remarks follow two streams: the substance of government in the 1980s, or *what* will be done; and the method of government, or *how* the society will be managed. The "what" can be treated briefly. Speaking of government at all levels, Kirby stated quite clearly that he did not foresee a retreat of government from provision of the present menu of services. These services have emerged as a result of public demand, and will be maintained as a result of public demand. All levels of government have become fixated upon the idea of providing services directly to the public. But a decision to support a social function can be separated from the way in which the support is provided. In future, there-

---

59 Michael J.L. Kirby, "Reflections on the Management of Government within a Democratic Society in the 1980's," The Plaunt Lectures delivered at Carleton University, April 10-11, 1980, mimeo., Carleton Information Office, Part II, pp. 3-5 and *passim*. I am greatly indebted to my colleague Dr. Sharon L. Sutherland for much of the critique of Kirby's reflections which now follow. See V. Seymour Wilson and Sharon L. Sutherland, "Reform as Exorcism." Paper presented to CPSA Annual Meeting, Montreal, June 4, 1980.

fore, we will see a variety of new forms in provision of services – voucher systems for welfare and educational services, involvement of the private sector in social services, and so forth. The "user-pay" concept will become more practicable through use of the newer delivery modes, Kirby predicted, and the public service will become more revenue dependent, smaller and more efficient, so that the overall tax burden is lightened in comparison for a more direct "purchase" of services by the citizen.

The management of society posed a more serious theoretical and practical problem for organizations in the public domain. It is important to outline Kirby's diagnosis of the distemper of our times, because his prescription for the reforms of the 1980s is contingent upon it. First, he said, the desires of the electorate tend to be internally contradictory. The classic example is the wish for increased services but lower taxation. Modern problems are complex, requiring great expertise to comprehend, and are further interwoven in complex ways. The onus is on government to provide to the public information which will enable it to understand clearly the "true nature of the problems society faces."[60] Further, Kirby's diagnosis proceeds, the public is alienated from government as a whole, and from the use of political parties as channels for communication between citizens and their government.[61]

The decline of parties and the rise of citizen alienation pose the problem of how to get an effective public contribution to government processes – the "democratic society." Kirby's prescription was manifold, including use of advisory committees, task forces, royal commissions, and inquiries modelled on the Berger inquiry. But, he cautioned, the role of the advisory committees is to be "purely one of advice," the aim being for consensus and a sophisticated public which understands that the ear of government is not necessarily connected to the arm.[62] Kirby's example of the process was one in which a private company allowed a committee of citizens to help choose the final site for a new power plant. Citizens provide advice on detail, rather than on the full scope of decisions.

Participation therefore takes place in some kind of an informal, direct democracy, and is not channelled through the traditional and formal representative democracy of the parliamentary system. Indeed, virtually the only reference in Kirby's lectures to the parliamentary nature of our government was a negative reference to the activist judiciary in the American system. Parliament will not lead in the tasks of problem definition and articulation of grievances. Rather, it will probably find itself in the position of being a forum for identification of undesired, "counterintuitive" effects of policy decisions taken by experts, elsewhere.

60 Ibid., Part 1, p. 4.
61 Ibid., pp. 25-30 and *passim*.
62 Ibid., Part II, pp. 30-2.

However, in academic circles at least, there is a current belief that modern western democracies during the 1960s and early 1970s rather grossly over-estimated the extent to which social problems were amenable to technological solutions.[63] Fundamental clashes of value over *who* should bear the primary cost of some societal problem were avoided in favour of proposals for "root and branch" solutions for the difficulty. Problems of sharing were avoided in favour of problems of productivity, so that all could be winners. It is further held by many analysts that this bubble has burst, and we are overdue for a return to hard problems of choice between equally desired values, in a climate of scarcity. Kirby most emphatically did not share this retreat from the technical in his lectures. Indeed, he diagnosed the opposite problem, saying that the public has a tendency to blame leadership for the perceived lack of solutions, whereas the difficulty stems precisely from the technological intractability of the problems. How prescient, Kirby says, were the words of John F. Kennedy in 1962. He quotes Kennedy:

The central ... problems of our time ... do not relate to basic clashes of philosophy or ideology, but to ways and means ... sophisticated solutions to complex and obstinate problems. What we need are not labels and cliches but more basic discussion of the sophisticated and technical questions involved in keeping a great economic machinery moving ahead ... Political labels and ideological approaches are irrelevant to solutions. ... Technical answers – not political answers must be provided ... [we] deal with questions which are beyond the comprehension of most men.[64]

Solutions to problems must therefore be sought by experts. The public in a "democratic society" is to be kept in touch with current formulations of problems, in order that it may be brought into consensus about "what constitutes reality and hence what is possible." One can deduce then that pure politics, in the sense of a free people freely choosing both how it will understand its world and what it will call problematic, have been eradicated by the technical complexity of reality.

The reader most likely has a sense of déja-vu in reading the summary of Kirby's lectures given above. The familiar themes of the men of ideas in organization theory keep cropping up again and again: Keynes' men of ideas, like Banquo's ghost, keep lurking in the background, reappearing at appropriate times and places. The main themes of organization theory are all here: the central questions of rationality (including economy and efficiency) in an increasingly technological society, the external

63 For representative discussions, see Richard R. Welson, *The Moon and the Ghetto: An Essay on Public Policy Analysis* (New York: Norton, 1977), and Guido Calabresi and Philip Bobbit, *Tragic Choices: The Conflicts Society Confronts in the Allocation of Tragically Scarce Resources* (New York: Norton, 1978).
64 Kirby, "Management of Government," Part I, p. 2.

contradiction obtaining between democratic norms and the actual policy-making practice of administrators, the role of leadership in surmounting these paradoxes of our times and so on. In the past it may have been that in public administration there was relatively little in common between the study of the relation of administration with politics and the study of internal management. The former united public administration with political science; the latter joined it with administration – both private and institutional – and organization theory.

In the 1980s we find this distinction increasingly eroded because the heretofore seemingly mundane questions of day-to-day administration have been shown to be crucial to the economic and ultimately political solutions best sought for our societies. The enduring questions posed above are, in my view, an attempt to get at the interconnecting linkages between organization theory and internal management on the one hand, and the relation of administration with politics on the other.

Where to look for answers in the corpus of organization theory is one thing; what we attempt to do with the answers remains another. Asking the right theoretical questions will not, of course, turn conflicting interests into parallel ones (although it might help); it will not make scarce resources free; it will not turn us all into rational and reasonable men; it will not, in short, provide a substitute for what is the ultimate in the political process – the accommodation of diverse values and interests in a complex society. But asking the right questions and seeking the answers wherever they may lead us certainly will help.

Public administration: federalism and intergovernmental relations

Audrey Doerr

Among other features in our constitution, the division of powers has provided the essential federal framework within which our public services have operated. However, as Professor Hodgetts has commented "... constitutions are notably rigid, and it has been largely within the public services – local, provincial and federal – that we find the main evidence of adaptation to clarifying conditions and emergent needs which have provided the necessary flexibility."[1] And there have been a variety of devices and techniques which have been used by governments to provide that flexibility and to accommodate the expansion of government functions beyond original jurisdictional boundaries. Nevertheless, the degree of accommodation which has been achieved between governments as a result of collaboration has not eliminated differences or resolved continuing conflicts in our federal system.

In recent years, the political stresses in Canadian federalism have been very apparent. For example, the election of the Parti Québécois in Quebec in 1976 has represented a major challenge to the federal and other provincial governments with respect to intergovernmental relations in Canada. The resource boom in Western Canada has also led to increased demands by political leaders in these provinces for a larger role and greater recognition in national policy-making. Conflicts between governments have been sharpened by federal-provincial confrontations on matters respecting constitutional reform which have spilled over into other areas as well. There is no longer a consensus among political leaders on the nature of our federal system and the way governments relate to one another. The processes of federal-provincial bargaining and negotiation often result in unresolved stalemates or disputes. Increasingly, the courts are being called upon to act as arbiters on major issues.

The purpose of this paper is to consider where we have been and where we may be going in the area of federalism and intergovernmental

The author is associate dean of graduate studies, Simon Fraser University.

1 J.E. Hodgetts, "Challenge and Response: A Retrospective View of the Public Service of Canada," CANADIAN PUBLIC ADMINISTRATION, 4 (December 1964), p. 409.

relations as it pertains to public administration. Although there are many facets to this subject, the following discussion will focus on the major developments and trends in two main areas: federal-provincial financial arrangements and the structures and processes of intergovernmental collaboration. Federal-provincial financial relations form the core of many of the substantive issues respecting the jurisdiction and influence of governments in Canada. The structures and processes of intergovernmental collaboration, on the other hand, influence the pattern of relations between governments which, in turn, influences the outcomes of those relations. As the highlights of practical developments and scholarly work will demonstrate, these areas have been ones of significant interest and concern.

The emerging problems in the practice of public administration on an intergovernmental basis will also be examined. Some new directions are discernible but there is also a high degree of uncertainty as a result of the processes of constitutional reform on the one hand and economic problems of recession on the other. Recent trends seem to indicate that it will be more difficult for governments to forge a national consensus on federal-provincial issues in the future. Thus, the agenda for students of public administration for research and training in the years ahead will include a variety of new problems respecting the relations between and among governments in Canada.

Major developments and problems

It may be argued that the modern period of the study of federalism and public administration was marked by the release of the report and studies of the Royal Commission on Dominion-Provincial Relations in 1940. Nevertheless, the Commission's philosophy with respect to provincial autonomy and its recommendations for financial devices and techniques which would give the provinces the freedom to determine the extent and the level of public services to be provided was not the direction federal-provincial relations were to take in the ensuing years.[2] It was the co-ordinate rather than the independent modes of activities which were to be emphasized and the literature is replete with descriptions and assessments of the different forms and stages of development of collaborative federalism in Canada.[3]

2 D.V. Smiley, "The Rowell-Sirois Report, Provincial Autonomy, and Post-War Canadian Federalism," *Canadian Journal of Economics and Political Science*, 28, no. 1 (February 1962), pp. 54-69.
3 For a discussion of these concepts, see D.V. Smiley, *Constitutional Adaptation and Canadian Federalism since 1945*, Documents of the Royal Commission on Bilingualism and Biculturalism (Ottawa: Queen's Printer, 1970). Other key references on the evolution of Canadian federalism include: Edwin R. Black, *Divided Loyalties: Canadian Concepts of Federalism* (Montreal: McGill-Queen's University Press, 1975); J.R. Mallory, "The Five Faces of Federalism," in P.A. Crépeau and C.B. Macpherson, *The Future of Canadian Federalism/L'Avenir du fédéralisme canadien* (University of Toronto Press, Les Presses de l'Université de Montréal, 1965).

Although federal-provincial financial arrangements have provided the foundation for major program developments, they have also reflected the difficulties and complexities of relations between governments arising from economic inequalities among them. The "search for balance" has been a continuing theme in this area. The processes of intergovernmental consultation which have involved the direct relations between ministers and officials of provincial and federal governments have sometimes appeared to supplant our system of responsible government as major policies and programs have been devised within these executive forums.

Financial relations

Federal-provincial financial arrangements in Canada have attempted to address four main issues. First, the respective expenditure functions of federal and provincial governments have not matched their borrowing and revenue-raising capacities. Historically, the federal government has had access to larger revenue sources although the primary spending responsibilities have been those of the provinces.[4] Secondly, the uneven fiscal capacities of the provincial governments have created problems of disparities in the quantity and quality of public services available to citizens in different parts of the country.[5] Thirdly, to the extent that there is competition between federal and provincial governments for tax money, the risk of administration and economic inefficiencies has existed. Finally, this same competition has often created obstacles to the implementation and development of effective fiscal policies for the promotion of economic growth and stability.[6]

The federal-provincial financial arrangements which have been renewed and modified every five years for the past four decades have dealt with these problems with increasing technical sophistication. In general, governments have come to maintain and to tolerate over time a sharing of tax revenues to meet respective expenditure requirements; a reasonably unified tax collection system; a general commitment to equalization to ensure that a minimum standard of public services is provided; and

4 The literature on this subject is extensive. Classic references include: G.V. La Forest, *The Allocation of Taxing Powers under the Canadian Constitution*, rev. ed. (Toronto: Canadian Tax Foundation, 1981), and *Natural Resources and Public Property under the Canadian Constitution* (Toronto: University of Toronto Press, 1969); A.M. Moore, J.H. Perry, D.I. Beach, *Financing Canadian Federation* (Toronto: Canadian Tax Foundation, 1966); and J.H. Perry, *Taxation in Canada* (Toronto: University of Toronto Press, 1961).
5 See, in particular, Douglas H. Clark, *Fiscal Need and Revenue Equalization Grants*, Tax Paper, No. 49 (Toronto: Canadian Tax Foundation, 1969); Allan M. Maslove, *The Pattern of Taxation in Canada* (Ottawa: Information Canada, 1973); and, R.J. May, *Federalism and Fiscal Adjustment* (Oxford: Clarendon Press, 1969).
6 See J.S. Dupré, "Political Economy of Federal Finance," in M.H. Watkins and D.F. Forster, *Economics: Canada* (Toronto: McGraw-Hill, 1964), pp. 299-300.

an extensive use of the federal spending power especially in the social policy field.[7]

An analysis of the first twenty years of the arrangements has been provided by Professor Burns in his 1980 book, *The Acceptable Mean: The Tax Rental Agreements, 1941-62.* Burns sets out the substantive issues in detail and considers the effect of the personal relations of politicians and officials in the various governments on the negotiations and the issues. In particular, his discussion of the change in 1957 from tax-rental to tax-sharing arrangements is important. This change marked a major turning point in joint financial relations. It loosened federal control of the tax arrangements, thus opening the door to the provinces to obtain access to larger shares of tax revenues and, at the same time, introduced a new concept of explicit equalization which was tied to the shared tax sources.[8]

Since 1962 the fiscal arrangements have been renewed four times. Two major changes to the revenue-sharing arrangements were made between 1962 and 1977. First, a "representative tax system" was introduced as the basis for equalization payments in 1967. Initially, there were sixteen provincial and municipal sources included in the formula; by 1977, there were twenty-nine sources. The second major change occurred as a result of an inordinate increase in revenue yield in one of the tax sources, non-renewable natural resources, due to the jump in oil prices in 1973. Limitations were placed on the amount of this revenue source to be included in equalization as a means of containing the cost of the program.[9] However, in the 1982-87 arrangements, the measurement of provincial fiscal capacity for purposes of equalization payments has been enlarged by removing the restrictions on resources revenues and by including municipal tax revenues in full. Moreover, the federal government has

---

7   These arrangements are enshrined in federal legislation. Thus, the primary source is the *Statutes of Canada* for the years in which the legislation was passed and/or amended. *The National Finances,* an annual publication of the Canadian Tax Foundation provides a summary of the five year agreements in a chapter on "General Payments to Other Governments." The Foundation also publishes *Provincial and Municipal Finances* biennially which provides similar analyses for this level of government. A good description of pre-1970 federal-provincial and municipal relations can be found in United States, Advisory Commission on Intergovernmental Relations, *In Search of Balance: Canada's Intergovernmental Experience* (Washington, D.C. 1971).
8   Burns, *The Acceptable Mean,* pp. 232-34. See also F.A. Angers, "Conséquences des nouveaux arrangements fiscaux proposé par le gouvernement Diefenbaker," CANADIAN PUBLIC ADMINISTRATION, 5 (March 1962), pp. 1-8; and V. Salyzyn "Federal-Provincial Tax Sharing Schemes," CANADIAN PUBLIC ADMINISTRATION, 10 (June 1967), pp. 161-66.
9   Only 50 per cent of non-renewable natural resource revenues were included. Secondly, total natural resource revenues were limited to one-third of total equalization transfers. See Robin M. Boadway, *Intergovernmental Transfers in Canada* (Toronto: Canadian Tax Foundation, 1980), p. 16.

changed the basic standard for these payments from a national average of per capita revenue yield to an average per capita yield of five provinces.

On the expenditure side of the fiscal arrangements, the use of the federal spending power in areas of provincial jurisdiction has been a contentious issue. Nevertheless, federal spending, especially in the form of conditional grants has supported the development of co-ordinate or horizontal arrangements of powers between governments. But conditional grants impose restrictions on the decision-making authority of the recipient governments with respect to the nature of the program, the purposes for which the money can be spent and, in some cases, the amounts available. Conflicts between governments have occurred particularly in cases in which objectives have been different. An example of this problem was the adult occupational training program. The central government's interest in economic development was not congruent with the Ontario government's interest in the educational considerations of the program.[10]

Two main developments have taken place in the last two decades, which had as their objective both the provision of greater flexibility and, hence, more autonomy to the provinces in the administration of these programs and the control of costs to the federal government. In 1965 the federal government passed the Established Programs (Interim Arrangements) Act to allow provinces to opt out of certain conditional grant programs, including hospital insurance, health grants, welfare and technical education. Tax abatements in lieu of grants were made available to provinces that wished to opt out. These arrangements were largely the result of pressure brought to bear by the province of Quebec in its drive for fiscal autonomy.[11] Quebec was the only province to adopt the opting out provisions.

By the seventies, the three largest shared-cost programs dealt with hospital insurance, medicare and post-secondary education. The federal government introduced the Established Programs Financing Act in the 1977-82 agreements to provide block-funding arrangements for these

10 For assesments of the impact of these programs, see D.V. Smiley, *Conditional Grants and Canadian Federalism* (Toronto: Canadian Tax Foundation, 1963); George C. Carter, *Canadian Conditional Grants since World War II* (Toronto: Canadian Tax Foundation, 1971); Boadway, *Intergovernmental Transfers*; and J. Stefan Dupré, *et al., Federalism and Policy Development: The case of adult occupational training in Ontario* (Toronto: University of Toronto Press, 1973).

11 Perhaps the most comprehensive expression of Quebec's case for fiscal autonomy is contained in: Province of Quebec, *Royal Commission of Inquiry on Constitutional Problems, Report,* 4 vols. (Quebec City, 1956) and, in particular, F.A. Angers, *Le problème fiscal et les relations fédérales-provinciales, annexes au rapport de la Commission Tremblay,* 2 vols. (Quebec City, 1956). An account of the later developments may be found in Claude Morin, *Quebec versus Ottawa: The Struggle for Self-Government, 1960-72* (Toronto: University of Toronto Press, 1977).

programs.[12] Provinces were not required to match the lump-sum payments nor were they required to adhere to more than a few general requirements in their expenditures.[13] The federal government, in turn, was able to establish limits on its expenditures on these programs as well as to encourage provincial governments to exercise restraint. The federal proposals for the 1982 legislation represented an apparent reversal of these provisions. The Established Programs Financing Act was amended to include a per capita formula for the federal contributions to all provinces for these programs. The proposals for the establishment of national standards for these programs and of a mechanism for maintaining them and for the development of alternative arrangements for financing post-secondary education and human resource development were not implemented pending further discussions with the provinces and other groups.[14]

In summary, the fiscal arrangements which were put in place during the war have, over the years, been adjusted to provide provinces with greater access to tax revenues assumed by the federal government, greater autonomy in the expenditure of federal grants and an equalization program. The provinces continue to press for more fiscal decentralization; the federal government takes the position that the system is already highly decentralized. A key problem in the political and scholarly debate on this subject is the lack of an objective definition of an appropriate balance in fiscal relations between governments.[15] The dynamic equilibrium of fiscal relations has, in fact, been represented by what governments have been prepared to accept or acquiesce in at a particular point in time.

Intergovernmental collaboration

In a federal system, coordination between governments normally occurs in response to problems of overlapping jurisdictions and conflicting legislation. In Canada, the establishment of formal mechanisms of consultation and cooperation resulted, for the most part, from the development

12 See Thomas J. Courchene, *Refinancing the Canadian Federation: A Survey of the 1977 Fiscal Arrangements Act* (Montreal: C.D. Howe Research Institute, 1979).
13 Robin W. Boadway, *Intergovernmental Transfers in Canada*, pp. 23-33; and, Ontario, Ministry of Treasury and Economics, *Ontario Papers on Federal Provincial Fiscal Arrangements* (Toronto, 1981).
14 Several studies had criticized the effect of block-funding on the operations of established programs. See Canada, *Canada's National-Provincial Health Program for the 1980s* (Saskatoon: Craft Litho, 1980); Parliamentary Task Force on Federal-Provincial Fiscal Arrangements, *Fiscal Federalism* (Ottawa: Supply and Services, 1981); and Economic Council of Canada, *Financing Confederation: Today and Tomorrow, Summary and Conclusions* (Ottawa: 1982). For their part, the provinces have been more concerned about possible reductions in the amount of federal funding and the effect of tightening-up provisions in the programs.
15 For example, see Richard M. Bird, *Financing Canadian Government: A Quantitative Overview* (Toronto: Canadian Tax Foundation, 1980), pp. 56-67.

of joint financial and administrative agreements between provincial and federal governments.[16] By the 1960s, the need for consultation on a permanent basis was presented as a basic tenet of co-operative federalism.[17] As government activities at all levels have increased and as a larger number of federal-provincial issues have been considered at the political level, the agenda for intergovernmental collaboration has extended to a broad range of policy matters. The use of federal-provincial first ministers' meetings as a forum of debate on constitutional questions since the late sixties has further enhanced and served to formalize the processes of intergovernmental collaboration.

The base structure of the machinery of federal-provincial relations has been described in detail by several authors.[18] At the political level, there are first ministers' conferences and ministerial meetings. At the administrative level, the committee structure includes meetings of senior officials, directors and technical officials. In some cases, intergovernmental secretariats have been established for the purpose of serving ministerial meetings.[19] The number and frequency of the meetings have increased enormously in the last twenty years.

The machinery of interprovincial coordination seems to be less formalized but provides for consultation and information exchange on a broad range of matters.[20] Although the processes of province-building have

16 See K.W. Taylor, "Co-ordination in Administration," in J.E. Hodgetts and D.C. Corbett, *Canadian Public Administration: A Book of Readings* (Toronto: Macmillan, 1960), pp. 145-61.
17 See Jean-Luc Pepin, "Co-operative Federalism," *The Canadian Forum*, Vol. 44, No. 527(December 1964), pp. 206-10, as reprinted in J. Peter Meekison, *Canadian Federalism: Myth or Reality* (Toronto: Methuen, 1968), pp. 320-29.
18 Edgar Gallant, "The Machinery of Federal Provincial Relations: I," CANADIAN PUBLIC ADMINISTRATION, 8 (December 1965), pp. 515-26; see also, R.M. Burns, "The Machinery of Federal Provincial Relations: II," ibid., pp. 527-34. In 1967, Gérard Veilleux undertook a historical study of the machinery which appeared in his book, *Les relations intergouvernementales au Canada, 1867-1967* (Montreal: Les Presses de l'Université du Québec, 1971). He subsequently updated the study in a paper, "L'évolution des mécanismes de liaison intergouvernementale," in Richard Simeon, ed., *Confrontation and Collaboration: Intergovernmental Relations in Canada Today* (Toronto: Institute of Public Administration of Canada, 1979), pp. 35-77.
19 Two main examples include the Canadian Intergovernmental Conference Secretariat and a technical committee, the Continuing Committee on Fiscal and Economic Matters. See, for example, A.R. Kear, "Co-operative Federalism: A Study of the Federal Provincial Continuing Committee on Fiscal and Economic Matters," CANADIAN PUBLIC ADMINISTRATION, 6 (March 1963), pp. 43-56.
20 There is not much literature on this subject. J.H. Aitchison, "Interprovincial Co-operation in Canada," in J.H. Aitchison, ed., *The Political Process in Canada* (Toronto: University of Toronto Press, 1963), pp. 153-70; R.H. Leach, "Interprovincial Co-operation: Neglected Aspect of Canadian Federalism," CANADIAN PUBLIC ADMINISTRATION, 2 (June 1959), pp. 83-99; and Ronald James Zukowsky, *Intergovernmental Relations in Canada: the year in review, 1980, Volume One: Policy and Politics* (Kingston: Institute of Intergovernmental Relations, Queen's University, 1981), pp. 99-101.

had an important impact on federal-provincial relations,[21] interprovincially the provinces have rarely been able to demonstrate or sustain a united front in dealings with the federal government. The main features of interprovincial consultation include the annual Premiers' Conference and other ministerial level meetings. For example, the Council of Ministers of Education is a forum which meets several times a year and is served by a small secretariat.[22] Regionally, there is a Council of Maritime Premiers and a Western Premiers' Conference which meet regularly. On occasion, the cabinets of Alberta and British Columbia have met jointly. The Maritime provinces have had the greatest experience with regional collaboration.[23]

The inclusion of municipalities in the national intergovernmental maze of co-ordinating mechanisms reached a peak in the early seventies.[24] The creation of the federal Ministry of State for Urban Affairs in 1970 acted as a catalyst for encouraging national and regional tri-level consultation but these efforts were short-lived and did not establish any permanent practices respecting municipal participation in intergovernmental forums. Rather, the provinces have tended to centralize relations with their local units in financial and program relations.[25] The municipal voice has not been silenced but it has been toned down on the national scene.

The benefits of intergovernmental consultation have accrued largely from the sharing of information, the harmonization of programs and policies and the joint determination of policy in areas such as economic or fiscal matters.[26] The main disadvantages have been products of the

21 Edwin R. Black and Alan C. Cairns, "A Different Perspective on Canadian Federalism," CANADIAN PUBLIC ADMINISTRATION, 9 (March 1966), pp. 27-45; and more recently, Larry Pratt, "The State and Province-Building: Alberta's Development Strategy," in Leo Panitch, ed., *The Canadian State: Political Economy and Political Power* (Toronto: University of Toronto Press, 1977), pp. 133-62.

22 The Hon. Brian R.D. Smith, Minister of Education, Province of British Columbia, "The Need for Intergovernmental Cooperation," in J.W. George Ivany and Michael E. Manley-Casimir, *Federal-Provincial Relations: Education Canada* (Toronto: OISE Press, 1981), pp. 58-62.

23 Cooperation among the maritime provinces has been the focus of several studies. In particular, see Dalhousie University, Institute of Public Affairs, *Intergovernmental Relations in the Maritime Provinces* (Fredericton: Maritime Union Study, August 1970); and Maritime Union Study, *The Report on Maritime Union Commissioned by the Governments of Nova Scotia, New Brunswick, and Prince Edward Island*, ibid. In Western Canada, there was some discussion of "union" in the early 1970s. See David K. Elton, ed., *One Prairie Province?* (Lethbridge: *Lethbridge Herald*, 1970).

24 Kenneth Cameron, ed., *Municipal Government in the Intergovernmental Maze* (Toronto: The Institute of Public Administration of Canada, 1980), p. 195.

25 Ibid.; see, in particular, papers by Dale E. Richmond, "Some Common Issues in Provincial-Municipal Transfer Systems," pp. 252-68; Jean-Louis Lapointe, "La reforme de la fiscalité municipale au Québec," pp. 269-80; and David Siegel, "Provincial-Municipal Relations in Canada: An Overview," pp. 281-317.

26 Don Stevenson, "The Role of Intergovernmental Conferences in the Decision-Making Process," in Simeon, ed., *Confrontation and Collaboration*, pp. 89-98.

processes themselves. Intergovernmental activities have often overshadowed the role of legislatures and Parliament in policy-making. The problems of secrecy, lack of accountability among governments and the accentuation of regional interests and cleavages raise questions about the desirability of further development of the machinery. As Professor Smiley has commented: "Executive federalism 'organizes into politics' the interests of governments and of those private groupings which are territorially concentrated. The system almost by its inherent nature weakens the influence of other interests."[27]

The effects that the processes of collaboration have had on policy and program development have been closely monitored by Professor Smiley, who has maintained a watching brief over the last several decades.[28] His assessments have been complemented by a number of policy studies. One of the first detailed analyses to link the processes of federal-provincial consultation with the substantive issues of policy formulation was Richard Simeon's book on federal-provincial diplomacy.[29] His approach, which focused on the process of direct negotiation and bargaining between and among politicians and officials in the formulation of policy, became a widely accepted view of federal-provincial policy making. In essence, Simeon's model characterized governments as having a "unified" interest in their dealings with other governments. More recently, Richard Schultz has offered a different model of analysis which focuses on the intra-governmental processes of intergovernmental negotiations.[30] Governments are not viewed as monolithic actors but rather as complex sets of interests engaged in the play of "bureaucratic politics." The impact of these patterns of internal relations are considered a primary determinant of the outcomes of negotiations between governments.

The case studies on federal-provincial policy-making demonstrate how a variety of frameworks and concepts may be applied to analyse policy issues. The chapters dealing with theoretical considerations in books by Malcolm Taylor, Ken Bryden, and Neil Swainson, for example, in the IPAC Public Administration series, provide important source material for

27   D.V. Smiley, "An Outsider's Observations of Federal-Provincial Relations among Consenting Adults," in Simeon, ibid., pp. 105-13.
28   See, in particular, his several editions of *Canada in Question: Canadian Federalism in the Seventies* (Toronto: McGraw-Hill-Ryerson, 1972 and 1976); *Canadian Federalism in the Eighties* (Toronto: McGraw-Hill-Ryerson, 1980); and earlier references in this text.
29   Richard Simeon, *Federal-Provincial Diplomacy: The Making of Recent Policy in Canada* (Toronto: University of Toronto Press, 1972).
30   Richard J. Schultz, *Federalism, Bureaucracy and Public Policy: The Politics of Highway Transport Regulation* (Montreal: McGill-Queen's University Press/IPAC, 1980).

students of Canadian public policy analysis.[31] Secondly, the case studies have provided an enormous amount of detailed information on major policy issues.[32] A particular feature of the analyses which should be noted is the role of interest groups and their attitudes and relations to governments. They have been critical factors in many cases in influencing the positions that governments have adopted in their intergovernmental negotiations. In fact, the conflicts between governments often appear to be as much a struggle between differing society values represented by groups as they are jurisdictional tugs-of-war.

In summary, the federal-provincial consultative and policy agenda of the sixties was devoted primarily to major social policy issues within provincial jurisdiction, although a growing involvement of provincial governments in national economic policy discussions was also apparent. During the seventies, federal and provincial governments shifted their priorities towards economic development concerns. Matters relating to the structure of the economy, the regulation of major industrial sectors such as non-renewable resources, foreign investment and monetary policy are some examples of current agenda items. But the processes within which these issues are considered have come to represent federal-provincial conflicts and tensions rather than to serve as means to ameliorate them.[33] New approaches are needed to break the pattern of "organized politics."

Emerging trends and future prospects

The processes of collaborative federalism, by and large, have emphasized technical solutions to political problems. The specialization of skills within public services has been a support as well as an instigator of complex

31 Malcolm G. Taylor, *Health Insurance and Canadian Public Policy* (Montreal: McGill-Queen's University Press/IPAC, 1978); Kenneth Bryden, *Old Age Pensions and Policy-Making in Canada* (Montreal: McGill-Queen's University Press/IPAC, 1974); Neil Swainson, *Conflict over the Columbia: The Canadian Background to an Historic Treaty* (Montreal: McGill-Queen's University Press/IPAC, 1979).

32 In addition to the case studies noted above, see, in particular, Keith Banting, *The Welfare State and Canadian Federalism* (Montreal: McGill-Queen's University Press, 1982); Dennis Guest, *The Emergence of Social Security in Canada* (Vancouver: University of British Columbia Press, 1980); Carl A. Meilicke and Janet L. Storch, eds., *Perspectives on Canadian Health and Social Services Policy: History and Emerging Trends* (Ann Arbor, Michigan, 1980); Anthony Careless, *Initiative and Response: The Adaptation of Canadian Federalism to Regional Economic Development* (Montreal: McGill-Queen's University Press/IPAC, 1977); and, Donald J. Savoie, *Federal-Provincial Collaboration: The Canada-New Brunswick General Development Agreement* (Montreal: McGill-Queen's University Press/IPAC, 1981).

33 Richard Simeon, "A Summary of Proceedings," in Simeon, ed., *Confrontation and Collaboration: Intergovernmental Relations in Canada Today*, pp. 1-16; and Garth Stevenon, *Unfulfilled Union* (Toronto: Macmillan, 1979), pp. 197-203.

and detailed policies and programs to deal with political demands and interests. This is demonstrated by the fact that a main product of collaborative federalism has been a large number of federal-provincial agreements.[34] These programs represent a large commitment to federal-provincial coordination and program administration in terms of human, financial and physical resources but they have also served to blur lines of responsibilities between governments which, in turn, has made accountability of elected and appointed officials difficult to obtain.[35]

The size and complexity of government has also advanced to the point that specialists have been needed to manage the processes of intergovernmental co-ordination. The creation of central agencies or units for this purpose has been a feature of organizational change within public services.[36] The process experts who work in these agencies are perhaps a new breed of public servant. They do not deal directly with substantive matters but rather develop strategies, coordinate policy and program activities across their respective governments and maintain liaison with their counterparts in other governments.

In the last several years, nevertheless, it has become apparent that those administrative techniques and coordinative processes which have supported adaptation and accommodation in the past no longer offer solutions to protracted political disputes. Matters which used to be handled quietly in federal-provincial official forums and committees are moving into the political arena. Governments appear increasingly unwilling to compromise or to cooperate. This changing attitude on the part of governments toward consultation may be a signal that relations between the public services of those governments will require major readjustments. This is not happening all at once, nor is it occurring across the full range of government activities. But a pattern is emerging. Let us look at some examples of recent issues.

Within months of the return of the Liberal government to office in Ottawa in 1980, three major issues of federal-provincial concern were placed on the public agenda: constitutional reform; the National Energy

34 See Kenneth Wiltshire, "Working with intergovernmental agreements – the Canadian and Australian experience," CANADIAN PUBLIC ADMINISTRATION, 23 (Fall 1980), pp. 353-79; and Federal-Provincial Relations Office, Federal-Provincial Programs and Activities: A Descriptive Inventory, 1979 (Ottawa, 1981).
35 See A.C. Cairns, "The Other Crisis of Canadian Federalism," CANADIAN PUBLIC ADMINISTRATION, 22 (Summer 1979), pp. 175-95; and, for a particular case study, Donald J. Savoie, "The General Development Agreement approach and the bureaucratization of provincial agreements in the Atlantic provinces," CANADIAN PUBLIC ADMINISTRATION, 24 (Spring 1981), pp. 116-32.
36 V.S. Wilson, "Federal Provincial Relations and Federal Policy Processes," in G.B. Doern and Peter Aucoin, Public Policy in Canada (Toronto: Macmillan, 1979), pp. 190-222; and T. Woolstenscroft, Organizing Intergovernmental Relations (Kingston: Institute of Intergovernmental Relations, Queen's University, 1982).

Program; and the renegotiation of the five-year fiscal arrangements. In each case, there were a number of common features respecting *form* and *process*. First, the proposals put forward constituted a form of unilateral federal action which represented the "national interest" as advocated by the federal government. Secondly, Parliament, not a federal-provincial conference, was the initial forum in which the federal government introduced its proposals. For example, the constitutional resolution was introduced in Parliament on October 2, 1980, a month after the federal-provincial first ministers' meeting on the constitution ended in disagreement. The National Energy Program was tabled by the Minister of Finance during the presentation of his budget on October 28, 1980. Finally, the federal government presented its proposals on federal-provincial financial arrangements to the parliamentary task force which was created for the purpose of reviewing the 1977 legislation and related programs in April 1981. This marked the first time a parliamentary committee had been struck to review the agreements.

The parliamentary hearings on the constitutional resolution and the fiscal arrangements sparked full-scale public debates involving a large number of interested groups and individuals in each case. In this way, the federal government was able to obtain public and parliamentary reaction to its proposals before it approached the provincial governments. In the case of the debate on the constitutional resolution, the public support demonstrated for the entrenchment of a Charter of Rights undoubtedly was useful to the federal government in strengthening its position vis-à-vis the provinces on this matter.

With respect to the *substantive* issues involved, each case was marked by bitter disagreement between the federal government and the provinces over the respective federal proposals. The entrenchment of a Charter of Rights had received the active support of only two provinces, Ontario and New Brunswick, with the other eight opposing. During the parliamentary consideration of the resolution, three references went to the Supreme Court of Canada concerning the legal and conventional practices of this approach to constitutional reform. The Court's rulings of September 28, 1981[37] prompted the federal government to pursue a last round of federal-provincial first ministers' negotiations. The final package to which a majority of provinces ultimately agreed in November 1981 was very much a "bargained version" of the original. The government of Quebec, however, was not a party to the final agreement.

In the case of the National Energy Program, the province of Alberta was singled out by the federal government in relation to the issues of

---

37 See Peter Russell, ed., *Leading Constitutional Decisions*, 3rd ed. (Ottawa: Carleton University Press, 1982), pp. 501-74.

fairness in petroleum pricing and revenue-sharing. Alberta's initial response was to stage gradual cut-backs on oil production until a bilateral agreement between Edmonton and Ottawa was reached nearly a year later. Other elements of the Program, especially those pertaining to "Canadianization" of the oil industry, have remained contentious ones to the producing provinces and especially the petroleum industry despite some subsequent modifications to the Program.

The federal proposals on fiscal arrangements marked a major departure from earlier agreements in substance and approach. For example, the federal government has now defined fiscal imbalance as one which relates to "the fact that one order of government has a large and persistent deficit or surplus in its accounts in relation to that of another order of government."[38] Previously, fiscal imbalance between federal and provincial governments was related to the fact that expenditure functions did not match respective borrowing and revenue-raising capacities. From the federal perspective, part of the deficit problem has been attributed to the increased costs of federal transfer payments to the provinces. The fact that provincial-municipal revenue and expenditure shares of the total government sector have increased in relation to those of the federal government has also become a source of federal concern. Interprovincially, the disproportionate increase in non-renewable resource revenues in the three western provinces has created a major fiscal imbalance between these provinces and the other seven. For the provinces, therefore, the purposes and the basis of the equalization program are key issues in addition to proposed changes in other types of transfer payments.

As the political struggles over jurisdiction and money continue, the current features of collaborative federalism are primarily ones of competition and conflict. Perhaps the most unfortunate outcome of recent federal-provincial disputes, especially the one on the constitution, is the lingering bitterness and distrust. At a time when conditions of severe economic recession would seem to require cooperation between governments, the atmosphere is charged with suspicion and disagreement. The last several years' experience of federal-provincial relations has not appeared to renew federalism; rather it seems to have been exhausted by it.

For public administration, one area which will be of particular concern in the years ahead relates to the large network of joint policy and program activities. The division of powers between governments remains

---

38 Department of Finance, *Federal-Provincial Fiscal Arrangements in the Eighties, A submission to the Parliamentary Task Force on Federal-Provincial Fiscal Arrangements*, by the Minister of Finance, Ottawa, April 23, 1981, p. 8.

an unresolved area of constitutional reform and any impact which the
Charter of Rights may have in clarifying the respective responsibilities
of governments will occur gradually as interpretations of particular cases
are handed down by the courts. The lack of agreement among governments in the past on matters respecting division of powers will probably
lead to the adoption of an ad hoc approach on these matters in the
future. On the one hand, governments may attempt to pursue their
interests in a unilateral fashion. For example, national and regional
orientations in federal policy and program activities which focus on
providing goods and services directly to individuals rather than to individuals through provincial governments are likely to become more apparent. The national interest and federal responsibility on matters affecting
the economy, resource development, trade, transportation, communications and so on can be advanced to support a broad range of federal
initiatives, especially through regulatory measures. On the other hand,
the provinces can be expected to maintain and expand their jurisdictional
interests and/or resist unilateral federal action. Greater attention may
also be directed to means of interprovincial coordination of policies and
programs.

One cannot foresee an immediate dismantling of the existing network
of joint policy and program activities, but a gradual adjustment in the
financial and administrative aspects of joint programs may be pursued.
However, the degree of interdependence and, indeed, vested interests
which have been built into a wide range of existing programs will make
major readjustments in them difficult to achieve. Even during periods of
restraint, there may be resistance by governments to consider the con-
solidation or even transfers of programs from one level of government
to another as means of clarifying responsibilities and reducing administrative costs.

Secondly, if the discussions of federal-provincial issues shift in a major
way from intergovernmental meetings to federal and provincial legislative forums, public administrators will be required to deal with politicians and interest groups more directly than in the past. Nevertheless,
by opening up the process in this way, the problems of secrecy and lack
of accountability associated with the processes of intergovernmental
collaboration may be tempered. Moreover, the refusal by the province of
Quebec, since November 1981, to attend any federal-provincial meetings
except those which deal with key issues such as the economy may create
pressure to examine the nature and form of intergovernmental consultation and develop alternative mechanisms. The federal government has
recently appointed a senior official of the Ministry of State for Economic
and Regional Development in each provincial capital to provide liaison
between the respective provincial government and Ottawa. It will be

interesting to see whether the role and activities of these federal coordinators will make any changes in the processes of federal-provincial relations.

The basic question is whether a search for new or at least different patterns of interaction between and among government administrations will yield solutions to deal with immediate problems and develop means to continue to make the system work. The major policy and program achievements of the past were the result, in large part, of the work of professionals in provincial and federal public services who shared common values and goals. Currently, the views of Canadian federalism which federal and provincial public servants must observe through these respective "windows" consist of a variety of scenes which reflect few common objectives. In pursuing the art of the possible, federal-provincial cooperation in the current political and economic context will require a good deal of imagination and courage.

Research and teaching agenda

Despite the fact that federal-provincial and intergovernmental relations are topics on which a wealth of literature has already been produced, current and emerging developments provide a lengthy list of items for future research such as the following:

1. Federal-provincial relations have created a variety of complex formal and informal organizational structures. Organizational analyses are needed to help us understand better the dynamics of change and adjustment in our federal system.
2. Alternatives to existing mechanisms of federal-provincial and intergovernmental coordination need to be explored. Intra-state techniques at the administrative level seems a particularly fertile area of research.
3. More work needs to be done in the area of program administration of federal-provincial agreements. Studies of provincial systems of health and social service systems, for example, could provide comparative models to assess standards of services and to help explain the operational dynamics of these programs.
4. Another major topic will be the impact of the Charter of Rights and constitutional reform generally on public administration. The implications of judicial review on these issues for the provision of public services and the role of the courts in federal-provincial policy-making may be considerable.
5. Policy studies are needed in the new priority areas of government activity. Assessments of what governments are doing in the economic and energy fields are two particular examples.

6. Finally, a continuing monitoring and analysis of federal-provincial and provincial-municipal fiscal arrangements is essential. Financial relations will remain a central element of public administration in this area.

By itself, federal-provincial and intergovernmental relations is an expanding field of specialization with a number of key sub-fields relating to substantive and administrative matters. It is also a topic which cuts across most subject areas in public administration from policy analysis to financial management. Hence, Canadian study programs in public administration may include specific courses on federalism and public administration as well as federalism components in courses on other subjects. Given the growth and complexity in the activities of governments and the practice of public administration in this area, it should follow that more rather than less attention will need to be devoted to this subject. Furthermore, as the study of provincial governments and administration expands, there should be a greater variety of course designs by which to approach the study of federal-provincial and intergovernmental affairs.

The traditional areas of federalism and public administration with which students need to be conversant will continue to be important, particularly in light of recent events. A knowledge of constitutional developments, an understanding of cultural dualism and an appreciation of the politics and management of federal-provincial and intergovernmental relations are essential. But an understanding of these areas should be complemented by general study of cultural, economic and social cleavages in Canadian society, the role of interest groups and the media, and French-English relations. Given the scope of relevant areas of study, it is certainly possible to anticipate the need for more Institutes of Intergovernmental Relations in universities such as the one at Queen's University in Kingston.

In practical training programs, courses for officials involved in federal-provincial relations should be devised or courses for senior managers should include a strong component on intergovernmental affairs. In this regard, particular focus should be placed on the development of diplomatic skills such as effective interpersonal communications and on relations with interest groups and the media. Despite the highly technical nature of many of the issues of federal-provincial concern, more generalists and generalist skills for specialists will be needed to support changing relationships between governments in the future.

Marsha Chandler
William Chandler

Public administration in the provinces

Canada is unique among federal nations because so much of the growth of the modern state has taken place at the provincial level. Today, the ten provincial governments annually account for approximately one-third of all government expenditures.[1] They regulate in a wide variety of fields, including housing, labour, trucking and agriculture. The provinces also own and operate their own airlines, ferries and railroads, as well as potash, oil, steel and hydro-electric companies. One of the most significant elements in the growth of the provincial state is the development of provincial public administration. This development involves more than a dramatic increase in size; provincial public services have also undergone considerable qualitative changes as they have sought to adapt to changing political, socio-economic and technological conditions. Internal structures and processes have been transformed, along with the relationship between the public services and their environment. Despite these alterations, longstanding questions of accountability, responsibility and responsiveness remain primordial concerns. If anything, these issues have become even more salient as the power of the bureaucracy has increased.

The purpose of this paper is to trace the study and practice of provincial public administration. The first part is an overview of various approaches and problems in the literature. Subsequent sections explore the patterns of provincial administrative development and the issues that have arisen along with that development. The last part of the paper looks to the future and proposes a research agenda for the eighties.

Studying provincial public administration

Analysis of public administration in Canada has tended to focus primarily on the federal level. Not only has the bulk of descriptive work centred on

Professor Marsha Chandler is with the department of political science and faculty of law, University of Toronto. Professor William Chandler is with the department of political science, McMaster University.

1 For summaries of each province's expenditures and revenues see the bienniel series, *Provincial and Municipal Finances* (Toronto: Canadian Tax Foundation).

the federal public service, but the questions and themes of analysis have been drawn mainly from the federal experience. The relative paucity of provincial research creates obvious difficulties for a review such as this. The gaps are too many and too wide to provide any easy focal point. The emphasis must be on the research and analysis carried out to date, not so much with a view to summarizing substantive findings but rather with the goal of providing an overview of the field and in the hope of identifying the central problems arising with the study of provincial bureaucracy.

Approaches

The four main approaches that have been used in the analysis of provincial public service are: cross-provincial studies, single-province accounts, issue or topic-oriented research and case studies. These approaches are not mutually exclusive. Each, however, represents a distinct perspective on the problem of understanding provincial public administration.

Cross-provincial studies

There is no textbook on provincial public administration, but some cross-provincial works do provide a general perspective on the topic. This is accomplished either by aggregating the provinces and generalizing common trends or by describing individual provincial practices. For example, Hodgetts and Dwivedi's *Provincial Government as Employers* provides a survey of the structures of provincial administration with an emphasis being on personnel management. Chapters from Chandler and Chandler, Bellamy *et al.* and Rowat include some comparative analyses of the policy formulation and implementation roles of the public service.[2] Although each tries to develop some generalizations, the main strength of these works is that they provide badly needed description of each province's administrative structures. Within the cross-provincial category one also finds comparative studies of specific aspects of provincial public administration, for example, collective bargaining arrangements, expenditure control by the legislature and administration of the provincial North.[3]

2 J.E. Hodgetts and O.P. Dwivedi, *Provincial Governments as Employers* (Montreal: McGill-Queen's University Press, 1974): for an updating of the employment data, see David Foote, ed., *Public Employment and Compensation in Canada* (Toronto: Institute for Research in Public Policy, 1980); M. and W. Chandler, *Public Policy and Provincial Politics* (Toronto: McGraw Hill-Ryerson, 1979); D. Bellamy *et al.*, eds., *Provincial Political Systems* (Toronto: Methuen, 1976), chapters 21-24; and D. Rowat, ed., *Provincial Government and Politics* (Ottawa: Department of Political Science, Carleton University, 1972), chapters 6-9.

3 On these topics see, respectively, Shirley Goldenberg, "Collective Bargaining in the Provincial Public Service," in *Collective Bargaining in the Public Service* (Toronto: Institute of Public Administration of Canada, 1973); Simon McInnes, "Improving Legislative Surveillance of Provincial Public Expenditure: The Performance of Public Accounts Committee and Auditors General," CANADIAN PUBLIC ADMINISTRATION, 20 (Spring 1977), pp. 33-86; and G.R. Weller, "Local Government in the Canadian Provincial North," CANADIAN PUBLIC ADMINISTRATION, 24 (Spring 1981), pp. 44-72.

Single-province accounts
The second, and most common, approach to the study of provincial public administration is found in research focused on a single province. Within this mode there are at least four distinct variants. First is the historical panorama best typified by the University of Toronto series. Most of these works were inspired by the late R.M. Dawson and modelled on his *Government of Canada*. They include Beck's *The Government of Nova Scotia*, Donnelly's *The Government of Manitoba*, Noel's *Politics in Newfoundland*, Schindeler's *Responsible Government in Ontario*, MacKinnon's *The Government of Prince Edward Island*, and Thorburn's *Politics in New Brunswick*. A similar recent study is Eager's *Saskatchewan Government*. In the course of describing the development of a single province's government, each provides an account of the administrative apparatus. A number of other single-province studies, such as Gow's *La Modernisation de la fonction publique au Québec*, focus specifically on the general historical development of the public service.[4]

Other single-province studies are narrower in scope. One group examines a particular aspect of provincial administration. Examples here include analyses of the cabinet–public service relationship in British Columbia and Newfoundland, of regulatory agencies, boards and commissions in Ontario, or budgeting in Saskatchewan.[5] Yet another group of studies of one province traces the development of a single bureau, department or program. These include Lambert and Pross' study of Ontario's Department of Lands and Forests, and Richardson's critique of the Design for Development Programme.[6] A final single-province source consists of provincial government reports. Based on the findings

4 See also, G. Wright, "The Administrative Growth of the Government of Alberta, 1905-1921," M.A. thesis (Edmonton: University of Alberta, 1952); Susan McCorquodale, "Public Administration in Newfoundland During the Period of Commission Government," Ph.D. thesis (Kingston: Queen's University, 1973); and James Ian Gow, "Modernisation et administration publique," in E. Orban, dir., *La Modernisation politique du Québec* (Montréal: Boreal Presse, 1976), pp. 157-86.
5 See Paul Tennant, "The NDP Government of British Columbia: Unaided Politicians in an Unaided Cabinet," *Canadian Public Policy*, 3 (Fall 1977), pp. 489-502; Ross Johnson, "Cabinet Decision-Making: Taking Issues Out of Politics," paper presented at CPSA meetings, June 1976; Peter Johnson and Graham White, "To Everything There Is An Agency: Boards, Agencies, and Commissions," Donald C. MacDonald, ed., *The Government and Politics of Ontario*, revised edition (Toronto: Van Nostrand, 1980); and D.M. Wallace, "Budget Reform in Saskatchewan: A New Approach to Programme Based Management," CANADIAN PUBLIC ADMINISTRATION, 17 (Winter 1974), pp. 586-99.
6 R.S. Lambert and A.P. Pross, *Renewing Nature's Wealth – A Centennial History* (Toronto: Ontario Department of Lands and Forests, 1967), and N.H. Richardson, "Insubstantial Pageant: The Rise and Fall of Provincial Planning in Ontario," CANADIAN PUBLIC ADMINISTRATION, 24 (Winter 1981), pp. 563-86. See also David Corbett, "Liquor Control Administration in British Columbia: A Study in Public Enterprise," CANADIAN PUBLIC ADMINISTRATION, 2 (March 1959), pp. 199-237.

of a task force or royal commission, these reports provide valuable insights into many aspects of government in which the bureaucracy is a key component, for example, Ontario's *Report of the Committee on Government Productivity* (1971), and Newfoundland's *Report of the Committee on Government of Administration and Productivity* (1972).

Issue-oriented research

This third approach centres on institutions or issues rather than provinces per se, as in studies of public ownership, ombudsmen, and pressure group/bureaucratic relations.[7] Although similar to cross-provincial studies, the issue-oriented approach does not try to touch upon each province's practices; rather the emphasis is on analysis of an issue, instrument or institution. Often the issue-oriented studies mix federal and provincial examples.

Case studies

This fourth approach may at times overlap with single-province research. However, the case study represents a distinct analytical perspective because it is built around a particular decision or set of decisions. The bureaucracy is treated as part of a wider policy network. Thus, although the case study may appear to be narrow in focus, it has the virtue of always placing the public service in the context of the broader political system. Dupré *et al, Federalism and Policy Development*, Swainson, *Conflict over Columbia*, and Feldman, *The Politics of Canadian Airport Development*, are case studies involving one or more provinces. Each provides a fascinating image of the workings of the public service and its relationship with other political actors and agencies.[8]

Problems of analysis

In 1968 Kernaghan, lamenting the general state of the study of public administration in Canada, noted that "despite all these indications of growth and change in the Canadian public service, Canadian public administration as a field of study has not yet come of age."[9] Unfortunately

---

7 See Allan Tupper, "The Nation's Business: Canadian Concepts of Public Enterprise," Ph.D. thesis (Kingston: Queen's University, 1977), or Donald Rowat, "Recent Developments in Ombudsmanship: A Review Article," CANADIAN PUBLIC ADMINISTRATION, 10 (March 1967), pp. 35-46, or Robert Presthus, *Elite Accommodation in Canadian Politics* (Toronto: Macmillan, 1973).

8 There are other, equally useful, case studies of narrower policy-making. See W. Williams, "Development of a Safety Program for Provincial Public Service," CANADIAN PUBLIC ADMINISTRATION, 11 (Winter 1968), pp. 468-84 or J.T. Morley, "The Justice Development Commission: Overcoming Bureaucratic Resistance to Innovative Policy-Making," CANADIAN PUBLIC ADMINISTRATION, 19 (Spring 1976), pp. 121-39. There is also a growing number of discussion cases relevant to the study of provincial politics in the IPAC Case Program in Canadian Public Administration.

9 "An Overview of Public Administration In Canada Today," CANADIAN PUBLIC ADMINISTRATION, 11 (Fall 1968), p. 294.

some fifteen years later these remarks are only too applicable to the situation at the provincial level. Despite the excellence of many individual pieces of research, the study of provincial public administration remains at a rather primitive stage. Although the most obvious problem has been the scarcity of systematic research itself, we can pinpoint several conceptual obstacles which have so far been inadequately dealt with and which have inhibited the study of provincial administration from developing into a systematic, cumulative body of knowledge.

A central difficulty in analysing provincial administration stems from the fact that the provinces are ten distinct political systems. This fact imposes the problem of whether and how to aggregate. For example, is it meaningful to speak of the total number of provincial public servants or crown corporations, etc., or is it necessary to break down all data by province? Do aggregated findings reveal general trends or do they obscure significant differences among provinces? A related issue is whether quantitative variations result in qualitative differences. Is the policy process in smaller provinces fundamentally different from that in Ottawa or in the larger provinces? Can we safely assume, for example, that New Brunswick's public service operates similarly to Ontario's, which is four times as large.

Uneven provincial coverage represents a second problem area for research. Without question, Quebec and Ontario have received far more attention than the other provinces.[10] Some excellent work on Saskatchewan notwithstanding, there is an almost total absence of studies of the public services in the western provinces. The Atlantic provinces have fared only a little better. Although Ontario and Quebec employ about half of all provincial public servants, generalizations based only on the experience of these two large provinces may not be representative of the structures and processes in the other eight.

A further difficulty for students of public administration is undoubtedly the absence of consistent definitions and comparable categorizations. Each province uses its own terminology which makes the search for pro-

10 Established in 1969, the Ecole Nationale d'Administration Publique of the Université de Québec deserves much of the credit for Quebec's pre-eminent position in provincial administration analysis. On Quebec, see such excellent works as Alain Baccigalupo, *L'Administration Québécoise* (Paris: Editions Berger-Levrault, 1976); André Gélinas, *Les organismes autonomes et centraux* (Québec: Presses de l'Université du Québec, 1975) and Patrice Garant, *La Fonction publique: Canadian et Québécoise* (Québec: La Presse de l'Université Laval, 1973). Supplement 3 (1976-78) of *Canadian Public Administration Bibliography* classifies and counts references to provincial administration. Taking into account that the definition of administration is wider than in this article, the frequency of references by province is as follows: Alberta, 68; British Columbia, 67; Manitoba, 18; New Brunswick, 22; Nova Scotia, 24; Ontario, 96; PEI, 3; Quebec, 261; Saskatchewan, 14. Some of the Quebec preponderance may be explained by the efficiency of ENAP documentation process for material in French.

vincial regularities and variations all the more difficult. Brown-John has discussed this problem with regard to regulatory agencies, while Prichard and Trebilcock have done so in the context of provincial public enterprise.[11]

Although the study of provincial public administration remains less developed than a twenty-fifth anniversary edition of the *Journal* might indicate, and even though we might wish for more evidence and analysis of the growth of the provinces' administrative machinery, the work completed to date does permit us to draw a general picture of the evolving nature of the public service. The next section chronicles the major trends in that development.

The changing public service

The last twenty-five years have witnessed many changes in both Canada's policy agenda and in the institutions and processes that constitute the political system. The maturation of the provinces, often referred to as province-building,[12] is without doubt among the most far-reaching of the transformations. The expansion of the provincial public sector has been a catalyst for a series of changes involving the bureaucracy. In this section the patterns of change and development are examined from five perspectives: size, scope and structure, cabinet and legislature, organization and process, personnel administration and federal-provincial relations.

Size, scope and structure

If one asks in what ways have provincial bureaucracies changed, the most immediate response is that they have grown substantially. Unfortunately, as Richard Bird points out "there are serious problems in obtaining a complete inventory of public sector employment in Canada at any point in time, let alone comparable estimates over time."[13] Does the term "provincial public employment" refer only to those directly employed by the province and within the scope of the civil service, or does it include non-federal hospital workers, teachers and professors, or workers in gov-

---

11 C. Lloyd Brown-John, *Canadian Regulatory Agencies* (Toronto: Butterworths, 1981); M.J. Trebilcock and J.R.S. Prichard, *Crown Corporations: The Calculus of Instrument Choice* (Toronto: Butterworths, forthcoming). The problem of definition of public ownership is not confined to the provinces; see J. Langford, "The Identification and Classification of Federal Public Corporations: A Preface to Regime Building," CANADIAN PUBLIC ADMINISTRATION, 23 (Spring 1980), pp. 76-104.
12 E. Black and A. Cairns, "A Different Perspective on Canadian Federalism," CANADIAN PUBLIC ADMINISTRATION, 9 (March 1966), pp. 27-45; L. Pratt, "The State and Province-Building," in L. Panitch, ed., *The Canadian State* (Toronto: University of Toronto Press, 1977).
13 "The Growth of the Public Service In Canada," in Foot, ed., *Public Employment and Compensation in Canada*, p. 25.

ernment enterprises? Using a narrow definition of government employment that includes only those who worked in provincial government departments, Hodgetts and Dwivedi found that the civil service employment had increased from 38,370 in 1946 to 209,760 in 1971, in other words by almost 500 per cent. Using a broader definition of provincial public employment that includes those directly employed as well as those in government enterprises, Statistics Canada counted almost 500,000 provincial employees in 1980.[14] Some 43 per cent of total public sector employees work for the provincial governments.

Another aspect of the changing bureaucracy involves the composition of the public service. Are those who fill key administrative roles the same kind of people as those who occupied such positions a generation ago, or have there been changes in social, educational and professional dimensions? Regrettably, beyond a very few surveys of Ontario and Quebec there has been no systematic analysis of these questions.[15]

There have been three avenues for the growth in the public service: enlarging existing departments, creating new departments and establishing non-departmental structures. In their survey of provincial employment, Hodgetts and Dwivedi found that a large part of the increase occurred in the traditional departments of welfare, health, highways, and education. However, extending the analysis in the 1970s, Foot *et al.* found that the rate of growth in education and transportation has fallen below average while the fastest growing employment areas were local development, recreation and culture, and social welfare and labour.[16] Since World War Two all the provinces have organized provincial responsibilities under an increased number of departments. Through the creation of such new departments as Energy, Environment and Federal-Provincial Relations, the average provincial cabinet in 1976 had grown to 18.6.

Non-departmental entities, which Hodgetts aptly refers to as structural heretics, are the other major vehicles for expansion of the public service. Since 1945 there has been a remarkable increase in regulatory boards, commissions and agencies. In Ontario alone there are now estimated to be over 700.[17] Although state enterprises have long been a part of the

14 Hodgetts and Dwivedi, *Provincial Governments as Employers*, p. 2; *Provincial Government Employment* (Ottawa: Statistics Canada), DBS 72-007.

15 See Roch Bolduc, "Les cadres supérieurs, quinze ans après," CANADIAN PUBLIC ADMINISTRATION, 21 (Winter 1978), pp. 618-39; Roch Bolduc, "Le Recruitement et la selection dans la Fonction publique du Québec," CANADIAN PUBLIC ADMINISTRATION, 7 (Summer 1964), pp. 205-14; and Harvey Rich, "From a Study of Higher Civil Servants in Ontario," CANADIAN PUBLIC ADMINISTRATION, 17 (Summer 1974), pp. 328-34.

16 *Provincial Governments as Employers*, p. 11; "The Growth and Distribution of Federal, Provincial and Local Government Employment in Canada," in Foot, ed., *Public Employment and Compensation*, p. 83.

17 Johnson and White, "To Everything There Is An Agency," p. 23.

provinical public sector, over half of the present crown corporations were created in the 1970s. Comparative and single province surveys reveal the broad range of policy areas in which there are provincial state enterprises.[18] As in other non-departmental structures, there is a broad variation in crown corporations; some, like Hydro Québec and Ontario Hydro are extremely significant institutions within the provincial political system, others are inconsequential. Some enterprises operate quite independently of governmental direction, others are closely tied to it. Although provincial enterprises vary in size, function and accountability, one generalization that can safely be asserted is that public enterprise has become a popular instrument of provincial policy.

Quantifiable measures of size, scope and structure are useful preliminary indicators of the changing public service. However, other changes, not so easily quantified, have also taken place in the internal dynamics of the bureaucracy and in its personnel management. In order to better understand these developments it is first necessary to consider the pressures emanating from other political institutions within the province.

Cabinet and legislature

The public service does not operate in a vacuum. Its links with both the cabinet and legislature constitute a complex system of interaction.[19] Important changes have taken place in this institutional setting and provincial public services have had to adapt to these external developments. Until after World War Two provincial cabinets operated as small, informal groupings which reflected the personality of a particular premier more than any standing organizational structure or enduring set of operating procedures.[20]

The growth of provincial powers and the consequent expansion of departmental structures has had direct implications for the method of organizing provincial responsibilities. Small portfolios facilitate clearer levels of ministerial responsibility and more coherent program development. On the other hand, multiplicity of departments increases the problem of coordination and may result in narrow views of public problems.

18   See A. Vining and J. Botterell, "An Overview of the Origins, Size and Functions of Crown Corporations," in Trebilcock and Prichard, *Crown Corporations*; Neil Swainson, "The Crown Corporation in British Columbia," paper presented at IPAC meetings in Halifax, 1981; *Public Enterprise in Saskatchewan* (Regina: Crown Investment Corporation, 1979); and Pierre Fournier, *Les Sociétés d'Etat et les Objectifs économiques du Québec: une évaluation préliminaire* (Quebec City: La Documentation Québécoise, 1977).
19   The system model is proposed by R. Jackson and M. Atkinson, *The Canadian Legislative System* (Toronto: Macmillan, 1974). See also, K. Kernaghan, "Power, Parliament and Public Servants," *Canadian Public Policy*, 3 (Summer 1979), pp. 383-96.
20   Much of this discussion of cabinet reform is drawn from Chandler and Chandler, *Public Policy and Provincial Policies*, chapter 4.

Small specialized departments may be more susceptible to pressure from client groups and more vulnerable to structural reorganization.

The increased scope of the public sector and greater interdependence among policy areas have led to structural and operational changes in both federal and provincial cabinets.[21] Besides increases in size, provincial cabinets have sought to expand their policy-making capacity through the adoption of four major reforms: creation of standing committees, an increase in staff assistance, establishment of horizontal portfolios, and the use of techniques for systematic policy choice and program evaluation.

The use of cabinet committees was one of the earliest reforms of cabinet. While provinces such as Ontario have gone somewhat further than the others, all the provinces have followed similar lines. They have moved toward greater coordination and control from the centre by Treasury or Management Boards and Planning/Priorities Committees, and to an increased division of labour through the use of standing policy committees.[22] Cabinet committees allow for specialization and more detailed consideration of policy than is possible before full cabinet. They also permit examination of issues that straddle departments. In the 1960s, when many of the provinces began to revamp their cabinets, they also developed secretariats to service the new arrangements. Besides providing an alternative source of information, cabinet secretariats are also important to policy integration.[23]

Another cabinet reform adopted by the provinces has been the establishment of horizontal, coordinating portfolios. Horizontal portfolios and policy ministers (or secretaries, as they are called in Ontario) are an at-

---

21 Among the studies of the changing provincial cabinet see G. Szablowski, "Policy-Making and Cabinet," in MacDonald, ed., *Government and Politics of Ontario*; J. Fleck, "Restructuring the Ontario Government," CANADIAN PUBLIC ADMINISTRATION, 16 (Winter 1973), pp. 56-72; K. Bryden, "Executive and Legislature in Ontario: A Case Study in Government Reform," CANADIAN PUBLIC ADMINISTRATION, 18 (Summer 1975), pp. 235-52; Micheline Plasse, "Les Chefs de Cabinets Ministériels au Québec: la transition du gouvernement libéral au gouvernement péquiste," *Canadian Journal of Political Science*, 14 (June 1981), pp. 309-36; D. Jarvis, "Cabinets," in Rowat, ed., *Provincial Government and Politics*; D. Brown, "Cabinets: Federal and Provincial Restructuring," in D. Rowat, ed., *Provincial Policy-Making: Comparative Essays* (Ottawa: Department of Political Science, Carleton University, 1981); and L. Ouellet, "L'appareil gouvernemental et législatif," in G. Bergeron et R. Pelletier, *L'Etat du Québec en Devenir* (Montréal: Boreal Press, 1981).

22 See Ken Bryden, "Cabinets" in Bellamy, *et al.*, *Provincial Political Systems*, pp. 310-22. For discussions of Ontario's traditional organization and subsequent reforms, see Schindeler, *Responsible Government in Ontario*, chapter 4, and R. Loreto, "The Cabinet," in MacDonald, ed., *Government and Politics of Ontario, rev. ed.*, pp. 20-35. On changes in Quebec, see Ouellet, "L'appareil gouvernemental et législatif."

23 Jacques Brunet, J. Houde et G. Savard, "La gestion ministerielle et les organisms centraux," CANADIAN PUBLIC ADMINISTRATION, 17 (Summer 1974), pp. 321-27. For the early development of secretariats in Saskatchewan, see George Cadbury, "Planning in Saskatchewan," in L. Lapierre, ed., *Essays on the Left* (Toronto: McClelland and Stewart, 1971). For Quebec, see André Bernard, *La Politique au Canada et au Québec* (Montréal: Les Presses de l'Université du Québec, 1976).

tempt to integrate within a single policy area, while the standing policy committees coordinate across policy areas. The most thorough-going movement toward horizontal agencies has been in Quebec and Ontario.[24]

A related attempt to improve cabinet decision-making has been the development of policy planning and systematic evaluation techniques. Although there are important differences among the techniques employed in various provinces, Planning, Programming and Budgeting (PPBS), Management by Objective (MBO), Management by Results (MBR) and Programme Management Information Systems (PMIS) have the common purpose of establishing a systematic process for decision-making. Despite initial enthusiasm, the provinces have been quite cautious in adopting rational policy techniques. Several of the provinces are really too small to utilize complex PPBS techniques, and even among the larger ones, two fundamental aspects of PPBS – detailed listing of priorities and policy evaluation – have proved difficult to implement.[25]

It is generally recognized that provincial legislatures are not directly involved in day-to-day decision-making. However, through the performance of the functions of law-making and surveillance the legislature has contact with the bureaucracy.[26] Several provinces have adopted reforms to facilitate the legislature in its law-making and surveillance func-

24 For a discussion of the concept of a policy field, see Committee on Government Productivity, *Interim Report Number Three* (Toronto, 1971). For an evaluation of these reforms see Szablowski, "Policymaking and Cabinet," and Bryden, "Executive and Legislature in Ontario"; for Quebec, see Ouellet, "L'appareil gouvernemental et legislatif."

25 For discussions of these provincial systems, see V. Fowke, "PPB for Provinces," CANADIAN PUBLIC ADMINISTRATION, 12 (Spring 1969), pp. 72-78; *Effective Management Through PPBS* (Toronto: Treasury Board of Ontario, 1968); *The Managing by Results and Goal Setting and Review Systems* (Toronto: Management Board Secretariat, 1975); D. Campbell, "Planning, Programming and Budgeting – the Ontario Government," *Cost and Management*, 49 (July-August 1975), pp. 6-13; Conseil du Trésor, *Le Systeme du Budget par programme et son application au Gouvernement du Québec* (Québec City, 1972); A. Ambroise et J. Jacques, "L'appareil administratif," in Bergeron and Pelletier, *L'Etat en Devenir*, pp. 129-32; D.M. Wallace, "Budget Reform in Saskatchewan: A New Approach to Program Based Management," CANADIAN PUBLIC ADMINISTRATION, 17 (Winter 1974), pp. 586-99; J.A. Riffel, H.N. Watts and J. Hudson, *Program Accounting and Budgeting in Alberta: Retrospect and Prospect* (Edmonton: Human Resources Research Council, 1972). See also R.M. Burns, "Budgeting and Finance," in Bellamy *et al.*, *Provincial Political Systems*, pp. 323-40; and G. Lemieux, "Budgeting and PPB," in Rowat, ed., *Provincial Government and Politics*, pp. 193-216.

26 On the functions of the provincial legislature and reforms to facilitate performance of those functions see: Philip Laundy, "Legislatures," in Bellamy *et al.*, *Provincial Government and Politics*, pp. 280-96; D.M. Street, "Provincial Assemblies," in Rowat, ed., *Provincial Government and Politics*; Chandler and Chandler, *Public Policy and Provincial Policies*, pp. 114-21; Donald M. MacDonald, "Modernizing the Legislature," in MacDonald, ed., *Government and Politics of Ontario*, revised edition, pp. 81-101; A. McLeod, "Reform of the Standing Committees of the Quebec National Assembly," *Canadian Journal of Political Science*, 8 (March 1975), 22-39; Claude E. Forget, "L'administration publique: sujet ou objet du pouvoir politique?" CANADIAN PUBLIC ADMINISTRATION, 21 (Summer 1978), pp. 234-42.

tions. One of the most significant measures has been the effort in some provinces to set up effective legislative committees. Besides providing a forum for the development and expression of policy ideas by members, committees, through consideration of the estimates, provide an important opportunity for oversight of the government. The post-audit of expenditures by Public Accounts Committees is an additional opportunity for surveillance. Another instrument of oversight is a Committee on Regulations, as established in several provinces. These committees review delegated legislation for form but only to a very limited degree for content.[27]

Organization and process

Changes in the organization and management of the provincial public services have come in response to their own increased size and scope and to developments in other institutions. Each province's administration has had its own unique development; however, there have been common features stemming from attempts to move toward more rational policy making. In an effort to improve the policy process, each province has sought to increase the coordination among programs, adopt a broader context for policy-making and increase its capacity for evaluating program effectiveness.

The traditional solution for the problem of coordination has been the hierarchical structure within departments. Central agencies acted mainly as control units determining whether departmental estimates were in keeping with governmental outlines, with individual ministers being able to appeal agency decisions to cabinet. Quite often cabinet acted less as a coordinator than as an arena for individual ministers to exert their political power. Policy reflected relative ministerial power more than anything else. The new approaches to policy-making have explicitly sought to make interrelationships explicit and to increase consideration across programs. Policy fields and functional cabinet committees have provided a structural basis for enhanced coordination among line departments. Inter and intra departmental committees have become common responses to the concern for coordination.

Although PPB systems have not been generally adopted, provincial governments have not simply retained the traditional methods of the past. Recent policy-making processes reflect the provinces' attempts to embrace the basic tenets of PPBS. This means, among other things, that compared to the traditional method, policies are now considered in a broader con-

27 See James McNally, "The Supervision of Delegated Legislation," in Rowat, ed., *Provincial Government and Politics*, pp. 217-50; and Ontario, *Royal Commission Inquiry in Civil Rights* (Toronto: Queen's Printer, 1968), Vol. 1, McRuer Report.

text. Budgeting is based on forward planning, whereby data and plans are cast in multi-year time frames. Furthermore, programs (and thus expenditures) must be justified against other programs and claims for funding. Multi-year planning obviously puts greater demands on officials, but the more fundamental change is the broader arena for justifying expenditures and programs. Proposals must now compete, not only in their own policy sphere, but also across policy sectors. This means that the recommendations of departmental officials have to persuade a larger audience.[28]

The third common development in the provinces' changing organization and process is the interest in program evaluation. Program evaluation is defined as "... the independent and objective assessment of a program to determine in light of present circumstances the adequacy of its objectives, design, and results, both intended and unintended."[29] Evaluation is a crucial part of rational policy-making; most provinces have become interested in evaluation as a direct result of their attempt to set up a comprehensive budgetary system. Unlike coordination or policy choice, evaluation takes place after implementation. It requires a distinct set of data for program output information. With the exception of early interest in Saskatchewan in the 1940s, Quebec in 1972 was the first province to institute evaluation, only for it to be discontinued and not reinstated until 1979. In most provinces in which effectiveness evaluation has been tried, it has been done on an ad hoc basis by central agencies.[30] Although recognized as important, utilization of program and policy evaluation is still very much in a state of flux. In several provinces it has only been tried in pilot studies. Even in Ontario, which has one of the most sophisticated systems of financial control, it is noted that "what is lacking is a systematic policy evaluation."[31]

Despite the emphasis here on a common developmental pattern of provincial public administration, it is important to recognize the unique, innovative role of Saskatchewan. Many reforms that were not even considered by other provinces until the 1960s and 1970s were adopted in

28   See Paul Leger, "Social Policy and Resource Allocation: A Problem of Choice," address to Canadian Conference on Historical Resources (Fredericton, 1977) for a discussion by the Secretary to the Cabinet Committee on Social Development of New Brunswick on the need for managers to think in broader social terms. The notion of a broader arena also is developed by Peter Aucoin, "Pressure Groups and Recent Changes in the Policy-Making Process," in A. Paul Pross, ed., *Pressure Group Behaviour in Canadian Politics* (Toronto: McGraw-Hill Ryerson, 1975), pp. 174-92.
29   Michael Hicks, "Evaluating Evaluation in Today's Governments, summary of discussions," CANADIAN PUBLIC ADMINISTRATION, 24 (Fall 1981), p. 351.
30   See H.G. Rogers *et al.*, "Evaluation in Practice: The State of the Art in Canadian Governments," ibid., pp. 371-86. For a discussion of the problems encountered in Quebec, see Bernard Bonin and Patrick Moran, "L'environment et la portée de l'évaluation," ibid., pp. 387-403.
31   This assessment comes from J. Simeon, "Policy-Making in the Cabinet," in MacDonald, ed., *The Government and Politics of Ontario*, revised edition, pp. 102-22.

Saskatchewan in the 1940s after the CCF came into power.[32] Central agencies were key components in the CCF's reform of the policy-making process. The Economic Advisory and Planning Board carried out broad policy and program planning and acted as a secretariat to the cabinet. Created in 1946, the Budget Bureau was an instrument for systematic budgetary review and program evaluation.

Personnel management

Not only have the policy structures and functions of the public service changed, provincial personnel management has also undergone a number of transformations.[33] The establishment of independent civil service commissions represented early efforts at reform through formation of a merit system. In 1917 British Columbia was the first province to create such a commission. In the next year Manitoba, Ontario and Alberta followed suit. Unfortunately these commissions did not alter provincial management practices. As Hodgetts and Dwivedi observed, "until World War Two, provincial agencies remained ineffective and weak and their contribution toward extending the merit system in personnel administration was just above negligible."[34] By the 1960s however, there were serious efforts in several provinces to strengthen the performance of modern personnel functions.

No single pattern emerged across all provinces. There were, however, some general trends. For the most part these management and development functions were performed by one or more central agencies. In several jurisdictions, as in the federal, the Treasury Board became an important actor in manpower management alongside the Civil Service Commission. In other provinces, British Columbia and Alberta for example, a strengthened Civil Service Commission presided over almost all personnel administration. In Quebec, a Department of Civil Service was created. By the late sixties the impact of the Glassco Commission on Government Organization began to be felt in provincial personnel management. Decentralization to departmental units became a significant

---

32 See Cadbury, "Planning in Saskatchewan," pp. 51-64, and Meyer Brownstone, "The Douglas-Lloyd Governments: Innovation and Bureaucratic Adaptation," in LaPierre, ed., *Essays on the Left*, pp. 65-80. For accounts that focus on the policies as well as the changes in structure and process, see J. Richards and L. Pratt, *Prairie Capitalism* (Toronto: McClelland and Stewart, 1979), and S.M. Lipset, *Agrarian Socialism* (New York: Anchor Books, 1965).
33 For some discussions of traditional personnel systems, see J.G. Channing, *The Effects of Transition to Confederation on Public Administration in Newfoundland* (Toronto: Institute of Public Administration of Canada, 1982); J. Leeke, "Patronage in Quebec," *Canadian Dimension*, 11 (July-August 1975), pp. 6-12; V. Lemieux, *Patronage et Politique au Québec: 1944-1972* (Québec: Editions Boréal, 1975).
34 *Provincial Governments as Employers*, p. 25. See also H. Scarrow, "Civil Service Commissions in the Canadian Provinces," *Journal of Politics*, 19 (May 1957), pp. 240-61.

element in personnel management. The trend toward transferring operational responsibilities to the departments has meant that civil service commissions are now left with three main functions: an advisory role on manpower policies, an auditing role, and a judicial role for individual complaints.[35]

As employers, provincial governments have had to respond to demands for worker participation in the determination of terms and conditions of employment. Collective bargaining, which now exists in every province, did not develop along any single path.[36] Seven provinces evolved toward collective bargaining through joint councils. Saskatchewan, Quebec and British Columbia moved to collective bargaining without earlier consultative procedures. Today, although all provinces have collective bargaining, they differ as to which agency is the employer spokesman in negotiations. The range of negotiable issues also varies from province to province, and finally, there are differences over what procedures are to be followed when negotiations break down. Half of the provinces (Nova Scotia, Prince Edward Island, Ontario, Manitoba and Alberta) deny the right to strike to government employees. The provinces that grant the right to strike also allow for voluntary arbitration, with the exception of Quebec which does not permit third-party involvement.

Federal-provincial relations

Federal-provincial relations provide yet another perspective on the changing provincial public service. The present structure of Canadian federalism is a far cry from the traditional concept of a compartmentalized division of jurisdictions between autonomous governments. In almost any field of activity both federal and provincial governments have some interest and claims to power. Even in those areas which presumably fall within only one jursidiction, policy-making often requires the cooperation of the other level. In short, a dominant feature of the Canadian federal system is the high degree of interdependence between the federal and provincial governments.[37] This has meant that federal and provincial governments interact regularly and often, across a wide range of fields. Each government is a factor in the other's decision-making and

35 Hodgetts and Dwivedi, chapter 2, and R. Dowdell, "Public Personnel Administration," in Kenneth Kernaghan, ed., *Public Administration in Canada* (Toronto: Methuen, 1977), pp. 208-27.
36 Shirley Goldenberg, "Public Sector Labour Relations in Canada," in B. Aaron *et al., Public Sector Bargaining* (Washington, D.C. Bureau of National Affairs, 1978), pp. 254-61. See also David Lewin and Shirley Goldenberg, "Public Sector Unionism in the U.S. and Canada," *Industrial Relations*, 19 (Fall 1980), pp. 239-56.
37 See Gérard Veilleux, "Intergovernmental Canada: Government by Conference? A Fiscal and Economic Perspective," and Richard Simeon, "Intergovernmental relations and the Challenges to Canadian Federalism," both in CANADIAN PUBLIC ADMINISTRATION, 23 (Spring 1980), pp. 33-53 and pp. 14-32.

federal-provincial relations have a significant impact on both political and administrative institutions within each government. Although there have been some general trends that have occurred in all provinces, it is quite clear that the effects of federal-provincial relations on bureaucratic structures and operations vary from province to province as well as from policy area to policy area.[38]

Although there were federal-provincial conferences and other, less formal interactions before World War Two, since that time federal-provincial relations have developed a great deal. From 1945 up until the 1960s these interactions were highly particularistic and isolated, carried on mainly by program specialists from the two levels.[39] From the early 1960s on, the nature of federal-provincial relations took on a political as well as a functional character and the provinces continuously challenged federal dominance in the relationship.[40] Institutional mechanisms were created to better cope with the increased complexity of federal-provincial relations. V.S. Wilson describes the two structural patterns that arose.

On the one hand, there has been a very strong inclination in some provinces (Alberta, Ontario and Quebec) to subordinate the organizational structure of intergovernmental relations to the political considerations involved in the process. On the other hand in other provinces (Nova Scotia, New Brunswick and Saskatchewan) organizational developments have been viewed less as a mechanism for political combat and more as an effort to filter out the operational and corporate level problems from the political level of intergovernmental relations, and hence to provide offices for coordinating federal-provincial relations at lower levels of the bureaucracy.[41]

The impact of the federal system goes beyond organizational changes. Cairns argues that each province has had to shift resources away from functional endeavours to use them to carry on federal-provincial relations. Competition between Ottawa and the provinces to expand their

38 For various examples, see Dupré *et al.*, *Federalism and Policy Development*; Richard Schultz, *Federalism, Bureaucracy and Public Policy* (Montreal: McGill-Queen's University Press/IPAC, 1980); and Anthony Careless, *Initiative and Response: The Adaptation of Canadian Federalism to Regional Economic Development* (Montreal: McGill-Queen's University Press/IPAC, 1977).
39 See D.V. Smiley, "Public Administration and Canadian Federalism," CANADIAN PUBLIC ADMINISTRATION, 3 (September 1964), pp. 371-88.
40 Richard Simeon, *Federal-Provincial Diplomacy* (Toronto: Queen's McGill University Press, 1972). For other accounts see Rand Dyck, "The Canada Assistance Plan; the Ultimate in Cooperative Federalism," CANADIAN PUBLIC ADMINISTRATION, 19 (Winter 1976), pp. 587-602; Martin Westmacott, "The National Transportation Act and Western Canada: A Case Study in Cooperative Federalism," CANADIAN PUBLIC ADMINISTRATION, 16 (Fall 1973), pp. 447-67; and Dupré *et al.*, *Federalism and Policy Development*.
41 V.S. Wilson, "Federal-Provincial Relations and Federal Policy Processes," in G.B. Doern and P. Aucoin, eds., *Public Policy in Canada* (Toronto: Macmillan, 1979), p. 199.

jurisdictions, as well as efforts to defend their existing powers, has resulted in an overall growth of government and a consequent increase in the executive machinery at each level.[42] Ottawa has served as a significant model for the provinces in several ways. Federal adoption of PBBS and collective bargaining were no doubt important precursors of provincial innovations, while federal commission reports have stimulated provincial studies and reforms.[43]

Interaction with Ottawa has directly affected the policy process within the provinces. Anthony Careless in *Initiative and Response* describes a pattern of initiation dominated by Ottawa, with the provinces having to take or leave federal plans. Other studies, for example, Simeon in *Federal-Provincial Diplomacy*, have described a process in which each government formulates its own policies and then negotiations begin as governments try to arrive at a common plan. Donald Savoie has characterized another pattern that has emerged. In the General Development Agreements, bureaucracy at both levels work together to plan and implement new policies. The consequences of the GDA approach have been to blur jurisdictional lines, to alter standing relationships between ministers and their officials, and to discourage public and interest group participation.[44]

Issues of the 1980s

Throughout much of the 1960s and 1970s, as the greatly expanded provincial bureaucracy sought to deal with an ever-increasing range of complex and multi-faceted policy problems, the guiding value remained effectiveness. The federal Royal Commission on Government Organization (1962) and the provincial studies that followed reflected the concerns of that period. They focused on organizational and managerial reforms to make the administrative process both more efficient and effective.

Heralded by the Royal Commission on Financial Management and Accountability (Lambert Commission), the primary concern of the 1980s is the role of a powerful bureaucracy in a democratic state. Indeed David Cameron contends that "the power of the bureaucracy and attempts to hold that power to public account constitute one of the cen-

---

42 Alan Cairns, "The Other Crisis in Canadian Federalism," CANADIAN PUBLIC ADMINISTRATION, 22 (Summer 1974), pp. 175-95.
43 After the Royal Commission on Government Organization (Glassco Commission), 1962, several of the provinces instituted studies of their administrative apparatus; for example, Royal Commission on Government in Saskatchewan, Operational Productivity of Government in Manitoba, Ontario Committee on Government Productivity, and Quebec Study of Administrative Practices.
44 D. Savoie, *Federal-Provincial Collaboration: The Canada-New Brunswick General Development Agreement* (Montreal: McGill-Queen's University Press/IPAC, 1981).

tral challenges facing contemporary public administration in Canada."[45] Certainly the concern over the power and responsibility of the bureaucracy is neither new nor confined to the provincial level. However, as the provincial public services have continued to grow and new policy techniques have enhanced the importance of information and expertise, the position of the bureaucracy in the political system has become an issue of increasing concern. The place of the bureaucracy may be viewed from two intertwined perspectives: the public sector's relation with its political masters – the issue of responsibility – and its relationship with the public – the issue of responsiveness.[46] These issues grow out of the fact that the bureaucracy, at the centre of the political process, constitutes a crucial institution in the formulation and implementation of policies to deal with public needs. Clearly the object is not to deny power to the bureaucracy, but rather to ensure that the power is used responsibly and responsively.

Power and responsibility

Administrative responsibility as it is used here refers primarily to objective accountability and is defined as the responsibility employees have to political and administrative superiors who may impose sanctions for failure to obey directions.[47] Objective responsibility is predicated on an institutional framework within which bureaucrats and political actors interact. Although the question of external control of the bureaucracy may arise at any point, traditionally accountability was possible through personal contact and involvement of senior officials and ministers. The legal and constitutional framework augmented these informal controls with lines of accountability drawn to legislators and judges.[48]

Four factors that have arisen in the development of the provincial state have substantially eroded the traditional framework of responsibility. These factors and the subsequent problem of responsibility apply in

45 David M. Cameron, "Power and Responsibility in the Public Service," CANADIAN PUBLIC ADMINISTRATION, 21 (Fall 1978), p. 364.

46 It does some violence to both concepts to restrict them as we have. Certainly it is recognized that responsibility to the public is indirect and that responsiveness can be to other political elites as well as to the public. However, for analytical purposes we found the distinction to be a useful starting point.

47 Kenneth Kernaghan, in "Responsible Public Bureaucracy: A Rationale and Framework for Analysis," CANADIAN PUBLIC ADMINISTRATION, 16 (Winter 1973), pp. 580-1, draws the distinction between objective responsibility and subjective responsibility. The latter refers to feelings of responsibility based on individuals' values and loyalties.

48 These are described in C.E.S. Franks, "The Legislatures and Responsible Government," in N. Ward and D. Spafford, eds., *Politics in Saskatchewan* (Don Mills: Longman Canada, 1968); Gerald le Dain, "The Supervisory Jurisdiction in Quebec," *Canadian Bar Review*, 35 (1957), pp. 788-829 and M. Woods, "Judicial Review of the Proceedings of Administrative Tribunals in Saskatchewan," *Cronkite Essays* (Toronto: College of Law, University of Saskatchewan, 1968), pp. 90-107.

varying degrees to all provinces. First of all, accountability has been diluted because of increased interdepartmental policy formulation. As administrators cope with multi-faceted problems through coordination across departments, lines of responsibility become harder to maintain. A second factor is the increasing volume of delegated legislation, an outgrowth of the increased regulatory activity that has characterized the growth of the state. Flexibility and discretionary powers are necessary to deal with the wide range of complex problems undertaken by provincial governments; however, here too the traditional structures of responsibility prove inadequate.[49] A related pressure is the overall increase in non-departmental agencies. Public enterprises are a case in point. As the provinces have increasingly turned to crown corporations as instruments of policy, a significant portion of the public sector operates outside the normal channels of accountability.[50] Finally, the well-documented growth of federal-provincial interdependence also serves to dilute the links necessary for responsibility between bureaucrat and cabinet and cabinet and parliament.[51]

As many of the characteristic developments of the modern state have tended to place much administrative activity outside the traditional channels of responsibility, students and practitioners in the 1980s are confronted with the dilemma of finding ways to ensure political control without introducing rigidities that put efficiency and effectiveness at risk.

Responsiveness

It is impossible to come to grips with the place of the public service in the political process without exploring the "other side" of its interactions – its relation with the public. Through the chain of administrative and political responsibility the public service is indirectly linked to the public. There are, however, important direct linkages which result from the bureaucracy's role in policy formulation and implementation. As part of the

49 See G.V. Nichols, "Safeguards in the Exercise of Governmental Discretion," CANADIAN PUBLIC ADMINISTRATION, 7 (December 1964), pp. 500-509; Schindeler, *Responsible Government in Ontario*; C.R. Tindal, in MacDonald, ed., *The Government and Politics of Ontario*, revised edition, pp. 36-49 and H.N. Janisch, "Policy-Making in Regulation: Towards a New Definition of the Status of Independent Regulatory Agencies in Canada," *Osgoode Hall Law Journal*, 17 (1979), pp. 46-106.
50 Saskatchewan has established a unique framework for effectively linking its crown corporations to the government. The original system, in place by the late 1940s, consisted of a statute establishing the corporations, ministers serving as chairmen of corporate boards, a central agency for crown corporations and a standing legislative committee. See *Public Enterprise in Saskatchewan* (Regina: Crown Investments Corporation, 1979).
51 See Audrey Doerr, *The Machinery of Government in Canada* (Toronto: Methuen, 1981), chapter 7. For a somewhat different view, see J.S. Dupré, "Reflections on the Fiscal and Economic Aspects of Government by Conference," CANADIAN PUBLIC ADMINISTRATION, 23 (Spring 1980), pp. 54-59.

process of policy formation the bureaucracy is the target or recipient of individual and group inputs. As such, civil servants in departments or quasi-independent agencies are the main channel for citizen involvement in decision-making. The nature of the relationship between the public and the bureaucracy raises the important questions of responsiveness.

Public participation in the political process depends on both information and opportunity. Both of these vary not only from province to province but also among policy areas. Information about planned or actual government policy is a necessary precondition to citizen involvement. Secrecy and inaccessibility as well as lack of funding are major barriers to informed public participation.[52] Although all provincial governments publicly favour greater access to information there has been only limited action to fulfill that objective. Nova Scotia and New Brunswick are the only provinces with freedom of information laws. Funding for public interest groups is at best available on an ad hoc basis.[53] The provinces have used white paper and green paper processes to inform and solicit responses to proposed government policies.

A recent survey of participatory practices across provincial Departments of the Environment described opportunities for public participation as "visibly subdued, conservative and piecemeal." It concluded that there was "great variation in the strength of the provinces' commitment to public participation" and although a few provinces, notably British Columbia, Alberta, Saskatchewan and Ontario have taken steps to provide opportunities for citizen participation, there are major inadequacies in citizen involvement in all provinces. Even where there is provision for citizen involvement, the process is often flawed, tending to be inconsistent, ad hoc, often confined to elite groups and occurring only in the later stages of the policy process.[54]

52 The seminal article on secrecy, published in 1965, is Donald Rowat, "How Much Administrative Secrecy?" *Canadian Journal of Economics and Political Science*, 31 (November 1965), pp. 479-98. For overviews of provincial responses to the demand for access to information, see B.R. Filipow, "Public Access to Policy Information," in Rowat, ed., *Provincial Policy-Making*; and B. Sandler, ed., *Involvement and Environment*, vol. 2 (Edmonton: Environment Council of Alberta, 1978). An insightful discussion of the effect of the high costs of information-seeking behaviour is found in Michael Trebilcock, "Winners and Losers in the Modern Regulatory System: Must the Consumer Always Lose?" *Osgoode Hall Law Journal*, 13 (1975), pp. 619-47.
53 See, for example, P. Everett, "Financial Assistance for Public Interest Group Participation in Environmental Decision-Making," *Environmental Law*, 10 (1980), 483-516.
54 Susan Finkle, "Public Participation: Departments of Environment," in Rowat, ed., *Provincial Policy-Making*. This excellent article provides a thorough comparison of the various practices of public participation in provincial departments. For other studies of public participation, see George Szablowski, *The Public Bureaucracy and the Possibility of Citizen Involvement in the Government of Ontario*, report prepared for Ontario Committee on Government Productivity (Toronto: Queen's Printer,

If responsiveness to public needs is a primary objective of the 1980s, a major precondition must be the provision of meaningful access by an informed citizenry. Scholars and practitioners have recognized that given the multitude of sometimes conflicting interests seeking accommodation, responsiveness is a complex problem. Moreover, Michael Pitfield has pointed out the problems that arise when officials are too open to demands. Policy-making can become ad hoc and fragmented with insufficient attention to a view of the whole and the interrelationships among programs.[55] A related problem resulting from unrestrained receptivity is that agencies and actors are more likely to be captured by well-organized interests. The point here is that responsiveness cannot simply be equated simply with openness. Hodgetts describes the broader concept of responsiveness:

> The test for government is how well its institutional arrangements work in identifying the interests that deserve to be incorporated in public policies and programmes; and how adaptable these institutions are in responding to changing values and circumstance.[56]

It is this understanding of responsiveness that brings out an important link between responsiveness and responsibility. The connection comes through inward accountability as well as external institutional framework. As Kernaghan has observed, "Responsiveness to the public whether citizens' groups, or to organized special interest groups, often requires the exercise of subjective responsibility because it depends on the public servants' perceptions of what influences they should respond to in making decisions."[57]

1971); J.O. Riordan, "The Public Involvement Program in the Okanagan Basin Study," *Natural Resources Journal*, 16 (1976), pp. 177-96; P.S. Elder, ed., *Environmental Management and Public Participation* (Toronto: Canadian Environmental Law Association, 1978); D. Fox, *Public Participation in Administrative Proceedings* (Ottawa: Law Reform Commission, 1979); H. Chapin and D. Duncan, *Citizen Involvement in Public Policy-Making: Access and the Policy-Making Process* (Ottawa: Canadian Council on Social Development, 1978); and J.D. McNiven, *Evaluation of the Public Participation Programme Embodied in the Prince Edward Island Development Plan* (Halifax: Dalhousie Institute of Public Affairs, 1974).
55 One outgrowth of the concern with responsiveness is a renewed interest in the representative quality of the public service, the argument being that a public service representative of the whole population will be responsive to the needs of the totality. See K. Kernaghan, "Representative Bureaucracy: The Canadian Perspective," CANADIAN PUBLIC ADMINISTRATION, 21 (Winter 1978), pp. 490-92; and M. Kirby *et al.*, "The Impact of Public Policy-Making Structures and Process in Canada," ibid., p. 411.
56 "Government Responsiveness to the Public Interest: Has Progress Been Made?" CANADIAN PUBLIC ADMINISTRATION, 24 (Summer 1981), p. 216.
57 "Changing Concepts of Power and Responsibility in the Canadian Public Service," CANADIAN PUBLIC ADMINISTRATION, 21 (Fall 1978), p. 404.

A research agenda for the eighties

By identifying major gaps in our knowledge and in pointing out unexplored analytical concerns, the preceding sections in this paper comprise a research agenda. The purpose of this section is to lay out systematically the deficiencies in the study of provincial public administration and to pose some specific and coherent directions for future research. The agenda put forward here consists of three overlapping stages: description, analysis and evaluation.

General descriptive studies of the structures and processes of provincial administration are the first order of the day. This means research that depicts historical development as well as current practices and trends in each province. Existing descriptive work on provincial executive machinery has tended to be confined to a single province. Far preferable for purposes of a general understanding of provincial administration are comparative studies that emphasize some aspect of public administration across several provinces.[58] Although there is an overwhelming number of topics that might be pursued, some important ones for which there is already some fragmentary material include cross-provincial comparisons of central agencies, of mechanisms for control of crown corporations, or of current manifestations of PPBS and other policy techniques.

Provincial research to date has been confined largely to describing structures rather than processes.[59] While this is understandable because structures are concrete and easier to identify, a knowledge of process is fundamental to an appreciation of the role of the public service.[60] It is in this regard that the writings of practitioners take on special importance and need to be encouraged.

Admittedly, in the early stages of study almost any descriptive material is welcomed. Once the field begins to mature and grow, some ana-

---

58 Some very insightful studies simply make comparisons across two provinces. See, for example, G. Veilleux, "The Ontario Labour Relations Board and the Quebec Rental Commission: A Comparative Analysis of Two Canadian Administrative Tribunals," CANADIAN PUBLIC ADMINISTRATION, 12 (Spring 1969), pp. 45-62 or H.V. Nelles, "Public Ownership of Electrical Utilities in Manitoba and Ontario: 1906-1930," *Canadian Historical Review* (December 1976).

59 Some very useful exceptions are S.H. Mansbridge, "Of Social Policy in Alberta: Its Management, Its Modification, Its Evaluation and Its Making," CANADIAN PUBLIC ADMINISTRATION, 21 (Fall 1978), pp. 311-23; Michael Bellavance, "Le Ministre de l'Education du Québec et la gestion de l'enseignement superieur," CANADIAN PUBLIC ADMINISTRATION, 24 (Spring 1981), pp. 73-91; and A.W. Johnson, "Biography of a Government: Policy Formulation in Saskatchewan 1944-1961," Ph.D. thesis (Cambridge, Mass.: Harvard University, 1963).

60 The study of provincial administration would very much benefit from analyses comparable to Richard French's *How Ottawa Decides* (Toronto: Lorimer, 1980) or from the kind of public debate that took place in the early seventies between Baker and LaFramboise over federal administrative reform.

lytical framework is necessary to guide research and data collection. It is only under the rubric of an analytical framework that critical connections are made and the dynamics of relationships set forth. From that base, hypotheses can be generated and data collected permitting the testing of propositions. A preliminary step in moving away from descriptive to the analytical stage might be accomplished by replicating or tailoring to the provinces work done at the federal level. These might include, for example, the in-depth study of central agencies as in Campbell and Szablowski's *The Superbureaucrats*, the testing of the bureaucratic politics model, or investigation of the bureaucratic phenomenon.[61] In each case, analysis at the provincial level could be based on analytical constructs and models found in federal studies. However, just as provincial parties and party systems are not replicas of those in federal politics, it may also be that provincial bureaucracy is not simply federal administration on a smaller scale. An important element in the research agenda is, therefore, some consideration or allowance in analysis for the possibility of significant differences between the functioning of bureaucracies at federal and provincial levels. This is not to assume that the provincial experience is necessarily different from the federal; rather the extent of parallels or discrepancies between the two levels remains a question to be investigated. The development of a distinctly provincial analysis might well be furthered through comparative analysis with other subnational units such as German Länder or Australian states. This perspective would help to bring out the administrative implications of multiple levels of government.[62] Greater refinement in the analysis of provincial executive machinery will be reached when students of the provinces are able to develop frameworks that can encompass various patterns and practices among the provinces. For example, Quebec, Ontario and Saskatchewan have consistently been leaders in adopting administrative reforms. Do the same factors explain these provinces' innovative behaviour?

Finally, the study of provincial administration must approach the question of "so what?" What are the distributive effects of adopting rational policy techniques, of different degrees of accountability, different ranges of discretion, etc.? In short, what are the social and political implications of variations in public administration? The object of evaluative research

---

61   *The Superbureaucrats: Structure and Behaviour in Central Agencies* (Toronto: Macmillan, 1979); M.M. Atkinson and K.R. Nossal, "Bureaucratic Politics and the New Fighter Aircraft Decision," CANADIAN PUBLIC ADMINISTRATION, 24 (Winter 1981), pp. 531-62. For a comparison of anglophones and francophones in the federal public service that applied the Crozier model to Canada, see Herman Bakvis, "French Canada and the Bureaucratic Phenomenon," CANADIAN PUBLIC ADMINISTRATION, 21 (Spring 1978), pp. 103-24.

62   See, for example, K. Wiltshire, "Working with Intergovernmental Agreements, the Canadian and Australian Experience," CANADIAN PUBLIC ADMINISTRATION, 23 (Fall 1980), pp. 353-79.

is to relate structure and process to outcomes, that is, to judge according to stated criteria the actions of the executive. Analysis tells us how power is exercised; evaluation tells us to what ends. Answers to such questions as what are the implication of the changing composition of the public service or the impact of increased citizen participation are not easy to ascertain. However, these are the kinds of questions that tap the essence of the governmental system because they link the workings of the bureaucratic level with the authoritative allocation of values.

Conclusions

In this paper, we have sought to chart what is by all accounts a field of study still in its infancy. Because research in provincial public administration is so sparse, it might have been possible to try to squeeze every available bit of information into this overview. We chose instead to review the approaches to the study of provincial administration and to sketch out the developments that have changed the character of provincial bureaucracies. Wherever possible, we emphasized general patterns rather than focusing on variations among the provinces. Those readers particularly familiar with one or more provinces will no doubt be all too aware of the limits of such generalizations.

The purpose of this paper goes beyond describing the transition from traditional administration to modern bureaucracy. Of at least equal concern are the directions and issues related to future development. The public service has shown itself to be a highly flexible and adaptive organism, and there is no reason to think that its evolution has ended. As political, social, economic and technological conditions continue to change, so too will provincial bureaucracies.

The development of the public service that has taken place in the provinces has occurred in the context of public sector growth. However, the rapid expansion of the state that marked the postwar decades has been replaced by an environment of cutbacks and restraint. Just as the public service reflected the earlier period and adapted to meet such challenges as formulating and administering the welfare state, and regulating the exploitation of natural resources, so it must now adapt to retrenchment and scarcity. As difficult as were the growing pains of the last thirty years, the shrinking pains promise to be even more challenging.

The nature and consequences of administrative adaptation and development must not be treated as arcane subjects to be cut off from the bulk of political analysis. The workings of the public service are a central part of the political process and no understanding of provincial politics can be undertaken without a thorough appreciation of administrative factors.

T.J. Plunkett
Katherine A. Graham
Whither municipal government?

Introduction

In his classic work published in 1954, the late K. Grant Crawford set out the twofold purpose of municipal government in Canada in the following terms:

> One is to carry out the duties imposed upon local authorities by the provinces which have created them, and to which they are ultimately answerable. The other is to carry out the wishes of the inhabitants of the area under their jurisdiction, within the scope and to the extent permitted by law.

He concluded by observing that "opinions differ as to which of these two purposes should be dominant, though legally and constitutionally, if not politically, the priority of the former cannot be denied."[1]

Despite the frequent recourse of municipal officials and others to the vaunted value of the autonomy of local government, it remains to be determined whether in the ensuing years there has been any significant shift in the balance as between provincially imposed responsibilities on local governments and the scope within which municipal officials can make decisions with some degree of autonomy.

This dichotomous municipal role, therefore, provides an important part of a framework for examining municipal government and public administration. Another element which needs to be incorporated within this framework is some assessment of the impact of urbanization on the institutional structures and on the decision-making processes of local government. The trends discerned from this overview will be considered in the light of their implications for the role of municipal administrators.

The significance of urbanization for municipal government lies not just in the scale of population growth, although this is not unimportant.

T.J. Plunkett is professor of public administration and director, School of Public Administration; Katherine A. Graham is assistant professor of public administration and director, Institute of Local Government, Queen's University, Kingston.

1 *Canadian Municipal Government* (Toronto: University of Toronto Press, 1954), p. 3.

Rather it is that the process of urbanization results in a more specialized and therefore more interdependent form of human organization, together with a much more complex social system. As a consequence, municipal decision-making, both political and administrative, is significantly affected by urbanization. As Higgins correctly suggests, urbanization raises two kinds of issues:

On the one hand there are urban problems such as transportation, planning, development and housing. Such policy areas tend to be relatively concrete, public and increasingly contentious. The other kind of issues produced by urbanization is stress on the actual decision-making structures and processes of major cities.[2]

This assessment will also provide an indication of developing trends and issues, areas of needed research, and the implications of these for education and training for public administration at the local level of government.

In this article the terms "municipal" and "local" government are used interchangeably.[3] Generally they refer to all incorporated units of local government, of which there are more than four thousand extant in Canada, ranging in population from those with less than 100 in population to a very few with more than one million inhabitants. Here, however, municipal or local government will imply urban municipalities, mainly cities, large towns and metropolitan units, of which there are now well over one hundred with populations exceeding 25,000 with at least twenty-five in excess of 100,000. This is not to suggest that the other units are less important but it is difficult, if not impossible, to deal effectively with both types of governments for the simple reason that the issues and concerns are very different.

The conventional role of municipal government

In part, the conventional view of the role of municipal government has been shaped and influenced by the philosophy of the urban municipal reform movement that was active from the latter part of the nineteenth century to the 1930s. The principal underpinnings of this movement in Canada were derived from the extensive literature developed by municipal reformers in the United States during this period. This is not to suggest that the municipal reform movement in Canada was simply a

2 Donald J.H. Higgins, *Urban Canada: Its Government and Politics* (Toronto: Macmillan of Canada, 1977), p. 163.
3 This reflects colloquial usage. There is a formal distinction, "municipal government" referring only to the municipal corporation and "local government" referring to the municipal corporation plus the myriad of local agencies, boards and commissions.

carbon copy of its American counterpart. What has come to be regarded as the conventional role of Canadian urban municipal government was the result of "factors indigenous to the Canadian political environment and from the influence of the American municipal reform movement."[4]

The expansion of U.S. cities during the latter half of the nineteenth century as the result of large-scale immigration furnished a power base for the emergence of strong political party machines in many large cities. In the view of municipal reformers this resulted in the extensive use of patronage in civic appointments and the awarding of contracts and franchises to party favourites. The resulting inefficiencies and break-downs in civic administration were thus attributed to these evils of politics. As a consequence, the reformers came to believe that politics did not have any place in municipal government. Hence, they advocated the non-partisan ballot and relatively small council elected at large. The institutional changes advocated by the reformers included first, the commission, and later, the council-manager, forms of government with the latter being derived from the corporate model of business enterprise. The aim of these various reforms was to secure a business-like approach to the provision of essential local services in an economical and efficient manner.

The early acceptance of non-partisanship in Canadian local government was closely linked to a belief in the purely service role:

An important strain in the ideology of non-partisanship present in the early thinking on municipal government was the belief that the purpose of local government was to provide services. The idea that ideal government involves administration, not "politics", was natural in these early communities when most important functions were dealt with by senior levels of government, and where the energy of the inhabitants was directed more toward the struggle for survival in an often unfriendly environment than toward internal rivalries.[5]

There were, of course, other considerations imbedded in the early reform movement.[6] Not the least of these was the desire of local elites to reduce popular participation in and control of municipal government and to ensure that it served the objectives of the economic establishment of the time. For the purposes of this article, the reform movement need not be explored further. The important point to be recognized is that it

4 Jack K. Masson and James D. Anderson, eds., *Emerging Party Politics in Urban Canada* (Toronto: McClelland and Stewart, 1972), p. 3.
5 J.D. Anderson, "Non-Partisan Urban Politics in Canadian Cities," in ibid., p. 10.
6 For further elaboration of the Canadian approach to municipal reform, see John C. Weaver, *Shaping the Canadian City* (Toronto: Institute of Public Administration of Canada, 1977); Alan F.J. Artibise and Gilbert A. Stettler, *The Usable Urban Past: Planning and Politics in the Modern Canadian City*, Carleton Library No. 119 (Toronto: Macmillan of Canada, 1979); and *The Canadian City: Essays in Urban History*, Carleton Library No. 107 (Toronto: McClelland and Stewart, 1977).

left a legacy that is still strongly entrenched: a denial of the essentially political nature of much local decision-making. In institutional terms it also left a legacy of municipal structures that have failed to provide for a responsible political executive and a representative municipal council. With few exceptions Canadian city councils are still relatively small and their members elected from large wards or districts. Moreover, few have managed to establish any kind of responsible political executive, the absence of which can lead to continuous tension between the elected council and the appointed administrators, particularly in the area of policy development. If policy development is viewed as the product of an interaction between politicians and administrators and based on some perception of public needs and interests, the question arises as to how policy is initiated under existing institutional arrangements. To whom, for example, does the administrator relate for policy guidance? The mayor or the entire city council? The former (who generally does not have much in the way of formal power as a political executive) may have little support in council while opportunities for conferring with the entire membership of the latter may be few indeed.

In some matters, the administrator may look to a functional committee of the council but this will not necessarily be an effective vehicle for considering a policy issue that involves several functional areas. In such circumstances the municipal administrator is often left with two alternatives: he or she can "sniff the wind" in an attempt to discern the policy thrust most acceptable to the council or take the initiative and eventually risk being identified, both in the minds of the council members and the public, of being a primary source of policy initiation within city hall. Thus, in some cities in recent times administrators have been publicly charged with being too powerful.

The impact of urbanization

What does urbanization mean for the development of municipal government in Canada? First, there is the matter of the scale of urban municipal government. The first census in 1871 revealed that there were only six cities and towns with a population in excess of 25,000 and only one of these exceeded 100,000. This group accounted for less than 9 per cent of the total Canadian population. Forty years later, in 1911, the census showed that there were now fourteen municipalities in the 25,000 and over population category and four of these had a population in excess of 100,000. These fourteen municipalities accounted for nearly one-quarter of the total population.

By 1941 about one-third of Canada's total population of just over 11.5 million resided in some thirty-five cities and towns with populations exceeding 25,000. Four of these were over 100,000 and another four

exceeded 200,000. However, it was in the period following World War
Two that Canada became a predominantly urban nation. Thus, just three
decades later, in 1971, more than 43 per cent of the total population
now lived in some ninety-four cities, each with a population in excess
of 25,000. More striking is the fact that the total population of these
cities was almost equal to the total population of Canada just thirty years
earlier.[7]

By 1976 the number of cities and towns with populations in excess
of 25,000 had increased to 109 and their total population now constituted
more than 46 per cent of the total population of Canada. But it has to be
noted that these census data include only cities and towns. In another
approach, the census defines the urban population as "all persons living
in an area of 1,000 or more and a population density of 386 a square
kilometre." Under this definition in 1976 "over 75.5% of Canada's population lived in an urban environment, with the degree of urbanization
ranging from 37.15 in Prince Edward Island to 81.2% in Ontario." The
most urbanized provinces, under the foregoing definition, were Ontario,
Quebec and British Columbia, all of which exceeded the national average of 75.5 per cent.

The urban population can also be considered in terms of metropolitan
areas. For census purposes a metropolitan area represents "the main
labour market of a continuous built-up area having a population of
100,000 or more."[8] Many such areas include several municipalities and
some may also be subject to a metropolitan or regional form of municipal
government which has responsibility for certain activities over the entire
area. In 1976 more than one-half (55.7 per cent) of Canada's total population was located in twenty-three metropolitan areas.

From the perspective of municipal government the most obvious effect
of this explosive urban growth has been the need to rapidly extend the
traditional range of local services to meet the needs of the new population. But other problems have emerged, which have been brought into

7 *The Canada Year Book, 1916-17, 1932*, and *1952-53* (Ottawa, Dominion Bureau
of Statistics), and *The Canada Year Book, 1978/79* (Ottawa, Statistics Canada). The
census compilation of data for municipalities in terms of population categories is
limited to cities, towns and incorporated villages; but what constitutes a city or town
is dependent upon provincial legislation. Thus the minimum population required for
a municipality to be designated a city varies from province to province. However,
there are other types of municipalities defined in provincial legislation which were
originally intended for non-urban areas. Some of these are now primarily urban in
terms of population size and density but would not be included in the census
tabulations of urban municipalities by population size groups. Thus, for example,
municipal districts in British Columbia, a few townships in Ontario, and the boroughs
of metropolitan Toronto would not be included. Many of these, however, would be
included in the population data relative to metropolitan areas.
8 *Canada Year Book, 1978-79*, pp. 136-37.

sharp focus by this urbanization. These include the control and regulation of development and redevelopment; the excessive escalation of land values; the choice of transportation alternatives between systems that move vehicles or move people; the provision of a new range of community services to meet the demands of urban life; the provision of housing for those individuals whose incomes are at a level that will not permit them to be supplied by the private market; and, finally, the need for effective environmental control. These demands brought pressures to bear on provincial governments, who responded by assuming a more interventionist role in municipal government. All of these issues had important consequences for provincial/municipal relations.

All these issues are vitally related to the determination of the quality of life that can be developed and maintained in any urban community. But decisions in these areas can no longer be determined by the purely administrative or technical criteria which has generally been the basis of traditional local government decision-making. The fact is that many of the issues provoke genuine conflict and controversy, which must therefore be articulated through and resolved by the local political process. Generally speaking, it is the failure of the local political process to provide an outlet for these legitimate cleavages of opinion that has been the cause of many angry confrontations at local municipal council meetings during recent years. Within the local municipal establishment such citizen discontent has all too often been considered a temporary aberration.

The conventional role of local government was based on the assumption that there was a community consensus with respect to the provision of a limited range of services, generally of the physical or "hard" variety and mainly related to property – for example, roads, streets, water and sewerage systems and protective services such as fire and police. This permitted municipal councillors to view their role as that of prudent trustees. Their main aim was to secure economical and efficient administration of these services so that the property owners would not be unduly burdened. It is hardly surprising, then, that this conventional role and the institutional arrangements which supported it have been found wanting in dealing with the value-laden conflicts underlying the issues generated in the modern urban community.

Municipal government has also been affected in other ways by urbanization. Most significant has been the vastly increased expenditure requirements arising from urbanization and the effect these have had on the local government revenue system. In 1951, for example, just three years before Crawford's book appeared, local governments were able to finance more than 60 per cent of their expenditure requirements from

Table 1: *Total Municipal Government Revenues by Source*
Selected years, 1951-1980

Year	Property taxation $ million	(% of total)	Provincial transfers* $ million	(% of total)	Other revenue $ million	(% of total)	Total
1951	468.6	(61.4)	67.7	(8.9)	226.3	(29.7)	762.6
1956	781.3	(62.8)	120.2	(9.6)	343.0	(27.6)	1,244.5
1962	1,379.3	(65.2)	251.0	(11.9)	482.1	(22.8)	2,112.4
1968	2,494.6	(41.7)	2,088.2	(34.9)	1,392.7	(23.3)	5,975.5
1974	4,076.8	(33.2)	5,841.3	(47.6)	2,351.6	(19.2)	12,269.7
1975	4,707.7	(32.0)	7,192.6	(48.8)	2,822.1	(19.2)	14,722.4
1980	8,288.7	(33.3)	11,426.0	(45.9)	5,189.6	(29.8)	24,903.3

SOURCE: *Financial Statistics of Municipal Governments*, Dominion Bureau of Statistics for the years 1951, 1956 and 1962, and *Local Government Finance*, Statistics Canada for the years 1968, 1974, 1975 and 1980. Data for 1980 are estimates.
*Does not include grants in lieu of taxes from provincial enterprises.

the tax on real property, while about 30 per cent came from other local sources (e.g., licence and permit fees, investment income, special assessments, etc.). Transfers from provincial governments accounted for less than 10 per cent of total revenue. Table 1 shows that by 1978 transfers from senior governments accounted for almost half of all local government revenue, and the property tax provided only one-third of total revenue. Thus, over a period of almost thirty years the composition of the local government revenue system has undergone a dramatic shift to the point where government transfers now play a dominant role in the support of local government expenditure requirements.

By far the greatest proportion of government transfers are in the form of conditional or specific purpose grants from provinces to municipalities. In 1980, more than 85 per cent of provincial grants to municipalities were either in the conditional or specific category.[9] This increased dependence on conditional transfers to municipalities was attributable both to provincial desire to sustain minimum standards for particular services and to a recognition of the inability of municipal government to underwrite an expanding range of activities through the property tax. No doubt this recognition was conditioned by political sensitivity to the property tax. As virtually the remaining lump-sum tax, any substantial increase, however necessary and justified, tends to produce a vocal reaction, particularly from individuals on fixed incomes or at the lower end of the income scale. Although generally regarded as an exclusively municipal tax source, about half of its yield is allocated annually to local

9 Canadian Tax Foundation, *Provincial and Municipal Finances 1981* (Toronto, 1981), p. 180.

educational authorities over which municipal governments have no control and for whom they are required by provincial statute to act as simply a tax collection agency.[10]

Implications for local decision-making

The greatly increased municipal dependence on provincial transfers has brought with it extensive provincial intervention in municipal decision-making. Most provincial conditional transfer programs establish minimum service standards or require provincial approval of a municipal program or project before a transfer is allocated. Virtually all provinces now provide a wide range of conditional transfer programs and these are not administered through a single department (e.g., Municipal Affairs), but involve most major departments. Thus, the number and increasing complexity of such programs has created both confusion and tension in provincial/municipal relations.

Provincial financial assistance programs are usually the product of a provincial department initiative in order to secure some degree of uniformity of service standards throughout the province. As a consequence, municipal governments have tended to institutionalize a functional approach to their operations which, in turn, "fuels functional loyalties and perpetuates a compartmentalized approach to provincial/municipal relations." In these circumstances it is not difficult for provinces to "achieve the universal application of a municipally oriented program in a specific functional area" without having to consider if it is "in harmony with the overall priorities of individual municipalities."[11] Alternatively, municipal governments have taken the initiative to secure provincial financing for a specific program, project or activity. However, the conventional municipal wisdom espoused by many provincial associations of municipal governments is that the proliferation of such programs and the assumption by a province of complete or partial responsibility for various locally provided services has created tensions and reduced the effectiveness of local decision-making.

While municipal governments make strong arguments in favour of enhanced local decision-making, the actions of municipal representatives sometimes deny the rhetoric of municipal autonomy. Illustrative of this

10 Since 1980, the Quebec government has assumed major responsibility for funding education. This move was accomplished by a corresponding decrease in provincial/municipal transfers as an impetus to municipal governments assuming full control over the property tax field.

11 Lionel Feldman and Katherine A. Graham, *Bargaining for Cities: Municipalities and Intergovernmental Relations* (Montreal: Institute for Research on Public Policy, 1979), pp. 6-7.

phenomenon is the observation contained in an Alberta report which could be applied also to the municipal scene throughout Canada:

> It is not infrequent that municipal politicians make statements to the effect that local taxes have to rise because the Province will not provide adequate assistance and if the taxpayers do not like it they should complain to their MLA's. Such statements are clear and deliberate attempts to shift the responsibility for local taxation to another level of government and do little to enhance the public perception of the role of local governments. There is much talk by municipal representatives ... about the need for reform of municipal finance in order to promote local responsibility and autonomy, but sometimes the impression is that the municipalities want to continue providing all the services demanded by their citizens without having to face the unpopular task of raising the necessary revenues. Frankly, the expressed intent of municipalities to be responsible and fully accountable for their actions is not always evident.[12]

In these circumstances, municipal governments tend to consider many important decisions entirely in terms of their impact on property taxation. Thus, for example, municipalities are often led to adopt planning and development policies on the sole ground that these might result in an improvement of the property tax base. The primary aim, therefore, is to encourage taxable assessment growth irrespective of undesirable social or economic consequences.[13]

Increased dependence on provincial transfers has helped to distort municipal priorities while dependence on property taxation as the principle source of locally raised revenue has tended to influence unduly planning and development policies. This suggests that the dual purposes of municipal government cited by Crawford over a quarter of a century ago remain. In fact, they have been exacerbated by the process of urbanization to the point where the balance between provincially imposed obligations on municipal government and the scope for relatively autonomous local decision-making has been tipped more heavily in favour of the former. Moreover, concern with the property tax base and the substantial share absorbed by local education authorities has helped to further circumscribe the area of local decision-making. Urbanization has also changed the nature of local government, rendering its conventional role inadequate for modern needs and unable to articulate, let alone resolve,

---

12 *Report of the Provincial-Municipal Finance Council on the Responsibilities and Financing of Local Government in Alberta, 1979*, p. 9. While these observations were intended to represent the views of Alberta municipalities they are often reflected in statements by municipal associations in other provinces.

13 See T.J. Plunkett, *The Financial Structure and the Decision-Making Process of Canadian Municipal Government* (Ottawa: Central Mortgage and Housing Corporation, 1971).

the conflict-ridden and value-laden issues that have emerged in most major urban centres. These themes raise vital questions with respect to the viability of municipal government in the future.

Local government or local administration

Other factors affect the role of local government. As a result of the earlier reform ideology, local responsibilities have become extremely fragmented and a variety of powers given to local boards and commissions. Such bodies are assigned responsibility by the province rather than the local council for specific services such as transit, hydro-electric distribution, parks, recreation, public housing, public health, libraries, etc.[14] While local councils may be required to provide varying degrees of financial support for these activities, they have relatively little ability to control or influence their direction. The effect of this development is to weaken the focus of responsibility and accountability in the local government. Moreover, it has helped to further circumscribe the area of local decision-making and shield certain activities from the wider political process:

... almost invariably, the justification for the creation of such bodies was that they would serve as a means of shielding various municipal functions from "politics". "Politics" in this context did not mean the process of making decision on matters of public policy. That process obviously went on. The only effect of the creation of special boards and commissions was that it helped to restrict decision-making to a small circle of people. The "politics" from which municipal functions were being shielded was not politics, per se, but democratic politics.[15]

Equally important, the existence of these bodies has helped to isolate the citizenry from the decision-making process. This fragmentation creates a context within which people are unaware of who is responsible for what function, or, even, that the function exists in the first place.

Special purpose boards and commissions create another significant political problem:

... often these bodies equate their individual and narrow interest with the general public interest. To the extent that this occurs as a result of insulation, the decision-making integrity of, and popular respect for, multi-purpose municipalities are threatened. The citizen, especially if he has a complaint, understandably tends to seek redress from his alderman. But that official may be powerless to assist if the fault lies with a special body.[16]

14 The establishment of such special purpose bodies is probably most extensive in Ontario and less so in the Atlantic provinces, Quebec and western Canada.
15 T.J. Plunkett and G.M. Betts, *The Management of Canadian Urban Government* (Kingston: Institute of Local Government, Queen's University, 1979), pp. 120-21.
16 Dominic Del Guidice and Stephen M. Zacks, "The 101 Governments of Metro Toronto" in Lionel D. Feldman, ed., *Politics and Government of Urban Canada*, Fourth Edition (Toronto: Methuen, 1981), p. 276.

It is interesting to note that while municipal spokesmen often decry the matter of fragmentation of responsibilities, municipal initiatives for remedial action are extremely rare. In this area municipal governments appear to reflect the same ambivalence we have already noted in their attitude towards their dependence on conditional provincial transfers.

The final point that must be examined is the effect the non-partisan tradition has on the role of local government and, more particularly, the citizens' perception of it. Non-partisanship is generally defended on the grounds that it preserves the independence of councillors who are free to make decisions without the need to compromise. But adherence to the doctrine of non-partisanship may well have an ideological bias in favour of the maintenance of the status quo. Moreover, the staunchest supporters of non-partisanship may form groupings which act like embryonic local political parties.[17]

A locally based responsible political party system is unlikely to emerge under present arrangements in most municipal jurisdictions where the elected council cannot determine or establish an accountable political executive.[18] One of the anomalies of the Canadian approach to urban municipal government is that while there is a strong commitment to responsible parliamentary government at the provincial and federal levels there is continued denial of its applicability, even in a modified form, to urban local government. As a result in most cities there is little coherence or direction to policy-making. Citizens experience difficulty in identifying and holding accountable a "government" and civic administrators frequently fail to obtain any sense of policy direction from their political masters.

The report of a review of the structure of the City of Winnipeg pointed to the lack of an identifiable government:

... the "government" is strictly government being the majority when any given vote is taken. Two successive votes may assemble quite different majorities, neither of which takes responsibility for the policy consistency of the decisions made or the executive follow through on the issues decided.

That is not responsible government; indeed, it is a recipe for irresponsibility. It invites short-sightedness, parochialism and haphazard decision-making. It

17 Examples would be NPA (Non-Partisan Association) which has long exercised a major influence on civic politics in Vancouver, and the ICEC (Independent Citizens Election Committee) which currently exercises a similar role in Winnipeg. See Masson and Anderson, *Emerging Party Politics*, and also *Report and Recommendations of the Committee of Review, City of Winnipeg Act* (The Taraska Report) (1976), and Paul Tennant, "Vancouver City Politics," in Feldman, *Politics and Government*, pp. 126-47.
18 At least two factors contribute to this: the ambiguous position of the mayor who is required to be elected at large but whose duties are primarily ceremonial and the general perception that municipal councils cannot delegate any of their responsibilities.

frustrates intelligent councillors, the administrative staff and the people who require decisions from city hall. It can breed, alternatively, stagnation and chaos in the city's multi-million dollar business.[19]

The Winnipeg report argued for an executive with the responsibility to govern, headed by the mayor who would be chosen by the council from among their members – a radical departure from present practice.

When many of the apparent characteristics of contemporary urban local government in Canada are taken into account (the tendency to adhere to a purely service role, increased dependence on conditional provincial grants, fragmentation of responsibilities, intergovernmental linkages based on professional and functional ties rather than on broad policy issues, lack of policy direction and the failure to furnish an identifiable government), we have to conclude that local governments are adhering to their role as agents of provincial interest to the detriment of their role as interpreters of the local scene. The most pessimistic view would therefore be that the second purpose of local government identified by Crawford nearly thirty years ago has been lost; what now exists may not be local government so much as a complex form of local administration.

Two questions remain: Can the trend be reversed? And what are the implications for municipal administrators?

Prospects and possibilities

If the trend toward provincial government domination is to be arrested or reversed, some of the tensions inherent in the current composition of many Canadian urban centres need to be magnified. As noted earlier, many local issues are value-laden and provoke genuine controversy requiring resolution by the local political process. Therefore, many Canadian local politicians and administrators will find themselves virtually forced to operate in a system which acts as a forum for articulation of local interests and the resolution of important issues. There are a number of factors supporting this suggestion.

Perhaps the first factor generating an increased political role for local government is its traditional property base and the importance of property interests to those in the property-owning classes or those aspiring to join their ranks. The recent meteoric rise (and sometimes fall) of property values in many Canadian cities means that now, more than ever before, acquisition and retention of private property represents the major

19 *Report and Recommendations* (Taraska Report), p. 56. This report noted that Winnipeg, unlike most Canadian cities, had most of the elements necessary for a responsible parliamentary system: a city council large enough to be representative of the diverse parts of the city, with councillors drawn from wards ... small enough to preserve the traditional responsiveness of local government (p. 56).

capital investment of many individuals. Accordingly, interests related to property, the traditional domain of local government, have become increasingly important and will likely continue to be so. Home as castle and the NIMBY syndrome (Not In My Back Yard) have become increasingly prominent themes in local politics.

There are, however, some important differences between the current expression of property interests in Canadian cities and such expressions in the past. In the first place, property interests can now be defined more broadly. Quality of life and ambiance in a neighbourhood can quite possibly have more prominence as local political issues than more traditional property-related matters such as potholes, water or waste disposal. Secondly, the composition of residential property ownership in Canadian cities appears to have become more varied in terms of ethnic distribution and income. This situation may well contribute to further politicization of local issues related to such things as policing, the provision of special education, recreation, and social services.

A second factor resulting in increased pressure for local governments to assume a political role stems from the characteristics of the rental population in urban areas. Along with homeowners, renters also use public parks, public transit and other locally provided services as mainstays of their existence. The rise of tenants' groups in the 1960s is a phenomenon that local governments have not yet completely recognized. While their prominence may fluctuate, the interests of tenants are increasingly diverse and focused at the local level. Moreover, tenants cannot any longer be considered either as persons without a real stake in the community or who cannot afford to own property. Tenants now represent the entire income spectrum and many rent by choice and not by necessity.

It is certainly the case that the scope for local decision-making has become narrower and is now subject to greater influence by provincial governments. Given this trend, it might be argued that it is only a matter of time before provincial governments formally assume local governments' responsibilities. However, few provinces would relish the task of having to undertake everything now assigned to local institutions. In fact, present institutional arrangements furnish at least two important benefits for provincial governments:

- a means of providing a range of services and activities in a variety of communities, each with differing needs, without extending the provincial administrative structures; and
- a means whereby provinces can avoid being held politically accountable for such services and activities provided through the local government system.

In this environment, the provinces have the best of all possible worlds.

They do not have to become involved too directly in the countless decisions that have to be made in dozens of different communities. Moreover, the provinces can, through legislation and the use of conditional transfers, influence the course of local decision-making while at the same time reinforcing a general public perception that the outcomes of such decisions are the responsibility of local decision-makers.

In this context, it is perhaps ironic that a third factor possibly contributing to the development of local government as an agent of local interest is the tendency which some provinces are beginning to exhibit of divesting administrative responsibility for certain "unwanted programs" to the local level but retaining policy control. For example, Ontario has proposed devolution of responsibility for administration of all family benefits programs to the local level. While this shift may mean that local governments become even more the administrative peons of provincial policy-makers, another possibility is that public sensitivity about locally administered programs will force local governments to act more strongly as agents of local opinion in intergovernmental discussions.

In order to do this, most urban governments in Canada would require a major overhaul of their political and administrative machinery. They may have to be pushed, rather than cajoled, into such necessary changes. To date, internal efforts to redefine the role of local government and its institutional apparatus have tended to accept the assumptions of a purely service role that is non-political in character. Thus, with respect to the need for securing better representation of the diverse areas within the larger cities, this matter is approached cautiously and usually rejected on the grounds that any expansion of council membership could make decision-making more difficult or encourage parochial thinking.[20]

Implications for public administrators at the local level

These trends and prospects for Canadian urban governments would seem to propel local government administrators into a situation of conflicting demands. On the one hand, pressure for increased services and more

20 The reports of two recent city-funded studies (in Edmonton and Vancouver) provide an interesting illustration of this restricted nature of attempts at municipal modification. In both reports there is an expression of concern that a representative system based on small wards might lead to parochial thinking. Thus, if a ward system is to be utilized there must be relatively few but very large wards. *Report of the City of Vancouver Governmental Review Commission* (Vancouver: City Hall, 1979) and *Task Force on City Government – City of Edmonton* (Edmonton: City Hall, 1980). Both reports advocated a system of dual election on an at-large and a large ward basis, and both their proposals on arrangements which had evolved in Kansas City. Other proposals contained in both reports were also based on the Kansas City experience. For a commentary on the Vancouver proposals, see Tennant, "Vancouver City Politics," pp. 143-44.

sophisticated services in urban areas has generated administrative interest in streamlining techniques of management and administration with their attendant systems and procedures. Such efforts, although necessary, may contribute to urban administrators becoming remote from public concern or being perceived as so. On the other hand, public pressure concerning local issues has subjected urban administrators to intense scrutiny. The emotionalism surrounding debates over expressways, day care and other matters has sometimes resulted in local administrators being pushed into the limelight and associated with a particular side on specific issues.

Whatever the prospects for Canadian local government, be it increasingly the agent of provincial government or of local political will, the future for urban administrators will not be easy. In general, they lack an identifiable reference point. One moment they are subject to the changing demands of their local councils; the next, they must satisfy the particular administrative requirements of a provincial department; or they must respond directly to a citizen initiative.

Municipal administrators are usually recruited on the basis of their technical or professional specialty. Their subsequent career development has frequently been confined within the department most interested in their expertise, for example, planning, public works, finance, etc. Having reached the senior level of management, many now find themselves operating in a turbulent political climate and a much more intricate network of intergovernmental relationships.

Most local administrators require specific professional development to cope with this unfamiliar multi-faceted role. They need to be drawn out of their specialized disciplines and subjected to professional development activities designed to instil a sense of the role of the public administrator, the specific political context of local government, the intergovernmental aspects of local government and the requisites of management in a complex municipal organization. In short, they need to become generalists in what some see as a specialist age.

The Canadian academic community can play a role in the development of such local administrators. An obvious vehicle is the offering of courses and programs in public administration and local government policy. Equally important is academe's potential research role.[21] For

---

21 For a recent review of Canadian literature on local government, see Donald H. Higgins, "Municipal Politics and Government: Development of the Field in Canadian Political Science," CANADIAN PUBLIC ADMINISTRATION, 22, no. 3 (Fall 1977), pp. 380-401. Since the publication of this article at least two theoretical approaches to local government have been published: Harold Kaplan, *Reform, Planning and City Politics; Montreal, Winnipeg and Toronto* (Toronto: University of Toronto Press, 1982) and Warren Magnusson, "Metropolitan Reform in the Capitalist City," *Canadian Journal of Political Science*, XIV, no. 3 (September 1981), pp. 557-85.

example, there is a need for much more precise information and analysis of the subtleties of municipal intergovernmental relationships. More research on the political and administrative interaction of elected and appointed officials at the local level is also desirable in order to develop a repertoire of specific case studies for teaching purposes. There are many other useful areas for research.[22] As Colton has noted:

The study of urban politics in Canada has recently been characterized as being in transition "from infancy to the early stages of puberty." Some, myself among them, will find this an excessively complimentary progress report. Whether it is on the mark or not, there is no question that the enterprise falls woefully short of the maturity that Canada's status as a society of city dwellers would have us expect.[23]

22 A list of possible research topics in the area of local government finance is set out in Katherine A. Graham, *Local Government Financial Management and Accounting: A Research Framework*, Research Monograph No. 3, The Canadian Certified General Accountants' Research Foundation (Vancouver, 1981).
23 Timothy J. Colton, *Big Daddy* (Toronto: University of Toronto Press, 1981), p. vi.

John W. Langford | **Public corporations in the 1980s: moving from rhetoric to analysis**

A recent press release from the federal Department of Energy, Mines and Resources notes that a bio-mass synthesis gas demonstration project is being undertaken by Biosyn, a general partnership of Canertech Inc. and Nouveler Inc. Biosyn, it was also announced, had just signed a contract with Omnifuel Gasification Systems (OGS). Canertech is a 25 per cent partner with the Ontario Energy Corporation in OGS. Rexfor, a shareholder in Nouveler, will be responsible for wood supply to the project. The research activity will be coordinated by the Institut de Recherche en Electricité du Québec (IREQ), and the National Research Council will be on the technical advisory committee.

Some readers will have recognized the fact that all of the above bodies are public corporations owned, wholly or in part, directly or indirectly, by the governments of Canada, Ontario and Quebec. The communique illustrates vividly the manner in which Canadian governments are continuing to penetrate the workings of the economy (particularly, in recent years, in the energy, natural resource and high-technology sectors), using the corporate form and the complicated structures of direct and indirect public ownership which this penetration has caused. Analogous illustrations could be used to demonstrate the employment, particularly by provincial governments, of public corporations and both non-profit and profit-making quasi-public corporations in the social policy area. The simple message is that in the twenty-five years since the inception of this journal, one of the most fascinating developments in Canadian public administration has been the ardour with which governments have embraced both public and quasi-public corporations (which I refer to simply as public

The author is associate professor, School of Public Administration, University of Victoria. The author gratefully acknowledges the financial assistance of the President's Committee on Faculty Research and Travel, University of Victoria, and the comments on an earlier draft of this paper by a number of colleagues including Ted Hodgetts, Bill Stanbury, Allan Tupper, Mark Sproule-Jones and Jim McDavid.

corporations throughout this paper) as appropriate vehicles for the design, coordination and delivery of economic and social policy.[1]

No essay on Canadian public corporations is complete without an indictment of the relevant academic disciplines for their indifference to this development. Unfortunately, this author is now denied the cathartic pleasure of the lonely scholar. In the last year, two books on government enterprise in Canada have been published, and three more are soon to appear.[2] In addition, the public corporate sector has been given much more extensive treatment recently in business and public administration texts and related journals.[3] By Canadian standards, an industry is being created where before there was only barren acreage worked by the occasional academic claim-staker. Amongst this surge of scholarly production are a number of excellent reviews of the Canadian literature on public corporations and the unfolding of "real world" developments up to the end of 1980. No effort will be made to go over that ground systematically again.

Some of this new wave of observers have argued that the critical focus of attention on public corporations has been far too narrow, fixed on the issues of control and accountability.[4] Alternative agenda of questions to be explored by academics have been suggested. There is no doubt that

1 Public and quasi-public corporations include all corporate organizations with which a government is involved, directly or indirectly, on a *continuing* basis through ownership, sponsorship or funding.
2 Marsha Gordon, *Government in Business* (Montreal: C.D. Howe Institute, 1981): Allan Tupper and G. Bruce Doern, eds., *Public Corporations and Public Policy in Canada* (Montreal: The Institute for Research in Public Policy, 1981); R. Prichard, ed., *Crown Corporations in Canada: The Calculus of Instrument Choice* (Toronto: Butterworths, forthcoming, 1983); and W.T. Stanbury and Fred Thompson, eds., *Managing Public Enterprises* (New York: Praeger, 1982); E.J. Dosman, *The Evolution of Ports Policy in Canada* (Montreal: The Institute for Research in Public Policy, forthcoming).
3 See, for example, Christopher Green, *Canadian Industrial Organization and Policy* (Toronto: McGraw-Hill Ryerson, 1980), chapter 9; V. Seymour Wilson, *Canadian Public Policy and Administration* (Toronto: McGraw-Hill Ryerson, 1981), chapter 12; Audrey D. Doerr, *The Machinery of Government in Canada* (Toronto: Methuen Publications, 1981), chapter 5; R.F. Adie and P.G. Thomas, *Canadian Public Administration: Problematical Prospectives* (Scarborough: Prentice Hall, 1982), chapter 8; John W. Langford and Neil Swainson, "Public and Quasi-Public Corporations in B.C." in O.P. Dwivedi, ed., *The Administrative State in Canada* (Toronto: University of Toronto Press, 1982), pp. 63-87; D.P. Gracey, "Federal Crown Corporations in Canada" in K. Kernaghan, ed., *Public Administration in Canada* (Toronto: Methuen Publications, 1982), pp. 59-70; John W. Langford, "Crown Corporations as Instruments of Policy" in G. Bruce Doern and Peter Aucoin, eds., *Public Policy in Canada: Organization, Process and Management* (Toronto: Macmillan of Canada, 1979), pp. 239-75; Allan Tupper, "The State in Business," CANADIAN PUBLIC ADMINISTRATION, 22 (Spring 1979), pp. 124-50.
4 See, for instance, Tupper, "The State in Business," p. 149.

this criticism is valid and that a future research agenda should include projects designed to examine such questions as the impact of public corporations on society and the so-called mixed economy, and the implications of the wide use of such vehicles for the role of the state in Canada. However, it is equally true that the stubborn fixation in the literature with the issues of control and accountability reflects the legitimate preoccupations of ministers and administrators with running a state apparatus swollen by a burgeoning corporate sector.

This essay – in the very few pages allotted to it by a ruthless editorial staff – briefly reviews the approaches being taken by governments, corporate management and academic analysts to the problem of administering public corporations. The politicians and bureaucrats are portrayed collectively – with no unkindness intended – as schizophrenics, in love with the corporate form as an instrument of public policy on the one hand, and frightened by the possibly dire consequences of its independent action on the other. The former side of the administrator's public personality has led to a vast increase in the employment of public corporations in recent years, while the latter side has spawned the rhetoric of executive control: governments must institute regimes which give them more powers of direction, control and scrutiny over corporations to assure their efficient, effective and accountable performance. Corporation managers have generally adopted a low public profile on the regime issue, but in political battles with their government masters they almost without exception adopt an unrepentant anti-control posture. Turning to the academic literature for discussion of the validity of these antithetical positions provides mixed results. Traditionally, this critical institutional design question has (mea culpa) been poorly served by Canadian academic analysts. However, there are some encouraging signs of the emergence of more robust theorizing and case studies on public corporations which could, with luck, result in some payoffs for administrators. Without a more rational approach to the administration of public corporations by politicians, bureaucrats, managers and academics, the mindless cycle of more public corporations and more government control of them can only lead to further organizational disarray within the Canadian administrative state.

The real world of public and quasi-public corporations

Politicians and bureaucrats must love public corporations because they persist in using them as instruments of public policy. The most casual attention to the media in recent months would suggest the unquenchable enthusiasm with which governments continue to resort to the corporate

form of organization to deliver a good or service. Some illustrations of this contemporary compulsion include:
- the transformation of the post office into a crown corporation, reducing the size of the traditionally defined federal public service by over sixty thousand employees;
- the passage of legislation to turn an existing crown corporation, the National Harbours Board, into a holding company for up to twenty-five local port corporations;
- proposals to create two federal-level state trading firms, Canagrex and a National Trading Corporation, to market agricultural products and commercial goods and services, respectively;
- proposals to make Canada's major airports into crown corporations;
- the establishment of Nova Scotia Resources Limited by the Nova Scotia government.

In addition to starting new corporate ventures, Canadian governments are also continuing to increase their overall corporate involvements through share purchases, takeovers and joint ventures initiated by existing public corporations:
- after a long court battle, the Société nationale de l'Amiente finally gained from General Dynamics a controlling interest in the Asbestos Corporation;
- the Ontario Energy Corporation's purchase of a 25 per cent interest in Suncor gives it a foothold in the oil patch;
- the Société de développement industriel du Québec and the Caisse du dépôt à placement du Québec have increased the Quebec's government's ownership share in companies which are judged to be of strategic significance to the Quebec economy (e.g., Alcan Aluminum, Domtar);
- the Canada Development Corporation and Petro-Canada have purchased controlling interests in companies such as Acquitaine Company of Canada and Petrofina Canada, respectively.

While Canadian governments and their spokesmen seem both incoherent and largely unconcerned about the reasons behind this passion for the corporate form or the effect that it may be having on the shape and nature of the administrative state, they are still filled with fear and loathing about the more immediate impact of the phenomenon on their capacity to govern: This is the essence of the love-hate relationship. Even while embracing corporate instruments with reckless abandon, politicians and administrators have become increasingly preoccupied with "bridling the beasts."[5] What they cherish for its potential for independent, innova-

---

5 A lovely metaphor from G.H. Beatty, "Bridling the Beasts," *Policy Options*, 3 (July/August 1981), pp. 35-38.

tive management, they paradoxically despise because it is outside of their complete control.

It is not without reason that practitioners are of two minds about public corporations. Not only do such corporations all too rarely do precisely what their governments want, but they frequently exhibit signs of mismanagement, and, occasionally, get their political masters and bureaucratic overseers into trouble. Events of the last decade suggest that the deployment of public corporations can create a wide variety of problems for the government responsible for them. We might list some of these problems:

– The untramelled creation, purchase or funding initiatives of individual ministers, public servants and existing public corporations have raised concerns about uncontrolled proliferation. While the federal government acknowledges its involvement in over five hundred public corporations and some provincial governments also number their corporate entanglements in the hundreds, governments at both levels neither know the full extent of their holdings nor have satisfactory means of containing the growth.

– In a related development, the growing incidence of diversification amongst major public corporations, largely through the creation or purchase of subsidiaries, has become a critical issue. The corporations argue that they must diversify, not merely integrate, for commercial survival. Governments fear that diversification will lead to the public purpose of a corporation being lost in the shuffle of a multi-market organization.

– Policy coordination failures have become commonplace as a result of the inability of cross-cutting and competing political, bureaucratic and regulatory structures to provide coherent direction in social or economic policy areas crowded with a wide variety of corporate entities. The confusing spectacle of the federal government attempting to bend the Canada Development Corporation (a mixed enterprise with hundreds of private shareholders) to its economic development priorities illustrates the frustration of policy-makers with the complex instruments they have created. Provincial social policy-makers are experiencing similar frustration in their efforts to assure effective services in the context of a delivery system studded with community-based corporate agencies.

– The increasing financial exposure of governments which are providing loans and loan guarantees to commercial public corporations has also become a source of anxiety. The issue of exposure has assumed prominence recently as a result of growing concern in a period of recession that billions of dollars of government loans cannot be repaid and that government guarantees may be activated.

– There have been substantial political costs associated with the tendency of public corporations to engage in commercial practices and activities (e.g., bribery, false invoicing) which may be commonplace in the market environment in which they operate, but are anathema to a public body.

– There have been insistent demands for stronger accountability linkages between the legislature on the one hand, and the ministers, bureaucrats, directors and managers involved in the operation of public corporations on the other.

– Uncertainties and controversy about the efficiency of corporations have raised questions about the putative benefits of the corporate form.

– Confusion concerning the legal status of public corporations with respect to their incorporation, taxation, prosecution and regulation has become a major problem. Issues related to the legal status of corporate employees as public servants have also arisen in the context of the trend to unionization of such employees, especially in provincial social service corporations.

The "Sturm und Drang" over privatization as a panacea for the ills besetting the public corporate sector seem to have largely passed into history.[6] The more common response of most Canadian governments in recent years has been to continue to pay lip-service to the need for corporate autonomy and initiative, but to demand significantly increased direction, control and scrutiny powers over public corporations than the limited financial control powers which they have traditionally been accorded. Details of the various reform proposals put forward by governments, auditors general and royal commissions since the mid-1970s are widely available and have been reviewed in the literature.[7]

There are two distinct approaches to regime-building which have received attention from Canadian governments in recent years. What might be labelled the "Saskatchewan model" is based on the establishment of a government holding company for the coordination of public corporations, affording the board of the holding company – made up of

6 The major example of the theory being put into practice, the privatization of the British Columbia Resources Investment Corporation, revealed long-run political costs which had not been anticipated at the outset. See T.M. Ohashi and T.P. Roth, *Privatization: Theory and Practice* (Vancouver: The Fraser Institute, 1980).

7 Accounts of recent federal proposals are available in Tupper and Doern, "Public Corporations and Public Policy in Canada," in Tupper and Doern, eds., *Public Corporations and Public Policy in Canada*, esp. p. 50; and John W. Langford, "The Identification and Classification of Public Corporations," CANADIAN PUBLIC ADMINISTRATION, 23 (Spring 1980), pp. 76-104. For examples of recent provincial regime-building activities, see also Gordon MacLean, *Public Enterprise in Saskatchewan* (Regina: Crown Investments Corporation of Saskatchewan, 1981); and Government of British Columbia, Ministry of Finance, *Discussion Paper: A New Financial Administration Act* (Victoria; August 1980).

ministers – strong powers of policy direction, financial control and scrutiny. The board becomes effectively a cabinet committee on public corporations. Ministers also serve on the boards of the various corporations, usually as chairmen. Accountability to the legislature is through the ministers, but legislative scrutiny of the performance of corporations is effected also through the operation of a standing committee on crown corporations, similar in structure to a public accounts committee. Recent announcements from the newly elected government of Manitoba indicate that it is preparing to adapt the Saskatchewan model to its particular requirements.

The other approach might be called the "Ottawa model." In it, public corporations are attached to the government through various portfolios and responsible ministers. The powers of direction, control and scrutiny over them are divided amongst the responsible minister, his department, the treasury board, comptroller general, department of finance, and relevant cabinet policy committees and secretariats. While there is usually no central agency devoted solely to the administration of corporations under this model, more recent proposals focus significant power on the treasury board and the economic development ministry. The extent of government's powers and their distribution are usually determined by the placement of a corporation in a classification system which, ideally, would locate all public corporations within a comprehensive set of schedules. Beyond the involvement of the auditor general, the Ottawa model makes no special provisions for either accountability to the legislature or legislative scrutiny, both of which tend to be underdeveloped, in part because of the number of players potentially involved in corporate decision-making.

Some of the recent proposals for the reform of the Ottawa model would strengthen the legislature's role vis-à-vis public corporations, but the central thrust is to upgrade government's authority in corporate decision-making by giving various components within the government increased or more effective powers in the following areas:
– appointment and dismissal of board members of parent corporations;
– clarification of the corporation's mandate and role;
– authorization of subsidiary creation, purchase or disposal;
– establishment of policy direction;
– approval of corporate plans and budgets;
– approval of borrowing proposals;
– efficiency and effectiveness evaluation;
– establishment of management practices (e.g., accounting and auditing procedures, dividend policy, reporting and disclosure procedures, rights and obligations of board members, commercial practices).

A variety of systems and techniques (e.g., the "single window," contracts, directives, compensation, memoranda of understanding, comprehensive audits) have been suggested to effect the shift in power from the corporation to the government, but the direction of the shift is always the same.

The trend towards increased government control has met with considerable opposition from the management of corporations, whose vision of appropriate power-sharing with government – driven largely by the private sector rhetoric of managerial freedom, innovation and accountability to customers or clients – remains almost diametrically opposed to recent proposals and government initiatives. Corporate opposition to the Privy Council Office's Blue Paper (entitled "Crown Corporations: Direction, Control and Accountability") and Bill C-27 (the subsequent crown corporation legislation) in Ottawa was a significant factor in the government's decision not to reintroduce the legislation after it died with the Clark government in late 1979. When the British Columbia government recommended an ambitious variation on the Ottawa model in a discussion paper in 1980, the howls of protest from the boards and managements of corporations forced the government to shelve its proposals. They have yet to reappear. When Ottawa attempted to increase its control over Canada Development Corporation decision-making by parachuting in a strong government supporter as chairman of the board, the corporation opposed the appointment and, in the end, prevailed. Rape crisis centres in British Columbia prefer to lose their funding rather than submit to the evaluation procedures laid down by the government in their annual contract.

Both the political clout of corporate management and the tendency of governments to assume powers "informally" when formal regime changes are delayed are two noteworthy features of recent efforts by Canadian governments to increase their power vis-à-vis public corporations. In the long run, however, the most significant aspect of recent developments may be the tendency of governments largely to ignore the rhetoric of corporate boards and managers, and instead to follow blindly the logic of their own rhetoric, which dictates that increasing their power in corporate decision-making is the only feasible way to deal with the corporate jungle which they have created. The problem is that the positions of both sides are largely driven by unsubstantiated myth. In the end, this becomes not much more than an empty battle of words which begs the question: Is it possible to move beyond rhetoric and argue on the basis of descriptive theory and case studies that one form of regime rather than another for a certain type of public or quasi-public corporation will lead to more efficient, effective and accountable performance? For help with this dilemma, one turns naturally to the academic literature.

The changing academic perspective

Until recently, the literature on the administration of Canadian public and quasi-public corporations has not offered much hope of analytical deliverance from the rhetorics of control dividing politicians and bureaucrats from board members and corporate managers.[8] Research has been narrowly focused on wholly owned or "crown" corporations, and the overviews and case studies have – by necessity, often, in view of the dearth of publicly available data – been largely descriptive in character. Commentaries on existing and proposed regimes of direction, control and scrutiny have been, for the most part, the territory of political scientists and lawyers – concerned about the viability of our system of responsible cabinet government and, at heart, outraged by the injury and untidy adjustments which the world of "structural heretics" is inflicting on the departmentally oriented concepts of ministerial responsibility and upward accountability. This is not to argue that the traditional analytical framework ignored the potential impact of regimes of direction, control and scrutiny on the efficient and effective performance of the corporation. The need to balance the demands for accountability with the need for unfettered and innovative corporate management has always been recognized, but the framework – rooted in the examination of formal authority structures – has lacked the analytical tools to examine these questions in anything but the most intuitive manner. There has been, for instance, little cross-pollination between the work of economists on the efficiency of public corporations and the traditional analysis of regimes.

Overall, academics, like practitioners, have been slow to recognize that the creation of control regimes is part of a much more complex institutional design question, involving the establishment of relationships between the characteristics of a particular corporation (e.g., age, size, task, financial dependency), the environment in which the corporation operates (e.g., the market place, the regulatory setting *and* the regime of direction, control and scrutiny itself), the behaviour of internal corporate actors (e.g., directors, managers) and the performance of the corporation (expressed in terms of values such as efficiency, effectiveness, and accountability). Looked at in this way, a regime of direction, control and scrutiny can be seen as one of several possible independent variables, the alteration of which, in interaction with other variables, will affect the efficiency, effectiveness and accountability of the public corporation.

Some recent literature provides grounds for optimism that the tradi-

8 For a review of the traditional literature, see Tupper and Doern, "Public Corporations and Public Policy," and Langford, "Crown Corporations as Instruments of Policy."

tional approach to the analysis of regimes of direction, control and scrutiny can be strengthened in three key areas.

1/ The analysis of the characteristic of public and quasi-public corporations and the environment in which they operate

Provoked by the Lambert Commission Report and British and American literature on quangos and the "contract state," efforts have been made to look more closely at structural heretics in corporate dress at the provincial and federal levels.[9] This endeavour has proceeded down three paths: the identification and description of the wide variety of public corporations; investigations of the rationales for the creation of this chaotic corporate universe; and less-developed attempts to use the analysis of corporate and environmental characteristics as a basis for classification and regime design.

The results of the first line of inquiry have been spectacular. The scope of investigation of the public corporate sector has widened enormously, focusing attention on the familiar wholly owned or crown corporations with varying degrees of commercial purpose, wholly owned corporations with no commercial purpose; (e.g., hospitals, universities); mixed or joint enterprises in which a government is either directly or indirectly through a holding company a part owner with other governments and/or private participants in the form of large numbers of shareholders or small numbers of corporate shareholders; vast arrays of subsidiary, sub-subsidiary, and associated corporations of wholly owned and joint enterprises in which government has some degree of indirect ownership interest; a mixed bag of profit-making and non-profit corporations regularly funded by government through fees, grants or contracts, usually to provide social or medical services, and, at the farthest reaches of the quasi-public corporate sector, "chosen instrument" or "sole sourcing" corporations.[10] In addition, efforts have begun to collect and analyse more data concerning the significance of the public corporate sector (in terms of indicators such as assets, sales revenue, employment, degree of private funding, unionization, etc.) relative to the rest of government and the relevant areas of the economy and society in which they operate.[11]

9 The Royal Commission on Financial Management and Accountability, *Final Report* (Ottawa: Department of Supply and Services, 1979), Part IV; Christopher Hood, "The World of Quasi-Government," paper prepared for presentation at the annual conference of the Public Administration Committee, York, September 1979; B.L.R. Smith, ed., *The New Political Economy: The Public Use of the Private Sector* (London: Macmillan, 1971).

10 See Langford, "The Identification and Classification of Federal Public Corporations"; John Shepherd, "Hidden Crown Corporations: The Private Corporation as a Chosen Instrument," paper presented to IRPP conference on Crown Corporations, Ottawa, October 1980.

11 See Tupper and Doern, "Public Corporations and Public Policy," pp. 3-10; A.R.

Growing appreciation of the diversity, size and significance of this corporate universe has also sparked renewed interest in the rationale question. The traditional "pragmatism," political culture and political economy explanations for the employment by Canadian governments of corporate instruments have been supplanted or supplemented by more finely tuned hypotheses – often with more predictive potential. Tupper has identified a number of fields of activity in which Canadian governments have been generally more inclined to resort to a corporate form of public ownership.[12] Marsha Chandler has looked at the historical data being developed on the use of public corporations by provincial governments in an attempt to establish the effects of political partisanship on the development of state enterprise.[13] Borcherding draws on property rights theory to argue that the choice of public ownership by government is a reflection of either the high monitoring costs associated with the use of other instruments (e.g., contracting out, subsidization, regulation) to deliver the desired policy, or the superiority of public enterprise as a vehicle for redistribution.[14] Also in the property rights/public choice mode, Trebilcock and Prichard developed a framework of analysis which attempts to explain and predict "instrument choice" through an exploration of the interaction between "fields of activity" variables and characteristics of a public corporation.[15] This ambitious effort brings together in one framework a large number of the explanatory variables which have been applied in isolation elsewhere, and also provides an intriguing check-list approach for decision-makers concerned about the appropriateness of resorting to the use of a public corporation in a particular set of circumstances.

Finally, the collection of data on the characteristics of public corporations is having a significant impact on efforts to classify them. While traditional analysis in the past has been critical of classification schemes that inappropriately group corporations for purposes of the establishment

---

Vining and R. Botterell, "An Overview of the Origins, Growth, Size and Functions of Provincial Crown Corporations," and John W. Langford and Kenneth J. Huffman, "The Uncharted Universe of Federal Public Corporations," both in Prichard, ed., *Crown Corporations in Canada*, chapters 4 and 5. See also J.L. Howard and W.T. Stanbury, "Measuring Leviathan: The Size, Scope and Growth of Governments in Canada," paper presented at the University of Lethbridge, April 1982.

12 Allan Tupper, "The Nation's Business: Canadian Concepts of Public Enterprise" (Ph.D. thesis; Queen's University, Kingston, 1977).

13 Marsha Chandler, "The Politics of Public Enterprise" in Prichard, ed., *Crown Corporations in Canada*.

14 Thomas E. Borcherding, "Toward a Positive Theory of Public Sector Supply Arrangements" in Prichard, ed., *Crown Corporations in Canada*.

15 M.J. Trebilcock and J.R.S. Prichard, "Crown Corporations: The Calculus of Instrument Choice" in Prichard, ed., *Crown Corporations in Canada*.

of regimes of direction, control and scrutiny, the basis of the criticism has always been intuitive. Ideas emanating from organization theory suggest ways in which the data being gathered on corporate and environmental characteristics (e.g., market place, age, size, task, technical systems, etc.) can be used for purposes of classifying public corporations and regime design. Corporations could be grouped on the basis of a cluster analysis of characteristics which are deemed to be relevant (in terms of impact on performance) to the structuring of organizations and their external control.[16] This approach would encourage the exploration of the interaction between "fixed" environmental features such as the regulatory framework within which a corporation operates and aspects of the regime (e.g., ministerial directive power); or between characteristics of the internal structure of the corporation (e.g., degree of centralization or decentralization) and the degree of external control by the government acting as shareholder.[17]

2/ The description and analysis of corporate management

The traditional approach to analysis of regimes of direction, control and scrutiny tended to be founded on strong views about the way boards of directors did and should operate, and on the place of senior managers in the decision-making process. However, these views were generally based on ideas drawn from poorly researched private sector analogies, formal roles as set down in legislation and intuitive evidence. There was no concerted effort to examine the actual behaviour of directors and managers, informal power structures and linkages, or the impact of management behaviour on corporate performance. Essentially, regime design and critique proceeded on the unspoken premise that directors and managers were robots who would subscribe to the mandate dictated by government and follow the rules set down in the formal regime, and – inevitably – perform efficiently. The generally secretive and uncooperative attitude of public corporate managers in Canada assured the perpetuation of this mythology by discouraging research access to corporate decision-making in the public sector.

Organization theorists and public choice/property rights analysts have suggested some innovative ways of conceptualizing corporate decision-making, and, particularly, the behaviour of public corporation managers

16 See Langford, "The Identification and Classification of Public Corporations," pp. 80-87.

17 See the general hypotheses concerning the relationship between environment, external control and structure in Henry Mintzberg, The Structuring of Organizations (Englewood Cliffs: Prentice-Hall, 1979), chapters 15 and 16; Jeffrey Pfeffer and G.R. Salancik, The External Control of Organizations (New York: Harper and Row, 1978); and L. Karpik, ed., Organization and Environment (London: Sage, 1978).

and directors which may assist regime analysts to rise above the myth of the public manager as either a public interest or free enterprise robot. Both schools of thought direct their attention to the impact of the incenive structures and constraints flowing from the internal characeristics of the corporation, the wider environment in which it operates and the specific regime of direction, control and monitoring established by the owners or funders on the behaviour of public enterprise managers and directors. They stress that these constraints and incentives will often be different from those affecting their private corporate counterparts.

The property rights school, at the most simplistic level, argues that because of the diffusion of effective ownership of public corporations across the electorate and the lack of equity involvement of the manager – the bureaucrats and their political masters – the incentives and constraints which would tend to make the manager take risks and behave in an efficient and innovative manner are significantly diminished. Complementing this deductive approach, the public choice theorists generally examine the specific utility functions of public managers and the constraints which they face, and from this base hypothesize that the manager's emphasis on "pay, power, and prestige", "independence" or "survival" inevitably leads to inefficient managerial behaviour and various forms of overproduction or inefficient allocation of resources by the enterprise.[18] More sophisticated statements of public choice/property rights theory suggest that the inevitability or degree of inefficient managerial behaviour is dependent on a variety of factors which can alter the utility functions of managers. Consider the following hypotheses:

– The more private the character of the goods produced, the more able the manager is to recover the cost of production through fees, and the more likely he is to do so to increase his independence from government funding.

– Competition in the marketplace serviced by the enterprise will tend to increase the efficiency of the manager.

– Public enterprises in smaller jurisdictions (provinces, municipalities) will be more easily monitored by shareholders or their representatives, and therefore management will be more efficient.

– Managers of public enterprises which transcend political jurisdictions are more likely to act efficiently through the realization of economies of scale.

– Managers of commercial public enterprises faced with clearly defined

---

18 See Borcherding, "Public Sector Supply Arrangements," Section IV; and J.R. Baldwin, *The Regulatory Agency and the Public Corporation: The Canadian Air Transport Industry* (Cambridge, Mass.: Ballinger, 1975).

economic goals are more easily monitored and tend, therefore, to behave more efficiently.[19]

The organization theory discipline has, to date, taken a less overt interest in the operation of public corporations in Canada than has the property rights/public choice school. However, the discipline has drawn on a wider array of descriptive theories capable of supporting case studies and generating hypotheses and complex utility functions concerning the patterns and motivations of public corporate management behaviour. The following suggests the kind of findings which a more concerted application of management science approaches might substantiate:

– A study of board members of Canadian public corporations indicates that directors do not play a major role in the decision-making, and relate this failing, in part, to the government's patronage abuses under regimes where the appointment power resides with the cabinet.[20]

– Raiffa suggests that when boards do become involved in corporate decision-making they will be more likely to act as a bargaining forum for a wide variety of interests than as an integrated entity reflecting "corporate" or "government" interests.[21]

– Zif explores the possibility that the behaviour of public enterprise managers is dependent on the degree to which he or she is oriented to business or political goals. He postulates that an increase in political orientation enlarges the likelihood that: sales rather than profit goals would be emphasized; low prices relative to costs would be charged; goals would be relatively unstable; goals would be stated in unclear or vague terms; performance evaluation would be carried out on an irregular basis; public support would be sought prior to action; and top management would be recruited from the public sector.[22]

– Aharoni postulates causal connections between environmental and internal characteristics of the corporation (e.g., financial independence, degree of government ownership, costs associated with monitoring man-

19 These hypotheses are put forward in Michael Denning, "The Public Ownership of Productive Resources: An Economic Analysis of Public Enterprise," a paper prepared for the annual meeting of the Western Political Science Association, San Diego, March 1982.

20 J. Peterson, *Canadian Directorship Practices: A Critical Self-Examination* (Ottawa: Conference Board in Canada, 1977), chapter 12; see also Canada, Ministry of Transport, *Air Canada Inquiry Report* (Ottawa: Information Canada, 1975), chapters 5 and 13.

21 Howard Raiffa, "Decision-Making in the State Owned Enterprise" in Raymond Vernon and Yair Aharoni, *State Owned Enterprise in the Western Economies* (London: Croom Helm, 1981), chapter 3.

22 Jehiel Zif, "Managerial Strategic Behaviour in State-Owned Enterprises – Business and Political Orientations," *Management Science*, 27 (November 1981), pp. 1340-47.

agerial behaviour) and the degree of "managerial discretion" exhibited by public managers.[23]

– Some empirical evidence is available concerning the difference between the goal orientations of directors and managers in public corporations: the former tend to be motivated by social responsibility and focus on socio-political goals, while the latter are motivated by self-interest and emphasize goals related to commercial objectives when involved in corporate decision-making. A causal relationship between organizational roles and attitudes is postulated.[24]

– Weaver demonstrates an admirable eclecticism in his study of Amtrak and the CNR, drawing on

> theories of bureaucratic politics and organization as well as theories of the firm to argue that differences in public enterprise behavior result to a large degree from variations in two constraints imposed by the owning government: the nature of the state-owned enterprise's financial dependence on government and the government's "command structure" for the enterprise. These constraints are likely to force upon state-owned enterprises one of two very different strategies: either to maximize their autonomy from government, or maximizing political support (survival) through a process of coalition building. Only under special circumstances will an enterprise have strong incentives to use "the public interest" as a guide in decision-making.[25]

Regardless of the validity of the theories and hypotheses outlined above, they are clearly addressing questions which are of immense significance to analysts and designers of regimes of direction, control and scrutiny. The linkage between regime design and management behaviour is critical. An understanding of the behaviour of managers and board members in a variety of environmental and structural settings opens up the prospect of creating regimes which, whatever their merits from the accountability perspective, do as little violence as possible to the values of efficient and effective management.

23 Y. Aharoni, "Managerial Discretion," in Vernon and Aharoni, *State Owned Enterprise in Western Economies,* chapter 13.

24 Miriam Dornstein, "Managerial Theories, Social Responsibility, and Goal Orientations of Top-Level Management in State-Owned Enterprise," *Journal of Behavioural Economics,* 5 (Winter 1976), pp. 65-91.

25 R. Kent Weaver, "The Politics of State-Owned Enterprise: Government Constraints and Corporate Strategies," paper prepared for the annual meeting of the Canadian Political Science Association, Montreal, June 1980, pp. 1-2. This eclecticism is also present in J.J. Richardson, "Problems of Controlling Public Sector Agencies: The Case of Norwegian Oil Policy," *Political Studies,* 29 (March 1981), pp. 35-50; J.J. Anastassopolous, *La Stratégie des Enterprises Publiques* (Paris: Dalluz, 1980); and R. Mazzolini, *Government Controlled Enterprise* (London: Wiley and Co., 1979).

3/ Talking about and measuring performance

The use of public corporations and the characteristics of regimes of direction, control and scrutiny within which they are to be managed are often justified in terms of performance values such as efficiency, effectiveness and accountability. The traditional analysis of regime design both by academics and practitioners makes regular reference to these values, arguing, for instance, in favour of contracts with quasi-public service corporations or comprehensive external auditing for quasi-commercial corporations on the grounds that such instruments, included in the appropriate regime package, will enhance efficiency or accountability. The problem here has always been that there is very little agreement on what "good" performance (in the context of these values) looks like or how it can be measured. Consequently, the descriptive and normative analysis of regimes is carried on without any consensus about how to address the issue of the ultimate purpose of the organizational design exercise.

This problem is least severe with respect to accountability. In the context of preserving the Canadian version of responsible cabinet government, there is some agreement on what satisfactory accountability would look like for wholly owned corporations. However, this consensus does not extend to cover the other components of the public and quasi-public corporate sector which were outlined earlier. There is, for instance, no established tradition of demanding that quasi-public service corporations be held to account at all. The uncertainty in these greyer areas is undoubtedly related to the widespread reluctance to examine the more fundamental issue of whether upward accountability and ministerial responsibility – two fundamental building blocks of the Westminster model – are anything more than anachronisms in the modern administrative state.

With respect to the values of efficiency and effectiveness, the issue is the relevance of the proposed measures to multiple goal corporate entities. The public administration literature is bulging with methodologies and critiques associated with the definition and measurement of efficiency and effectiveness – most recently grouped under the rubric of comprehensive auditing – and the application of various techniques to public and quasi-public corporations has been suggested. Where the corporation is an enterprise, analogous to a private sector firm, the most common approach has been to focus on its efficiency in terms of measures such as profit, marginal cost pricing, rate-of-return on investment, and total factor productivity.[26] A substantial literature (largely in the public choice/

26 See, for instance, W.G. Shepherd, "Public Enterprises: Purposes and Performance, and Strategy and Structure," and A.Y. Lewin, "Public Enterprise, Purposes and Performance: A Survey of Western European Experience," in Stanbury and Thompson, eds., *Managing Public Enterprises.*

property rights tradition) records studies which have been made of the efficiency of the commercially oriented public corporations – on the basis either of comparisons with analogous or competing private firms or theoretically derived ideal levels of performance.[27] While the thrust of these studies is that public corporations must be and are inefficient and wasteful (either relatively or absolutely), a harder look at the data suggests to some analysts that the results are inconclusive or ambivalent, regardless of whether the public corporations are operating in a monopolistic or competitive market place.[28] The inappropriateness of simple efficiency measures for public and quasi-public corporations is reflected in the misleading fixation with waste in the type of study noted above and the irrelevance of such measures to corporations delivering more overtly public services (e.g., education, health care). The obvious move is to some recognition of social benefit, and the measurement of efficiency either through the exploration of the relationship of dollar costs to "output measures of a physical or index nature" (i.e., cost-efficiency approaches as practised in departmental program evaluation) or through measures of the "absolute value" of the service based on demand information gained through pricing techniques (direct or imputed) or the use of a Clarke tax.[29] The former rejects "bottom-line" accounting, while the latter attempts to retain it.

The recognition that the output of a public corporation – virtually by definition – contains some social benefits (or there would be no point in having it public) forces into the open the fact that public corporations almost inevitably have multiple goals. It is this phenomenon more than anything else which must be clarified in the discussion and measurement of efficiency and effectiveness. Introducing mechanisms such as "compensation" for the pursuit of non-economic goals does not allow the monitors of efficiency to return to simpler measures; it merely deflects difficult calculations of the relationship between dollars and social benefits to a different forum. The discussion and measurement of effectiveness (the relationship between the desired output and the benefits received) or cost-effectiveness, already intrinsically difficult due to uncertainty, the unavailabiilty or high cost of data, and high manpower requirements, is

27 See Borcherding, "Public Sector Supply Arrangements"; C. Eckel and A. Vining, "Toward a Positive Theory of Joint Enterprise," in Stanbury and Thompson, eds., *Managing Public Enterprises*, and D.W. Caves and L.R. Christensen, "The Relative Efficiency of Public and Private Firms in a Competitive Environment: the Case of Canadian Railroads," *Journal of Political Economy*, 88 (October 1980), pp. 958-76.
28 See M. Denning, "Public Ownership of Productive Resources," pp. 29-35.
29 See, for example, W.G. Shepherd, "Public Enterprise in Western Europe and the United States" in the H.W. de Jong, ed., *The Structure of European Industry* (The Hague: Martinus Nijhoff, 1981) pp. 289-320; and J. Cutt, "Accountability, Efficiency, and the 'Bottom Line' in Non-Profit Organizations," CANADIAN PUBLIC ADMINISTRATION, 25 (Fall 1982).

further complicated by the problems associated with ranking goals and establishing the rules for making trade-offs in conflict situations in which, not only are there multiple goals, but there are also multiple proponents or principals to interpret or set goals.[30]

Obviously, the identification and measurement of good performance for public and quasi-public corporations is not a problem which will be solved overnight. However, the fact that the task is difficult is not an excuse for continuing to accept platitudinous statements. The clear danger is that without a more sophisticated approach to the concept of performance in the context of multiple goals and proponents, there will be an acceptance by academics and practitioners of simplistic criteria such as profit or labour productivity, and a consequent reduction in concern about social output. Alternatively, a "soft" approach to the measurement of social benefits creates the potential for unnecessarily inefficient performance in their name. Furthermore, as the discussion of management behaviour has already suggested, because of its linkages to goals, the concept of performance adopted becomes a key factor in our understanding and manipulation of the relationship between corporate environment (including the regimes of direction, control and scrutiny), internal corporate characteristics, management behaviour, and performance.

Concluding observations

The lesson to be drawn from recent developments is that the administration of Canadian public corporations can and should be approached more rationally and systematically in the future by politicians, bureaucrats, managers and academics. Ideally, politicians and bureaucrats would be persuaded that if it makes political sense to employ public corporations as instruments of policy, it also makes political sense to try to create an environmental setting which will optimize their performance rather than merely falling back unthinkingly on increased control as a cure-all for what is intuitively seen to be inadequate performance. Similarly, corporate managers would be persuaded to discard their traditional "hands-off" rhetoric and explore the proposition that the environment, incentive and constraints which affect them as participants in the public corporate decision-making process are not and *should* not be the same as those affecting their private counterparts. It would be unkind, but not inaccurate, to note that to the degree that their private sector counterparts have accepted the contemporary concept of corporate social responsibility,

30 Y. Aharoni, "Performance Evaluation of State-Owned Enterprises: A Process Perspective," *Management Science*, 27 (November 1981), p. 1342.

they have themselves discarded the "free" enterprise myth to which public sector managers continue to cling. Finally, in this ideal world, academics have an obligation to move beyond description and myth to examine and operationalize the type of institutional design hypotheses which have been outlined above. They also would be expected to extend to the classroom the intellectual eclecticism required to move research on the public corporate sector to a new plane. It is inappropriate to continue to suggest to students that decisions about regime design for non-departmental agencies can be made with only passing reference to the realities of corporate management behaviour and the values of efficiency and effectiveness. The administration of public and quasi-public corporations deserves more sophisticated analytical attention.

Richard Schultz # Regulation and public administration

A student of Canadian regulation confronts immediately a fascinating paradox. On the one hand, regulation has long been a fundamental weapon in the arsenal of governmental power in Canada, indeed so fundamental that it has been described as "the hidden half of government."[1] On the other hand, students of Canadian politics and specifically public administration, until very recently, have largely ignored this subject area. In this respect, Krislov's comment about bureaucracies is most apt for regulatory activities and processes: they are "the late bloomers of modern political structure. They grew silently, inexorably in the underbrush – seldom noticed, little analysed."[2]

This paradox is currently being confronted, however, as more students and scholars – some undoubtedly following the "intellectual polls" and recognizing a hot political topic – not only show an increasing awareness of the salience of the issues raised by government regulation but more significantly are prepared to follow up that awareness with a commitment to undertake research in the field. Consequently much of the "underbrush" is in the process of being cleared. Notwithstanding this most welcome change, it seems fair to suggest that the academic study of regulation in Canada, particularly that in public administration and political science generally, is still very much in its early stages. Accordingly, this review article cannot follow too closely the editorial format suggested.

In particular, any attempt to review the literature would be most premature at this stage for it could not avoid emphasizing more what is not, rather than what is, known. The approach of this paper, therefore, will

The author is director of the Centre for the Study of Regulated Industries and associate professor in the Department of Political Science, McGill University.

1 G. Bruce Doern, ed., *The Regulatory Process in Canada* (Toronto: Macmillan, 1978), p. 1.
2 Samuel Krislov, *Representative Bureaucracy* (Englewood Cliffs, N.J.: Prentice Hall, 1974), p. 40.

be first to concentrate on major current developments and problems and to review the literature from this perspective and secondly, and more extensively, to identify those areas and issues where research should be undertaken.

Before turning to these aspects, several introductory comments are in order, some providing background commentary on the study of regulation and others more germane to the scope of this review. The first point to be made is that it is instructive to note that by far the largest component of recent research on regulation in Canada has been government or quasi-government inspired and funded. The federal Department of Consumer and Corporate Affairs, the Science Council of Canada, the federal Law Reform Commission and, most notably, the Economic Council, particularly in its Regulation Reference, have all been instrumental in the phenomenal increase in research in regulation in the last few years.[3]

Without stipulating a cause-and-effect relationship in light of the preceding, the second dominant characteristic of available research is the very strong emphasis on the substance of governmental regulatory activities rather than on regulatory processes and techniques. While there are, of course, some major exceptions to this bias, it is worth noting that it represents what the Standing Joint Committee on Regulations and other Statutory Instruments criticized as an all too common bias in Canada, namely "to assume that the means employed to achieve the ends of policy are of little consequence and a mere matter of administrative convenience."[4] The committee went on to note that this "is a criticism which can be directed not only at well intentioned and hard pressed servants of the Crown but also at commentators and academic political scientists who find the policy content or ends of subordinate law fascinating and the propriety of the means to achieve those ends of little consequence." The relevance of this comment to students of public administration should be apparent.

It is also of direct relevance to the scope and concentration of this paper. Although several Canadian public administration specialists, most notably Bruce Doern, have contributed valuable studies of substantive regulatory policy issues, this paper will largely ignore those studies in order to concentrate on those issues of more immediate relevance to the concerns of public administration rather than public policy more gen-

3 A comprehensive bibliography is to be found in W.T. Stanbury and Fred Thompson, *Regulatory Reform in Canada* (Montreal: Institute for Research on Public Policy, 1982).
4 House of Commons and Senate, Joint Standing Committee on Regulations and Other Statutory Instruments, Thirty-Second Parliament, *Fourth Report*, in Senate *Debates*, 17 July 1980, p. 759.

erally.[5] Moreover, the constraints of space, as well as the author's competence, given the magnitude of government regulation, compel a concentration on a limited sector of government regulation, namely that by agencies which possess some degree of institutional autonomy or independence. In other words, departmental regulation which is the primary, but not exclusive, instrument for so-called "social regulation," such as in health, safety, product quality and environmental matters, will not be discussed.[6] Finally, similar constraints will force an emphasis on federal rather than provincial regulation. These emphases should not be interpreted as suggesting that either departmental or provincial regulation is of little consequence. Rather they merit reviews on their own; the former constitutes the most significant growth area in regulation while the latter provides an opportunity for some very useful interprovincial and federal-provincial comparative studies of many of the issues to be surveyed below.

Current developments and problems

From the perspective of public administration, only two issues have received any sustained degree of attention from researchers or governments. The first is the debate that has emerged about political control over, or alternatively, the accountability of, regulatory agencies. The second, which derives from the claim that regulatory activities are too costly, involves the development of various cost-benefit tools for the assessment of such activities and the concomitant debate over the merits of employing such tools. We shall discuss these in turn. Before doing so, however, it is worth noting one area where, although the problems are identifiable and persistent, they have not received a commensurate degree of attention. The area in question is that of the relationships between the federal system and government regulation, and particularly the significance for public administration of the impact of the federal system on regulatory activities and *vice versa*. Given the increased attention paid to regulation in the past decade, this was surely one area calling for research. This was particularly the case since the "burden of overlapping federal and provincial jurisdictions" was one of the two fundamental issues that prompted the creation of the recently completed

5 See, for example, G. Bruce Doern, "The Political Economy of Regulating Occupational Health: the Ham and Beaudry Reports," CANADIAN PUBLIC ADMINISTRATION, 20, no. 1 (Spring 1977), and "Science and Technology in the Nuclear Regulatory Process: the Case of Canadian Uranium Mines," ibid., 21, no. 1 (Spring 1978), and G. Bruce Doern *et al.*, *Living with Contradictions: Health and Safety Regulation and Implementation in Ontario*, Study No. 5, Royal Commission on Asbestos (Toronto: the Commission, 1982).

6 For a good study of departmental regulation, see W.T. Stanbury and Susan Burns, "Consumer and Corporate Affairs: Portrait of a Regulatory Department," in G. Bruce Doern, ed., *How Ottawa Spends Your Tax Dollars* (Toronto: James Lorimer, 1982).

Regulation Reference of the Economic Council of Canada. Despite the centrality of this concern, the Economic Council in both its reports and its research almost completely ignored this part of its mandate.[7]

Regulatory agency accountability

A recent study for the Law Reform Commission concluded that "the political theory underlying the adoption of an independent regulatory model was never fully thought through, or, when it was thoroughly examined the political implications of its adoption were either not given a uniform interpretation or not unanimously accepted."[8] This is a particularly apt observation. It is germane to what is perhaps the one area of government regulation that has received considerable academic and public scrutiny, namely the nature and scope for agency independence and the various mechanisms and their effectiveness for ensuring that, in our parliamentary system, politically accountable authorities are ultimately responsible for "political" decisions. In fact, it would be accurate to state that the largest component of the literature relevant to public administration concentrates on these issues. Academic students in several disciplines, particularly law and political science, have developed general assessments of the effectiveness of existing accountability regimes and these have been supplemented with numerous case studies of conflicts involving accountability and independence issues. It is worth noting that on this topic the academic literature to a large degree preceded the public debate, indeed encouraged it, and then focused the analysis and assessment of various reform proposals. Subsequent to the academic research, the Law Reform Commission, the Privy Council Office, the Lambert Royal Commission on Financial Management and Accountability, the Parliamentary Task Force on Regulatory Reform and most significantly the Economic Council in its interim report for the Regulation Reference entitled *Responsible Regulation*, have all emphasized in varying degrees the centrality of the accountability issue in any discussions of, and prescriptions for, regulatory reform.[9]

7 See T. Enemark, "Reforming Regulation: A Federal-Provincial Affairs Perspective," *Canadian Public Policy*, 13 (Winter 1982), pp. 40-44.
8 Lucinda Vandervort, *Political Control of Independent Administrative Agencies* (Ottawa: Law Reform Commission of Canada, 1979), p. 9.
9 The primary public sector reports on this topic are: Royal Commission on Financial Management and Accountability, *Final Report* (Ottawa: Minister of Supply and Services, 1979); Economic Council of Canada, *Responsible Regulation* (Ottawa: Minister of Supply and Services, 1979); Law Reform Commission of Canada, *Independent Administrative Agencies* (Ottawa: Minister of Supply and Services, 1980); and Parliamentary Task Force on Regulatory Reform, *Report* (Ottawa: Minister of Supply and Services, 1981). For academic analyses of the accountability issues, see H.N. Janisch, "Policy Making in Regulation: Towards a New Definition of the Status of Independent Agencies in Canada," *Osgoode Hall Law Journal*, 17, no. 1 (April

In terms of the specific issues involved in the general accountability debate, two in particular stand out. The first pertains to the statutory mandate of the agencies, the nature of, and scope for, "policy-making" discretion thereby delegated and how that discretion can be effectively confined and structured by accountable political authorities. The debate has been lively on the merits and demerits of the concept of a "policy directive." By means of a directive, the cabinet would be empowered to rank alternative and potentially competing goals as well as to offer interpretations of such goals and the regulatory agencies would be bound to treat such directives as authoritative and binding as the statutes themselves.

The federal government over the past half-decade has proposed that a directive power be incorporated in statutes governing the transportation, communications, energy and nuclear regulatory commissions. While the principle has been endorsed by academics as well as the Economic Council, the Law Reform Commission and the Lambert Commission and many other commentators, there is widespread concern about specific aspects, in particular how the directive process itself should be structured and how much discretion should be delegated to the government of the day to be able, in effect, to amend statutes. The debate has concentrated not on the principle but on what the appropriate roles of the agency, the public and Parliament itself should be in the process. Rather than being prepared to share its powers in the directive process, the government has been inclined in the face of protest to withdraw the proposal or where there is insufficient pressure to push on with its original proposal.[10] To the extent that the power of directive is ensconced in statute, future students will have ample opportunity to assess how it has been implemented and whether the fears of its critics were merited.

One of the primary objections to the directive proposal relates to the second aspect of the accountability issue. That aspect is the provision for various types of appeals from regulatory decisions to the cabinet. Although the "political appeal" mechanism is distinctively Canadian inas-

---

1979); C. Lloyd Brown-John, *Canadian Regulatory Agencies* (Toronto: Butterworths, 1981); J.E. Hodgetts, "Government Responsiveness to the Public Interest: Has Progress been Made?", CANADIAN PUBLIC ADMINISTRATION, 24, no. 2 (Summer 1981); Richard Schultz, "Regulatory Agencies in the Canadian Political System," in Kenneth Kernaghan, ed., *Public Administration in Canada*, 3rd ed. (Toronto: Methuen, 1977), pp. 333-44; and Richard Schultz, "Regulatory Agencies and the Dilemmas of Delegation," in O.P. Dwivedi, ed., *The Administrative State in Canada* (Toronto: University of Toronto Press, 1982), pp. 89-106.
10   It appears that the Privy Council Office, however, is considering another attempt to integrate a broad-based directive power without any of the checks that almost all advocates on that power have recommended. See Privy Council Office Review Group on Regulatory Reform of Crown Agencies, "Final Report," November 1981.

much as it is not available to either American or British political authorities (or indeed most provincial governments), we have not had an extensive analysis of how it emerged and evolved.[11] In terms of current problems, two issues are central. The first concerns the procedures to be followed in appeals to cabinet.[12] At present there are no firm procedures that guarantee those who may have participated before the agency in the first place any role in the appeal process. They are not assured that their position will be presented to cabinet or an opportunity given to answer the positions of other participants. To put the situation in its starkest relief, contrary to the agency process which must respect "natural justice," before cabinet political factors account for all. This situation has been criticized by many, including the Lambert Commission, the Economic Council and, in one instance, the Federal Court. One of the most pressing issues, therefore, is the extent to which the political appeal process can be opened up so as to respect the interests of affected parties as well as the members of cabinet. This will surely become even more pressing in future years if use of such an appeal mechanism continues to grow.

Closely related to the procedural issues involved in the political appeal process is a question of whether such an appeal should not be abolished altogether.[13] This question is linked to the preceding discussion concerning the introduction of a policy directive. The essence of the debate for proponents of abolition is that if the government possesses the power to issue a policy directive prior to a decision then it should not possess a power to have a "second go" after the regulatory body has made a decision. The argument is that such a second go will demoralize both the regulators and affected parties, except, of course, those successful in the appeal. On the other hand, those who defend maintenance of an appeal to cabinet even with a directive power do so on the grounds that

---

11 For two preliminary discussions, see Albert S. Abel, "Appeals Against Administrative Decisions: III. In Search of a Basic Policy," CANADIAN PUBLIC ADMINISTRATION, 4, no. 1 (Spring 1961), and Arthur R. Wright, "An Examination of the Role of the Board of Transport Commissioners for Canada as a Regulatory Tribunal," CANADIAN PUBLIC ADMINISTRATION, 6, no. 4 (Winter 1963). One of the interesting aspects of the development of the political appeal mechanism is that S.J. McLean, the author of the two reports which led to the creation of the Board of Railway Commissioners, did not include such a mechanism in his initial report but did so in his second. Aside from this anomaly, which has not yet been explained, the reports are worthy of an extensive study in themselves. The reports, written in 1899 and 1902, are found in the House of Commons, No. 20a, 1-2 Edward VII, 1902, *Sessional Papers*.
12 For a discussion, see the articles by Janisch cited in footnote 9 and T. Gregory Kane, *Consumers and the Regulators* (Montreal: Institute for Research on Public Policy, 1980), esp. chapter 4.
13 Both the Lambert Commission and the Economic Council as well as several academics have recommended the abolition of political appeals if a directive power is introduced. The Parliamentary Task Force on Regulatory Reform advocated their maintenance even with a directive power.

cabinet, being ultimately responsible to Parliament, must continue to have a review power. While the issues have been raised and defined, it remains to be seen, if and when a directive power is introduced, how the two powers co-exist. This will surely provide opportunity for further study.

Regulatory costs and benefits

The second, indeed the primary, issue that has captured the attention of regulatory reformers is that of the costs and benefits of regulation. The issue here is whether the social and economic benefits of regulating programs and activities are commensurate with their associated social and economic costs. Much of the push for regulatory reform, particularly one variant – namely, deregulation – has been premised on establishing that in many instances the costs far outweigh any benefits. For students of public administration who are interested in the evaluation of government activities, the resulting debate over cost-benefit analysis in its various forms is instructive.

In the first place, given the competing and conflicting political values and philosophies at issue, there are important principles involved, the most important of which is the neutrality of cost-benefit analysis. Those who seek to defend government regulatory activities often take the position that, while costs should not be ignored, an emphasis on counting costs and benefits may be fundamentally flawed. The flaw results from a bias which can readily identify costs but cannot so easily capture benefits. In the words of one such American critic, "given the state of economic art, mathematical cost-benefit analyses are about as neutral as voter literacy tests in the Old South."[14]

The second issue, not unrelated to the first, is more practical. There is debate whether it is possible in practice to develop the tools for establishing and measuring the costs and benefits of regulation. In this respect, the debate has something in common with earlier, though more comprehensive, efforts such as management by objectives and PPBS to monitor the efficiency and effectiveness of government programs.

At present, the regulatory arena is providing the most recent laboratory for the evaluation and assessment of government programs. Starting in 1976, the Treasury Board and the Department of Consumer and Corporate Affairs undertook a study of the feasibility of employing cost-benefit analysis to government regulations. This culminated in a 1978 decision to establish a "socioeconomic impact analysis" program for all

14 Mark Green, quoted in Suzanne Weaver, "Inhaber and the Limits of Cost-Benefit Analysis," *Regulation* (July/August 1979), p. 14. See also, Steven Kelman, "Cost-Benefit Analysis – An Ethical Critique," *Regulation* (Jan./Feb. 1981) and letters thereon in subsequent issues.

new, major regulations in the areas of health, safety and fairness regulation, i.e. "social" regulation.[15] More recently, the Economic Council has recommended that this program should be expanded to provide an analysis of the economic impact of all new regulations, economic as well as social.[16] Finally, the Joint Standing Committee on Regulations and other Statutory Instruments has proposed that prior assessment should include not only the economic impact but the policy impact of regulations.

The assessment of the costs and benefits of regulatory activities may confront the same obstacles, and the same end, of prior attempts to undertake similar assessments. In time the assessments will themselves require assessment and evaluation. It would be premature at this stage to offer any conclusions about their utility. Students of public administration undoubtedly have a role to play in monitoring the performance of the assessment program and in providing evaluations of its effectiveness.

A research agenda

In a field of study as diverse as public administration, research agendas tend to be highly idiosyncratic. This being the case, it would seem appropriate that the underlying selection criteria should be identified. In the case of the agenda that follows, two basic criteria have been instrumental – the political and the institutional features of the regulatory process. The emphasis on the political nature and significance of regulatory agencies and processes is derived from my perspective in which regulatory agencies are seen to be the result of, and participants in, the political process.[17] They are centrally involved in politics and policy-making. In some respects this political view of the regulatory process is similar to recognition of the political role of the larger administrative world. In others it is unique to agencies which are delegated powers in a highly exceptional manner for our parliamentary system. The second criterion pertains to the unique institutional characteristics associated with regulation by agency, especially the collegial nature of agency decision-making. For a student of public administration, the administrative and political consequences of institutional design must surely be central. In what follows, although a host of research issues could have been identified, only five of the most important in terms of the two criteria are discussed.

15 See the "Series of Studies on Government Regulatory Activity" published by the Treasury Board and Consumer and Corporate Affairs in 1977-1980. On the impact analysis program, see Treasury Board of Canada, *Administrative Policy Manual*, chapter 490 (Ottawa, December 1979), especially Appendix E. According to an anonymous referee of this article, it is noteworthy that only three socioeconomic import analyses have been completed in the first four years of the program.
16 Economic Council of Canada, *Responsible Regulation* (Ottawa: Minister of Supply and Services, 1979), chapter 6.
17 See Schultz, "Regulatory Agencies and the Dilemmas of Delegation."

Origins of the commission form

Although our first independent regulatory agency, the Board of Railway Commissioners, was created only sixteen years after its American counterpart, it is somewhat disconcerting to note that we have yet to produce a comprehensive account of the origins of any of our agencies.[18] We do not have anything comparable to the classic American studies such as Cushman's *The Independent Regulatory Commissions* or Bernstein's *Regulating Business by Independent Commission*.[19] We need Canadian equivalents not simply to fill gaps in our historical knowledge, although I believe filling such gaps is worthy enough reason for undertaking the task; rather, I believe that historical analyses of the origins and administrative evolution of our regulatory agencies can contribute to an understanding of contemporary policy issues and to the general debate about the nature, role and value of regulation in Canada.

In undertaking such studies, researchers can be guided by a rich set of hypotheses developed in the American literature as well as studies in Canada of other forms of institutional innovation. Three particular competing explanations stand out in the literature. The first is the functional specialization hypothesis which argues that agencies, like other innovations, result from the emergence of a new task which existing institutions are incapable of handling.[20] In the case of regulatory agencies, it is claimed their development was necessary because neither the courts nor the legislatures nor cabinets could cope with the new function.[21] The alternative hypotheses which have provided much of the focus, as well as the heat, for the current debates over deregulation, involve competing views of the importance of the "public interest" versus the power of "private interests."[22] In short, we have a wealth of theories, partial and whole, yet a dearth of empirical research in Canada. Given the increasingly common view of regulatory agencies as part of the larger political

---

18   On the BRC and its successor, see Wright, "Role of the Board of Transport Commissioners," and A.W. Currie, "The Board of Transport Commissioners as an Administrative Body" in J.E. Hodgetts and D.C. Corbett, eds., CANADIAN PUBLIC ADMINISTRATION (Toronto: Macmillan, 1960), pp. 222-40. For a useful preliminary attempt in Canada, see Carman D. Baggaley, *The Emergence of the Regulatory State in Canada 1867-1939* (Economic Council of Canada, Regulation Reference, Technical Report No. 15, September 1981).
19   Robert E. Cushman, *The Independent Regulatory Commissions* (New York: Oxford University Press, 1941) and Marver H. Bernstein, *Regulating Business by Independent Commission* (Princeton: Princeton University Press, 1955).
20   This hypothesis is advanced, for example, in J.E. Hodgetts, *The Canadian Public Service* (Toronto: University of Toronto Press, 1972) particularly in chapter 7.
21   See the McLean Reports.
22   The debates are admirably summed up in Barry M. Mitnick, *The Political Economy of Regulation* (New York: Columbia University Press, 1980), chapter 3. See also Robert Cairns, *Rationales for Regulation* (Economic Council of Canada, Regulation Reference, Technical Report No. 1, October 1980).

process, it would be valuable to know what forces and interests shaped their emergence and the nature of powers assigned to them. A natural extension of such research would be to analyse the evolution of these agencies, paying particular attention to the changing nature of their responsibilities and powers and their relationships with other key participants in the regulatory process.

Regulatory agencies and their political environment

The concern for the relationships among agencies and key external actors in the regulatory process leads us to the second area that calls for research. If regulatory agencies are born of politics, as two of the three preceding hypotheses predict, and if they are delegated significant powers affecting the interests of both the regulated and their customers, not to mention society generally, then it follows that they will exist within an environment that can be expected to be rife with political conflict and controversy. Consequently a central research interest must be how regulatory agencies operate within that environment. More specifically, the concern is how do regulatory agencies as institutions persist and then how do they protect and possibly enhance their organizational mission. Equally important is how and why they lose power. These questions are vital to students of regulatory agencies because the answers can illustrate important themes about the nature of the administrative process, especially the inter-organizational dynamics and the relationships between public and private power.

Without attempting to develop an elaborate research agenda on this topic, some questions can be identified. The significance of these questions can be highlighted by reference to specific incidents involving regulatory agencies. The first question is fairly straightforward – namely, what are the sources of political support that regulatory agencies can draw on? The American literature here is replete with references to the "iron triangle" of agency-congressional-regulated interest relationships, but it is obvious that such triangles are unlikely to develop in Canada given the different institutional system. Accordingly, if agency persistence and enhancement is to occur one needs to examine the relationships between agencies and a diverse group of actors such as departments, regulated interests, public interest groups, the media, and parliamentarians. In addition, research should focus on the role of expertise as a source of political support. Associated with the question of support is that of the nature of the strategies employed by regulatory agencies to marshall and exploit such support, especially when their "missions" are threatened or they seek to expand. Finally, given the author's argument that the regulatory function is multi-dimensional, research is needed on how the evolution of regulatory functions has affected the sources and patterns of political support.

Three examples can be briefly introduced to illustrate the significance of the preceding questions. The first concerns the 1943-44 decision by the Board of Transport Commissioners to grant Canadian Pacific Airways a licence in violation of explicit government policy.[23] The result was that the government introduced legislation to strip the board of its air responsibilities and to create a new regulatory agency with only an advisory role. The facts of this case are well known. What has not been analysed are the politics involved. Did the BTC simply commit administrative suicide? Did it misread its position vis-à-vis key political actors, notably the cabinet and Trans Canada Airlines? Did it overestimate the perceived political strength of Canadian Pacific? In short, there is a valuable case study waiting to be written about the BTC–CP Air decision from the perspective of the relationships between the regulator and its key political constituencies.

A similar study needs to be undertaken of the 1976 decision to transfer telecommunications regulation from the Canadian Transport Commission to an expanded CRTC. This transfer challenges basic hypotheses in the bureaucratic and regulatory politics literature. Was the transfer voluntary or not? Why did the CTC, not known to be modest or ineffective in its defence of its territorial imperatives, not contest the transfer?[24] Furthermore, the transfer goes directly against the conventional wisdom found in theories about agency-industry relationships. The telecommunications transfer should be all the more intriguing to students of the politics of administrative systems because it preceded a successful defence by the CTC of its jurisdiction against a "raid" by the Department of Transport. The department, seeking to redress the errors of 1967, introduced legislation that would establish the minister and his officials as the primary sources of policy-making in the transport sector. The attempt would have been successful had it not been for the broad-based industry support that developed for maintaining the institutional status quo.[25]

Numerous other examples could be cited, but the preceding should suffice to justify the contention that the dynamics of agency interactions with key actors in their environment merit research attention. At a mini-

23 See D.C. Corbett, *Politics and the Airlines* (Toronto: University of Toronto Press, 1965) and John Baldwin, *The Regulatory Agency and the Public Corporation* (Cambridge, Mass.: Ballinger, 1975).

24 See John W. Langford, *Transport in Transition* (Montreal: McGill-Queen's University Press/IPAC, 1976) and Richard J. Schultz, *Federalism, Bureaucracy and Public Policy* (Montreal: McGill-Queen's University Press/IPAC, 1980).

25 The legislation and industry responses are discussed in Trevor D. Heaver and James C. Nelson, "The Role of Railway Regulation in National Policy in Canada," *Journal of Transport Economics and Policy*, 14 (1980).

mum, a focus on agency-industry relationships can illuminate in one arena some of the dynamics of what Hodgetts identified as a commonplace feature of the modern administrative state, namely the growth "in the *direct* exchanges between the public service and its clients . . . that supplants or supplements the conventional, indirect methods of routing demands through the more visible, representative institutions."[26] Such a research focus in particular can aid in our understanding of the relationships between public and private power and private and public purpose. Moreover, research that concentrates on commission-constituency relationships is relevant to wider concerns about institutional design. Such relationships may, for example, be largely responsible for the federal government's decisions to create several non-independent regulatory agencies in the past few years such as FIRA and the Petroleum Monitoring Agency.

Commissions and collegial decision-making

Although a central focus of public administration has long been on the significance of structure and organizational design, it is remarkable that this has not resulted in attention being paid to what is perhaps the single most important characteristic that distinguishes regulation by commission from almost all other components of the administrative system, the collegial nature of agency decision-making. With very few exceptions, agency decisions are the responsibility either of panels of commissioners or of the commission as a whole. Yet I know of no study in Canada that has attempted to address the significance of this feature of the regulatory process.[27] This has not been the case in the United States where study after study has criticized the collegial nature of regulatory decision-making and claimed that it is a crucial determinant of the perceived inadequacies of regulatory performance.

Only recently have such critiques been challenged and found wanting by David Welborn in his masterful study, *The Governance of Federal Regulatory Agencies*. In this study, Welborn defined his central analytical problems to be the following: Within these organizations, who may be said to regulate and on what basis? What are the relevant capacities and effects of chairmen, commissioners and staff, and how do they interact in processes leading to critical regulatory determinations? He then

26   J.E. Hodgetts, *The Canadian Public Service*, p. 346.
27   For two preliminary discussions, see John D. Hylton, "Collegial Decision-Making," in Seminar for Members of Administrative Tribunals (March 1979) *Selected Proceedings* (Ottawa: Law Reform Commission, 1979), and Harry J. Boyle, "The Chairman as Chief Executive Officer," ibid. (March 1980), *Speakers Remarks and Excerpts from Discussion Periods* (Ottawa: Law Reform Commission of Canada, 1980).

developed a more detailed set of questions which are worth repeating at length:

What resources do chairmen and members have to influence agency activity? What are the constraints? How do sets of resources and constraints play against one another to produce certain results? To what extent is the distribution of influence in regulatory agency governance stabilized and institutionalized? What, in general, can be said as to the potency of the *positions* of chairman and member, as contrasted with the potency of individual incumbents? . . .

To what extent does the commission form constrain policy and program coordination, adaptability, appropriate allocation of resources and agency activism? What are the implications of patterns of governance for the concepts of collegiality and independence and for understanding and improving regulatory performance?[28]

If there is one basic area of commonality in Canadian and American regulatory agencies, it is with respect to collegial decision-making. An attempt to replicate Welborn's study in the Canadian context, therefore, would make an important contribution to our knowledge and understanding of this vital characteristic of the regulatory process.

Regulation and public enterprise

If the preceding research topic is one shared by Canadian and American regulation, this is one that gives rise to the greatest difference between the two regulatory systems. Every major sector of regulated activity at the federal level is characterized by the presence of a crown corporation. One consequence has been that the regulatory system has normally been tilted in favour of the crown corporation. At the outset, for example, the government-owned Intercolonial Railway was not subject to the authority of the Board of Railway Commissioners. The CBC for many years was both regulator and competitor and continues to enjoy special status under regulation.[29] Until 1977, Air Canada had a similar privileged position vis-à-vis its regulator and its competitors.

While these facts have long been known, we have little research on the actual impact of the mix of private and public enterprise under regulation on the nature of regulatory goals or on the dynamics of the regulatory process. In terms of some of our earlier discussion, given the "chosen instrument" status of crown corporations, there has been an immediate impact on the range of objectives pursued via regulation. More specifically, regulated sectors involving crown corporations have been charac-

28 David M. Welborn, *The Governance of Federal Regulatory Agencies* (Knoxville: University of Tennessee Press, 1977), p. 13.
29 See Frank W. Peers, *The Politics of Canadian Broadcasting 1920-1951* (Toronto: University of Toronto Press, 1969) and *The Public Eye: Television and the Politics of Canadian Broadcasting 1952-1968* (Toronto: University of Toronto Press, 1979).

terized by a much wider set of non-economic, social objectives and this fact accounts for the limited relevance of much of the American literature, particularly that of economics, to the debates over the merits of deregulation. Similarly, regulating a crown corporation may shape the dynamics of the regulatory process and the consequent relationships. It is not idle, for example, to speculate that in Canada for many years the "iron triangle" consisted of the regulatory agency, the government department and the crown corporation. An alternative hypothesis that may be particularly relevant in view of the reluctance to embrace the deregulation ideology in Canada is that the demand for deregulation has been undercut by a realignment of political forces with the crown corporation an active ally of private sector participants. A final hypothesis is that a crown corporation, with its own concerns about its degree of independence from government, may prove to be a willing and useful ally for a regulatory agency with similar concerns.

Regulation and compliance

There is ample evidence in recent years that problems involving compliance with regulatory orders and decisions are emerging as important aspects of the regulatory process.

A few examples will illustrate some of the issues. Miners and lumberjacks have chased out of their camps members of the RCMP intent on seizing their illegal television satellite-receiving antennas (prompting one wag to say that the RCMP may always get their man but they can't get their dish). In the field of cable television, the Quebec government in the mid-seventies provided equipment and used the provincial police force to aid and abet a Quebec-licensed cable operator's efforts to frustrate the CRTC. In atomic energy regulation, a federal official has claimed that Ontario Hydro was able to disregard Atomic Energy Control Board regulations in a manner that would prompt a public outcry if it was attempted by a private enterprise.[30] Even without these highly publicized, possibly exceptional, examples, other incidents involving more normal, presumably routine, situations could be cited.

If regulation is the "hidden half" of government, then compliance is the ignored half of the regulatory process. The preceding examples, however, suggest that this ignorance should be attacked.[31] Compliance processes and politics raise significant issues for our understanding of regu-

30 See the *Globe and Mail*, August 9, 1979, p. 2.
31 I am grateful to John Langford for suggesting the importance of this topic and for drawing to my attention the draft working paper by Howard R. Eddy entitled "Sanctions, Compliance Policy and Administrative Law" prepared for the Law Reform Commission of Canada. Steven Kelman's *Regulating America, Regulating Sweden* (Cambridge, Mass.: The MIT Press, 1981) emphasizes the importance of compliance politics in the study of government regulation.

latory agency behaviour and the complex of relationships within which that behaviour occurs. Many of the concerns identified with respect to prior topics can be phrased in terms of compliance policy issues. Among these would be the nature of agency compliance and sanction powers, the enforceability of regulatory goals and public policies in face of external change, the distribution of political power within the regulatory system and the potential for selective or discriminatory enforcement, and finally agency reliance on other governmental actors for enforcement and the impact of this reliance on compliance strategies and sanction decision-making.

Conclusion

All specialists are inclined to reduce and redefine the world to fit their particular perceptions of what is important. In the case of public administration and the study of regulation, the argument here is that such a process may not be completely invalid. While some of the issues identified in this review are intrinsic to the regulatory process itself, many others are relevant to much larger concerns. Certainly this is the case for the issues of accountability, the growth of regulation and its effectiveness evaluation and the general issues of the dynamics of the regulatory process. If research on some of these topics is undertaken, the findings should help us grapple with more general issues about the nature of the administrative state and the roles of public and private power in our society. In this review the emphasis has been on the need for research. One hopes that the current interest in regulation is not simply faddish and that for the golden anniversary of *Canadian Public Administration*, the next reviewer will be able to report that the research has been undertaken and has indeed contributed to an appreciation of these issues.

René Dussault
Louis Borgeat

Le droit administratif: une réalité omniprésente pour l'administrateur public

Les normes juridiques occupent une place de plus en plus importante dans les administrations publiques modernes. Pendant longtemps, ce phénomène a caractérisé certaines sociétés européennes, qui étaient dotées d'un système de droit administratif autonome et complet, distinct du droit judiciaire ordinaire. Aujourd'hui, il s'étend à toutes les sociétés développées, y compris celles qui, comme la nôtre, appliquent à l'administration publique essentiellement le même droit qu'aux particuliers.

Créée par un Parlement souverain, la loi est toujours apparue comme le fondement même de nos sociétés démocratiques. De nos jours, toutefois, les normes juridiques prennent des formes plus variées : réglementation, jurisprudence des tribunaux judiciaires et administratifs et, depuis peu, directives administratives. Ces formes connaissent un essor tel qu'elles en sont venues à encadrer de façon très précise l'action des administrateurs publics, en particulier celle des gestionnaires. L'insertion dans la Constitution d'une Charte des droits liant les gouvernements ne fait que renforcer cette omniprésence du droit.

Dans un tel contexte, le gestionnaire ne peut pas adopter une attitude indifférente ou négative à l'égard du droit et de ses diverses manifestations. Récemment, on soulignait avec justesse que « dans un régime où le droit constitue le langage par excellence de l'activité politique et le principal instrument de régulation sociale, la méconnaissance du droit chez les citoyens et la méfiance qu'ils entretiennent encore à l'égard de tout ce qui relève du domaine juridique affectent les fondements mêmes de la démocratie ».[1] Cela est encore plus vrai du gestionnaire public, car, dans notre régime constitutionnel, le gouvernement et l'administration publique sont assujettis à la « Rule of law », c'est-à-dire au principe de la légalité. Le droit établissant le cadre de son action, l'administrateur public doit bien connaître les bases de cette discipline, au même titre

Les auteurs sont avocats et professeurs à l'Ecole nationale d'administration publique, à Sainte-Foy, Québec.

1 Jean-Guy Belley et Pierre Verge, professeurs à la Faculté de droit de l'Université Laval, *Au fil des événements*, 21 janvier 1982, p. 7.

que les parlementaires. Il doit, en particulier, en connaître les sources, la portée, l'objectif fondamental et les nouvelles orientations.

Les sources du droit administratif

Le droit comporte essentiellement deux grandes divisions : le droit public et le droit privé. Le droit privé régit les relations des individus entre eux alors que le droit public régit l'organisation et le fonctionnement de l'Etat ainsi que ses relations avec les citoyens. Il se divise en un certain nombre de grandes catégories, telles que le droit international public – qui régit les relations entre les Etats – le droit criminel et pénal, le droit administratif et le droit constitutionnel. Alors que le droit constitutionnel est relativement stable, du fait qu'il prévoit l'infrastructure même de l'Etat, le droit administratif présente un caractère essentiellement évolutif. Ce droit administratif a comme source la Constitution bien sûr, mais surtout les lois, les règlements, les directives administratives et les décisions des tribunaux. S'y ajoutent, bien qu'elles soient de moindre importance, la prérogative royale, la coutume et la doctrine.

La Constitution, dans tout pays démocratique, est la loi fondamentale. Dans plusieurs pays où le droit est d'inspiration britannique, la Constitution comporte des éléments écrits et d'autres non écrits. Les premiers se trouvent dans des textes de loi, les autres dans des conventions constitutionnelles. Le Canada et les Etats membres de la fédération n'échappent pas à cette règle. C'est une loi du Parlement de Westminster, datant du 29 mars 1867 et entrée en vigueur par proclamation le 1er juillet de la même année, qui leur sert de Constitution. Cette Loi constitutionnelle de 1867,[2] à laquelle s'ajoutent un certain nombre d'autres lois du même nom, constitue la norme juridique suprême que doivent respecter aussi bien le Parlement du Canada que celui des membres de la fédération lorsqu'ils adoptent des lois. Cette loi fondamentale a trois objectifs majeurs : indiquer qui exerce les pouvoirs législatif, exécutif et judiciaire de l'Etat, déterminer le partage des compétences législatives entre les deux ordres de gouvernement et, enfin, donner aux citoyens des garanties juridiques en matière de religion et de langue. Le nombre des droits individuels garantis par la Constitution s'est grandement accru par l'adoption de la Charte canadienne des droits, insérée dans la Loi constitutionnelle de 1982.

La loi est l'expression de la volonté politique des représentants élus de la population dans ce qu'elle a de plus stable.[3] Elle transcende les programmes politiques, les « livres » de toutes couleurs, les discours inauguraux : elle seule manifeste de façon concrète la volonté des diri-

2   U.K. 1867, chap. 3, dont le titre fut *British North America Act* jusqu'à l'adoption de la *Loi constitutionnelle de 1982*, article 53.
3   Voir Louis-Philippe Pigeon, *Rédaction et interprétation des lois*, 2e éd., Québec, 1978, p. 1.

geants élus. Il va sans dire que pour l'administrateur public la loi constitue une donnée fondamentale avec laquelle il doit savoir compter, d'autant plus qu'elle est la source des pouvoirs réglementaires et autres de plus en plus étendus confiés à l'Exécutif ou aux autres organismes du gouvernement.

Tout comme la loi est la voix des parlementaires, le règlement est la voix principale de l'Exécutif. Il s'agit essentiellement d'une norme de conduite générale autorisée par la loi et applicable aux citoyens ou à certaines catégories d'entre eux. Contrairement à la loi, qui vient du Parlement, le règlement vient de plusieurs organes, dont le principal est le gouvernement. Il porte quelquefois d'autres noms : ordonnance, règle, tarif, etc. Etant donné sa portée générale, le règlement se distingue d'une décision administrative individuelle. Son caractère unilatéral le distingue également du contrat administratif, qui exige le consentement d'un co-contractant. L'importance du règlement comme source de droit est capitale, car il est devenu un outil indispensable à l'application des lois. Le nombre annuel de règlements dépasse actuellement celui des lois, aussi bien au fédéral qu'au Québec.

La directive est une norme de l'Administration régissant l'activité de ses fonctionnaires. Elle se fonde rarement sur une disposition expresse de la loi. Elle découle plutôt des pouvoirs généraux d'administration, confiés à des ministres ou à des organismes centraux du gouvernement. Contrairement au règlement, la directive a donc une origine implicite et vise d'abord l'organisation interne de l'Administration et ses fonctionnaires. Ce n'est que par l'usage que ceux-ci en font qu'elle peut éventuellement toucher les citoyens.

La jurisprudence est la voix des tribunaux. Elle est l'ensemble des décisions rendues par le pouvoir judiciaire à l'occasion de litiges. En règle générale, les tribunaux n'ont pas à faire le droit, mais seulement à l'appliquer à des situations particulières. Ce principe fondamental connaît toutefois certaines exceptions lorsque le droit est imprécis ou même silencieux. Les tribunaux ont le devoir de trancher les litiges qui leur sont soumis, peu importe l'état du droit à l'égard du point soulevé. Ils exercent ainsi une fonction créatrice suppléant aux lacunes de ce droit. Les arrêts des tribunaux sont particulièrement importants en droit administratif, dont beaucoup de règles ne se retrouvent pas dans les lois ou les règlements, mais seulement dans de grandes décisions jurisprudentielles. Etant donné le bouillonnement intense que connaît ce domaine, le principe de l'« autorité du précédent », qui veut que les décisions des tribunaux supérieurs lient les instances inférieures (appelé aussi *stare decisis*), joue un rôle considérable dans l'établissement d'une certaine sécurité juridique en droit administratif.

La prérogative constitue le résidu des pouvoirs que l'Exécutif peut exercer sans l'autorisation d'une loi. A l'origine, le souverain bénéficiait de tous les pouvoirs. Petit à petit, il s'est vu dépouiller de ses privilèges et de ses droits particuliers. Aujourd'hui, ses pouvoirs sont généralement encadrés par des lois du Parlement et interprétés par des tribunaux indépendants. Même s'il demeure chef de l'Etat, le souverain est devenu une personne à peu près comme les autres et ce sont les organes de l'Etat qui exercent ses pouvoirs en vertu de la Constitution. C'est donc dire qu'aujourd'hui le gouvernement, héritier du pouvoir royal, ne détient ses pouvoirs et ne peut les exercer qu'en vertu des lois du Parlement. Seules quelques exceptions subsistent : on les appelle prérogatives. Par exemple, comme le soulignait récemment la Cour suprême du Canada, « la préro- gative royale met la Couronne dans une situation privilégiée en tant que créancière, en ce qui concerne l'héritage de terres à défaut d'héritiers ou relativement à la propriété de métaux précieux et *bona vacantia* ».[4]

La coutume est une règle de droit implicite, née de la répétition con- tinue d'un acte public et paisible ou de son omission, en l'absence d'une règle de droit précise.[5] En droit public, elle est souvent assimilée aux conventions constitutionnelles, comme celle voulant que le représentant du souverain demande au chef du parti qui a la confiance du Parlement d'assumer la fonction de Premier ministre ou encore celle voulant que ce soit ce dernier qui appelle les députés à des fonctions ministérielles. La coutume existe également en droit privé. Par exemple, au Québec, le fait pour la femme mariée de prendre le nom de son mari est encore largement considéré comme la norme, alors que la loi n'a jamais créé cette obligation.

Quant à la doctrine, il s'agit essentiellement des analyses et commen- taires que peuvent faire les juristes sur la législation et la jurisprudence et dont s'inspirent les tribunaux et les législateurs dans leurs activités. Ces textes peuvent prendre la forme d'articles, de monographies ou de traités.[6]

---

4 Renvoi: *Résolution pour modifier la Constitution*, (1981), 1 R.C.S. 753, p. 877.
5 Voir Henri Brun et Guy Tremblay, *Droit constitutionnel*, Québec, 1982, p. 43.
6 A l'instar des sources plus fondamentales du droit administratif comme la législa- tion, la réglementation et la jurisprudence, la doctrine a connu un développement phénoménal depuis une dizaine d'années. A titre d'exemple, on peut citer au Canada anglais : R.F. Reid and H. David, *Administrative Law and Practice*, 2e éd., 1978; – D.J. Mullan, *Administrative Law*, 2e éd., 1979; – J.M. Evans, H.N. Janisk, D.J. Mullan and R.C.B. Risk, *Administrative Law Cases, Text and Materials*, 1980; – S.A. de Smith, *Judicial Review of Administrative Action*, 4e éd., 1980, (préparée par le professeur J.M. Evans de Toronto). Au Canada français, voir R. Dussault, *Traité de droit administratif canadien et québécois*, 1974; – P. Garant, *Droit administratif*, 1981; – D. Lemieux, *Le contrôle judiciaire de l'action gouvernementale*, 1981; – Pierre Lemieux, *Le contrat administratif*, 1982; – G. Pépin et Y. Ouellette, *Principes de contentieux administratif*, 2e éd., 1982; – L. Borgeat, R. Dussault et L. Ouellet, *L'Administration publique québécoise: organisation et fonctionnement*, 1982. Voir aussi *Royal Commission Inquiry into Civil Rights*, 1968 (rapport McRuer); – Groupe de travail sur les tribunaux administratifs au Québec, 1971 (rapport Dussault); – Commission de réforme du droit du Canada, *Le contrôle judiciaire*, 1977.

La portée du droit administratif

Bon nombre d'administrateurs publics connaissent bien certaines manifestations concrètes du droit administratif, par exemple la réglementation, pour avoir dû en tenir compte dans certains dossiers. Cependant, peu d'entre eux ont une vue d'ensemble de son impact sur leur environnement quotidien et c'est sur ce sujet qu'il convient de s'attarder. Le droit administratif comporte deux grandes fonctions : prévoir les règles d'organisation et de fonctionnement interne de l'Administration et aménager les relations entre celle-ci et les citoyens.

La prévision des règles d'organisation et de fonctionnement interne de l'Administration

Voyons à tour de rôle comment le droit administratif encadre la structure, le fonctionnement et les actes de l'Administration.

La structure de l'Administration. Si la structure de l'Etat relève du droit constitutionnel, celle de son Administration ressortit davantage au droit administratif. L'un des premiers objets de cette discipline est en effet de veiller à l'organisation du gouvernement, de ses ministères et de ses organismes. Au Québec, par exemple, les règles de fonctionnement du Conseil des ministres et de ses principaux comités se retrouvent dans une législation et dans un ensemble de décrets qui déterminent notamment qui assume la présidence du Conseil ainsi que le mode de fixation de son quorum.[7] Il en est de même pour les ministères. Ils sont créés par une loi qui définit leurs rôles ainsi que les pouvoirs du ministre et de son sous-ministre. Elle établit aussi quelques règles de base pour le fonctionnement administratif du ministère, comme la délégation du pouvoir de signer des contrats. Quant aux très nombreux organismes décentralisés, c'est aussi par législation qu'ils sont généralement constitués. Par conséquent, il faut se référer à leur loi constitutive pour connaître leur degré d'autonomie et l'importance des contrôles dont ils sont l'objet,[8] ce qui permet de les ranger dans l'une ou l'autre des nomenclatures générales établies par les auteurs de droit administratif ou de science politique, dont aucune n'a toutefois reçu de consécration officielle par la loi : conseils consultatifs, tribunaux administratifs, régies et commissions, offices

---

7 *Loi sur l'exécutif*, L.R.Q., chap. E-18 et décrets 1900 à 1908, du 9 juillet 1981. L'article 9 de cette loi prévoit que le réaménagement ou le transfert des fonctions confiées à un ministère peut se faire par décret.

8 Par exemple, l'organisme est-il constitué en corporation distincte de la Couronne ? Si oui, en est-il un mandataire ? Ou encore, l'organisme voit-il ses employés régis par la Loi sur la fonction publique ou est-il un employeur distinct ? Doit-il soumettre un rapport d'activité au Parlement ? Doit-il s'autofinancer ou bénéficie-t-il de crédits votés annuellement par le Parlement ou pris sur le Fonds consolidé du revenu ?

et bureaux, sociétés d'Etat...⁹ C'est donc, en définitive, le droit administratif qui établit les règles fondamentales de l'organisation de l'Administration. Ce fait est souvent méconnu des fonctionnaires, qui ignorent généralement le fondement même de la structure administrative dans laquelle ils travaillent et, surtout, où cette structure se situe dans l'ensemble de l'appareil administratif et comment elle s'y intègre.

Le fonctionnement de l'Administration. Tous les ministères et les organismes n'ont pas les mêmes responsabilités. Certains sont de nature horizontale et rendent des services aux autres ministères; d'autres sont sectoriels et oeuvrent auprès de clientèles déterminées. En matière de gestion des ressources humaines, financières et matérielles, ils doivent tous, pour réaliser les objectifs qui leur sont propres, suivre une procédure uniforme, qui constitue le dénominateur commun de leur activité. Or, le fondement et le cadre de cette procédure sont surtout de nature juridique.¹⁰ En matière de gestion financière, par exemple, l'article 53 de la Loi constitutionnelle de 1867 exige que les crédits nécessaires au fonctionnement du gouvernement soient votés par l'Assemblée ou par le Parlement. Ce vote prend place à l'occasion de la présentation d'un certain nombre de lois sur les subsides ou portant affectation de crédits.¹¹ Ces lois ne touchent que les programmes ou crédits, à l'exclusion de leur subdivision, ce qui a pour conséquence de rendre impossibles les virements de fonds entre programmes ou crédits.¹² Ces lois, par ailleurs, ne prévoient l'adoption que des « crédits annuels », par opposition aux « crédits permanents » dont certaines lois ont déjà prévu qu'ils « sont puisés à même le fonds consolidé du revenu », ce qui les dispense d'un vote annuel par l'Assemblée ou par le Parlement.¹³

9 Au fédéral, la classification offerte dans la *Loi sur l'administration financière*, S.R.C. 1970, chap. F-10, annexes « A », « B », « C » et « D », laisse de côté une foule d'organismes gouvernementaux qui ne sont pas constitués en corporation et qui pourtant sont décentralisés. Pour une critique de cette classification, voir le *Rapport de la Commission royale sur la gestion financière et l'imputabilité* (commission Lambert), Ottawa, mars 1979, pp. 328 et suivantes.

10 Pour une présentation détaillée de ces trois grands processus de gestion au Québec, voir L. Borgeat, R. Dussault et L. Ouellet, *op. cit.*, note 6.

11 On trouve habituellement trois de ces lois pour chaque année financière: la loi n⁰ 1 octroie en bloc un quart ou un tiers des crédits totaux des prévisions budgétaires; la loi n⁰ 2 vote ensuite le reste du budget lorsque tous les crédits ont été étudiés; la loi n⁰ 3 est requise lorsqu'il y a présentation d'un budget supplémentaire. Voir par exemple, L.Q. 1981, chap. 1, 15, 21, et S.C. 1980-81-82, Projet de loi C-63, C-80, C-86, C-99.

12 Trois façons permettent de pallier le manque de fonds dans un programme ou crédit : le recours au « fonds de suppléance » ou « éventualités du gouvernement » (programme 4 du ministère québécois des Finances ou 5c du Conseil du Trésor fédéral); le mandat spécial du Lieutenant-gouverneur ou du Gouverneur général (lorsque l'Assemblée ou le Parlement ne siègent pas et que survient une dépense imprévue et urgente); le budget supplémentaire.

13 Par exemple, remboursement des emprunts, salaires des juges, rentes des fonctionnaires, transferts fiscaux aux provinces.

De façon plus particulière, les grands paramètres de l'activité financière se retrouvent tant au fédéral qu'au Québec dans la Loi sur l'administration financière,[14] ses règlements et les très nombreuses directives émanant du Conseil du Trésor. Il en va de même dans la plupart des provinces canadiennes. A la lecture de ces textes, on constate par exemple que c'est en vertu d'une norme juridique précise que les précisions budgétaires sont préparées sous la surveillance du Conseil du Trésor, que les ministères peuvent, à l'intérieur d'un même programme ou crédit et avec l'approbation préalable de ce conseil, effectuer un virement d'un élément ou d'une décision à l'autre et que les subventions octroyées peuvent être autorisées en bloc et non une par une.[15]

Les actes de l'Administration. L'Etat peut restreindre les droits et les libertés des citoyens de plusieurs façons. Le Parlement le fait par des lois qui créent des obligations et des interdictions. L'Administration peut faire la même chose par la voie de règlements qui ont la même force que les lois. Elle peut également lier par contrat un citoyen envers elle. Elle peut aussi, dans l'exercice de pouvoirs quasi judiciaires, octroyer ou refuser d'octroyer des permis ou des prestations. Elle peut, enfin, accomplir un très grand nombre d'actes à caractère purement administratif dans l'exercice des pouvoirs discrétionnaires qui lui sont conférés.

Fort divers, ces actes sont parmi les plus importants de l'Administration. Parce qu'un grand nombre d'entre eux ont pour effet de porter atteinte aux droits des citoyens ou de leur imposer des obligations, ils ne peuvent être accomplis que dans un cadre juridique très précis. Ainsi, le droit administratif veut qu'un règlement ne puisse imposer des taxes, des impôts ou des sanctions, ni avoir un effet rétroactif, sans que le législateur ne l'ait autorisé par une loi. De la même façon, un contrat conclu par un ministre ou un sous-ministre dans son domaine de compétence « apparent » pour le citoyen contractant liera l'Administration même en l'absence d'un pouvoir précis de contracter.[16] Egalement, l'exercice de pouvoirs quasi judiciaires et même administratifs est assujetti à des garanties procédurales de plus en plus importantes. Ce sont là des contraintes que les tribunaux ont jugé bon d'imposer à la suite de litiges particuliers.

L'aménagement des relations entre l'Administration et les citoyens

Le droit administratif offre aux citoyens divers moyens de se pourvoir contre l'Administration et de faire contrôler l'exercice de ses pouvoirs.

14 L.R.Q., chap. A-6; pour le fédéral, voir *supra*, note 9.
15 Au Québec, ces règlements et directives sont regroupés dans le *Répertoire des politiques administratives*, Conseil du Trésor, trois volumes; pour le fédéral, voir le *Manuel de la politique administrative*, Conseil du Trésor, cinq volumes.
16 *Verreault et fils Ltée* v. *Proc. gén. du Québec*, (1977) 1 R.C.S. 41.

Certains visent à prévenir ou à faire annuler les actes illégaux, d'autres, à obtenir réparation pour les dommages subis.

La légalité de l'action administrative. Nous avons mentionné précédemment que l'Etat est assujetti à la « Rule of Law », c'est-à-dire au principe de la légalité. Pour les fonctionnaires, le respect de la loi comporte trois aspects principaux : le respect de la Constitution, qui s'applique non seulement au législateur, mais aussi aux fonctionnaires qui agissent pour l'Administration; le respect des limites de leurs pouvoirs, telles qu'elles sont établies par les lois et les règlements; et enfin, le respect, dans l'exercice de leurs fonctions, de certains principes fondamentaux d'équité, tel celui de donner à l'intéressé l'occasion d'être entendu avant la prise d'une décision qui le concerne. Dans le cas où la règle de la légalité est transgressée, on parle d'excès de compétence et d'acte *ultra vires*. L'intéressé peut faire annuler l'acte illégal devant le tribunal compétent au moyen de diverses procédures dont les principales sont les brefs d'évocation, de *certiorari* ou de prohibition et l'action en nullité. L'ensemble des règles qui s'appliquent dans cette situation forme ce que l'on appelle le droit du contrôle judiciaire de l'Administration et constitue l'un des aspects les plus importants et les plus développés du droit administratif contemporain.

La responsabilité civile de l'Administration. Lorsque l'Administration ou l'un de ses fonctionnaires, à la suite ou non d'une illégalité, a commis une faute entraînant des dommages, la Couronne peut être tenue de verser une compensation financière à la victime. Il s'agit de l'application à l'Etat des principes de responsabilité prévus au Code civil ou dans la Common law, et applicables à tout citoyen dans notre société. En effet, en introduisant dans la législation des admissions générales ou particulières de responsabilité pour les fautes des fonctionnaires, le législateur est venu limiter ou anéantir, selon le cas, la portée de la prérogative d'immunité de poursuite (« The King can do no wrong ») dont bénéficiait traditionnellement la Couronne.[17] Il faut souligner, par ailleurs, que le rôle particulier de l'Etat à l'intérieur de la collectivité a rendu nécessaires certaines adaptations de ces principes issus du droit privé. Par exemple, l'évaluation de la responsabilité de l'Etat pour les fautes commises dans l'exercice de pouvoirs, comme ceux de réglementer, de rendre justice ou d'octroyer des permis, a fait naître des règles particulières en ce qui touche sa responsabilité civile. Ces particularités appartiennent au droit administratif, qui vient ici compléter le droit commun applicable. On dit alors que le régime de responsabilité ainsi établi pour l'Administration est complémentaire ou dérogatoire par rapport au droit ordinaire.

---

17 Voir, pour le fédéral, la *Loi sur la responsabilité de la Couronne*, S.R.C. 1970, chap. C-38.

L'objectif fondamental du droit administratif

L'ampleur, la diversité et la complexité des interventions de l'Administration dans la société contemporaine exigent qu'elle poursuive des objectifs d'efficacité, de rapidité et de rentabilité, sans perdre de vue, cependant, que sa raison d'être fondamentale demeure l'intérêt public. Aujourd'hui, il ne suffit pas que l'Administration prétende assurer l'intérêt public en agissant selon les règles qui lui paraissent les plus efficaces. Elle doit aussi se préoccuper de connaître leurs répercussions sur les citoyens. La société dans son ensemble s'attend à ce que les mesures d'intérêt collectif ne briment pas indûment les intérêts des groupes d'individus. On touche ici, à notre avis, à l'objectif fondamental du droit administratif moderne : établir un équilibre juste et réaliste entre les nécessités administratives et les droits des particuliers. Ce point d'équilibre n'est pas fixe, mais se déplace constamment suivant l'évolution des deux principales sources du droit administratif, la législation et la jurisprudence.

L'équilibre des droits dans la législation

A l'occasion des derniers conflits mondiaux pour le gouvernement fédéral, et depuis 1960 au Québec, l'Administration s'est vu octroyer par le législateur des pouvoirs d'intervention considérables. Ceux-ci s'exercent dans les programmes sociaux, dont l'application exige un contrôle étroit des bénéficiaires, et dans l'activité économique, dont peu de secteurs ont échappé à une réglementation quelconque. Pour faire contrepoids à ces pouvoirs de l'Administration, le législateur a senti le besoin de donner aux citoyens des recours généraux ou particuliers, qui s'ajoutent à ceux qui existent en vertu du système judiciaire traditionnel concernant le contrôle de la légalité de l'action administrative et le contentieux de la responsabilité civile.

Les recours généraux. Certains de ces moyens sont généraux, en ce sens qu'ils touchent l'ensemble de l'activité gouvernementale. C'est le cas, au Québec, du Protecteur du citoyen, qui a compétence à l'égard de l'ensemble de la fonction publique, et de la Commission des droits de la personne, dont la compétence touche l'ensemble de la collectivité, mais qui exerce un contrôle important sur l'Administration en raison du pouvoir d'intervention contre la Couronne prévu par sa loi organique. C'est le cas également des organismes créés récemment dans plusieurs juridictions pour assurer l'accès des citoyens à l'information gouvernementale. Dans l'exercice de ses fonctions toujours plus nombreuses, l'Administration est appelée à constituer, à détenir et à faire circuler une quantité importante d'informations de toute nature. Il peut s'agir de rapports relatifs à la conception, au développement ou à l'évaluation de programmes gouvernementaux, ou de renseignements sur des citoyens ou des groupes, par exemple, pour assurer l'octroi de prestations ou de permis de toute sorte. Dans un cas comme dans l'autre, on reconnaît de plus en plus la nécessité de permettre aux citoyens d'avoir accès à ces informations; d'une part, les rapports élaborés par l'Administration peuvent être utiles à des personnes ou à des groupes qui n'en font pas partie; d'autre part, il paraît juste que le citoyen puisse contrôler les renseignements que possède l'Administration à son sujet, étant donné les préjudices graves pouvant résulter de leur inexactitude.

Ainsi, le gouvernement fédéral a légiféré pour permettre aux citoyens d'avoir accès à leur dossier personnel lorsque les renseignements qui y sont contenus servent de fondement à une décision administrative les concernant;[18] il vient de faire de même à l'égard de l'information gouvernementale.[19] Le Québec, pour sa part, vient d'adopter un projet de loi qui fait suite au rapport Paré.[20] En Ontario, le rapport Williams attend toujours qu'on y donne suite.[21] Le droit administratif apportera en cette matière une clarification utile à l'ensemble de la collectivité.[22]

Les recours particuliers. D'autres recours se limitent à des interventions administratives particulières. Deux exemples québécois, tirés des domaines social et économique, illustrent cette réalité.

Dans le cadre des différents régimes de sécurité sociale qu'il administre, l'Etat québécois consent des avantages à diverses catégories de personnes. La décision concernant les droits d'une personne à des prestations est prise par des fonctionnaires dans le cadre des lois instituant ces régimes et des règlements en découlant. Pendant longtemps, le législateur a attribué un caractère définitif à ces décisions de l'Administration. Aujourd'hui, il estime nécessaire de donner aux citoyens des garanties supplémentaires d'impartialité en leur accordant un droit d'appel devant un tribunal administratif spécialisé : la Commission des affaires sociales. La décision ultime en cas de conflit entre l'Administration et un citoyen se trouve ainsi confiée à un tiers dont les attributions sont quasi judi-

18 *Loi canadienne sur les droits de la personne*, S.C. 1976-77, chap. 33.
19 *Projet de loi sur l'information gouvernementale*, Bill C-43, 1980, adopté en juin 1982.
20 *Information et liberté. Rapport de la Commission d'étude sur l'accès du citoyen à l'information gouvernementale et sur la protection des renseignements personnels*, Québec, ministère des Communications, 1981; – Projet de loi n° 65, *Loi sur l'accès aux documents des organismes publics et sur la protection des renseignements personnels*, L.Q. 1982, chap. 30.
21 *The Report of the Commission on Freedom of Information and Individual Privacy*, Toronto, Queen's Printer, 1980.
22 Il s'agit d'un domaine où, en l'absence de normes juridiques précises, l'Administration comme les citoyens vivent une situation d'incertitude et même de confusion. En l'absence de règles pour les guider, les fonctionnaires adoptent tout naturellement une attitude de prudence et de réserve, qui prive indûment les citoyens de renseignements dont la publicité ne mettrait pas en péril le bon fonctionnement de l'Administration.

ciaires. Il s'agit d'une façon d'établir un meilleur équilibre entre les parties en présence.

Le législateur veut assurer le même équilibre lorsqu'il va au-delà de son rôle d'Etat-providence pour intervenir directement dans l'activité économique. La récente loi québécoise en matière de protection de l'environnement en fournit une bonne illustration.[23] Les pouvoirs qu'elle octroie à l'Administration et les contraintes qu'elle impose aux entreprises sont d'une ampleur sans précédent au Québec : autorisations préalables pour toutes sortes d'opérations, études d'impact préalables, pouvoir du ministère de l'Environnement d'édicter des ordonnances et de les exécuter aux frais des entreprises en cas de refus de leur part, démolition des installations construites en violation de la loi, etc. En contrepartie, la personne visée dispose, dans la plupart des cas, d'un droit d'appel devant la Commission municipale du Québec. On retrouve ici le même principe qu'en matière de sécurité sociale : prévenir, en conférant la décision finale à un tribunal, une situation où l'Administration serait seule maîtresse de l'application de sa propre législation.[24]

L'équilibre des droits dans la jurisprudence

Ce souci d'équilibre entre l'Administration et les citoyens, on le retrouve également dans les décisions des tribunaux, dont le droit administratif, nous l'avons vu, est largement tributaire. Il se manifeste souvent de façon spectaculaire lorsque les tribunaux, en vue de sauvegarder les droits d'un particulier dans ses relations avec un organisme public, décident d'écarter un principe qu'ils ont établi antérieurement ou donnent une portée insoupçonnée à une disposition législative. Des exemples de ce genre de décision n'ont pas manqué au cours des dernières années. Le plus célèbre est sans contredit l'arrêt *Nicholson,*[25] dans lequel la Cour suprême du Canada a décidé d'obliger l'Administration publique à « agir équitablement » même dans les cas où elle n'est pas tenue de respecter les règles de la justice naturelle parce qu'elle ne touche pas directement les droits d'un citoyen. La cour a ainsi reconnu à une personne menacée de perdre son emploi le droit de connaître les reproches qu'on lui adresse et de s'expliquer, même si elle est en période de probation préalable à un engagement permanent. L'impact pratique de cet élargissement d'une règle de justice naturelle, appliquée jusqu'ici aux seules décisions de

---

23 *Loi sur la qualité de l'environnement,* L.R.Q., chap. Q-2.
24 Voir également la section II.1 de la loi qui crée le Bureau des audiences publiques sur l'environnement, une structure permanente de consultation destinée à entendre les intéressés sur toute question désignée par le ministre de l'Environnement.
25 *Nicholson* v. *Haldimand-Norfolk Regional Board of Commissioners of Police,* (1979) 1 R.C.S. 311.

nature judiciaire ou quasi judiciaire, peut être considérable pour un grand nombre d'organismes administratifs au Canada.

Plus récemment, un juge de la Cour supérieure du Québec, dans l'affaire *Lapierre* c. *Proc. gén. du Québec*,[26] retenait la responsabilité civile du gouvernement au bénéfice du père d'une fillette chez qui une vaccination contre la rougeole, faite dans une clinique gouvernementale, avait provoqué, sans faute de quiconque, une encéphalite virale aux conséquences désastreuses. Cette décision, qui introduit la notion de responsabilité « sans faute » à l'encontre de l'Administration, constitue une innovation dans notre droit administratif. Ses effets dans le cas d'accidents survenant à l'occasion de programmes gouvernementaux (fluoration, isolation, etc.) pourraient se révéler très importants. Cette affaire a cependant été portée devant la Cour d'appel du Québec et se rendra probablement jusqu'en Cour suprême du Canada.

Les décisions qui précèdent expriment la même préoccupation, celle de protéger l'individu face à une intervention croissante de l'Administration. Rappelons toutefois qu'en vertu du principe de la suprématie de la loi et de celui de la souveraineté du Parlement, le législateur peut toujours modifier la portée d'une règle de droit établie par la jurisprudence, sous réserve bien sûr des limites qui lui sont imposées par la Constitution. L'administrateur public, pour sa part, n'échappe pas davantage aux enjeux de cette problématique du droit administratif moderne, qui exige déjà beaucoup des législateurs et des tribunaux. Dans ses conseils, ses décisions et ses actions, il doit participer à la réalisation du fragile équilibre entre les interventions de l'Administration et les droits des citoyens.

Les nouvelles orientations en droit administratif

L'avenir du droit administratif est intimement lié à celui de l'Etat. Le développement phénoménal qu'a connu cette discipline au cours des dernières décennies n'est qu'une conséquence de l'accroissement du rôle de l'Etat dans notre société. De la même façon, les changements d'attitude auxquels nous assistons depuis le début de la présente décennie à l'égard du rôle de l'Etat auront une incidence directe sur l'évolution même du droit administratif. Sans prétendre être exhaustif, nous croyons pouvoir affirmer que le droit administratif connaîtra, au cours des années 1980, une certaine évolution dont les principales caractéristiques sont les suivantes : clarification des relations entre les tribunaux administratifs et judiciaires; ralentissement du démembrement intensif de l'Etat; accroissement du contrôle parlementaire sur l'activité administrative; meilleur encadrement des décisions touchant les citoyens; assouplissement des

26   (1979) C.S. 970. Voir également *Manitoba Fisheries* v. R., (1979) 1 R.C.S. 101.

règles de gestion des ressources; diminution des prérogatives et immunités de la Couronne; enfin, utilisation d'une technologie permettant de rendre le droit plus accessible.

Clarification des relations entre les tribunaux administratifs et judiciaires

La question des tribunaux administratifs a toujours soulevé beaucoup d'inquiétudes dans les milieux judiciaires. Le développement d'une justice administrative parallèle, pour nécessaire qu'elle soit, provoque une certaine résistance, ne serait-ce que parce qu'elle sous-entend une certaine inaptitude du système judiciaire à résoudre les problèmes engendrés par le développement de l'administration publique moderne.

Au-delà des questions pourtant fort importantes de la procédure et des règles de preuve devant les tribunaux administratifs,[27] il faudra aussi apporter une solution raisonnable aux difficultés constitutionnelles mettant en cause l'existence même des tribunaux administratifs dans les provinces. Les tribunaux judiciaires supérieurs ont en effet donné à l'article 96 de la Loi constitutionnelle de 1867, qui prévoit que l'Exécutif fédéral nomme les juges des cours supérieures, de districts et de comtés, une portée telle qu'un nombre considérable de tribunaux administratifs provinciaux ont vu leurs pouvoirs déclarés inconstitutionnels, notamment le Tribunal des transports et le Tribunal des professions au Québec, la Régie du logement en Ontario et au Québec et le Tribunal de la famille en Colombie-Britannique.[28]

Ce litige constitutionnel devrait forcer la réflexion des deux ordres de gouvernement sur la place de la justice administrative dans une société comme la nôtre. Celle-ci ne doit-elle être qu'un réseau de justice parallèle plus expéditive ou plus spécialisée, ou bien un forum judiciaire distinct rendant des décisions fondées non pas uniquement sur le droit mais sur des critères d'intérêt public davantage sujets à interprétation ? Dans le même ordre d'idées, il faut se demander jusqu'à quel point il est opportun de maintenir dans la législation les dispositions privant l'autorité judiciaire de son pouvoir de contrôle sur la légalité de l'activité administrative et s'interroger sur la nature du droit d'appel qu'il convient de donner devant les tribunaux ou autres instances administratives. Le respect accru que l'on attend des tribunaux judiciaires à l'égard des décisions

27 Yves Ouellette, « La procédure et la preuve devant les juridictions administratives », (1979), 39 *R. du B.* 704.
28 *Proc. gén. du Québec et le Tribunal des transports* v. *Farrah*, (1978) 2 R.C.S. 638; – *Crevier* v. *Proc. gén. du Québec*, Cour suprême du Canada, (1981) 2 R.C.S. 220; – *Re Loi de 1979 sur la location résidentielle*, (1981) 2 R.C.S. 714; – *Propiq* v. *Régie du logement*, (1982) C.S. 111; – *Renvoi relatif à l'article 6 du Family Relations Act de la Colombie-Britannique*, Cour suprême du Canada, 26 janvier 1982.

des tribunaux administratifs, et dont on retrouve déjà certaines manifestations,[29] passe nécessairement par de telles clarifications.

Ralentissement du démembrement intensif de l'Etat

Au cours des vingt dernières années, l'administration publique au Canada a vécu une période de démembrements intensifs. La création d'une multitude d'organismes du gouvernement, dont plusieurs investis d'une personnalité juridique distincte de la Couronne, a conduit à un éparpillement qui risque de mettre en péril non seulement la faculté de gouverner de l'Exécutif, mais aussi la garantie démocratique que constitue un contrôle parlementaire réel sur les activités administratives. En effet, ce contrôle ne saurait être mieux assuré que par la technique de la responsabilité ministérielle appliquée aux activités d'un ministère. Au cours de la présente décennie, les contraintes budgétaires et la prise de conscience accrue de la nécessité de ne pas émietter indûment le coeur de l'appareil administratif, si l'on veut que la responsabilité ministérielle devant le Parlement continue d'avoir un sens, feront en sorte qu'on créera beaucoup moins de nouveaux organismes administratifs : on cherchera plutôt à faire exercer des fonctions nouvelles par des organismes existants ou par la structure ministérielle proprement dite.

Accroissement du contrôle parlementaire sur l'activité administrative

De nos jours, beaucoup s'entendent pour dire que les parlementaires, le gouvernement et l'administration publique doivent établir un meilleur équilibre entre l'adoption de lois, de règlements ou de programmes nouveaux et l'évaluation de ce qui existe, sur le plan de l'opportunité, de l'efficacité et du coût. L'une des conséquences de cette préoccupation est que l'accent sera mis sur une réforme du Parlement visant à doter les parlementaires de meilleurs outils de contrôle. Cette réforme est déjà en cours si l'on considère le rôle joué par le Protecteur du citoyen et le Vérificateur général ainsi que les fonctions élargies attribuées aux commissions parlementaires par exemple pour le contrôle des règlements, des engagements et des dépenses ou des sociétés d'Etat. Cependant, beaucoup de chemin reste à parcourir si l'on veut vraiment faire jouer aux parlementaires un rôle de contrôleurs de l'administration publique. A cet égard, les rapports annuels des divers vérificateurs ou auditeurs généraux au Canada, ainsi que certains rapports d'enquête ou d'étude

29 *Jacmain* v. *Attorney General of Canada*, (1978) 2 R.C.S. 15, p. 29, par le juge Dickson, dissident; – *CUPE* v. *New Brunswick Liquor Corporation*, (1979) 2 R.C.S. 227, pp. 235-236.

tels que, au fédéral, le rapport Lambert[30] et, au Québec, le rapport Vaugeois,[31] contiennent des pistes à explorer sans plus tarder.

Meilleur encadrement des décisions touchant les citoyens

Sous le couvert d'un contrôle de la légalité, les tribunaux contrôlent de plus en plus l'opportunité de l'action administrative, si bien que la règle de droit devient peu à peu la règle de discrétion des tribunaux judiciaires; considérons, par exemple, l'extension, par la voie de l'obligation d'équité, des principes de justice naturelle à l'activité purement administrative de l'Etat, le contrôle accru des erreurs de droit, etc. Le législateur lui-même tend à encadrer de plus en plus, par des règlements et des directives, l'exercice des pouvoirs des fonctionnaires et accorde aux citoyens des droits d'appel inédits contre leurs décisions. Cette attitude se répercute même sur les tribunaux administratifs, régies et commissions auxquels la Cour suprême du Canada donnait récemment le droit d'adopter des énoncés politiques et des directives leur permettant d'encadrer l'exercice de leurs pouvoirs de façon à leur donner plus de cohérence et une plus grande sécurité.[32] Le risque d'arbitraire des autorités administratives dans leurs décisions touchant les citoyens s'en trouve ainsi considérablement diminué. La plus grande sécurité qui en résulte pour l'Administration et le citoyen devrait amener une utilisation accrue de cet encadrement.

Assouplissement des règles de gestion des ressources

Que ce soit en matière de ressources humaines, financières ou matérielles, le gestionnaire public a des règles très précises à suivre. On y retrouve toute la gradation des normes juridiques en vigueur dans l'Administration. Une loi-cadre établit des principes généraux, qui sont ensuite précisés par un ensemble de règlements, eux-mêmes quelquefois détaillés par des directives administratives. S'y ajoutent parfois des politiques administratives dont le fondement échappe au droit. De plus, à l'intérieur de cette structure normative, seuls ceux qui bénéficient d'une délégation d'autorité sont habilités à prendre des décisions; souvent, celles-ci doivent être assorties d'une autorisation d'un organisme de contrôle.

Toutes ces règles, dictées par le souci légitime de limiter la discrétion

---

30 *Supra,* note 9.
31 *L'Assemblée nationale en devenir : pour un meilleur équilibre de nos institutions,* Québec, 28 janvier 1982. Voir le projet de loi 90 de 1982, *Loi sur l'Assemblée nationale du Québec.*
32 *Capital Cities Communications Inc.* v. *Canadian Radio Television Commission,* (1978) 2 R.C.S. 141.

des fonctionnaires, ont aussi eu pour effet de restreindre et de diluer considérablement leur responsabilité. Deux importants facteurs militent en faveur de leur modification. D'abord, la nécessité de réduire les dépenses publiques au minimum va amener des mesures visant à stimuler la productivité de l'Administration et des fonctionnaires, ce qui impliquera nécessairement une plus grande autonomie de gestion. Ensuite, la volonté de valoriser la fonction de gestionnaire va de pair avec une augmentation de sa part de responsabilité et une plus grande décentralisation des pouvoirs. Bref, d'une gestion trop fortement axée sur la sécurité, l'Administration passera vraisemblablement à une gestion orientée davantage sur la productivité, à l'instar du secteur privé. Il en résultera sur le plan juridique une remise en question et une élimination graduelles d'un certain degré de détail dans la réglementation. Par exemple, en matière de gestion financière, on viendra sans doute à accepter un jour qu'une fois les autorisations accordées pour les enveloppes budgétaires globales des ministères, l'intervention du Conseil du Trésor pour approuver des dépenses une à une n'est pas vraiment nécessaire et devrait se faire moins fréquente.

Diminution des prérogatives et immunités de la Couronne

La Couronne, dans le système britannique, bénéficie traditionnellement d'un régime d'exception par rapport aux citoyens. Ces exceptions proviennent à la fois de prérogatives non écrites et d'immunités établies expressément par le législateur, ces dernières ayant cependant tendance depuis quelques années à remplacer les premières. A mesure que l'Etat dépasse le cadre de l'Etat-gendarme pour passer à l'Etat-providence, dispensateur de biens et de services, son activité s'assimile de plus en plus à celle d'un particulier, de sorte que le fondement de ces exceptions s'estompe quelque peu. Les tribunaux, en tout cas, sont de plus en plus circonspects à leur égard.

C'est ainsi que, lors de la contestation de la loi permettant l'expropriation de la société Asbestos, les tribunaux ont accordé une injonction empêchant le gouvernement d'exproprier les actifs immobiliers de la compagnie avant que le débat entourant la constitutionnalité de cette loi ne soit clarifié; cette injonction prononcée contre la Couronne était une première.[33] De même, dans *Banque de Montréal c. Proc. gén. du Québec*,[34] la Cour suprême du Canada a refusé à la Couronne l'appli-

33 *Société Asbestos Ltée* v. *Société nationale de l'amiante*, (1979) C.S. 848, (1979) C.A. 489 et (1979) C.A. 342. Voir aussi *Proc. gén. du Québec* v. *Société Asbestos Ltée*, (1980) C.A. 341.
34 (1979) 1 R.C.S. 565. Voir *Proc. gén. du Québec* v. *Labrecque et autres*, (1980) 2 R.C.S. 1057, p. 1083.

cation de son privilège de ne pas se soumettre aux règles de prescription parce que la transaction en cause était de nature contractuelle et semblable à celle pouvant lier des particuliers. Dans le même esprit, les tribunaux ont tendance, dans leur décision, à réduire les contraintes de forme et de procédure dans les recours contre l'Administration.[35] Cette volonté de la Magistrature d'interpréter restrictivement les privilèges et immunités de la Couronne devrait s'affirmer encore davantage dans les années à venir.

Utilisation d'une technologie permettant de rendre le droit plus accessible

Le droit administratif tire sa source de documents et d'instruments dont le nombre et la variété, nous l'avons vu, n'ont d'égal que leur dispersion. On a assisté, ces dernières années, à d'importants efforts d'inventaire et de mise en ordre de cette documentation : les lois et les règlements sont maintenant refondus régulièrement et parfois sur une base permanente; les directives administratives sont plus visibles parce que répertoriées; la jurisprudence est maintenant disponible presque instantanément grâce au système des « résumés », publiés bien avant les recueils; la doctrine, beaucoup plus imposante qu'auparavant, a fait des efforts considérables pour exposer de façon synthétique l'état de ce droit en pleine évolution. Il n'en demeure pas moins que celui-ci se caractérise encore par une grande instabilité et défie souvent la compréhension.[36] Cette situation est une cause de difficultés aussi bien pour le citoyen et l'administrateur public, à qui s'applique avec toute sa force la maxime « nul n'est censé ignorer la loi », que pour le praticien de ce droit, qui est lui-même dans l'impossibilité de suivre complètement l'évolution extrêmement rapide de la discipline.

Aujourd'hui, le soutien qu'offrent l'informatique et la télématique devrait permettre, en documentation juridique comme ailleurs, des développements spectaculaires pour accélérer la compilation, la mise à jour et le repérage des données. Déjà, au Québec, c'est grâce à l'informatique que s'effectue la refonte des lois sur feuilles mobiles, qui donnent à celle-ci un caractère permanent. D'autres innovations, dans un avenir relativement proche, devraient permettre aux professionnels du droit et ensuite à l'ensemble des citoyens, à l'aide d'écrans disponibles sur l'ensemble du territoire, d'avoir accès à une information constamment

35 Voir *Duquet* v. *Ville de Sainte-Agathe*, (1977) 2 R.C.S. 1132; – *Vachon* v. *Proc. gén. du Québec*, (1979) 1 R.C.S. 557. Voir de façon générale sur cette question, L.-P. Pigeon, « Les rigueurs de la loi », allocution prononcée en septembre 1978 à la Conférence des avocats et notaires de la fonction publique du Québec.
36 Claude Tellier, « Les problèmes relatifs à l'information juridique », (1973) 33 *R. du B.* 196; – Denis Lemay, « L'information juridique au Québec : état de la question », (1978) 19 *C. de D.* 987.

à jour et rendue facilement utilisable par des instruments perfectionnés de recherche et de dialogue avec les banques de données. Ainsi mis à la disposition du public par l'intermédiaire de la technologie, le droit pourrait peut-être atteindre une accessibilité et une simplicité qu'il n'a jamais eues jusqu'ici.

Conclusion

Au cours des vingt dernières années, le droit administratif a connu une montée spectaculaire au sein de l'Administration, entraînant pour le gestionnaire public certaines exigences nouvelles.

Une montée spectaculaire du droit administratif

Cette montée du droit administratif est intimement liée à l'apparition d'une préférence marquée pour la norme juridique, d'un enthousiasme pour les droits et d'une accentuation du rôle des tribunaux.

Une préférence pour la norme juridique. Le droit ne saurait être une fin en soi. Il est un instrument au service des choix sociaux et des valeurs que se donne une collectivité. Concrètement, il est utile lorsqu'une norme est nécessaire pour orienter ou limiter la liberté d'agir des individus ou des groupes. Ainsi, si le droit est aujourd'hui aussi présent dans l'Administration, c'est parce qu'on préfère souvent la norme objective et publique à la discrétion des fonctionnaires, fussent-ils les mieux intentionnés. Le droit ne doit pas être perçu toutefois comme un remède à toutes les difficultés d'organisation et de fonctionnement que connaît l'Administration ni, à l'inverse, comme la cause de ces difficultés. Dans l'administration publique comme ailleurs, il faut prendre le droit pour ce qu'il est : une discipline dont l'objet est de prescrire des normes de comportement pour les membres de la collectivité. Or, il faut être conscient des limites de cet instrument d'intervention sur la société. Une norme est, par définition, générale et impersonnelle. Elle touche aveuglément et avec la même rigueur tous ceux qu'elle vise; son application peut, dans certaines circonstances, créer des situations absurdes ou même injustes. Le feu rouge, manifestation la plus élémentaire de la règle de droit, est utile, voire indispensable aux heures de pointe; il devient souvent une source de frustration lorsqu'il fonctionne encore aux petites heures du matin. De la même façon, le droit des individus à l'égalité, qui prohibe toute forme de discrimination, est certes un principe valable; son application l'est moins si ce droit empêche de traduire dans les faits un consensus social voulant qu'on favorise ouvertement une catégorie de personnes envers qui la collectivité estime avoir des dettes historiques, culturelles ou sociales.

Un enthousiasme pour les droits. Dans nos sociétés modernes, le rôle considérable joué par le droit administratif dans l'aménagement des relations entre l'Etat et le citoyen n'a rien de passager. L'enthousiasme manifesté pour les droits et recours de toutes sortes et pour l'intervention des tribunaux a pour conséquence que la science et la « culture » juridiques étendent de plus en plus leur emprise sur l'organisation et le fonctionnement de l'administration publique. Au Canada, en raison de l'absence prolongée d'une Charte des droits intégrée à la Constitution et aussi de l'attitude traditionnelle des membres de la Magistrature, qui s'attachent d'abord à une interprétation littérale des textes, ce fait a toujours été moins apparent qu'aux Etats-Unis. Il est appelé toutefois à prendre beaucoup d'ampleur au cours des prochaines années.

Un rôle accru pour les tribunaux. Dans ce contexte, le sens de l'équilibre devient plus important que jamais. A première vue, on pourrait facilement être tenté, dans certains milieux, de tenir pour acquis qu'il est souhaitable que la « culture » juridique, sous-jacente à l'action des tribunaux, étende son emprise. Suivant cette ligne de pensée, l'emprise du droit serait de toute façon moins dangereuse à long terme que celle des administrateurs publics et même des législateurs, fussent-ils élus démocratiquement. Il s'agit là d'une question fort délicate. Bien sûr, personne ne conteste le rôle essentiel des tribunaux comme protecteurs des droits individuels et comme interprètes des normes juridiques adoptées par une assemblée démocratiquement élue. Toutefois, les citoyens, tout comme les administrateurs publics d'ailleurs, savent fort bien que trop de légalisme, autant qu'une trop grande subjectivité dans le processus d'interprétation et d'application des lois, peuvent fausser les objectifs des politiques publiques. Quoi qu'il en soit, on aura beau penser dans plusieurs milieux, y compris dans la fonction publique, que les juges devraient devenir moins techniques, plus présents dans la société et plus ouverts aux volontés exprimées par le processus démocratique – New Deal, Asbestos, Régie du logement – il faut reconnaître qu'il y a des limites objectives dans le processus de décision, que les juges ne sauraient franchir sans risquer de tomber dans l'arbitraire. L'administrateur public des années 1980 doit donc être en mesure de mieux comprendre et d'intégrer à sa vie quotidienne le processus de décision judiciaire car celui-ci est appelé à y accroître sa présence et son influence.

Des exigences nouvelles pour le gestionnaire public

L'administrateur public moderne doit adopter une attitude plus respectueuse envers la règle de droit, développer de bons réflexes juridiques et acquérir une formation légale mieux adaptée à ses besoins.

Une attitude plus respectueuse de la légalité. Régi comme tout autre citoyen par la règle de droit, l'administrateur public ne peut se permettre de prendre des risques en ce qui concerne la légalité de ses actes; il y va de la légitimité et de l'image de l'Etat tout entier. Parce qu'il est proche des législateurs, l'administrateur public bénéficie d'une position privilégiée. Il peut, plus facilement que le citoyen ordinaire ou les administrateurs de l'entreprise privée, obtenir une modification législative pour régler un litige sur une question d'interprétation ou tout simplement pour résoudre un problème qui pourrait l'être par voie administrative. Il peut donc avoir tendance, souvent inconsciemment, à attacher moins d'importance à la stricte légalité car, peut-il croire, il pourra toujours faire changer la loi ou le règlement en cause, si cela se révèle nécessaire.

Ce serait une grave erreur que de raisonner ainsi. L'administrateur public doit être conscient de l'importance de rester dans le cadre de la légalité tout autant que peut l'être celui d'une entreprise privée, qui sait très bien que tout manquement à la légalité est susceptible d'entacher sa réputation et de nuire à son entreprise. Il est d'ailleurs incité à agir en ce sens par le ministère de la Justice, premier gardien de la légalité à l'intérieur de l'administration publique. Mais plus profondément, son respect de la loi devrait s'appuyer sur une conviction personnelle, qui à notre avis implique une connaissance concrète de ce qu'est le droit administratif, de sa portée et de sa signification. Bref, pour être à l'aise avec le principe de la « Rule of Law », l'administrateur public doit avoir développé une certaine « culture » et de bons réflexes juridiques.

De meilleurs réflexes juridiques. Dans le secteur public comme dans le privé, on reconnaît que le gestionnaire moderne doit savoir s'entourer de spécialistes rompus aux techniques les plus complexes : comptabilité, informatique, économique, analyse des systèmes, recherche opérationnelle, droit, etc. On insiste toutefois pour qu'il soit un « généraliste » apte à manier les données de plusieurs disciplines et à garder une certaine autonomie vis-à-vis des spécialistes qui le conseillent. Dans le domaine du droit en particulier, l'administrateur public doit acquérir des connaissances et des réflexes qui lui permettent de dialoguer efficacement avec les avocats et les notaires gouvernementaux.

Les connaissances que l'administrateur public doit acquérir ne sont évidemment pas du même type ni du même niveau que celles qui sont nécessaires au juriste. Ce que l'administrateur public doit posséder, c'est une certaine « culture » juridique, une sensibilité à son environnement juridique, beaucoup plus qu'un catalogue de données précises en droit administratif. Sans chercher à être un expert, il doit en savoir suffisamment sur la portée de cette discipline pour reconnaître les situations nécessitant le recours préventif ou curatif à des experts en droit. Lorsqu'il a obtenu leur avis, il doit être capable de le comprendre, d'en discuter avec eux et de confronter leur point de vue avec le sien. En droit comme ailleurs, il ne s'agit pas, pour le gestionnaire, de se substituer à ses conseillers, mais plutôt d'avoir le réflexe de recourir à leurs services au bon moment et d'être capable de saisir la portée et les limites de leurs conseils, pour conserver l'essentiel de sa tâche de décideur.

Une formation juridique mieux adaptée. L'enseignement qui permet d'acquérir ce genre de connaissances est d'un type particulier. Il n'est pas dispensé dans les facultés de droit où l'enseignement est destiné à de futurs juristes qui ont besoin d'une connaissance verticale de l'ensemble du droit administratif. On le retrouve essentiellement dans des institutions donnant des cours pratiques ou des sessions d'information, dans des disciplines directement liées à l'activité et à l'environnement de l'administrateur public. En droit, cet enseignement devrait viser certains objectifs de base qui, à notre avis, sont les suivants :

– démystifier la complexité du droit administratif : les règles de droit qu'il comporte sont adoptées et interprétées par des citoyens (parlementaires et juges) n'ayant aucune supériorité intrinsèque sur les autres, mais dont la principale caractéristique est d'exercer des fonctions spécialisées à l'intérieur de l'Etat; ces règles n'ont en conséquence pas toujours la complexité qu'on leur attribue;
– faire comprendre la portée de cette discipline en mettant en évidence le rôle important que joue le droit administratif dans l'organisation et l'activité de l'Administration et dans ses relations avec les citoyens;
– faire connaître les principales sources de ce droit, les grands principes qui guident son évolution, l'objectif fondamental qu'il poursuit et l'enjeu qu'il représente pour l'administrateur public et le citoyen.

Malheureusement, la forme de cet enseignement relativement nouveau reste encore à préciser et à mettre au point. Sa nécessité et même son utilité doivent encore être démontrées, car, pendant trop longtemps, le droit a été considéré comme un frein à l'activité de l'Administration plutôt que comme l'encadrement destiné à prévoir, à l'avantage de tous, la marge de manoeuvre de ceux qui agissent au nom de cette Administration.

Paul G. Thomas # Public administration and expenditure management

Introduction

Prior to the last two decades public budgeting was portrayed in the literature as primarily a neutral, technical exercise concerned with ensuring strict financial control. It was seen as a dry and dusty domain ruled over by accountants with quill pens and abacuses. This earlier image of the budgetary process was unrealistic, as many participants recognized. Politics has always figured prominently in deciding what goes into the budget. During the nineteenth century, political uses of the budget included spending designed to assist in the re-election of the party in power and the adoption of imaginative but dubious accounting methods designed to produce surplus or balanced budgets. Today, budgeting is perceived in the academic literature primarily in political terms: as a complex and shifting set of relationships among various institutions and actors, which records whose preferences and interests will prevail over one or more years. The modern budget serves a variety of purposes, in addition to the original goal of control, and as a result the complexity of the process has increased. The tools of the trade have also changed. Today's budget actors run computer simulations of the economy, conduct performance measurements and cost/benefit analyses of programs, and practice "comprehensive auditing."

The budgetary process is riddled with political pressures. Ministers win more political credit for launching new programs than for successfully administering existing ones. Bureaucratic incentive structures, in the past at least, have rewarded program innovation and additional spending, and have given little recognition to the need for management and the serious evaluation of programs. Pressure groups lobby for new programs and the enrichment or maintenance of existing ones. Whatever decision-making

The author is associate professor of political studies, St. John's College, University of Manitoba. The author would like to thank Mr. James Egan for his valuable research assistance and two anonymous reviewers for their constructive comments on an earlier draft of this article.

techniques are adopted, their impact is limited by the political environment in which budgets are prepared.

Abandonment of the earlier, shallow interpretation of budgeting has undoubtedly led to greater understanding and realism. However, upon reading the contemporary literature one wonders whether "ultra-realism" is now the prevailing fashion and whether this outlook leads, in turn, to a dead end in terms of a willingness and a capacity to recommend new budgetary approaches. After all, if politics, of both the partisan and the bureaucratic variety, determine everything of importance in budgeting, then the search for a more "rational" budgetary process is futile and will produce only perpetual disappointment. Naive faith in the latest budgetary gadget is dangerous, but equally dangerous perhaps is a thoroughgoing pessimism which denies any potential for constructive institutional reform.

In light of this overall theme, this paper examines the theory and practice of contemporary budgeting in Canada. A series of questions are investigated. What does budgeting consist of? How have our notions about budgeting evolved? What have been the consequences of such changes for the types of organizational arrangements created, the sorts of personnel involved with budgetary activity, and the patterns of relationships which emerge among various decision-makers? What is the current state of knowledge about the budgetary process? It has been suggested that "budgeting is one of the few areas in public administration in which there is a body of knowledge and theory useful enough to apply to the real world."[1] Is this true?

Budgetary reform movements appear to be a hardy perennial of administrative life. Have we been beset by fads involving new techniques, usually imported from the private sector or the United States? As new purposes and techniques have been added, has the result been to overburden the budgetary process? Are the purposes assigned to budgeting always consistent with one another? If not, how should we reconcile such purposes? In thinking about future reforms, should we seek to streamline the process; can we safely add to its complexity; or should we simply leave well enough alone?

Given slow growth in public revenues and the apparent strong public concern about the level and rate of expenditure growth, adherence to the status quo may well be an untenable position for any government to adopt. Past approaches to budgetary decision-making were premised upon constant growth in public spending. Are alternative approaches available which would help us to cope with the increased conflict that

---

1 Thomas H. Hammond and Jack H. Knott, *A Zero-Based Look at Zero-Base Budgeting* (New Brunswick: Transaction Books, 1980), p. x.

must accompany maintenance or retrenchment of public spending? Can the public service deliver restraint if this is demanded by the political leadership?

These are enormously difficult questions and it is impossible to answer them adequately in a single, short paper. Therefore, a few words about the scope of the paper are in order. Public budgeting involves both the raising and the spending of tax dollars, although it is mainly the latter which will concern us here.[2] In recent years we have witnessed a break-down of the so-called Keynesian consensus regarding the use of fiscal and monetary policy to direct the economy. Various economic theories – monetarism, supply-side economics, post-Keynesian approaches and others – compete for acceptance as the new orthodoxy.[3] While the debate over the economic role of the budget is best left to the professional economists, it should be noted that explanations for current economic problems are closely linked to attitudes about the current level and nature of government spending. The wider significance of the budget and the ideological disagreements it arouses must be noted, all too briefly unfortunately, so as to avoid any implication that the mechanics of budgeting are all-important. Contrast, for example, the view of certain economists that within government decision-making, economic-efficiency concerns are being subordinated to social policy considerations, with the neo-Marxian argument that government spending to assist capital accumulation and to reduce social discontent produce a "fiscal crisis" in which demands for spending outstrip revenues.[4]

Given such divergent perspectives on public spending – and there are many others – there will never be complete agreement over what the budget should consist of, even over how it should be prepared, because such a happy state of affairs presumes that all conflict within society could be eliminated. Since the budget ultimately deals with power, with who gets included, excluded, rewarded and punished, it will always be a controversial subject. The current "crisis in economic theory" and the apparently intractable nature of current economic problems increase con-

2 Two valuable works on the revenue budget process are: David A. Good, *The Politics of Anticipation: Making Canadian Federal Tax Policy* (Ottawa: School of Public Administration, Carleton University, 1980), and Douglas G. Hartle, *The Revenue Budget Process of the Government of Canada: Descriptions, Appraisals, and Proposals* (Toronto: Canadian Tax Foundation, 1982).
3 See "The Crisis in Economic Theory," *The Public Interest*, Special Edition (1980).
4 Two good articles which present the first view are: Thomas J. Courchene, "Towards a protected society: the politicization of economic life," *Canadian Journal of Economics*, XIII, 4 (November 1980), pp. 556-77; and Rod Dobell, "How Ottawa Decides Economic Policy," *Policy Options*, 1, 3 (September/October 1980), pp. 12-19. For the neo-Marxian perspective, the leading work is James O'Connor, *The Fiscal Crisis of the State* (New York: St. Martin's, 1973), and for the application of his thesis to the Canadian situation, see Leo Panitch, ed., *The Canadian State: Political Economy and Political Power* (Toronto: University of Toronto Press, 1977).

flict. A public mood of disillusionment and declining expectations surrounds budgeting as an economic activity and this pessimism spills over into other dimensions of the process.

A further preliminary word on the scope of the paper is necessary. In relation to the expenditure side of the process, the remainder of the paper concentrates on developments at the national level. This focus conforms with an unfortunate tradition within the Canadian public administration literature. Despite the fact that for a number of years now the provincial and municipal governments have done more of the spending within the federal system, far less has been written about their financial procedures.[5] An up-to-date, comparative study of provincial and municipal budgetary approaches would be extremely valuable, but it cannot be attempted in this article.

Review of the literature

Notions about what budgeting involves have changed over time and have affected the types of organizations, personnel, information and relationships involved in the process. Writing in 1973, Donald Gow identified three main budgetary purposes which corresponded to three historical stages through which the expenditure budget process had evolved at the national level in Canada.[6] The first stage involved an emphasis upon control, defined narrowly in terms of the accuracy and probity of financial reporting. Over time the concept of budgetary control has acquired multiple meanings, but a concern to ensure the legality and honesty of public spending remains a basic purpose of all budget systems. Such control is a prerequisite to the use of the budget for other purposes. In a cabinet-parliamentary system, control is important both within the executive arm of government and in terms of rendering the executive accountable to the legislature.

In Canada, the emphasis on the legal aspects of control reached its peak during the 1930s with the creation of the post of the Comptroller of the Treasury. Comprehensiveness, unity, clarity, specific authorization, and accuracy were the criteria to be met if internal and external control were to be realized.[7] The emphasis was mainly on input costs, as re-

5 See Richard M. Bird, *Financing of Canadian Government: A Quantitative Overview* (Toronto: Canadian Tax Foundation, 1979), pp. 14-16.

6 Donald Gow, *The Progress of Budgetary Reform in the Government of Canada* (Ottawa: Economic Council of Canada, Special Study No. 17, 1973), p. 2. Gow borrowed his threefold classification from Allen Shick's perceptive article on the U.S. experience, "The Road to PPB: The Stages of Budget Reform," *Public Administration Review*, XXVI, 4 (December 1966), pp. 243-58.

7 For a useful discussion of these criteria, see Kenneth W. Knight and Kenneth W. Wiltshire, *Formulating Government Budgets, Aspects of Australian and North American Experience* (St. Lucia: University of Queensland Press, 1977), chapter 3. See also H.R. Balls, "Control and coordination of public expenditures," *Canadian Tax Journal*, IX (May-June, 1962), pp. 159-65.

flected in the designation of 30 Standard Objects of Expenditure. Detail and accuracy were necessary to ensure that expenditures occurred according to the intent of legislative bodies and there were requirements for strict pre- and post-audits of all spending. The main personnel associated with this type of budgeting were auditors, accountants and lawyers.

With the growth in the scope and complexity of government operations, especially in the postwar period, it became more difficult to meet these tests of successful budgeting. Insistence on detail, for example, clashed with the principle of clarity of presentation when the size and types of public spending increased. Also, the belief developed that the problems of legal control were largely solved. Insistence upon excessively rigid controls was stifling for departmental managers, the Glassco Commission warned in the early sixties.[8] Furthermore, the savings produced by adherence to strict rules were miniscule compared to the total volume of public spending.

During the fifties and sixties concern about control subsided, only to be revived recently in response to the tight budgetary situation and revelations by the Auditor General and others that a breakdown had apparently occurred. However, the term "control" has taken on different, much wider meanings within contemporary budget debates. To the original concern about *legal* control were added concerns about *managerial* control (i.e., the efficiency of government departments and agencies), *strategic* control (i.e., the allocation of spending among various areas of government activity and the assessment of the results of programs in terms of realizing stated objectives), and the *macro-economic* aspects of control (i.e., the use of government spending for fiscal policy purposes).[9] As will be discussed later, these various aspects of control are related and an emphasis on one aspect may lead to the development of budgetary procedures which hinder rather than help the others. We will see in a moment how this emphasis upon the broader aspects of control has developed.

When the problems of legal control were deemed to be solved, effective management was added to the purposes of budgeting. The budget was seen as a management tool to ensure the economical and efficient operation of departments and programs. The introduction of labour-saving equipment, the streamlining of paper processing, the careful deter-

8 Canada, Royal Commission on Government Organization, *Report*, I (Ottawa: Queen's Printer, 1962), pp. 91-93.
9 See Peter Else, "New Developments in Budgetary Decision-Making: A Review," in David Coombes, *et al.*, eds., *The Power of the Purse: The Role of European Parliaments in Budgetary Decisions* (London: George Allen and Unwin, 1976), p. 339, for a discussion of the ambiguous use of the concept of control.

mination of manpower needs, and the introduction of performance measurement procedures to relate results achieved to resources used, are among the typical activities associated with managerial control. As one of·the few processes which brings together in one location information on the diverse and far-flung operations of government, the budget provides an opportunity to identify contradictions, duplication and mismanagement. Of course, there is no guarantee that all defects will be identified, or that those which are will be cured.

Legal and managerial control take as given the objectives and structure of existing programs. Beginning in the late sixties, the emphasis shifted to the use of the budget to set long-range priorities and to evaluate existing programs. The shift was heralded by the introduction of Planning, Programming and Budgeting (PPB), but the change also coincided with the development of a more active cabinet committee system (including the important Priorities and Planning Committee), the separation of the Treasury Board Secretariat from the Department of Finance, and the expansion of central agencies for purposes of strategic planning.[10] The new arrangements and procedures were intended to integrate a variety of processes, some of which operated annually and others over a longer term. Such processes included: the identification of priority problems, the launching of major policy reviews, the review of individual departments, the evaluation of senior personnel, the preparation of the government's legislative program, and the preparation of the revenue and spending budgets. Making all these pieces fit together was a tough job, which was never fully accomplished. Since budgeting was recognized as being connected to numerous other processes, it became a much more complicated activity.

Pushed by the criticism of the Glassco Commission that Ottawa had been slow to adopt modern budgetary techniques and by the "demonstration effect" of the U.S. experience with PPB, the system was introduced across all departments during the late sixties. It was intended to lead to a merger of analysis, planning and budgetary allocation. Installing analysis and planning within the budgetary process has proven to be the most difficult of the budgetary goals to obtain. For the past two decades debate has raged between the so-called pragmatic incrementalist and the

10 Useful sources which place budgetary developments within the context of broader changes to policy-making structures in Ottawa during the seventies include the following: Richard French, *How Ottawa Decides* (Toronto: James Lorimer, 1980); Douglas Hartle, *The Expenditure Budget Process in the Government of Canada* (Toronto: Canadian Tax Foundation, 1978); H.V. Kroeker, *Accountability and Control, The Government Expenditure Process* (Montreal: C.D. Howe Research Institute, 1978); and R. Van Loon, "Stop the music: the current policy and expenditure management system in Ottawa," CANADIAN PUBLIC ADMINISTRATION, 24, 2 (Summer 1981), pp. 175-99.

rational program budgeters over the extent to which analysis and planning must be subordinated to political considerations in budgeting. A review of this debate reveals that PPB was neither a panacea nor a hoax, but that it was definitely oversold and probably was introduced too quickly.

The leading proponent of incrementalism in budgeting is Aaron Wildavsky, an American political scientist. In his seminal work, *The Politics of the Budgetary Process* (1964), Wildavsky went beyond the traditional concern with the mechanics of budgeting to treat the budget as "political things." Budgeting was "at the heart of the political process" because the government's proposals for the raising and the spending of the tax dollars reflected decisions on how the benefits and burdens of programs would be shared among different groups within the society.[11] Wildavsky portrayed this process at the national level in the United States as enormously complex and completed under great pressures of time. In response to such pressures, decision-makers resorted to a number of "aids to calculation." Principal among these was the incremental method. In part, the method consisted of treating the expenditure base as given and focusing attention on the increases requested each year. Accepted notions of "fair shares" were developed among decision-makers. Decision-making was fragmented, made in sequence by various bodies and coordinated through repeated attacks on problems and multiple feedback mechanisms. In the final result, the budgetary changes that occurred were marginal or incremental in nature.

In his initial work, Wildavsky focused on incrementalism as a method of calculation. Later, in more explanatory and predictive efforts, Wildavsky and his colleagues focused on incrementalism as process, defined as a stable pattern of relationships among actors over several years.[12] In Wildavsky's studies, the relationship involved the U.S. Congress and bureaus acting through the Office of Management and Budget. It is not necessary to discuss here the way in which Wildavsky sought to "model" these relationships; it is sufficient to reiterate the importance of distinguishing the process of incrementalism from the product. Conceivably, non-incremental processes could produce both incremental and non-

11 Aaron Wildavsky, *The Politics of the Budgetary Process* (Boston, Mass.: Little, Brown, 1964, revised editions in 1974 and 1978), pp. 4, 5. See also Aaron Wildavsky, *Budgeting: A Comparative Theory of Budgetary Processes* (Toronto: Little, Brown, 1975), chapter 12. While the suggestion that budgeting involves politics now seems to be a commonplace, at the time that Wildavsky first wrote it represented a truly original viewpoint.
12 M.A. Dempster and Aaron Wildavsky, "On Change: Or, There is No Magic Size for an Increment," *Political Studies*, XXVII (1979), pp. 371-89, and Otto Davis, Michael Dempster and Aaron Wildavsky, "Towards a Predictive Theory of Government Expenditure: U.S. Domestic Appropriations," *British Journal of Political Science*, IV (1974), pp. 419-52.

incremental outcomes. The challenge is to predict when surrounding conditions will give rise to non-incremental procedures and results.

A large number of critiques have been levelled at the writings of Wildavsky et al. over the years. Some of the criticisms are methodological, involving questions of the appropriateness of indicators of budgetary change within the American system, and these need not detain us here. Another line of criticism calls for a clearer distinction between process and outcomes; a complaint which Wildavsky dealt with explicitly in a subsequent work.[13] Failure to specify what size of a monetary increase or decrease constitutes an incremental change was perceived as a further difficulty. On this point, Wildavsky replied that identifying increments depends on the purpose of a particular research project. For a study of expenditure growth patterns, a 10 per cent increase might be seen as large, given that at this rate a budget would increase by 100 per cent in only seven years. For someone concerned about the comprehensiveness of budgetary calculations, the discovery that analysis was confined to 15 per cent of spending above and below the expenditure base might lead to the label "incrementalism" being applied. There is, in other words, no magic figure; it all depends on the purposes of the research.

Two other challenges to the incremental model deserve mention. Lance Le Loup and William Moreland suggest on the basis of their studies that the "normal" strategy of moderation posited by the incremental theorists is more myth than reality.[14] They argue that not all agencies within the U.S. government behave in the same way. A strategy of moderation may be desirable for agencies seeking stability and support for their initial requests, but it will not lead to agency growth and may produce decline. It is their finding that, the more assertive an agency, the lower the relative proportion of requests approved, but the greater the absolute budget growth. However, a high degree of assertiveness is not equally available to all agencies. "Agency assertiveness is a function of several factors: the values, attitudes, and orientation of agency administrators, the extent of external support for the agency and its programs, and the environmental constraints."[15] Le Loup and Moreland recognize that their conclusions, based upon an investigation of only agricultural agencies in the period 1946-71, must be tentative. Their perspective, however, recognizes that the behaviour of organizations within the budgetary process will not be uniform and will vary over time. An offensive strategy may well have worked successfully in an expansionary period, but presumably a more

13 Dempster and Wildavsky, "On Change," pp. 374-76.
14 Lance T. Le Loup and William B. Moreland, "Agency Strategies and Executive Review: The Hidden Politics of Budgeting," *Public Administration Review*, XXXVIII, 3 (May/June, 1978), pp. 232-39.
15 Ibid., p. 238.

defensive posture is appropriate under the current circumstances of expenditure restraint.

A related criticism is that incrementalism ignores non-incremental policy pursuits.[16] In addition to being fewer in number, non-incremental policies have the character of being relatively indivisible. That is to say, some policies are relatively monolithic in structure, and do not consist of a large number of separable sub-programs and activities. Such policies are beset by "organizational thresholds" or critical mass points. They must expand greatly if they are to expand at all. Cumulative development of policies through piecemeal, incremental increases is not possible. Non-incremental policies are also seen as essentially unstable for they are "devoid of middle ground between self-generating states of growth and decay."[17] In the United States, the space program and urban renewal efforts have been identified as non-incremental policy pursuits.

As has been seen, much of the debate over incrementalism has been based upon American data. It could be argued that the Canadian system of government is inherently less prone to incrementalism than the United States. In Canada, authority and power are concentrated in the cabinet, Parliament is not a strong force within the budgetary process, and the bureaucracy is more subject to unified political direction. This contrasts with the U.S. system of separation of powers, the powerful budgetary role assumed by the Congress, and the divided loyalty of the bureaucracy to the president and to authorizing committees of Congress. Despite these differences, it would be surprising to find that Canada was entirely free from incrementalism since it arises mainly in response to the daunting complexity of modern budgeting.

The classical budgetary process as it operated in Canada before the late sixties, with its emphasis upon input control and a narrow definition of efficiency, lent itself to an incremental style of decision-making. The process treated the expenditure base as given and focused attention on the increments calculated on the additional inputs required (manpower, supplies, etc.) rather than on objectives and outputs. Departments rarely sought to evaluate the effectiveness of their programs, except, perhaps, to prepare a case for an enriched version of these programs. They haggled with the staff in the Treasury Board Secretariat over the size of their annual increments. The process operated on a much smaller scale than today and seemed to be characterized by considerable predictability. The cabinet had ultimate decision-making authority, but given the fact of virtually completed budgets built from the "bottom up" on a de-

16 Paul R. Schulman, "Nonincremental Policy Making: Notes Towards an Alternative Paradigm," *The American Political Science Review*, 69, 4 (December 1975), pp. 1354-70.
17 Ibid., p. 1356.

partmental basis, plus the normal constraints of complexity and the pressures of time, the actual decision-making capability of ministers was limited.

Bruce Doern attempted to measure the extent of incremental outcomes involved in the budgetary pattern of the federal government over the decade 1960 to 1970.[18] He identified three types of expenditure additions. An "incremental-bureaucratic" process accounted for approximately 45 per cent of the expenditure growth over the period. This growth consisted of the normal expansion of programs in line with population growth and inflation. Secondly, there was an "incremental-uncontrolled" expenditure process where growth was due to "uncontrolled" forces such as provincial actions in the context of shared-cost programs. About 20 per cent of the expenditure increase fell into this category. Thirdly, about 35 per cent of the growth was accounted for by new initiatives by the cabinet. New programs, once created, became part of the incremental controlled pattern. Doern readily acknowledged that the percentages assigned to the three categories were somewhat arbitrary since he was working mainly on the basis of information presented in public documents.[19] Some of the new programs ascribed to cabinet leadership may have owed much to bureaucratic power and initiative. While Doern identified incremental outcomes, he did not investigate whether stable (incremental) patterns of interaction between departments and central budget actors had produced these results.

The Doern study concluded at the point in time when the new PPB system was taking hold. PPB was intended to overcome the incremental pattern of decision-making based upon existing departmental structures. It was to usher in an era of integrated, top-down expenditure planning.[20] It involved the setting of specific objectives, the assessment of alternative

18 See G. Bruce Doern, "The Budgetary Process and the Policy Role of the Federal Bureaucracy" in G. Bruce Doern and Peter Aucoin, eds., *The Structures of Policy-Making in Canada* (Toronto: Macmillan, 1971), pp. 79-106.
19 Ibid., pp. 83-86. See also footnote 10 on page 106.
20 The literature on PPB is voluminous. For the origins in the U.S., see David Novick, ed., *Program Budgeting: Program Analysis and the Federal Government* (Cambridge, Mass.: Harvard University Press, 1965), and Leonard Merewitz and Stephen H. Soshnick, *The Budget's New Clothes: A Critique of Planning; Programming Budgeting* (Chicago: Markham, 1971). Other useful general studies are Douglas G. Hartle, *A Theory of the Expenditure Budget Process* (Toronto: Ontario Economic Council, 1976), pp. 37-46, and James Cutt, "The Program Budgeting Approach to Public Expenditure: A Conceptual Review," CANADIAN PUBLIC ADMINISTRATION, 13, 4 (Winter 1970), pp. 396-426. On the introduction of the system to Canada, the following are readily available sources: H.R. Balls, "Planning, Programming and Budgeting in Canada," *Public Administration*, 48 (Autumn 1970), pp. 289-306; E.J. Benson, "Budget Breakthrough: Adoption of PPB," *Canadian Tax Journal*, XVI (May-June 1968), pp. 161-67; and A.W. Johnson, "Planning, Programming and Budgeting in Canada," *Public Administration Review*, 33, 1 (January-February, 1973), pp. 23-30.

means of reaching them, and the regular measurement of progress towards such objectives.[21]

To the extent that PPB was oversold, disappointment with its actual results was inevitable. It was relatively easy to move from the earlier input orientation and to express expenditures in terms of objectives. Nevertheless, the process of clarifying objectives was protracted, controversial, and in many cases incomplete. Many departmental objectives remained so vaguely stated that they could not be challenged meaningfully and could not be measured.

PPB was also intended to overcome the tendency of incrementalism to disregard the future implications of current spending. Program forecasts over five years would prevent departments from sneaking in major commitments with an initial modest request (affectionately known as "the camel's nose" problem) and would permit a more orderly reallocation of spending on different activities according to priorities set by cabinet. In practice, most departmental forecasts continued to be based upon detailed budgets prepared by individual managers throughout departments and future spending was usually an extrapolation from the past with some provision for departmental aspirations.[22]

The more fundamental purpose of PPB was to bring objective and quantitative analysis into budgetary decision-making, particularly in order to submit the expenditure base to careful scrutiny. From the outset the Treasury Board realized that the introduction of quantitative analysis would be a difficult and uneven process. For example, while the Board encouraged the use of cost/benefit analysis, it admitted that the benefits and costs of certain programs would be difficult to quantify. Still, the process of conducting the analysis would be useful for decision-makers, some analysis would be better than none, and efficiency considerations would be more systematically incorporated into budgetary decision-making. The Board attempted to implement an elaborate system of measuring program effectiveness (the so-called Operational Performance Measurement System), but this was later scaled down to more modest requirements.

To meet the analytical requirements of PPB there was an influx of systems analysts, operation research specialists, and social scientists from a variety of disciplines. The main organizational home for these specialists was the Planning Branch of the Treasury Board Secretariat and the leadership was provided by Douglas G. Hartle, who was deputy secretary to the Board from 1969 to 1973. At the time, Hartle was an enthus-

21 Government of Canada, *Planning, Programming Budgeting Guide* (Ottawa: Queen's Printer, 1969), p. 8.
22 Auditor General of Canada, *Annual Report and Supplement, 1975* (Ottawa: Supply and Services, 1976), p. 47.

iastic and sophisticated advocate of applied microeconomics as a means of improving program evaluations and strategic planning within government. According to Richard French, the Planning Branch's concern with overall government goals led to conflict with the Privy Council Office, which was jealous of its franchise on the provision of policy advice to the prime minister and cabinet.[23] The Branch also alienated its most important potential ally, the Department of Finance, by trespassing on its domain of broad economic management. Finally, the analysis of the Planning Branch was not integrated with the more detailed work on the spending forecasts and internal management being done by the Program Branch of the Secretariat. French concludes that Hartle and his staff produced an "intellectual *tour de force* without an audience to appreciate it."[24] It is unclear, however, whether the failure to utilize the analysis was primarily the result of bureaucratic infighting, the basic differences in outlook between the politicians and the professional policy analysts, the entrenched nature of existing budgetary routines, or some combination of these factors and others. We return to this question later in the paper.

It appears that PPB has been nowhere completely and successfully implemented.[25] The Government of Canada may have enjoyed relatively more success with PPB than other jurisdictions, partly because our constitutional system concentrates authority consistent with the centralizing bias inherent in PPB and because of the greater stability (at least until recently) within our economic and political environment. Optimists argue that while some of the formal requirements of PPB may be gone, its residual impact can still be seen. Governments have become more self-conscious about the selection of goals, the arrangement of programs around goals highlighted some outdated, overlapping and misguided efforts, and some of the incremental rules of thumb have been weakened by the introduction of efficiency and effectiveness considerations into budgetary debates.[26]

Current developments and problems

In response to a worsening revenue picture in the late 1970s and to criticisms that its existing budgetary procedures contained a bias in favour of increased spending, the Government of Canada introduced a new expenditure management system in 1979. The new system sought to ensure

23 French, *How Ottawa Decides*, pp. 32-45.
24 Ibid., p. 35.
25 Wildavsky, *Budgeting, passim.*
26 See Timothy E. Reid, "The failure of PPBS: real incentives for the 1980s (The past is not prologue)," *Optimum*, 10, 4 (1979), pp. 23-36, and John C. Strick, "ZBB: An Innovation or a Rediscovery of Old Concepts," *Canadian Tax Journal*, 28, 1 (January-February 1980), pp. 43-52.

that groups of ministers who wanted to spend were also required to save. It also sought to ensure that policy decisions would be made and expenditure limits set at the same time. To achieve these goals, ministers serving on five cabinet committees covering different policy sectors were entrusted with the task of managing ten resource envelopes. The amounts to be placed in each of the envelopes was to be determined by the Priorities and Planning Committee, based upon the advice of the Minister of Finance.

There is not the space here to describe the details of the new system and, since it has been used for only one full budgetary cycle, it is premature to offer definitive judgments on its success.[27] Several of its purposes and probable consequences deserve to be mentioned. First, the new system increases the political content of budgeting and reduces the potential impact of so-called objective analysis. No longer will budgets be built completely from the bottom up; instead the cabinet through its committees will determine the broad patterns of spending. As part of this more political approach, the Priorities and Planning Committee of cabinet, and the Minister of Finance who advises it, gain influence because of their role in allotting money to the various policy sectors. The Treasury Board, as a statutory committee of cabinet, was previously responsible for setting departmental budgets. With the transfer of this task to the five policy committees, Treasury Board is left with determining the level of financial and manpower resources required to deliver efficiently programs approved by the policy committees and it is also expected to identify the "cross-envelope" financial implications of departmental proposals.

At this stage in the development of the new process it is unclear whether ministers and their departments will maintain the discipline necessary to make it work successfully. By restricting ministers to what is available within their envelopes, there is supposedly pressure on them to review programs within their policy sectors and to reallocate funds to more effective programs. This benefit is unrealized at this point because most departments are not in a position to provide evaluation results which would enable ministers to assess ongoing programs.[28] Most min-

---

27 For details, see Canada, Treasury Board, *Guide to the Policy Expenditure Management System* (Ottawa, 1980), Policy and Expenditure Management System – Second Draft of Submissions Manual (January 1982). For commentary, see Sandford F. Borins, "Ottawa's Expenditure 'Envelopes': Workable Rationality at Last?" in G. Bruce Doern, ed., *How Ottawa Spends Your Tax Dollars, National Policy and Economic Development, 1982* (Toronto: James Lorimer, 1982), pp. 63-86; Rod Dobell, "Pressing the Envelope," *Policy Options*, 2, 5 (November/December, 1981), pp. 13-18; and R. Van Loon, "Stop the music."

28 Useful discussions of the new system have taken place in the Standing Senate Committee on National Finance, *Proceedings*, May 28, 1981, November 19, 1981, and March 24, 1982.

isterial reviews to date focus on new programs and expansions of existing efforts.

Each envelope contains both operational and policy reserves and already the concern has been expressed that these reserves might become so large as to breach the financial discipline of the envelope system.[29] The new system also involves multi-year costing, something which was intended to be part of PPB. It is unclear how seriously ministers treat such forecasts. While expenditure limits are identified for policy envelopes, firm three-year budgetary ceilings for departments have not been adopted because they would impose, in the Liberal government's view, an excessive rigidity on budgetary decision-making. On the other hand, if forecasts are revised regularly, financial discipline will be lost. Under the new system, ministers have gained some collective influence over spending, but at some cost in terms of individual ministerial independence. Ministers will be tempted to exploit the openings mentioned above in order to protect against the loss of resources and personal prestige.

Earlier budgetary approaches such as incrementalism and PPB supported innovation and growth within government. Economic stagnation and reduced growth in public revenues have caused a search for new mechanisms to check spending, to terminate ineffective programs and to control bureaucracies. Program evaluation has recently become fashionable in Ottawa, with prospects for a high level of activity for the foreseeable future. In 1978 the Office of the Comptroller General (OCG) was created as the central agency responsible for the promotion of evaluation. To date the OCG's approach has been cautious and pragmatic. Departments remain responsible for the actual conduct of evaluations, with the OCG providing advice and monitoring the results to ensure objectivity.[30] Program evaluation remains more of an art form than a science. Successful evaluation faces numerous obstacles, such as nebulous goals; the lack of appropriate data and personnel; a variety of methodological problems; ensuring the timeliness of evaluation findings; the use of evaluation for symbolic, ritualistic purposes; and the capacity of departments to resist the implementation of evaluation results.[31]

The Trudeau government promised to make its internal evaluation

29 Senate Committee on National Finance, *Report*, March 24, 1982, p. 5.
30 One recalls at this point Douglas Hartle's shrewd observation that "Asking the public service manager to subject his operations to recurrent comprehensive evaluation is like asking the dog to carry the stick with which he will be beaten."
31 See IPAC's national seminar edited by Michael Hicks, "Evaluating Evaluation in today's government," CANADIAN PUBLIC ADMINISTRATION, 24, 3 (Fall 1981), and G. Bruce Doern and Allan M. Maslove, eds., *The Public Evaluation of Government Spending* (Montreal: Institute for Research on Public Policy, 1979), and J.M. Jordan and S.L. Sutherland, "Assessing the Results of Public Expenditure: Program Evaluation in the Canadian Federal Government," CANADIAN PUBLIC ADMINISTRATION, 22, 3 (Fall 1979), pp. 581-609.

studies available to Parliament. Even with access to such studies, it is doubtful whether Parliament under modern conditions can hold governments accountable in any meaningful fashion for their budgetary performance. Reforms to the procedures for granting supply over the last decade have increased only marginally Parliament's surveillance of financial matters.[32] Further reforms, such as those recommended in the Lambert Report, might prevent Parliament from losing further ground, but would not secure a major place for the institution within the budgetary process.[33]

Since 1977 the Auditor General has been authorized to report on behalf of Parliament, not only whether probity and efficiency have been achieved in government spending but also whether departments have created adequate procedures for evaluating the effectiveness of their programs. The Auditor General has developed comprehensive or value-for-money auditing, which, according to its sponsors, will provide a usable indicator of effectiveness performance within organizations operating on a non-profit basis. To its detractors, the new method offers the allure of a simplistic slogan whose precepts cannot be fulfilled in practice and which really amounts to a disguised philosophical attack upon the alleged evils of "big government."[34]

Emerging trends and future prospects

Disillusionment with PPB and the perceived need for financial restraint has led to the latest budgetary fashion – zero-based budgeting (ZBB). Contrary to the past pattern of budgetary ideas migrating from the United States to Ottawa and then to provincial capitals, ZBB has not been adopted to date in Ottawa. ZBB began its life in private industry, was adopted by a number of American states, and was implemented in Washington by President Carter. In Canada, several provinces and municipalities have installed ZBB systems.[35]

32   Paul G. Thomas, "Parliament and the Purse Strings," in Harold D. Clarke, Colin Campbell, F.W. Quo and Arthur Goddau, eds., *Parliament, Policy and Representation* (Toronto: Methuen, 1980), pp. 160-80.

33   Douglas G. Hartle, "The Report of the Royal Commission on Financial Management and Accountability (The Lambert Report): A Review," *Canadian Public Policy*, 3 (Summer 1979), pp. 366-82, and Paul G. Thomas, "The Lambert Report: Parliament and Accountability," CANADIAN PUBLIC ADMINISTRATION, 22, 4 (Winter 1979), pp. 557-70.

34   See the case for value for money auditing by James J. Macdonell, "Value for Money: The Accountability Equation" (Paper to the IPAC Conference, Winnipeg, August 1979), and the criticisms of S.L. Sutherland, "On the Audit Trail of the Auditor General: Parliament's Servant, 1973-1980," CANADIAN PUBLIC ADMINISTRATION, 23, 4 (Winter 1980), pp. 616-45.

35   The literature on ZBB has become voluminous. The "father" of ZBB is Peter Phyrr, *Zero-Base Budgeting* (Toronto: John Wiley, 1973). See also Hammond and Knott, *A Zero-Based Look at Zero-Base Budgeting*. The better articles are: E.J.

An alleged virtue of ZBB is its flexibility. However, most systems involve three operational steps: the identification of decision units within organizations; the preparation by unit managers of "decision-packages" involving analysis of spending above and below the expenditure base of the preceding year; and the ranking of these packages in terms of their contribution to the overall goals of the organization. Despite the title, most working ZBB systems do not involve a complete re-examination of all spending; what it attempted is a marginal analysis of spending above and below the base.[36] For all its claims at being a form of rational budgeting, ZBB is best described as a more sophisticated form of incremental budgeting. Its greatest virtues are the formal requirement for the preparation of alternative funding levels and the greater involvement of lower-level management in the budgetary process. To the disappointment of many of its early advocates, ZBB has not led to major reductions in spending or to major reassignments of funds. Nor has it helped much in identifying issues, setting objectives, or even determining alternative methods of reaching those objectives.

The Ministry of Revenue within the Government of Ontario has claimed some success with a combination of ZBB and managing by results (MBR).[37] The process has been under development since 1975. For the 1981-82 cycle, a preliminary ranking of decision-packages was added to the process for the purpose of communicating ministry wide goals to operating managers before they began the documentation of their packages. This feature represented a modification to the standard ZBB approach of building budgets completely from the bottom up. Another feature of the ministry's approach involves managers, in effect, making commitments to achieve certain results in exchange for specific funding. Monitoring the commitment contracts is done on the basis of regular reports on indicators of performance agreed to in advance. The ministry relates its success to the adoption of a pragmatic, adaptive approach, avoidance of a panacea syndrome and the provision of continuous training to its staff.

Clynch, "Zero-Base Budgeting in Practice: An Assessment," *International Journal of Public Administration*, 1, 1 (1979), pp. 43-64; Donald F. Harder, "Zero-Base Federal Style," *Public Administration Review*, 27, 4 (July-August 1977), pp. 400-407; Thomas P. Lauth, "Zero-Base Budgeting in Georgia State Government: Myth or Reality," *Public Administration Review*, 28, 5 (September-October 1978), pp. 420-29; George Neufeld, "Learning from Zero-Base Budgeting," *Optimum*, 9, 3 (1978), pp. 40-52; Allan Shick, "The Road from ZBB," *Public Administration Review*, 38, 2 (March-April 1978), pp. 177-80; and John C. Strick, "ZBB: Innovation or Rediscovery."

36 See Shick, "The Road to ZBB," and Thomas P. Lauth, "Zero-Base Budgeting in Georgia."

37 Government of Ontario, Ministry of Revenue, *Integrated Zero Base Budgeting and Managing by Results for 1982-83* (Toronto, October 1981). The ministry publishes both an operating manual and a text for a presentation on the system.

The dilemmas of budgetary reform

As the above review makes clear, a consensus on how to conduct budgeting is always temporary because the budget is subject to the political process within a changing society. Budget techniques are judged as much by their effects on relative budget shares as by their achievement of such neutral process goals as increased information and analytical clarity.

Budgets have been asked to serve a variety of purposes not always consistent with one another. Probably we have expected too much of the budgetary process, which tends to be wedded to past decisions and takes place under great pressures of time. The process has proven to be a poor vehicle for the identification of issues, the preparation of policy plans, the assessment of alternatives and the evaluation of results. It is necessary to weigh more carefully the trade-offs involved with changes to budgetary procedures.[38] Should we sacrifice policy flexibility for greater planning? Should departmental autonomy be stressed at the cost of central policy direction? Will an insistence on detailed control lead to excessive red tape and information overload? These dilemmas are intensified when it is realized that the categories are related. A loss of control over budget detail can lead to a loss of policy control. In view of these dilemmas, what should be the response to the complexity of the contemporary budget?

One response is to leave well enough alone. This attitude reflects disenchantment with past reforms which have not lived up to their advance billing. Moreover, wider political forces are seen as more important than administrative gadgets in determining budgetary outcomes. Past reforms have allegedly been undone by political considerations. In this view, changes to budgetary procedures will be made pragmatically and incrementally as political circumstances permit. In the present turbulent economic environment, stability in the budgetary process is perceived to be desirable.

An alternative viewpoint insists on further changes to deal with the deficiencies of the existing budget process. A variety of proposals have been made which would extend the purposes of budgeting and further complicate the process. Thus the Lambert Report has called for an integration of budgeting and personnel policy through a restructured and retitled Treasury Board to be called the Board of Management.[39] The report also recommended a modified "sunset" approach whereby all statutory programs would have their funding lapse after five years unless

38 See the useful article on this theme by Naomi J. Caiden, "Dilemmas of Budget Reform," *Policy Studies Journal*, Special Issue No. 4 (1980-81), pp. 1215-26.
39 Canada, Royal Commission on Financial Management and Accountability, *Final Report* (Ottawa: Supply and Services, 1979).

recommended for renewal by the responsible minister and reapproved by Parliament. These and a variety of other changes proposed would make budgeting more comprehensive but it is conceivable that by asking the budget to do more it may actually do less. Before we can safely add to the purposes of budgeting, we should be clearer about the organizational potential and costs of such changes. Some of the goals being sought can, perhaps, be better realized outside the budgetary domain.

The difficulty of forecasting the impacts of changes leads to some discussion of the gaps in our knowledge of the budgetary process. The incorporation of goals into budgetary analysis has proven to be a perennial difficulty. Rather than constantly lamenting the refusal by politicians to state their goals precisely, it would be better for social scientists to investigate why politicians seek to obscure their goals and how this apparent "fact" of political life can be dealt with inside the budgetary process. Robert D. Behn has written recently about the need to make analysis more relevant to the needs of the politicians.[40] He suggests that the analyst is concerned with efficiency and outputs, and ignores sunk costs, while the politician is concerned with distribution and inputs, and seeks to justify sunk costs. Obscuring goals is required to build a consensus in support of programs. Politicians tend also to adopt a shorter time perspective than analysts, who do not have to worry about demonstrating program success before the next election. The analyst must incorporate such considerations of political feasibility and political stategy into his analysis if he wishes to ensure its relevance. Economically rational systems like PPB and ZBB do not meet the tests of political rationality.

Our understanding of the politics of the national budgetary process would be improved by a series of case studies of the growth of individual departments and programs.[41] Such case studies would help to offset the unfortunate tendency to treat the bureaucracy as a single, homogeneous body rather than what it actually is, a conglomeration of very diverse entities. System-wide reforms take too little account of the needs of different units. Budget maximization, which is often held to be a uniform drive within the bureaucracy, may be a strategy open to only certain organizations. Colin Campbell and George Szablowski, and Michael Hicks looked at the approach followed by the Treasury Board Secretariat in dealing with departments under the former budgetary process but their research should be updated in light of the new expenditure man-

40 Robert D. Behn, "Policy Analysis and Policy Politics," *Policy Analysis*, Vol. 7, 2 (Spring 1981), pp. 199-226.
41 Bruce Doern and his colleagues have taken a step in this direction with their annual volumes on national expenditures.

agement system. We also need to learn more of the departmental side of the budgetary story.[42]

More attention should be paid to federal-provincial negotiations over budgetary matters. For example, part of the conventional wisdom of practitioners is that joint programs are more resistant to budgetary controls. A comparison of the expenditure growth patterns of shared-cost programs to other programs, supplemented by interviews with the principal actors, might confirm or deny this hypothesis.

In terms of budgeting at the provincial and municipal levels, we lack up-to-date descriptive material, let alone in-depth analysis. Is budgeting less formalized and more personal within the smaller provincial governments? What budgetary freedom do such jurisdictions enjoy if over 60 per cent of their revenues are transfer payments from Ottawa? Will smaller jurisdictions have the managerial capacity to operate more elaborate budget systems? Do pressure groups have more access to key budget decision-makers at the provincial level? Do provinces face as great a problem in terms of control over non-departmental spending? Many of these same questions arise at the municipal level as well.

The most significant challenge for at least the next decade is how to manage restraint within government in the face of gloomy economic forecasts. Since the mid-seventies, governments in Canada have attempted to practise expenditure restraint, a process made more painful by reason of the fact that the brakes were being applied to public spending after a decade of rather explosive growth.[43] Even though there is no generally accepted formula for calculating revenue availability, the dominant political perception today is one of scarcity. Coping with slow growth and even retrenchment will be difficult and conflict-ridden. The public has come to expect services and improvements to them. It also believes that there is waste and mismanagement within governments. While Canadians would like to see their governments go on a "Weight Watcher's diet," they do not wish to see them beheaded.

One approach to achieving restraint is the crash austerity program, such as that applied by the Progressive Conservative government in Manitoba after 1977. Such an approach involves a number of dangers. By relying upon readily accessible items to achieve savings, the reductions may occur in the wrong place. For example, the imposition of a general

42   Colin J. Campbell and George Szablowski, *The Superbureaucrats: Structure and Behaviour in Central Agencies* (Toronto: Macmillan, 1979), pp. 40-49, and Michael Hicks, "The Treasury Board of Canada and its clients: five years of change and administrative reform, 1966-1971," CANADIAN PUBLIC ADMINISTRATION, 16, no. 2 (Summer 1973), pp. 182-205.
43   See the volume edited by Peter Aucoin, *The Politics and Management of Restraint in Government* (Montreal: Institute for Research in Public Policy, 1981).

hiring freeze and a reliance upon attrition to reduce staff costs will penalize more efficient and labour-intensive organizations. Secondly, rapidly imposed reductions will not permit adequate calculations of the secondary and longer-term costs, and who will bear them. While the crash austerity program may have a desirable shock effect on the bureaucracy, it may not produce permanent mechanisms to control spending.

In a recent article, Daniel Tarschys offers the general outlines of a "rational decremental" strategy as an alternative to the hazards of forced retrenchment.[44] He admits that the five features of his strategy do not constitute a working budget system, but represent a general approach. First, budget analysis must be marginal in nature, but it should be focused on potential reductions. Secondly, analytical tools should be employed with greater selectivity and discrimination. Thirdly, it is necessary to opt for a medium-to-long-range perspective in order to permit orderly reallocations of funds and to reduce the social frictions caused by a slowdown in spending. Fourthly, decision-makers should seek maximum support for restraints among the affected agencies and outside groups. A final feature of the rational decremental approach is the inclusion in programs, at the time of authorization, of mechanisms to permit reduction or termination.

Though helpful in some respects, Tarschys' proposals involve some difficulties. His advice to concentrate on potential reductions raises the question of whether organizations can be dismantled incrementally in the same fashion that they were built up earlier.[45] A cut in one function may have negative reverberations throughout an organization. Morale within declining organizations will be poor; younger, able employees will leave; and the productivity of the unit will decline. Phased reductions based upon prior notice and consultations with affected groups could well be counter-productive. Those who benefit from programs will complain immediately and loudly; others who favour restraint in general terms will be silent. Therefore, Robert Behn's advice to would-be terminators is that they don't float trial balloons and that they seek to identify the costs of particular programs so that a constituency in favour of termination can be developed.[46] Paradoxically, organizations may be required to spend more money in the short term in order to enhance long-term productivity or to terminate programs. Cutback management is a difficult and largely

---

44 Daniel Tarschys, "Rational Decremental Budgeting: Elements of an Expenditure Policy for the 1980s," *Policy Sciences*, 14 (1981), pp. 49-58.
45 See Charles Levine, "More on Cutback Management: Hard Questions for Hard Times," in Charles H. Levine, ed., *Managing Fiscal Stress: The Crisis in the Public Sector* (Chatham, N.J.: Chatham House, 1980), pp. 306-307 for a discussion of the "paradox of irreducible wholes."
46 Robert D. Behn, "How to Terminate a Public Policy: A Dozen Hints for the Would-Be Terminator," in ibid., pp. 327-42.

unpractised art. There are no obvious and easy solutions to many of the problems involved.

Another suggested response to restraint is the adoption of a new method of government financing called "full-cost revenue dependency." Under such a system, departments would measure the costs of providing certain services and sell them to the public. There is not the space here to review all the arguments for and against revenue dependency. Its advocates do not see it as a complete substitute for expenditure restraint.[47] However, it would relieve some of the mounting burden on ministers involved in coping with restraint. Since revenue-dependent public services would be subject to market forces there would be less need for ministerial involvement. Revenue dependency would drive efficiency considerations into government operations by providing an incentive for managers to cut unnecessary activities and to perform required activities at the lowest cost.

A host of objections from a variety of sources would be raised against any concerted move toward revenue dependency. To their credit, the authors of the most recent Canadian study anticipate many of these objections and offer some persuasive rebuttals.[48] The question they are least successful in answering is how to secure the implementation of their idea. There will be a public backlash against any proposal to charge for services which are perceived as being "free" at present. Richard Bird suggests that the idea must be applied on an experimental basis with respect only to new programs if it is to stand any chance of winning political acceptance.[49] Support from the public service will also be necessary and departmental managers may see more threats than rewards flowing from the adoption of market-like approaches.

This final point raises the wider issue of incentives within bureaucratic structures. Most commentators agree that there are at present few incentives for restraining expenditures and for adroitly managing cutbacks. For example, there is the familiar pattern of frenzied spending towards the end of each fiscal year so that departments are not left with surpluses that might harm their future budget prospects. What are the possibilities and problems associated with allowable budget carryovers from one fiscal year to the next?[50] How can we reward agencies for achieving econ-

47 A.R. Bailey and D.G. Hull, *The Way out: A More Revenue-Dependent Public Sector and How It Might Revitalize the Process of Governing* (Montreal: The Institute for Research on Public Policy, 1980).
48 Ibid., chapter 5.
49 Richard Bird, *Charging for Public Services: A New Look at an Old Idea* (Toronto: Canadian Tax Foundation, 1976), p. 96.
50 See Leonard G. Lee, "The 'spend-or-lapse' syndrome in program budgeting," *Optimum*, II, 2 (1971), pp. 32-39 for a useful discussion.

omies? Do real savings require more departmental freedom over the hiring and firing of personnel and what obstacles stand in the way of such an approach? Substitution of a new set of incentives would involve a fundamental re-examination of existing budgetary and personnel policies.

Conclusions

No budget system is forever. We must learn to avoid the panacea syndrome. While reforms have often been launched on the basis of inflated promises, such hyperbole may have been necessary to win initial acceptance and past reforms have usually left a useful residue of new personnel, knowledge and skills. The budget has become overburdened. Some thought should be given to streamlining the process and finding non-budgetary means to meet the challenges of restraint. Politics will always play the major part in budgetary decision-making, but this does not deny completely the contribution of managerial technologies or the potential for constructive institutional reform. Realism should not lead to anti-management bias in public administration education. There are plenty of challenges ahead for both practitioners and students of the budget process.

Kenneth Kernaghan
P.K. Kuruvilla

Merit and motivation: public personnel management in Canada

Introduction

The competence and performance of public employees are key determinants of successful policy formation and execution. Thus, the task of managing the human resources of Canadian governments[1] is an extremely important one. Yet it is widely recognized that public personnel management has been distressingly neglected not only by politicians and senior bureaucrats but also by public administration scholars.

The personnel management system is vast and complex and it operates in a highly political environment. Indeed, the past and current problems of the system can be attributed in large part to a lack of political will to reform it. Political leaders have paid lip service to the importance of personnel management. For example, as early as 1969, the federal cabinet declared that "without greatly improved executive personnel and public service management, the government will not be able to elaborate policies and implement programs in a speedy, imaginative and progressive manner. . . ." During the 1970s, these words were not translated into action much beyond the appointment of commissions and committees which investigated personnel problems.[2]

Professor Kernaghan is with the department of politics and the school of administrative studies, Brock University. Professor Kuruvilla is with the department of political science, Wilfrid Laurier University.

1 Much of the material in this essay is relevant to all levels of Canadian government but space limitations require a focus on the federal government. For a study of public personnel administration in Canada's provinces, see J.E. Hodgetts and O.P. Dwivedi, *Provincial Governments as Employers* (Montreal: McGill-Queen's University Press, 1974). See also the section on personnel management in the essay in this volume by Marsha and William Chandler on "Public Administration in Canada's Provinces."

2 The most notable of these are *Employer-Employee Relations in the Public Service of Canada: Proposals for Legislative Change* (the Finkelman Report) (Ottawa: Information Canada, 1974); Special Joint Committee of the Senate and the House of Commons on Employer-Employee Relations in the Public Service, *Report to Parliament*, February 26, 1976; the Royal Commission on Financial Management and Accountability, *Final Report* (the Lambert Report) (Ottawa: Supply and Services, 1979); and *Report of the Special Committee on the Review of Personnel Management and the Merit Principle* (the D'Avignon Report) (Ottawa: Supply and Services, 1979).

Responsibility for deficiencies in the personnel management system has also been ascribed to the Treasury Board and the Public Service Commission – the central agencies charged with managing and operating the system. The D'Avignon Committee observed that "the basic problems in personnel management are not laid at the doorstep of managers, employees or bargaining agents"; rather the problems are a lack of leadership, excessive and inflexible regulation, managers who are ill-equipped for managing and an absence of accountability for the proper management of human resources.[3]

The federal government has recently taken initiatives to improve the personnel system. It is notable that academic scholars have contributed little to proposing, designing or understanding these initiatives.

This brief essay cannot provide a comprehensive list much less a detailed examination of all the issues in public personnel management.[4] Thus, our purpose is to examine a number of major problem areas and emerging trends.

We begin with a discussion of *merit* which is the most pervasive and enduring theme in public personnel management. To understand the concept of merit, one must distinguish between the merit *principle* and the merit *system*. The merit principle requires that "1/ Canadian citizens should have a reasonable opportunity to be considered for employment in the public service" and "2/ Selections must be based exclusively on merit, or fitness to do the job."[5] The merit system "is the mechanism in use at any time by which these goals are achieved. . . . A merit system is an administrative device *which can and should be adapted to changing circumstances*."[6] The Public Service Commission has argued that "the policies and practices devised to ensure the application of merit . . . should continue to provide for appointment to, and career advancement within the Public Service to be based on the merit of each individual but taking into account the requirements of . . . other principles."[7] These other principles are efficiency and effectiveness, sensitivity and responsiveness, equality of opportunity, and equity. Moreover, the D'Avignon Committee concluded that "if the public service is to attract the talent it needs, legislation must permit selection on the basis of . . . the individual's ability to meet . . . more than the requirements of a specific set of duties."[8]

---

3 *Report*, p. 5.
4 But see Special Committee on the Review of Personnel Management and the Merit Principle, *A Working Paper* (1978), and *Report* (1979).
5 R.H. Dowdell, "Public Personnel Administration," in Kenneth Kernaghan, ed., *Public Administration in Canada*, 4th ed. (Toronto: Methuen, 1982), p. 196.
6 Ibid. (Emphasis added).
7 Public Service Commission, *Public Service and Public Interest* (Ottawa: Supply and Services, 1978), p. 12.
8 *Report*, p. 78.

Despite the advances in organizational theory during this century, organizational practice in the public personnel field continues to be based largely on the scientific management school of thought which emerged in the early decades of this century. But "current organizational theory, which views organizations more in terms of social systems, suggests that individuals should know the results expected of them, have some influence over the work they perform and over the possible application and development of their own abilities to varying tasks in support of those results. . . ."[9] It is evident that a less rigid interpretation of merit must be complemented by enhanced concern about motivation.

The personnel policies of our public services must reflect what we have learned from administrative theorists about the behaviour of people in organizations. The objective of public personnel administration is to supply a sufficient number of well-qualified and well-motivated persons at the appropriate time to ensure successful development and implementation of government policies and programs. Greater emphasis has traditionally been placed on providing well-qualified rather than well-motivated public employees. Given the evolution of public personnel administration in the unique Canadian environment and the recency of important insights into organizational behaviour, this emphasis is understandable. The longstanding concern about the quality of the employees' preparation and performance must now, however, be joined by increased attention to the quality of their working life and its effects on their performance.

There have been few significant events, developments and reforms in the public service that have not affected public personnel management in general and merit in particular. Merit has been pursued within the broader context of the administrative values[10] that have been most prominent in the evolution of the Canadian public service. It is suggested that the most dominant values have been and continue to be accountability, political neutrality, economy, efficiency, effectiveness, integrity, responsiveness and representativeness.[11] The priority which public servants assign to each of these values at any given time is a reflection of the desires and expectations of the various actors in the political system who control or influence public servants. Among the most important of these actors are political superiors. Indeed, the uniqueness of personnel management in the public as opposed to the private sector can be explained in large measure by the political environment within which public ser-

9   Ibid.
10   An administrative value is an enduring belief that influences the choices made by individuals, groups or organizations in the public service from among available means or ends.
11   See Kenneth Kernaghan, "Changing Concepts of Power and Responsibility in the Canadian Public Service," CANADIAN PUBLIC ADMINISTRATION, 21 (Fall 1978), pp. 389-406.

vants work.[12] The politics of public personnel management is a central, but much neglected, explanatory factor in the development of the field in Canada.

The literature

Collectors of public "administrivia" will be fascinated to learn that *Canadian Public Administration Bibliography*[13] contains 505 entries under the heading of public personnel administration. Yet academics and practitioners agree that there appears to be a conspicuous absence of notable writings in this field. A careful review of the literature shows that in this instance appearance is reality. Moreover, many publications are notable more for their existence than for their excellence. Books, monographs and cases are especially scarce.

The importance of personnel policies and practices in Canadian governments is not reflected by the research and writing devoted to their examination. A relatively small proportion of the burgeoning academic literature on Canadian public administration is concerned with personnel matters, with the possible exception of the issue of collective bargaining. In recent years, a good deal of thought and analysis has been given to personnel problems by practitioners working within the privacy of government offices, especially in the Treasury Board and the Public Service Commission. While the outside world has seen the results of some of this work in the form of policy decisions, government officials have revealed relatively little of the data and dialogue that led to these decisions.

Rather than singling out for special attention in this section a small number of especially valuable contributions to the literature, we have drawn attention to these and to other significant publications in the footnotes throughout this essay.

Current developments and problems
Background

The evolution of public personnel management in Canada[14] can fruitfully be viewed in terms of the effect on merit and to a lesser degree on

12 See Dowdell, "Public Personnel Administration," pp. 194-96.
13 W.E. Grasham and Germain Julien, *Canadian Public Administration Bibliography* (Toronto: Institute of Public Administration of Canada, 1972), plus Supplements 1, 2 and 3 dated 1974, 1977 and 1979.
14 For an excellent account of the development of public personnel administration in Canada which focuses on the evolution of the Civil Service Commission between 1908 and 1967, see J.E. Hodgetts, William McCloskey, Reginald Whitaker and V. Seymour Wilson, *The Biography of an Institution* (Montreal: McGill-Queen's University Press, 1972). For the impact on personnel administration of the evolution of the Treasury Board, the Public Service Commission, departmental management and employer-employee relations between 1867 and 1970, see J.E. Hodgetts, *The Canadian Public Service* (Toronto: University of Toronto Press, 1973).

motivation of the shifting but abiding importance of the administrative values noted above. During this century, personnel management has been affected by a different mix of administrative values as the priority of the various values has risen and declined. The period before 1967 was characterized by the interplay of the values of political neutrality, economy and efficiency. After 1967, the public service felt the effects of reforms generated in the previous period and responded to the problems that emerged in the 1970s by carrying out further reforms and appointing bodies of inquiry to make recommendations bearing on both current and anticipated problems. Public service managers in general and personnel administrators in particular were bombarded by changes that greatly affected personnel policies and practices. Among the most important issues were collective bargaining, service-wide classification revision, language training and new management techniques.

A larger number of administrative values contended for precedence during these years. The former emphasis on economy and efficiency was supplemented by vigorous concern for effectiveness. Disclosures of mismanagement and of inefficient and ineffective use of public funds led to widespread anxiety about the accountability of public servants. Revelations of numerous ethical offences involving government officials aroused unprecedented concern about the integrity of these officials.[15] The representativeness of the public service became a major issue as the claims of women, native peoples and the handicapped were added to those of French-speaking Canadians. The Trudeau government's promises of participatory democracy gave responsiveness a higher place among the bureaucrats' value priorities. Finally, the importance of political neutrality was renewed with the increased recognition of the changing role of bureaucrats in the political system. It was acutely evident by the end of the 1970s that the traditional concept of merit would have to be re-evaluated and re-interpreted to take account of other governmental concerns and objectives affecting personnel management. Indeed, in recent years, the Public Service Commission has repeatedly proposed, and the Treasury Board has accepted, the argument that the principles noted earlier should govern all aspects of personnel management. In addition, the government as a whole has put great emphasis on accountability.

On balance, the values of efficiency, effectiveness and accountability dominated the bureaucratic agenda during the 1970s. Their importance was clearly demonstrated by the publication in the last year of the decade of the reports of the Lambert Commission and the D'Avignon Com-

15 See Kenneth Kernaghan, "Codes of Ethics and Administrative Responsibility," CANADIAN PUBLIC ADMINISTRATION, 17 (Winter 1974), pp. 527-41.

mittee. We shall see that the recommendations in these reports have already had a major impact on public personnel management in the 1980s.

In the pursuit of accountability in the personnel management system, the roles and responsibilities of the Public Service Commission and the Treasury Board have been clarified. This has been achieved by formal agreement between the two bodies rather than by the legislative reallocation of responsibilities proposed by the Lambert Commission and the D'Avignon Committee. Except for appointments and appeals, statutory authority for personnel management belongs to the Treasury Board. The Public Service Commission, however, performs other personnel activities (e.g., staff training and development, language training) at the request of the Board or cabinet and in areas of shared responsibility with the Board (e.g., human resource planning, managing the Management Category). The Board is responsible for all other areas of personnel management, including organization of the public service, human resource policy, training and development policy, classification, discipline and collective bargaining.

Problem areas

In this section, attention is focused in turn on three broad spheres of public personnel management: staffing, training and development, and employer-employee relations.

According to the D'Avignon Committee, the current system of staffing "is viewed by managers as slow, inflexible and inefficient; by bargaining agents as misguided and inequitable; and by many employees as frequently failing to ensure that their qualifications are fairly and objectively assessed."[16]

In the key areas of staffing, namely recruitment and selection, the Public Service Commission has statutory authority. It establishes and enforces selection standards and it appoints the more than four thousand members of the Executive (EX) and Senior Management (SM) groups within the Management Category. Most other appointments are made by individual departments under authority delegated by the Commission.

Among the several problems in the staffing area is the abuse of delegated staffing authority. In 1967, no staffing authority had been formally delegated to departments; in 1982, delegated staffing authority covered about 98 per cent of public service appointments. The Commission establishes basic staffing policies and guidelines and then checks departmental compliance with them through its Staffing Audit and Review Program. The stated aim of the Commission in this area is to strike an

16 *Report*, p. 183.

appropriate balance between protecting the rights of employees and providing managers with the flexibility they need "to be accountable for their actions and to provide effective and efficient management."[17]

The major problems connected with delegated staffing authority include insufficient or non-existent documentation (e.g., statements of qualifications, lists of interview questions, rating guides, and selection board reports); inadequate training of managers in staffing; imprecise delineation of staffing responsibilities between managers and staffing officers; departures from established rules and regulations in making acting appointments; and inadequate controls over personal service contracts. The Commission asserts that it is now conducting a more thorough audit of departmental staffing actions.

The delegation of staffing authority was a partial response to problems in a second area of staffing, namely long delays and procedural rigidities in recruitment and selection. The Commission reports that a 1981 study showed that, compared to three large Canadian corporations, its selection processes "generally took 34 working days longer to complete a promotional competition, largely because of statutory notice requirements (20 days) and subsequent rights of appeal (a further 14 days)."[18]

Data Stream, another mechanism designed in part to speed up the staffing process, has been renamed the Management Resources Inventory System (MRIS) to reflect recent changes in its coverage. Data Stream was introduced in 1970 as an up-to-date computerized inventory of skills, knowledge, experience and other relevant data on about 110,000 public servants. For a variety of technical and psychological reasons, this mechanism was widely distrusted as a means of identifying potential candidates for vacancies. Its successor, MRIS, contains more complete data on about 25,000 employees at the senior levels of the service. With the great majority of employees now excluded from the inventory, the poster distribution system has again become an important staffing tool. This means of advertising has been criticized, however, as inadequate in ensuring that employees are aware of job vacancies.

A third staffing problem is the perception of many employees that selection board procedures do not necessarily result in the choice of the most meritorious candidate. There is unhappiness about the relative weighting given to the factors of knowledge, abilities, sensitivity, potential for advancement and seniority. There is concern also about the inadequate training of board members in selection techniques, about the inadequacy of the interview technique for predicting probable success

17 *Annual Report, 1981* (Ottawa: Supply and Services, 1982), p. 4.
18 Ibid., p. 13.

and assessing the relative merits of candidates with roughly the same qualifications, and about bureaucratic patronage resulting from the bias of board members towards certain candidates.

In that the plural of the word anecdote is not data, it is difficult to provide hard information on selection problems. But a former Public Service Commissioner recently wrote that despite efforts to adhere to the merit principle, "we know" . . . that "managers are understandably inclined to favour their immediate staff, whose work they have already seen, over other candidates"; that "managers tend to select in their own image"; that "performance appraisal information, although improving in quality, is still not as reliable a yardstick of performance and potential as we would like it to be"; that "interviews, even if structured, are an imperfect predictor of success in a job"; that "written examinations, while undoubtedly more objective, may in fact be no more reliable a predictor"; and that "the criteria for certain jobs tend to be overblown or to be of questionable relevance to successful job performance."[19]

– A fourth staffing problem is the scarcity of personnel of requisite quality in certain occupational groups (e.g., computer science programmers and systems analysts, engineers, and auditors). The difficulty of recruiting qualified personnel in these fields is attributable to a variety of factors, including competition with industry, universities and other levels of government. It has become very difficult to make public service employment sufficiently competitive with the private sector, especially at the senior levels of the service. A parity of salary scales between the two sectors is necessary to attract qualified people to government service, to discourage able public servants from leaving government and to promote mobility between the public and private sectors. Equally important, however, is improved human resource planning in the public sector which will enable and encourage government to convey to post-secondary institutions its future personnel needs.

A final problem in the staffing area is reconciling the merit principle with the need for a representative public service. The government's stated objective is to ensure equality of access to public service positions and thereby a more equitable representation of traditionally under-represented groups. The "designated target groups" are francophones, women, native peoples and the handicapped. The D'Avignon Committee asserted that "merit will need to be accompanied by explicit recognition of the need for special treatment" for members of under-represented groups.[20] The subject of representative bureaucracy has been considered

19 John Edwards, "Equal Opportunity in the Public Service," *Dialogue*, 6 (February 1982), p. 4.
20 *Report*, p. 89.

at length elsewhere[21] but it is important to note here that, despite vigorous efforts and substantial progress by the federal government, the groups mentioned above are still under-represented in the public service, particularly in senior positions.

The importance of a second major sphere of personnel management, *training and development*,[22] is too frequently underrated. The D'Avignon Committee asked how we can justify the cost of failure to provide adequate training "in terms of the resulting deadwood, reduced productivity . . . lessened service to the public, and poor public image."[23] The Committee was especially critical of the role of central agencies in this sphere. The Treasury Board is responsible for overall policy direction; the Public Service Commission conducts central training courses and programs and provides advice and assistance to departments; and individual departments provide programs to meet their particular needs. The D'Avignon Committee asserted that training "must be viewed as an essential cost of doing business" but "is often viewed as a necessary evil." Moreover, "the higher one goes in the bureaucratic pyramid, the more evil it becomes until in some quarters it seems to be viewed almost as an unnecessary evil."[24]

It is now widely acknowledged that sound training and development programs must be based on a clear understanding and articulation of their basic objectives within the framework of a corporate management philosophy. Moreover, there must be a government-wide commitment to providing adequate human and financial resources for training despite some imperfections in the training system. It is true that some persons have been trained in skills largely or completely unrelated to their current position or any likely future position and that the quality and benefits of training are difficult to measure. This is insufficient reason for treating training expenditures as the first budgetary item to be cut in time of austerity. The danger of this shortsighted approach is demonstrated by this Catch 22 situation:

. . . having failed to provide adequate training so that people can perform at an effective level, we (the public, the government, Treasury Board, the PSC,

21 See ibid., pp. 103-24 and *Equal Opportunity Programs in the Public Service of Canada* (Ottawa: Public Service Commission, May 1981). A review of Canadian literature on this subject is included in Kenneth Kernaghan, "Representative Bureaucracy: the Canadian Perspective," CANADIAN PUBLIC ADMINISTRATION, 21 (Winter 1978), pp. 489-512.

22 For an examination of several issues in this sphere, see the essays in Kenneth Kernaghan, ed., *Executive Manpower in the Public Service: Make or Buy* (Toronto: Institute of Public Administration of Canada, 1975).

23 *Working Paper*, p. 176.

24 *Report*, pp. 211, 210.

senior managers in relation to junior managers . . .) castigate these people for not performing adequately.[25]

The abuses can be substantially remedied by expending training funds only on programs designed to meet carefully identified needs, by better evaluation of these programs, and by holding managers accountable for the effective training of their staff.

The ineffective management of training results in part from the fact that the training of many of the managers themselves has been neglected. For example, a large number of managers are poorly trained in personnel management and they rely heavily therefore on personnel administrators who understand the complexities and specialties of the personnel system. Yet most of these administrators are specialists (in staffing, classification, etc.) rather than generalists who understand the organization's objectives and are sensitive to the line managers' operational and personnel needs.

To improve the management of the personnel function, managers must be held actually rather than just formally accountable for personnel management. But at the same time, the training and experience of an appropriate number of personnel administrators must be broadened beyond one or two specialties so that they can effectively assist line managers.[26]

The bases on which candidates are selected for training are sometimes questionable. Managers often select employees who are among the least competent and promising because they are most easily spared. On other occasions, employees are chosen who don't want or need the training. In general, employees covet opportunities for developmental training which prepares them for promotion. The polar positions on selection for training are 1/ that there should be competition for all training opportunities, and 2/ that selection should be left entirely to managerial discretion.

A related concern is that training and development opportunities are inequitable in that they are uneven from one department to another. Moreover, although most of the Public Service Commission's courses are offered in both official languages, the vast majority of departmental courses are conducted only in English.

The third major sphere of personnel management – *employer-employee relations* – is sufficiently large and contentious to merit at least a separate

---

25   D'Avignon Committee, *Report*, p. 213.
26   See Treasury Board Secretariat, *Report of the Study Group on Improved Personnel Administration in the Public Service* (Ottawa: September 1981).

essay. We have, therefore, confined our discussion here to certain issues bearing on collective bargaining and the right to strike.[27]

The Public Service Staff Relations Act of 1967 provided federal public servants with opportunities for significant input into the determination of the terms and conditions of their employment. It granted to employee associations the status of trade unions with the rights to collective bargaining, compulsory arbitration, conciliation and strike action. It also established a formal grievance procedure permitting third-party adjudication to resolve employee grievances about the terms and conditions of employment. The Public Service Staff Relations Board administers the act.

The act was intended to furnish an effective mechanism for dispute settlement. It is acutely evident, however, that its provisions and operation have not satisfied fully the government, the employees or the general public. The government's dilemma is that it is caught between the unions' complaints that the act has stacked the cards against them and the public's disaffection with work stoppages and with wage settlements that are perceived to be too generous.

Public service unions have argued consistently that the act's unduly rigid and restrictive provisions do not allow adequate scope for satisfactory bargaining. Their primary complaints are: 1/ the blanket denial of collective bargaining rights to several classes of government employees (e.g., managerial employees, the RCMP); 2/ the employer's right to "designate" employees whose duties are "necessary in the interest of the safety and security of the public" and who will therefore be deprived of the right to strike; 3/ the exclusion from negotiation and arbitration of all staffing matters of vital concern to employees (e.g., selection and recruitment, job security, classification); and 4/ the requirement that bargaining agents must choose either the conciliation-strike or the arbitration route of dispute settlement before the present contract expires and that the route chosen must remain in effect until the next round of bargaining.

The unions have been campaigning for changes in the act to bring about what they believe would be a more equitable balance in the rights of the employer and the employees. At the same time, however, the government has generally taken a hard-line approach to employer-employee relations.

At the government's invitation, Jacob Finkelman, the chairman of the

27 For a bibliography on these matters, see Sandra Christensen, *Unions and the Public Interest: Collective Bargaining in the Government Sector* (Vancouver: The Fraser Institute, 1980), pp. 89-95.

Public Service Staff Relations Board, prepared a report in 1974 proposing changes in the act, most of which favoured the employees. The government referred Finkelman's report to a Special Joint Committee of the Senate and the House of Commons on Employer-Employee Relations in the Public Service. Many of the recommendations made by the Committee in 1976 were similar to those of the Finkelman report. But the recommendations were more restrictive in such areas as penalties for illegal strikes, managerial and confidential exclusions, and union voting procedures. The unions opposed the Committee's recommendations as repressive and anti-union.

During 1978, the government introduced in Parliament two similar bills to amend the act by imposing greater restrictions in the collective bargaining process on employees. Bill C-28, which replaced Bill C-22, died on the order paper when Parliament was dissolved for the 1979 election. Among the proposed amendments most severely criticized by the unions were: 1/ the creation of a "managerial category" and the removal from the bargaining unit of persons with senior professional and managerial responsibilities and persons earning more than $33,500 per year; and 2/ the removal of the existing Pay Research Bureau from under the umbrella of the PSSRB and the establishment of a new national Pay Research Bureau to compile data showing total compensation comparability between the public and private sectors. The Management Category was subsequently created without amending the act but the proposal affecting the Pay Research Bureau has not been adopted. The unions have argued against efforts to seek comparability between public and private sector compensation levels.[28]

The D'Avignon Committee recommended that the scope of collective bargaining be expanded to include the determination of broad personnel policies (e.g., selection standards, open versus closed competitions, access to developmental training).[29] Negotiation on such matters would not take place under the Public Service Staff Relations Act but rather through a National Staffing Council composed of representatives of each bargaining agent and of corporate and departmental management. This recommendation has not met with a favourable response at the senior levels of government.

28 See P.K. Kuruvilla, "Collective Bargaining in the Canadian Federal Public Service, in Kenneth Kernaghan, ed., *Public Administration in Canada* (Toronto: Methuen, 1982), pp. 216-25. But see also *Unions and the Public Interest* in which Professor Christensen proposes in general the elimination of the right to strike over compensation and in particular the creation of a wage board to set public sector wages on the basis of comparability with the private sector.
29 *Report*, chapter 8.

The single most promising

government initiative designed to meet this challenge is the creation of
the Management Category which was formally announced in July 1980.
This development is the culmination of persistent pressures during the
1970s for improved public service management; it is also the foundation
for pursuing this objective during the 1980s. The Public Service Commission views the Management Category not as a panacea but as one
means of enhancing management performance in an era of increased
emphasis on the values of accountability, efficiency and effectiveness.[30]

The Management Category consists of the Executive (EX) and Senior
Management (SM) groups. The category includes senior public servants
who have responsibility for policy development; program formulation
and delivery; the design and operation of management machinery; and
the management of personnel, finances and public affairs. The EX group
is composed of five levels up to and including most assistant deputy
ministers and the SM group is made up of a single level immediately
below the EX group.

Among the primary objectives of the formation of the category are:
1/ to establish a simplified staffing system designed to attract, develop
and retain management talent; 2/ to establish a single classification
system for all managerial personnel; 3/ to replace appointment-to-position
by appointment-to-level so as to enable deputy ministers to redeploy
senior managers in response to changing needs; 4/ to increase the accountability of managers by specifying accountabilities in job descriptions; 5/ to provide training and development programs to give managers
the knowledge and skills required to manage in a context of increased
accountability; 6/ to establish a new compensation system that will
ensure fair and equitable compensation both within the public service
and in relation to the private sector; and 7/ to set up a pay system
clearly linked to performance, including rewards for superior and outstanding achievement.

Other notable initiatives have been taken or planned. The reallocation
of responsibilities between the Public Service Commission and the Treasury Board is being increasingly refined to clarify their respective accountability and to lessen the reporting requirements for departments. The
accord between the two bodies minimizes for the foreseeable future the

30 See *The New Management Category* (Ottawa: Public Service Commission, May
1981).

266 CANADIAN PUBLIC ADMINISTRATION

probability of the major structural reform recommended by the Lambert Commission and the D'Avignon Committee.

In the staffing sphere, the Commission is seeking greater flexibility through a gradual shift from a service-wide to a departmental approach "to improve the efficiency of staffing and to increase the accountability of those exercising delegated responsibility."[31] This will require an increase in the nature rather than the extent (already at 98 per cent) of delegated staffing authority; that is, the Commission will strive to reduce staffing rules and regulations and to tailor the terms and conditions of delegated authority to the particular needs of individual departments.

The shortage of certain skills in the labour market will continue to be reflected in the public service. But human resource planning to remedy skill shortages must also take account of the demographic imbalance in the decision-making groups of the present public service. There is limited room at the top levels of the administrative hierarchy to accommodate the career aspirations of a large number of public servants who have been hired and promoted rapidly since 1965.[32]

The Commission and the Treasury Board are continuing their difficult task of eliminating administrative and attitudinal barriers to equality of opportunity for under-represented groups. Foremost among the problems perceived by the central agencies is convincing managers that equal opportunity is compatible with the merit principle.[33] However, many managers would like the central agencies to make adjustments to the merit system which will facilitate efforts to achieve equal opportunity.

In the sphere of training and development, the Management Category will continue to have a significant impact. Managers will receive more training in personnel management and measures will be taken to enhance the service and advisory roles and the "professionalism" of personnel administrators.

Treasury Board has modified its staff training policy to distinguish between training required for clearly identified organizational needs and education that employees may wish to pursue for their own purposes. Henceforth, job-related training will be heavily emphasized and employees will "have primary responsibility for their own career advance-

31 Public Service Commission, *Strategy Document for 1982/1987* (Ottawa: Supply and Services, 1982), p. 8.
32 For an examination of this problem, see Nicole Schwartz-Morgan and Charles Moubarek, *Nowhere to Go?* (Montreal: Institute for Research on Public Policy, 1981).
33 For an account of the Commission's policy and initiatives in this area, see its *Annual Report, 1981*, pp. 17-19.

ment and personal development."[34] The Commission has responded by eliminating most personal development courses to concentrate almost solely on job-related courses. There is concern that the rigid application of this policy might conflict with the need to provide well-qualified persons from within the service to meet the human resource requirements of the 1980s.

In the sphere of employer-employee relations, there are no simple or generally acceptable solutions to the present discontent. In general, the government is inclined toward restricting rather than liberalizing the rights of employees in the collective bargaining process. Proposals for reform of the process range from expanding the scope of matters subject to collective bargaining to legislative prohibition of the right to strike.[35] At the time of writing, the government is in the process of suspending collective bargaining on monetary issues and the right to strike for a period of two years as part of its wage-restraint program. It is difficult to predict the effects of this measure on employer-employee relations in the public sector, but it is likely to have a damaging impact on employee motivation.

Research and teaching

Many of the items on the research agenda in public personnel management are evident from the preceding discussion of key problem areas. Other studies, notably the D'Avignon Report, have identified additional problems that require examination and resolution. As noted earlier, research on public personnel management in Canada is at a rudimentary stage. Much of the research has been done within the government rather than by academic scholars. If the product of this in-house research was more actively publicized and distributed, it might have a stimulative effect on academics. The drawback to many government studies, especially those deemed appropriate for wide circulation, is that they tend to obscure or minimize the politics and problems of the personnel management system. They also lack the critical analysis and theoretical underpinnings that are more characteristic of scholarly writings.

We need basic descriptive studies of the personnel management system so that an enhanced understanding of its components and complexities can serve as a foundation for more sophisticated empirical and analytical work. At a broad level, we require an examination of such central issues as the reconciliation of the merit principle with such values as efficiency and representativeness; the appropriate balance between

---

34 "Authorizing Staff Training," draft entry for *Personnel Management Manual*, June 1982.
35 For an examination of the various models for collective bargaining in the public sector, see Christensen, *Unions and the Public Interest*, pp. 49-62.

the centralization and decentralization of the personnel function; and the effects on the personnel system of technological advances, particularly in the information and communications fields.

While we recognize that the research priorities of observers of the personnel scene differ, we see the need for specific studies on the following matters:

1. the speed and integrity of the staffing process;
2. the quality and reliability of performance appraisals;
3. the burden on departments of the reporting requirements of central agencies;
4. the quality and effects of training programs;
5. the emphasis on job-related training and the decline of developmental training;
6. the changing roles of line managers and personnel administrators in the performance of the personnel function;
7. the adoption of new techniques of dispute settlement, including final offer arbitration;
8. the expansion of the scope of collective bargaining;
9. the overhaul of the classification system to reduce the number of occupational categories and, therefore, of collective agreements;
10. the rights of public servants to participate in political activity and engage in public comment; and
11. the level and means of motivation in the public service.

The scarcity of analysis of such issues and of straightforward descriptive materials impedes understanding and improvement of the personnel system. It also hinders the design and teaching of satisfactory university and government courses on public personnel management.

Conclusions

Many managers need to appreciate better that their most precious assets are human resources and that the effective management of these resources is essential to achieving organizational and government objectives. The challenge is to design and operate a personnel management system that ensures a high level of merit and motivation in the public service.

Academic scholars and administrative practitioners have paid little explicit attention to motivation. It is difficult to discern the influence that such organization theorists as McGregor, Argyris, Maslow, Hertzberg and Likert might have had on recent reforms of personnel policies and practices. Membership in the Management Category has the potential to satisfy such high-level needs as esteem and self-actualization; yet official statements on the category mention motivation only in the context of lower-level needs, notably compensation. For example, a central objective of the Management Category is "motivating managers to maximize their efficiency and effectiveness by establishing a uniform compensation system with rewards for high achievers." We need solid empirical studies of the effect of compensation and other rewards on the motivation of senior managers.[36]

Highly motivated senior managers provide an influential role model for their subordinates. These managers might also stimulate higher levels of motivation through greater emphasis on Quality of Worklife (QWL), "a process for work organization which enables . . . employees to actively participate in shaping the organization's environment, methods, and outcomes."[37] QWL is at an early stage of development in the federal public service[38] and at present appears to be a low priority concern.

Current efforts to enhance motivation are regrettably offset by such demotivating factors as embittered employer-employee relations and the negative public image of the bureaucracy. The Lambert Commission correctly observed that "the regard in which the public servant is held by those he serves – both the Government and the people – is, in the final analysis, the standard by which he measures the value of his contribution to society."[39] Thus, the successful management of human resources requires that the traditional focus on merit be complemented by increased concern about motivation. If the motivation of public servants is low, they cannot reasonably be expected to pursue vigorously, much less to achieve, the values of efficiency, effectiveness and accountability.

36 See, for example, David Zussman, "Bonuses and Performance in the Public Sector," *The Canadian Psychologist* (in press).
37 Treasury Board, draft of statement on "Quality of Worklife" for the *Personnel Management Manual*, 1982.
38 See Eric Trist and William A. Westley, *QWL in the Federal Public Service* (Ottawa: Labour Canada, June 1981).
39 *Report*, p. 8.

6600